The Rise of a Jazz Art World

This book presents a unique sociolo~
in the twentieth century. Anal~ ·
peting discourses in America
and others transformed the m~
distinct worlds of high art and ┴   ,azz
art world is shown to be a uniqu   ⌐se community struggling in various ways   ⌐oxy. Cultural
politics in America is shown to be ⸝   ⌐⸝, and often contradictory process of constant re-interp.   ┴ his work is a compelling
social history of American culture th⸝⸝ incorporates various voices in
jazz, including musicians, critics, collectors, producers, and enthusiasts.
Accessibly written and interdisciplinary in approach, it will be of great
interest to scholars and students of sociology, cultural studies, social
history, American studies, African-American studies, and jazz studies.

Paul Lopes is Assistant Professor of Sociology at Tufts University,
Massachusetts. He was Director of the Communications and Media
Studies Program at Tufts from 1994 to 2001. He is also a saxophonist
and has played in jazz, reggae, and rock groups.

The Rise of a Jazz Art World

Paul Lopes

CAMBRIDGE
UNIVERSITY PRESS

PUBLISHED BY THE PRESS SYNDICATE OF THE UNIVERSITY OF CAMBRIDGE
The Pitt Building, Trumpington Street, Cambridge, United Kingdom

CAMBRIDGE UNIVERSITY PRESS
The Edinburgh Building, Cambridge CB2 2RU, UK
40 West 20th Street, New York, NY 10011-4211, USA
477 Williamstown Road, PortMelbourne, VIC 3207, Australia
Ruiz de Alarcón 13, 28014 Madrid, Spain
Dock House, The Waterfront, Cape Town 8001, South Africa

http://www.cambridge.org

© Paul Lopes, 2002

First published 2002

Printed in the United Kingdom at the University Press, Cambridge

Typeface Plantin 10/12 pt.   *System* LaTeX 2$_\varepsilon$ [TB]

A catalogue record for this book is available from the British Library

Library of Congress Cataloguing in Publication data
Lopes, Paul Douglas.
The rise of a jazz art world / Paul Lopes.
   p.   cm.
Includes bibliographical references (p.) and index.
ISBN 0 521 80191 5 – ISBN 0 521 00039 4 (pb)
1. Jazz – History and criticism.   2. Music – Social aspects.   I. Title.
ML3508 .L67   2002
781.65′09 – dc21   2001043259

ISBN 0 521 80191 5 hardback
ISBN 0 521 00039 4 paperback

Contents

Acknowledgments

This book is the culmination of a long intellectual journey. The journey began at the Institute for Jazz Studies (IJS) at Rutgers University in Newark. Its supportive atmosphere allowed me to roam freely among its archives. I was able to follow every clue and personal intuition to gain the fullest understanding of the history of jazz as possible. In my early excursions into jazz history, I also had the opportunity to talk with Dan Morgenstern, the director of IJS. As someone who was an active participant during the modern jazz renaissance, his insights on the jazz art world were tremendously helpful. IJS also supported me through the Morroe Berger – Benny Carter Jazz Research Fund established by the great alto saxophonist, bandleader, arranger, educator, and union activist, Benny Carter. Five years after my time at IJS, I had an opportunity to advance my research and analysis a final crucial step forward with my appointment as an Annenberg Scholar at the Annenberg School for Communication at the University of Pennsylvania. At Annenberg I was able to search backwards into the early twentieth and late nineteenth centuries to understand more clearly the broader significance of the rise of a jazz art world. And the intellectual exchange among the most talkative group of scholars I have had the pleasure to spend time with was also truly inspirational. My book in no small way attests to the immeasurable value of IJS as a repository of jazz history and the valuable contribution of the Annenberg Scholars Program to the interdisciplinary exchange of ideas.

A number of individuals also helped this project with their insightful commentary and advice. Our conversations and correspondences were invaluable. Since the beginning of my project, Ron Lembo and Bob Dunn have provided critical advice as well as strong support for the intellectual path I had chosen. A special thanks as well goes to Reebee Garofalo, Howard Becker, Jim Ennis, Margaret Cerulo, Paula Aymer, and Andrew Hrycyna for their comments on my work. And I give a warm thank you to the Great Barrington Group for their perceptive conversations about cultural sociology and breaking disciplinary boundaries. I also appreciate the guidance provided by Ann Swidler and Todd

Gitlin in the initial stages of my project at the University of California, Berkeley.

Of course, such a long and exhausting journey to discovery is only possible with the support of friends and family. I was blessed during my student days in Madison, Wisconsin to have met a group of friends that have remained close to me over the years regardless of the geographic distance between us. Rick Schroeder, Tidiane Nigaido, Daniel Schneider, and Luis Garcia-Abusaid have always given me the strength to live up to my fullest potential and remain true to my convictions. A warm hug goes out to Leslie Reagan, Dorothy Hodgson, Ewa Golebiowska, Judith Biewener, Tim Sturgeon, Kathy Hauenstein, Eric Gordy, Susan Ostrander, David Brotherton, Jeanine Lopes, and my younger brother David for their support and friendship. I also send out another round of warm hugs to the members of the "I Club," Judith, Leah, Elizabeth, Anders, Luis, and Mona, for their support as I faced the trials and tribulations of my graduate years at Berkeley. Finally, my deepest gratitude goes to my older brother Les who has been a personal inspiration, and has remained an avid supporter and trustworthy confidant throughout my life.

Introduction

The quest for cultural legitimacy

> I say this because jazz, the music I play most often, has never really been
> accepted as an art form by the people of my own country... I believe
> that the great mass of the American people still consider jazz as lowbrow
> music... To them, jazz is music for kids and dope addicts. Music to get
> high to. Music to take a fling to. Music to rub bodies to. Not "serious"
> music. Not concert hall material. Not music to listen to. Not music to
> study. Not music to enjoy purely for its listening kicks.
>
> Dizzy Gillespie, "Jazz Is Too Good For Americans," *Esquire*, June 1957: 55

In 1957 jazz trumpeter Dizzy Gillespie criticized the continued lack of
respect in America for jazz as more than a lowbrow entertainment.
Gillespie's criticism came surprisingly at a time when jazz was enjoying a resurgence in national recognition as well as a booming commercial
market in recordings and live performances. It was in fact the peak of a
renaissance in jazz music – a rebirth of jazz as a high art movement that
over the two decades of the 1950s and 1960s transformed American
music. Inspired in the 1940s by a new style of jazz called bebop, musicians during the renaissance explored various styles of jazz performance,
composition, and improvisation. Their musical exploration generated a
long list of stylistic nomenclatures: cool jazz, hard bop, soul jazz, west
coast jazz, east coast jazz, mainstream jazz, free jazz, third stream jazz,
black music, fusion jazz, bossa nova and others. This renaissance in jazz
firmly secured this music as a major American art tradition that continues
up to the present day.

Dizzy Gillespie, however, was not alone in feeling that jazz in the 1950s
still did not garner the respect and rewards it deserved. This shared feeling
among jazz artists reflected a long-standing ambiguity in the United States
toward this music's place in American culture: one that continued to
haunt jazz even during the renaissance. Since the first jazz craze of 1917,
this music confronted a variety of distinctions that positioned it as far less
than legitimate. At the same time, however, this music also was quickly
claimed by some as an authentic and legitimate American art form. Was
jazz a lowbrow deviant form of entertainment or a complex and subtle
art equal to the classical tradition in Western music? Who made these

1

strangely polar opposite claims about jazz and why? Gillespie's and others' continued disappointment about the state of jazz at mid-century reflected a long history of struggle over the meaning and practice of jazz music.

Jazz as a cultural movement at mid-century, however, involved not only jazz artists. It also included record producers, concert producers, club owners, music critics, magazine publishers, and diverse audiences. All these various actors in jazz made up what sociologist Howard Becker (1982) calls an art world. So while artists brought their own meanings and practices to bear on jazz music, others joined them in fashioning the meaning, practice, and success of jazz as an art form. Of course, the rise of this jazz art world was a collective expression of a large number of individuals who did not necessarily all share a single purpose – individuals would pursue a variety of interests in jazz and hold a variety of views towards this music. Yet this collective coalescence around jazz music led to the eventual success of an art world that initiated a renaissance in jazz music during the 1950s and 1960s.

I will show how the rise of a jazz art world and the renaissance in jazz music at mid-century were expressions of a long struggle over the meaning and practice of music making in America reaching as far back as the nineteenth century. The distinctions and challenges that emerged in the 1950s cannot be fully understood without reference to the struggles which preceded them. The rise of a jazz art world involved more than a mere pretension to the status of serious high art on the part of musicians and others. The story of jazz in the twentieth century is far more complicated, and provides far more insight into the cultural distinctions that informed American culture during this period, than such a simple view might suggest. The social history of the jazz art world and jazz music reveals interactions and conflicts between a variety of cultural distinctions active in American music. As the historian Lawrence Levine (1989: 18) argues: "Jazz in fact is one of those forces that have helped to transform our sense of art and culture . . . a music that in fact bridged the gap between all of the categories that divided culture." The rise of a jazz art world did indeed entail transformations in categories of art and culture in America, but it did so often in contradictory ways and certainly encountered resistance along the way. Such contradictions and obstacles were the products of the cultural, social, and institutional forces that supported the distinctions that divided American culture and society during the first half of the twentieth century.

The genealogy of the modern jazz renaissance

General histories of jazz usually locate its original home beginning at the turn of the century in the red-light district of Storyville in New Orleans.

They follow this folk music's outward migration from the American South beginning in the second decade of the twentieth century. In the Jazz Age of the 1920s, jazz histories focus on the classic jazz ensembles and early beginnings of big band jazz as this music became the nation's most popular music. Jazz continues as a popular music during the swing big band era of the 1930s and 1940s. Then a modernist turn to high art occurs after World War II with a small coterie of bebop musicians leading the way to the modern jazz period. Jazz histories present a musical evolution from folk art to popular art to high art. Ted Gioia's (1997) *The History of Jazz* is a recent example of this type of general history with Marshall Stearns' (1956) *The Story of Jazz* having defined the standard jazz history. These works aim at establishing the lineage of a jazz music tradition. They played an important role in the rise of a jazz art world and continue to play an important role today.

Most jazz histories, however, are implicated in the jazz art world's quest to create and maintain a distinct music tradition called jazz, and therefore, never move much beyond this narrative to address the broader contexts of music and culture in America. Further, since they focus on establishing the lineage of jazz practices in which improvisation became the predominant art, these histories follow this practice backwards to the original performers of jazz improvisation, usually ending at the turn of the century with the blaring cornet of Buddy Bolden in New Orleans. But my work is less interested in the cultural lineage of improvisation and early jazz, than in the genealogy of the *modern* jazz renaissance in the mid-twentieth century. In the 1920s, jazz was adopted by an artistic culture different from the one in which most Southern American musicians performed early jazz. This was the artistic culture of professional musicians, particularly musicians active in the popular society orchestras of the Jazz Age that later were transformed into "big bands" in the 1930s. The high art turn among jazz musicians that defined this music at mid-century should be traced backwards through this artistic culture in order to understand its cultural and social contexts.

A focus on jazz musicians as professional musicians is not a completely new approach to jazz. Following an early essay by Wen Shih Hsio (1959) which pointed to the significance of professional black musicians as part of an emerging black middle class in the 1920s, Thomas J. Hennessey (1994) and Scott DeVeaux (1997) focus on the professionalism and middle class aspirations of black musicians. Hennessey emphasizes the middle class aspirations and professionalism of urban black musicians in the development of swing music, while DeVeaux makes a similar emphasis in relation to the birth of the modern jazz style bebop. My work significantly expands on these works by first addressing both black and white professional musicians in understanding the quest for cultural legitimacy that both groups of artists shared. It also expands on these previous works by placing the performance and aesthetic strategies of these professional musicians in the context of fundamental transformations and conflicts in American music from the late nineteenth century to the mid-twentieth century.

The ultimate course in the evolution in meaning and practice of jazz music in the twentieth century came from the actions of these professional musicians. The turn to high art during the modern jazz renaissance, in particular, could not have occurred without the willing consent of these musicians or their holding the dispositions necessary to make such a turn possible. Why did professional musicians have such aspirations and dispositions as artists who essentially performed for a popular music market? What was the context of these aspirations and dispositions in terms of the production and consumption of music in America since the late nineteenth century? And finally, why was "jazz" adopted as the name given to the music professional musicians performed in their quest towards high art legitimacy?

The jazz art world

While professional musicians were refashioning jazz music, a jazz art world of magazines, records, books, clubs, and concerts developed to support this music. This art world provided the organization, production, criticism and audiences to make jazz a distinct genre and specialized market in American music. The first developments of this art world appeared in the 1930s and continued to grow in the 1940s, but had few opportunities to move beyond the cognoscenti of the jazz scene. By the 1950s, however, changes in the music industry helped the jazz art world become the bedrock of a jazz renaissance. Throughout the period of this renaissance, the jazz art world remained essential to the success of jazz musicians and their music.

Howard Becker (1982) points to the important role non-artists in art worlds perform in the production and reception of an art form. Jazz producers were active in the production of jazz music both live and recorded. Jazz critics produced jazz criticism and jazz history, while also promoting jazz outside the jazz art world mostly in writing for magazines and newspapers. Jazz audiences obviously provided the patronage essential to the financial viability of this art world. Producers, critics and audiences, however, also were important in shaping the sound and meaning of jazz music. While professional musicians developed their own understanding of the significance of jazz music, producers, critics and audiences also actively formed their own understanding and appreciation of this music's significance as an art form.

In fact, the high art turn in jazz was only one aspect in this art world's quest to fashion and legitimate a new music tradition in America. In the broader scope of this art world, folk, popular, and modern styles of jazz would have a place in the development of jazz history, jazz criticism, jazz recordings, and live jazz performance. Not all participants in the jazz art world actually welcomed the high art turn in jazz among professional musicians. Jazz traditionalists who first lamented the commercialization of jazz during the Swing Era would become the "moldy figs" who saw modern jazz as a betrayal of the true roots of this music. Traditionalists versus modernists, however, was only one of many conflicts in the emerging jazz art world with the race question hovering like a dark storm cloud over the collective will to make jazz a unique American art. The jazz art world was at times quite a contentious community with enthusiasts and musicians battling each other over the meanings and practices associated with jazz.

The literature on jazz unfortunately barely addresses the history and significance of the jazz art world or the role of non-artists in the history of jazz. Only recently have works begun to broaden the historical purview on jazz. David W. Stowe (1994), Scott DeVeaux (1997), and Lewis A. Erenberg (1998), for example, have addressed certain aspects of this art world during the 1930s and 1940s, while DeVeaux (1991), John Gennari (1991), Steven B. Elsworth (1995) and Krin Gabbard (1995) have addressed jazz criticism. My work is the first to present a full history of the jazz art world during the crucial period of the 1930s to the end of the modern jazz renaissance. It looks not only at the impact of this art world on jazz music and jazz musicians, but the different meanings and associations non-artists brought to jazz as an art form during this period.

In integrating a history of the jazz art world with the history of professional musicians we can better understand the nature of the transformations jazz music underwent in the first half of the twentieth century. This approach to the social history of jazz broadens our understanding of the significance of jazz as both an American art form and as a major cultural movement in the twentieth century. What brought about such a coalescence of diverse individuals around jazz music? What different meanings and interests did they bring to jazz? How can we understand the various conflicts that emerged in this cultural movement? And finally, what future impact did this art world have on jazz music following the modern jazz renaissance?

High art and popular art in American music

The rise of a jazz art world and the transformations in jazz music up through the modern jazz renaissance direct us toward looking seriously at the *cultural politics* of American music. Changes in jazz as an art form during the twentieth century were expressions of the encounters of professional musicians and others with the various distinctions inscribed in the meanings and practices of American music, with artists also struggling simply to make a livelihood. Unique characteristics in music production and music consumption engendered their own expression of the more general cultural politics that defined both high art and popular art in America.

Scholars such as Paul DiMaggio (1991, 1992) and Lawrence Levine (1988) point to a significant transformation in the relation between high art and popular art beginning in the late nineteenth century. While the question of cultivated high art versus vernacular popular art had long been part of American culture, the clear delineation between two distinct *social worlds* of high art and popular art did not emerge until this period. DiMaggio and Levine see the key in the evolution of two distinct social worlds of art in the development of elite-supported high art organizations – symphony orchestras, opera companies, fine art museums, repertory theaters, and dance companies. The rise of these high art organizations also occurred in combination with the introduction of high art appreciation, scholarship, and training in universities and colleges. The relative autonomy from commercial markets enjoyed by the new high art world, which came to full fruition in the early part of the twentieth century, provided a greater control over high art in terms of art forms, artists, art appreciation, and audiences. The boundaries erected by this new elite art world set the general distinction in America between high art and popular art during the twentieth century. This distinction lay not only in the art forms themselves, but in the separation of cultural organizations, communities of artists, spaces for exhibition and performance, communities of consumers, and in distinct modes of art appreciation and art criticism. As a social world of high art developed, therefore, the general difference between the high and the popular became more clearly defined through each of these forms of division.

DiMaggio (1982) and Levine also show how the exclusive social world of high art in the United States originally functioned as a form of social distinction for a new urban elite who associated themselves with the patronage and consumption of high art. The wealth of an industrializing American economy in the last half of the nineteenth century created a growing urban elite at the same time it attracted large numbers of immigrants and migrants to major American cities. The urban elite envisioned a new American social hierarchy in which they formed a status community that rested comfortably above the popular classes. An exclusive social world of high art affirmed the legitimacy and facilitated the reproduction of this social hierarchy. High art consumption signified the natural and moral foundations of social distinctions of class, race, or ethnicity inscribed in this social hierarchy. The contours between high art and popular art, therefore, were not simply objective borders of aesthetic quality, artistic talent, and sophisticated tastes, but products of a cultural politics of distinction designed to legitimate a specific culture and the social class associated with its consumption. While high art appreciation would eventually spread beyond this early urban elite status community, its social function of distinction would remain, and more importantly, the social world of high art production and consecration would remain unchanged into the middle of the twentieth century.

At the same time that an exclusive social world of high art emerged in the United States, popular art in this country also went through important transformations. Lewis A. Erenberg (1981) and David Nasaw (1993) show how the late nineteenth century witnessed the beginnings of a rapid expansion and diversity in commercial popular entertainment that continued until the Great Depression. Many in the social world of high art and other self-ordained defenders of American culture were not particularly pleased by this rapid growth in popular entertainment. Their ire only increased as popular entertainment distanced itself more and more from any relationship to the supposedly legitimate cultivated arts and relied more on such vernacular practices as ragtime and jazz. Producers and artists in popular entertainment also confronted an increasingly diverse audience, particularly a growing middle class ready to enjoy popular entertainment, but not necessarily in the manner and form enjoyed by working class audiences. Producers and artists, therefore, became important *mediators* of commercial popular entertainment. They refashioned numerous practices and meanings in popular art in order to serve diverse audiences as well as to deflect critics. Whether confronting the disdain of highbrow critics, the fear of moral crusaders, or the tastes of diverse audiences, artists and producers constantly negotiated various social distinctions – class, race, ethnic, gender, and moral – articulated in popular entertainment.

Popular entertainment went through another major transition in the 1930s. The Great Depression wreaked havoc on live popular performance. The vitality of popular art suffered considerably from the economic and social devastation of the depression. At this time, a new mass media system of radio, film, and records appeared, and to a large degree shifted popular performance and popular consumption. This system was dedicated to a mass market on a national scale and could not replicate the more diverse popular entertainment that preceded the 1930s.

Decision-makers in this new system, therefore, conceived a much narrower aesthetic for popular entertainment. The same negotiation of social
distinctions in popular art remained, but within a market dominated by
a more centralized system of production and consumption. This transformation would have an effect on how artists, producers, and audiences
understood their place in the world of popular entertainment as well as
the nature of the commercial popular music market.

We will see in detail how professional musicians and others negotiated these various transformations and distinctions in American culture
from the late nineteenth century into the mid-twentieth century. The
professional class of musician was unique in American culture in being a large community of artists whose dispositions originally developed
before the high-popular divide in America and yet continued as a major community of artists in popular entertainment once this distinction
was established. It was further unique in the role of African American
artists who had a presence in music far greater than in any other art form
in America, significantly shaping its practices and professional culture.
The key question is how jazz came to signify various contours of status,
distinction and identity in American music confronted by professional
musicians and others. How did the cultural politics around high art and
popular art shape the evolution of jazz music and a jazz art world? And
finally, where did jazz fit into this cultural politics during the modern jazz
renaissance?

Transforming American culture

My book is not the first work to address jazz music in the context of high
art and popular art in America. Other works addressing this subject, however, have focused specifically on the high art turn in jazz. Work by Amiri
Baraka (1963), Richard A. Peterson (1972), Lewis Erenberg (1989), and
Diana Crane (1992) attempt to explain the factors behind this turn to high
art, while work by Andrew Ross (1986) and Nelson George (1988) simply focus on its elitist pretensions. From the perspective of these works,
the high art turn in jazz was a post World War II movement of middle
class, college or conservatory educated musicians who formed a new elite
community of artists. This view, however, fails to recognize the complex
transformations of jazz music in the first half of the twentieth century in
the broader historical context of the high and the popular in American
music. It also fails to acknowledge the diverse social class and race composition of the jazz art world and this art world's overall alternative vision
of American art and society. As such, this previous view of modern jazz
does not recognize how it was the end product of a long process that

challenged and transformed the reigning cultural hierarchy in twentieth-century America.

The evolution in the meanings and practices of jazz music over time traversed numerous boundaries of cultural distinction in America. This traversing of cultural boundaries forces us to understand why such boundaries existed in American culture and why musicians and others were compelled to transgress them. One needs to remain one step re-moved from the basic assumptions of the high-popular distinction in judging this cultural movement in order to recognize that the social and aesthetic distinctions embedded in this dichotomy were themselves constructed over time and how this movement attempted to transfig-ure these distinctions. The jazz art world was socially heterogeneous in terms of class, race, and education, although it remained a predomi-nantly male preserve. This very social heterogeneity undermined the basic conventions and assumptions active in high art and popular art. Fundamental questions of what constituted American culture in terms of social status and social identity were significantly challenged by the jazz art world.

The greatest challenge in the evolution of jazz music in the twentieth century was in disturbing the racial hierarchy in American culture. One problem in focusing only on the high art turn in jazz is that such a narrow emphasis tends to revert to questions only of social class and aesthetics, although even here the complexity of this turn in jazz is usually lost. It ignores how a racial hierarchy was intertwined with the class dynamics in high art and popular art in America. From the beginning, the defin-ing of American high art and American popular art always included the question of race with institutions carefully policing the segregation of African American culture. A two-dimensional cultural hierarchy, there-fore, located social status and social identity along parallel racial and class distinctions. In this sense, the early development of high art and popular art involved the construction of an American identity along both class and racial lines.

The jazz art world certainly faced its own contradictions and its own elitist tendencies in attempting to lift jazz music and jazz musicians to some higher cultural status. The jazz art world, however, ultimately staked claim to a unique tradition in American music that bridged various cultural distinctions active in both high and popular art in the United States. This art world was a unique combination of both populism and elitism – a celebration of the artistry of popular culture and a striving of many for high art status. It revealed in many ways the conflict-ridden na-ture of American democratic culture that celebrated the "common man" yet was infused with race, class, aesthetic, and moral distinctions of status and identity in cultural production and cultural consumption. But this does not mean that it did not represent a significant challenge to the American cultural hierarchy at the time. This book explores how this art world and jazz musicians created a tradition in American music that contributed significantly to refashioning America's understanding of art and society.

1 Before the jazz age: professional musicians and good music

We often hear complaints from musicians, especially band and orchestral, that they do not receive as much consideration and respect from the public as men of similar social status, but in other trades or professions... The musician, who is worthy the name, devotes his time unremittingly to his art, hence slander, or misapprehension, goes on unrefuted, so far as he is concerned. He is generally a man of a speculative turn of mind, dwelling apart, in realms of fancy, from the hurry-scurry of the world, apt to be sensitive and feel slights easily, but withal a good, honest citizen, who attends to his own business; and does not interfere with that of his neighbor... let some of those gentlemen who despise the musician, or who think his calling is an easy one, take a violin, or any other instrument in hand for a moment, try the most simple tune, or endeavor to play a common scale, *then* give their opinion... For the unremitting toil of the musical career, as well as for the social qualities of the musician, we claim that *true* musicians are worthy of the highest respect and consideration.

Editorial, *Metronome*, May 1885: 4

The first issue of *Metronome* was published in January 1885 and quickly established itself as a major national magazine for professional musicians in the United States. The Carl Fischer Company, a supplier of musical instruments and music sheets, published this "ad sheet" in New York City. *Metronome* remained a major magazine for professional musicians for 75 years, charting the rise and fall of the professional musician in American popular music until finally ending publication in 1961. As the editorial in May 1885 suggests, professional musicians in the late nineteenth century felt unappreciated as respectable professional artists. They also felt less than respected as tradesmen working to secure a livable wage. As professionals and tradesmen these musicians also would confront the question of the place of "good" music in popular performance.

The growth of a professional class of musician in the United States centered on the bands and orchestras that performed in cities across the country in the nineteenth century. These bands and orchestras were based on their European equivalents and borrowed their instrumental techniques and repertoires from Europe. Professional musicians shared a basic artistic culture founded on this European model of music making. Their ethos reflected a view of themselves as the best practitioners of music making in America – a skilled artisan class of trained and literate musicians. During this period, however, professional musicians constantly shifted between different performance contexts and music organizations within this shared artistic culture. And when performing for the general public, bands and orchestras would certainly add "popular" music to their standard European repertoire.

The May 1885 editorial in *Metronome* points to how professional musicians leading into the twentieth century viewed their role as providing the finest music available in America, what musicians and educators referred to as "good" music. "Good" music referred to the European music repertoire and legitimate techniques of professional bands and orchestras. Since most professional musicians performed for the general public, however, popular tastes and popular music constantly challenged the conception of their role in creating and promoting "good" music. Whether by choice or circumstance, most professional musicians became enmeshed in the relationship between what music historian H. Wiley Hitchcock (1988: 54–5) calls the cultivated and vernacular traditions in American music. The cultivated tradition was "a music almost exclusively based on continental European models, looked to rather self-consciously; an essentially transatlantic music of the pretenders to gentility." The vernacular tradition was "a music based on established or newly diffused American raw materials; a 'popular' music in the largest sense, broadly based…whose 'success' was measured not by abstract aesthetic standards but by those of the marketplace."

Hitchcock points to "an eventually profound schism in American musical culture" between the cultivated and vernacular traditions. Into the early decades of the twentieth century, however, most professional musicians bridged these traditions in their professional lives and in popular performance. The schism between these traditions, however, became more and more contentious as popular entertainment and popular music by the turn of the century was experiencing a tremendous growth that challenged the role of European cultivated music in the popular performances of professional musicians. Simultaneous to the growth of commercial popular music was the growth of a more insular patron-supported world of European cultivated music in symphony orchestras, grand operas, music societies, schools, and special journals. And as the sociologist Neil Leonard (1962) argues, elite "traditionalists" developed this exclusive social world of cultivated music specifically to distance themselves from popular entertainment and the popular classes.

The schism between these traditions at first was an ideological debate about the nature of popular performance and the role of the vernacular among peers who shared a common music culture. This schism, however, became more and more a reality of the social organization of music making in America. In the developments of a commercial market and a patron-supported art world, the production and performance of music in America centered more and more on two distinct traditions of music – European high art music and American popular art music. The professional class of musician in the United States itself would eventually divide along these two distinct paths. And as this direction in American music progressed, the original ideal of "good" music would itself be transformed. The promotion and ideal of "good" music originally shared by a single professional class of musician would move along two distinct routes, an old route of European cultivated music and a new route of American popular music.

What is often overlooked in the split between a European cultivated tradition and an American vernacular tradition, is how the American vernacular was itself being "cultivated" by professional musicians as well as Tin Pan Alley composers. As the commercial market in popular music expanded in urban cities, professional musicians secured the most lucrative jobs and applied their professional ethos of "good" music to popular performance and popular music. Meanwhile Tin Pan Alley composers were developing a more sophisticated popular song for vaudeville, musical theater, social dance, and eventually sound film that became the reigning popular music for the first half of the twentieth century. Ironically, the schism between the cultivated tradition and the vernacular tradition occurred at a time in which they most closely came together as professional musicians and composers brought their concept of "good" music to bear on the vernacular tradition in the commercial market of popular music.

These developments in the cultivated and the vernacular in American music also were enmeshed in the racial divide in American culture and society. While both white and black urban musicians developed as a professional class, and shared the basic ethos of providing "good" music to their audiences, the racial divide in American music would locate black professional musicians in a segregated market and in a distinctly subordinate position. At the same time, the formulation of the ideal of "good" music itself would confront the place of the black vernacular in American music as well – particularly as the black vernacular came to define American popular music. The black professional musician, therefore, would experience and respond to the developments between the cultivated and vernacular traditions in unique ways.

The directions that "good" music would eventually take among professional musicians articulated class, race, and professional distinctions in American music. This chapter discusses the early developments in the break between the cultivated and vernacular traditions and the fate of "good" music in America. It shows how the unique combination of social distinctions that affected American music in the late nineteenth and early twentieth century set up an equally unique development of two distinct "cultivated" music traditions – the high and the popular. It was this development of two traditions among professional musicians that would eventually lead to the evolution of jazz music as high art.

Professional musicians: the vernacular tradition and "good" music

It will soon be time for bands to make up their programmes for the summer, and every leader should see that there is sufficient variety in his repertoire to suit all classes of listeners. Many arguments have arisen as to just what ought to be given, some being of the opinion that only popular selections should be heard while others think that leaders should confine their work to classical music... By close observation a director can gauge the tastes and needs of his patrons and give entertainments that will prove beneficial. In no instance should he assume to reform tastes of the public or to revolutionize prevailing methods too suddenly. If he does, he will be looked upon as a conceited, disagreeable person and will utterly fail in his mission. Should he find that popular music creates more enthusiasm than anything of a classical nature, he ought to give only the best of popular selections, leading his listeners on to a higher and higher grade until finally the very music they disliked at first will prove the more enjoyable. (Editorial, *Metronome*, April 1895: 4)

As vernacular music became commercialized in written sheet music and popular performance in the nineteenth century, professional bands and orchestras incorporated this music into their performance repertoire. For professional musicians, however, "good" music referred to the European music tradition of classical, opera, and dance music. Popular songs based on vernacular music were viewed as a necessary burden to appease the tastes of the less cultivated classes, and of course, to secure a living wage. In simple terms, professional musicians carried an ethos of cultivated music making but often performed for popular audiences an eclectic repertoire that included American vernacular music. This was not necessarily a contradiction for the profession; it was such a balance that for many musicians made their role a democratic one – a type of cultural mediator introducing popular audiences to cultivated European music and performing vernacular-based popular music in a refined manner. "Our orchestras and bands are up to the times, also, and better able to interpret in a fitting manner compositions of every kind." (*Metronome* 9-1895: 12) As an 1889 editorial in *Metronome* advised its readers, the "bandmaster *must* play for the public. Doing so, his programmes are varied and calculated to suit all kinds of tastes, from those who enjoy a minstrel song to those who revel in the highest art forms." (*Metronome* 8-1889: 5)

Among early professional musicians performing popular music in the late nineteenth century, band organizations were the most common and performed as marching bands, band orchestras, and social dance orchestras. Brass band organizations included government and commercial bands. The big season for popular performances was the summer as these bands were employed in public parks throughout the country. Band orchestras, however, also performed on special occasions at special concerts, to large jubilees, to presidential inaugurations. The social orchestra, which often included strings, performed popular European dances such as the cotillion, waltz, lancer, and polka.

The most famous band organizations in the late nineteenth century were those of Patrick Sarsfield Gilmore and John Philip Sousa. As organizations of professional musicians performing for popular audiences, the Gilmore and Sousa bands performed an eclectic repertoire and prided themselves on mediating the various tastes of their audiences while bringing "good" music to the public. As *Metronome* noted in 1895 "perhaps the greatest charm of Sousa's concerts is the rare variety of music and of musical effect which characterize them. At one moment he is in the midst of a Wagner overture or a Schubert symphony, and the next he is rollicking off into a jolly plantation dance, or a lively and inspiriting march." (*Metronome* 2-1895: 4)

Sousa was continuing the tradition of his predecessor P. S. Gilmore, whose mantle he would take after Gilmore's death in 1892, the same year Sousa left as bandmaster of the United States Marine Band to embark on a commercial career. The self-defined role of professional musicians uplifting the tastes of popular audiences can be seen in this 1888 *Metronome* (4-1888: 10) editorial acclamation of Gilmore in response to a critic's review in the *New York Herald*:

Mr. Gilmore constantly gives evidence that he understands the public and knows how to cater to all tastes. He knows better than any man that the public, willing to be led, cannot be driven, and prepares his programmes accordingly. He baits the public with favorite compositions, and thus entraps them to listen to better things; consequently his audiences are representative in the best sense, and the educational work he performs is inestimable.

This critic seems to have followed the error common to his class, of viewing all popular music as claptrap. Such views may to some extent be correct. On the other hand, and speaking as a musician, we know much passing as high-class music that is pure rubbish, while many so-called popular works have the elements, development and vitality that will assure them life long after much that is now lauded by a clique will be thoroughly dead, buried and forgotten as the critic on the *Herald*.

The defense of Gilmore's approach to popular performance besides defending his eclectic repertoire, although defending somewhat equivo-cally popular music, also included another common refrain in *Metronome*. As professional musicians performed their eclectic repertoire for popular audiences, they would remind their stuffy critics of the elite nature of clas-sical orchestra concerts and the privileged class who patronized them. In its defense of Gilmore, the *Metronome* editorial referred to the elite nature of classical concert performances in New York City. "The orchestral con-certs in this city, truly excellent in their way, are undeniably supported by a class only, consisting of from two to three thousand people. Anyone in the habit of attending these concerts knows this to be true, as he finds the same faces around him at each performance. The music is unquestion-able, rendition admirable, but the great public does not come in contact therewith, and hence is not benefited thereby. Gilmore's concerts, on the contrary, reach all classes and do good everywhere." As John Philip Sousa later commented about elite classical concerts and their symphony con-ductors, "I think I have done more missionary work for the better class of music than all the rest of them put together." (*Music* 7-1899, ref. Bierley 1973: 142)

Most early "populist" professional musicians still were somewhat am-biguous about performing for popular audiences since "good" music was still mostly defined as legitimate European music in opposition to American vernacular music – these musicians sought a balance between "good" music and popular tastes with the emphasis on "good" mu-sic. Of course, the position of early populist professional musicians still found them constantly defending themselves as educators of popular taste against the elitists of European cultivated music, or the moralists of re-ligious music, who found the catering to lowbrow tastes an unseemly affair. While there was a debate as to whether musicians should entertain or should elevate their audiences, an 1897 editorial in *Metronome* could "see no reason why people should not be both elevated and entertained at the same time by music. This does not mean that musicians should force upon their audiences music of such grade that cannot be compre-hended." (*Metronome* 8-1897: 3) Yet in defending the public, populist professional musicians in the late nineteenth century still retained the view of European cultivated music as "good" music, whether symphonic, opera or dance music. John Philip Sousa summed up the populist mission of professional musicians performing for popular audiences in reflecting on his earlier career in the late nineteenth century in "Bandmaster Sousa Explains His Mission in Music" in *Musical America* on April 16, 1910.

It seemed to me, in my early life, that the principles of this type of music might be so far elaborated and utilized as to reach the entire world directly and effectively. . . . My theory was, by insensible degrees, first to reach every heart by simple, stirring music; second, to lift the unmusical mind to a still higher form of musical art. This was my mission. The point was to move all America, while busied in its various pursuits, by the power of direct and simple music. I wanted to make a music for the people, a music to be grasped at once. (John Philip Sousa, *Musical America* (Bierley 1973: 119))

The debate over "good" music, vernacular music, and popular audiences was not only a debate over musical tastes and music making but was infused with a strong moral undercurrent as well. Advocating for professional musicians in the late nineteenth century included a claim of the morally uplifting quality of "good" music. In an 1888 *Metronome* article "Good Music Not Inimical To Good Morals," Philip G. Herbert Jr. strongly supported the moral character of music making – arguing against the position held by "many moralists, and especially by the writers of Puritanical schools." Herbert lamented the view held by some that "any man who devoted himself wholly to music, its culture, its study and aesthetic bearings . . . is apt to be morally irresponsible, music having weakened his moral fibre." (*Metronome* 5-1888: 16)

The moral undercurrent in the debate over music making in America in the nineteenth century at first was a general question about secular music, both cultivated and vernacular, and the secular musician. But as the "genteel" tradition of cultivated European music making won greater favor among the moral guardians of American culture, moral questions focused more on vernacular music, popular audiences, and popular musicians. The populist professional musician, therefore, in defending his profession as a self-selected cultural mediator of the cultivated and vernacular traditions in American music had to deal with the convolution of aesthetic and moral arguments.

"Good" music in the late nineteenth century positioned vernacular-based popular music as well as popular audiences in both aesthetic and moral arguments – cultivated music was, as H. Wiley Hitchcock (1988: 54) argues, "to be appreciated for its edification – its moral, spiritual, or aesthetic values." Populist professional musicians were able to distance themselves in relation to the vernacular as educators of public taste in which "good" music played an important role in their performances as well as a cultivated rendition of vernacular-based popular music. They also were able to distance themselves to the vernacular in the distinction between their performances and venues for the public and those performances and venues of the purely vernacular in minstrelsy and variety shows in touring troupes, dance halls, and saloons. In general, a gap in terms of venues and repertoire existed between the "legitimate" world of public performance of professional musicians and the commercial world of vernacular music in the minstrel shows and variety shows of the nineteenth century.

While proclaiming their democratic roles in popular performances, populist professional musicians reproduced the class distinctions operating in the aesthetic and moral arguments over "good" music. The nineteenth century ideal of "good" music masked the concerns of the urban elite and middle class in America over the culture and power of the much larger working class population. The American vernacular represented the tastes and values of the working class against the tastes and values of the urban elite and the middle class. While in essence professional musicians themselves were working class and most came from working-class families, their professional ethos of cultivated music making reproduced the middle class ideology of aesthetic and moral superiority to the working class. The distancing in performance repertoire, style, and venue of professional musicians from the vernacular music of saloons, dance halls, and lower class minstrel shows, allowed these musicians to position themselves above the rabble of the pure vernacular, and intervene in public performances to mediate the cultivated with the vernacular.

The question of the relation between "good" music, vernacular music, and the professional musician, however, became more and more contentious as the world of American popular music entered a period of commercial expansion and development by the turn of the century. The last years of the nineteenth century signaled an important change in American popular performance. As the music historian Gilbert Chase (1987) and the social historian David Nasaw (1993) both argue, these years marked the beginning of a major commercial expansion in American popular music, part of a more general change in American popular entertainment. The commercial expansion of popular entertainment was a boost to previous band venues such as parks during the summer season. This expansion also moved American popular music into new performance venues designed to cater to a broader audience by class and gender. The new popular entertainment of vaudeville, musical theater, and musical revues, was geared to attract a broader public and their success boosted the construction of theaters across the country. Other popular entertainment venues for music that appeared were amusement parks, hotel lobbies, dance halls, and even restaurants because every "restaurant that wishes to be known as something better than an eating house is employing a good orchestra." (*Metronome* 10-1904: 14)

The rise of Tin Pan Alley song coincided with this boom in popular music entertainment and in the process created a new popular music during this period. (Chase 1987) As the music historian Charles Hamm (1983, 1979) argues, these composers standardized the popular song format while acting as mediators of the American vernacular – co-opting and transforming vernacular song into the commercial market of sheet music and live entertainment. With the success of Tin Pan Alley, professional musicians performed more and more vernacular-based popular music as compared to the balance of the cultivated and the vernacular of popular performances in the past. And like professional musicians, Tin Pan Alley composers mediated commercial popular music by translating the vernacular into compositions of "good" music – what the music historian Reebee Garofalo (1997) refers to as "mainstreaming" the vernacular.

As new "legitimate" forms of popular music and entertainment venues emerged, the professional musician entered new performance contexts. The movement to more vernacular-based music in popular performance by professional musicians, however, re-ignited the debates about "good" music and the fact that "composers write what the people want. If there is a demand for any particular class of music, the composer naturally turns to that." (*Metronome* 10-1904: 14) The debate between the "standards" of the cultivated tradition and the "popular airs" of the vernacular became a constant refrain. A *Metronome* editorial in 1904, for example, decried the new Tin Pan Alley song preferred in the new popular entertainment: "Time and again it has been asserted in this paper that the managers who produce the lighter form of musical entertainment misjudge the public in offering trash as the only thing likely to 'take'. . . [T]he managers insist in making the librettists and composers lower themselves to the darkest cellar level of taste and intelligence. There are, no doubt, thousands who prefer trash, but there are tens of thousands who would enjoy fun spiced with such good music of its kind as we used to have in the days of Offenbach, Lecocq, Strauss, Suppé, and Sullivan." (*Metronome* 12-1904: 7)

H. M. WEBER, director of the Toxaway Inn Orchestra, at Cape Toxaway, N. C., has proven himself a musician of splendid capabilities as well as a director of much magnetism. His programmes have been the delight of guests stopping at the inn, and one and all have been of the highest class of music rendered by splendid musicians. Mr. Weber evidently believes that the only good programme should be made up of good music and caters very little to popular tastes, and he has found in past experiences that good music (provided you have capable musicians to interpret it) is by far a greater attraction than the common ordinary rags. ("Among the Orchestras," *Metronome*, October 1904: 14)

At the turn of the century, the musical style most associated with the commercial rise of the American vernacular was ragtime music. Its challenge to "good" music became a regular refrain among critics of the increasing part played by American vernacular music among the popular performances of professional musicians. At least critics were not alone in their fears as "the daily papers in every part of the country are at last awakening and paying some small attention to the pernicious influence which the general run of trashy rag-time stuff is having on our public and musical tastes." (*Metronome* 3-1903: 11)

The laments of critics of the rise of Tin Pan Alley song and the American vernacular in the performances of professional musicians in vaudeville and musical theater continued even as this profession occupied the most lucrative jobs in the commercial market of live popular music performance. The continued defenders of the old definition of "good" music, however, could not stop the movement of a large part of their professional class, and the general paying public, into the American vernacular. *Metronome* was an "ad sheet" that advertised mostly music instruments and music sheets, and by the end of the first decade of the twentieth century Tin Pan Alley songs sheets began competing equally with the more traditional European based repertoire of bands and orchestras of the past. The previous balance between European "good" music and American vernacular music was shifting in the opposite direction in the popular performance of professional musicians in the early decades of the twentieth century. As the articles "The Degeneration of Our Popular Song" and "The Influence of Good and Bad Music" in *Metronome* in 1914 show, this shift in popular performance continued to upset the upholders of "good" music.

It is true that there are still a few writers who pride themselves on trying to keep up the interest of the music-loving public by writing good class songs, and who will not prostitute their talents by the writing of degrading ragtime and suggestive songs to please the taste of the perverted public... Where are our American classic composers today? There are practically none. They are swept aside in the great maelstrom of commercialism. The classical composer starves in his attic, while the illiterate one-fingered piano pounder gathers in the shekels from a generous public. ("The Degeneration of Our Popular Song," *Metronome*, January 1914: 18)

The lamentable craze for the so-called rag-time music is nothing but an outgrowth of bad taste, and while some of these pieces may be a wholesome change from the traditional and conventional, and while some of these productions, from good authors, are not without a certain freshness and pure naïvete, that is no reason for people to get "loony" about it and refuse to listen to the standard and legitimate, and give these jerky and stuttering pieces an overdue attention. ("The Influence of Good and Bad Music," *Metronome*, February 1914: 20)

The dance craze in the second decade of the twentieth century added fuel to the fire of controversy among professional musicians over "good" music and the American vernacular tradition in music. The new craze for dance was spurred on by the popular dance duo of Irene and Vernon Castle and their supporting dance orchestra directed by the black professional musician James Reese Europe. It spread among the public in rags, two-steps, foxtrots, and tangos – syncopated dance – and generated equal criticism to that of ragtime music. Professional musicians, however, quickly recognized syncopated dance's inevitable rise. "[H]as anything taken hold of the public with such a firm grip as the present desire for dancing... Assailed and defended with equal violence, this amazing phenomenon of the twentieth century has ceased to be an incident and bids fair to assume the proportions of an epoch...it is some years since the first ripple of the turkey trot and the tango broke upon these shores, and the tidal wave which immediately followed had inundated the ball rooms, the hotels, the cafés, invaded the sacred precincts of home and even threaten to engulf religious institutions." (*Metronome* 6-1914: 13) While religious institutions survived the dance craze, the popularity of syncopated dance did transform American popular music. Against the best hopes of its detractors, social dance music became a leading form of popular music entertainment.

The first decades of the twentieth century saw the rise of vaudeville, musical theater, musical revues, social dance, and Tin Pan Alley song – the development of a vibrant commercial popular music market based on the American vernacular tradition. And while defenders of "good" music constantly assailed the rising success of American vernacular music, professional musicians and composers were adopting American vernacular as the center of their careers. Older forms of band and orchestra performances for popular audiences continued alongside this development, but a significant shift was occurring in the repertoire and focus of professional musicians in popular performance. The new popular orchestra organizations of professional musicians that emerged in the early twentieth century were molding the instrumentation, arrangement, and legitimate techniques of older band and orchestras with vernacular-based popular music.

In the early twentieth century, professional musicians in adopting the American vernacular were transforming it through their professional ethos of "cultivated" music making. Many professional musicians began presenting the new American vernacular as "good" music. A process was beginning where professional musicians in moving to performance contexts where "popular" music predominated were shifting their ideal of "good" music to the performance of the American vernacular. It was this gradual transformation among professional musicians and in the American vernacular during this period that led to the jazz orchestras and big bands that dominated American popular music from the 1920s to the 1950s.

Black professional musicians: the black vernacular and "good" music

By the end of the nineteenth century black musicians were successfully establishing their own professional class. *Metronome* was a magazine for white professional musicians, however, and until the 1930s ignored these developments among black musicians. Racial segregation assured that the development of music as a profession among black urban musicians ran along parallel lines, including segregated venues, union locals, and music organizations. A growing commercial market for black entertainment, however, which grew in relation to the growth of black communities in major cities across the country, provided the foundation for black urban musicians to develop professionally. While these two professional classes of urban musicians developed separately they shared a similar ethos as well as similar performance roles. They also shared similar musical techniques and music repertoire, although black professional musicians did distinguish themselves in their adoption of the black vernacular in popular music making. Black artists, however, had a somewhat distinct relationship to the development of an American vernacular tradition and European cultivated tradition among professional musicians that played a role in their articulation of these traditions in the early years of the twentieth century.

The music historian Eileen Southern (1997) in *The Music of Black Americans* describes how the professional class of black musicians by the end of the nineteenth century performed across the country in popular bands and orchestras. Like their white counterparts, black professional musicians based their performances on instrumental techniques and music repertoires from Europe. The black middle class in the nineteenth century adopted similar attitudes as the white middle class, aesthetic and moral, about what constituted "good" music and this was reflected in the performances of black professional musicians. The music historian Samuel A. Floyd (1995) argues, however, that black professional musicians in the late nineteenth century while predominately following

European traditions were adopting black vernacular rhythms in their "ragging" of dance tunes in some popular performance – one basis of the ragtime craze at the turn of the century.

Just like white professional musicians and white Tin Pan Alley composers, in the early years of the twentieth century black professional musicians and black composers became active in musical theater, vaudeville, musical revues, and dance. Black entertainment districts were growing in black communities in major cities of the Great Migration including the establishment of major theaters for theatrical performances, musical revues, concerts, and film. Professional musicians were not only performing for black audiences in these new districts, however, but also began attracting white audiences. The musical *In Dahomey* that premiered on Broadway in New York City in 1903 also marked the beginnings of black professional musicians "crossover" to popular performances for white audiences outside the black community. (Shaw 1986) These black musical revues, unfortunately, as in earlier black minstrelsy, made use of racial stereotypes to entertain white audiences. Black professional musicians like William Marion Cook who wrote *In Dahomey*, however, while struggling with the perpetuation of such stereotypes still viewed the success of these musical revues as a major advancement for their professional class.

The dance craze for syncopated rhythms in the second decade of the twentieth century significantly pushed the "crossover" of professional black musicians to white entertainment districts as well as attracted white audiences to black entertainment districts. It represented a major financial boost to this profession and the start of integration of a more shared dance culture among black and white audiences based on the black vernacular in music and dance. The popularity of syncopated dance influenced not only social dances but also musical revues. In New York City, the emerging center of the popular music industry, black professional musicians not only performed for the social dances of white elite and middle class patrons, but also found jobs performing, composing, and arranging in conjunction with musical revues such as the famous Ziegfeld Follies. The famous composer and writer James Weldon Johnson in one of his regular contributions to the black newspaper *New York Age* in 1915 noted the great success of black musicians in his response to a white musician's complaint of this change in fortunes for his black contemporaries in the *New York Globe*. "The writer is evidently a New York musician, and he cannot understand why the Negro musicians of this city are making competition so strong for their white professional brothers... When he refers to the colored players as 'so-called-musicians' he may think he is slurring them, but, instead, he is slurring the white society people, and hotel and café proprietors who prefer Negro musicians... There are good and sufficient reasons why Negro musicians are preferred at social affairs. Modern music and modern dancing are both Negro creations. Since ragtime has swept the world and become universally known as American music, there have been attempts to rob the Negro of the credit of originating it; but this is in accord with an old habit of the white race; as soon as anything is recognized as great, they set about to claim credit for it." Johnson, however, ended his piece with a warning to his black professional brethren. "And let us add a word to the Negro musician upon efficiency in his work. He cannot afford to run along merely upon his great natural gift... Let the Negro musician improve and develop himself." (Johnson 1995: 284–6)

In the rise of popular music entertainment, the black professional musician, like his white counterpart, played an intermediary role between "good" music and vernacular music. William Howland Kenny (1993) and Thomas J. Hennessey (1994) both point out how black professional musicians applied to their popular performances the legitimate techniques of music making based on the cultivated tradition – the application of the idea of "good" music. As American vernacular music became more prevalent, particularly the black vernacular, these musicians incorporated this music in their repertoire while applying cultivated techniques to its performance for popular audiences. However, just as the professional class of white musicians was debating the proper balance of the cultivated and the vernacular in popular performances, the professional class of black musicians grappled with a similar balance between "good" music and the black vernacular. But again like their white counterparts, except for the black elite and segments of the black middle class, the market of popular tastes was demanding popular music incorporating the vernacular, particularly the larger market of white audiences who could easily get "good" cultivated music from white professional musicians. As Samuel B. Charters and Leonard Kunstadt (1962: 25) point out, the black professional musician "had to decide between a career as an unsuccessful serious musician or a career as a popular entertainer, playing music that the public expected Negro musicians to play."

The ideal of "good" music in America, however, was not only a question of vernacular versus cultivated music. The criticisms of ragtime and syncopated dance in the early twentieth century were also about the rising influence of the black vernacular in American popular music. The "pernicious" quality of ragtime given obsessive attention by critics of the vernacular was tied to its roots in black vernacular music. Ragtime was "the same old tune, invented in such remote times that it must be classed as ab-original rather than original." (*Metronome* 3-1903: 6) There was no doubt that ragtime was "a genuine creation of Negro blood." (*Metronome* 3-1903: 11) For critics, the clearest links to the black vernacular were the rhythmic qualities of ragtime and syncopated music. "It perpetuates and embodies the rhythm of those crude instruments of noise and percussion, which, in their original African home, awakens the fanatic enthusiasm of the natives for their religious and grotesque dances... Two centuries of continued importation of slaves naturally checked the spread of civilization among them." (*Metronome* 3-1903: 11) "To show its demoralizing tendency on the public discrimination, it is simply necessary to call attention to the fact that when in music, rhythm is dissociated from melody and harmony, the tendency is decadent and leads directly back to the primitive, the negro, and the savage." (*Metronome*, 1-1917: 44) The criticism of ragtime and syncopated dance also included laments of the popularity of "coon" songs at the turn of the century – these songs followed the earlier tradition of minstrel music of the nineteenth century.

The question of "good" music, therefore, had different ramifications for black professional musicians than white professional musicians. The racist connotation of "good" music was active in both attitudes about black vernacular music and about black musicians. The pejorative primitivism associated with black culture as applied to black vernacular music had important implications for black professional musicians. These ramifications involved the fears and prejudices of the black elite and middle class in terms of the implications for "the race" of the popularity of the black vernacular. The black community in general, however, held black professional musicians in high regard as one of the few professions open to their community – a burden that carried the extra weight of upholding the image of their community. As black vernacular music gained popularity in the early years of the twentieth century in ragtime music and syncopated music, however, black professional musicians had to balance the biases in performing the idioms of the black vernacular in their own communities.

The ramifications of the black vernacular for black professional musicians also involved the fears, attractions, and prejudices among European Americans. Outside the black community, these musicians had to confront the fears of the black vernacular, while also taking advantage of the new demand for "syncopated" music. In entertaining white audiences, however, black professional musicians also had to contend and adjust to the prejudicial views on the talents of black artists. In adopting the black vernacular, black professional musicians were viewed as less cultivated than the same white professional musicians who incorporated black vernacular rags and syncopated music in their performances – ironically in part because the black professional musician could rag much better than his white counterpart.

Hennessey (1994) points to the racist assumptions of white audiences about black professional musicians in the early twentieth century. Not wanting to offend their white audiences, black professional musicians, who were musically literate and trained in legitimate techniques of music making, would sometimes perform for white audiences without music stands, often pretending to spontaneously create their performance of written and pre-arranged songs. Hennessey makes specific reference to the most popular orchestras of the Clef Club organization of black professional musicians in New York City who were riding the wave of the dance craze for syncopated music. Of course, the musicians of the Clef Club also performed music from the European cultivated tradition in both classical concerts and more eclectic popular performances – they were among the top professional black musicians in New York City. The president and conductor of the orchestra was James Reese Europe. As Eubie Blake, a member of the Clef Club Orchestra, remembered "that Europe Gang were absolute reading sharks. They could read a moving snake and if a fly lit on that paper he got played." (Blesh 1971: 205) The effect of the Clef Club "performances" of the illiterate black musician in confirming the racial construction of "good" music can be seen in the acclamation of "Negro genius" by Natalie Curtis-Burlin in *The Musical Quarterly*. In remembering her experience listening to Clef Club musicians rehearse and perform seven years earlier Ms. Curtis-Burlin exclaims:

Indeed, the men of a European orchestra, each carefully schooled to automatic accuracy in his given role, would be baffled if called upon to do the almost inhumanly difficult things that these intuitive black players did naturally... The average Negro, in music, seems inspired as compared to the letter ridden, unimaginative, uncreative, and prosaic (however correct) white performer.

"Oh, yes," the conductor said, "they can catch *anything* if they hear it once, or twice, and if it's too hard for 'em the way its written, why, they just make up something else that'll go with it." (Natalie Curtis-Burlin, *The Musical Quarterly*, October 1919: 502–4)

Racial consciousness in American music created a clear distinction between white and black professional musicians. In adopting the black vernacular, as Kenny (1993) argues, black professional musicians were definitely distinct *musically* from their white counterparts in performing the American vernacular. The question remained, however, in how this distinction was interpreted by white professional musicians and white audiences. Was this distinction a matter of the "primitive" or "natural" talents of black professional musicians or a matter of the unique development of a distinct popular idiom by "skilled" artisans of the craft of music making? The struggle for black professional musicians was not only in legitimating the black vernacular, but also in legitimating their own status in American music.

The struggle of black professional musicians in legitimating their status in American music involved not only their own internal debates over "good" music and the black vernacular. As the black vernacular gained greater appeal among white audiences, white professional musicians increasingly incorporated the black vernacular in their music making. White Tin Pan Alley composers also increasingly incorporated the black vernacular such as the famous rags of the most successful white composer of the period, Irving Berlin. The dance craze in particular set in motion the greater co-optation of the black vernacular by white popular artists that culminated in the Jazz Age of the 1920s. Given the racist attitudes about black professional musicians and the segregation of the music market for black musicians and composers, white professional musicians and composers would lay claim to being the true cultivators of the black vernacular.

Black professional musicians and composers, however, "cultivated" the black vernacular through the synthesis of this idiom with the cultivated composition, instrumentation, arrangement, and legitimate techniques that these musicians shared with their white counterparts. Like white professional musicians, black professional musicians were experiencing a shift in their understanding of "good" music as they applied their professional ethos to the American vernacular. It was the formation of the "syncopated" orchestras of black professional musicians in the early twentieth century, and their growing popularity, which became the foundation of the jazz orchestras and swing big bands of the 1920s, 1930s, and 1940s.

Mediating the popular: the popular music market and non-professional musicians

Related to the question of "good" music among early white and black professional musicians was the question of the professional musician versus the non-professional musician in entertaining the public. As *Metronome* made constantly clear, professional bands were composed of highly skilled artisans "whose sole vocation is music, and who follow the art as a means of livelihood." These bands' "splendid musical performance will prove a great drawing card with the public and eventuate in greater profits than could be realized from the policy of engaging an inferior band for less money." Such inferior bands included the large number of part-time musicians who supported themselves in other trades, often performing for company bands, who were "the natural enemy of the professional bands." Other bands were of "amateur" musicians, "numerically the strongest of the group," who were "crude compared by a professional standard, but it must be remembered they are often situated in primitive communities." As for government bands, "there is not much to be said as the conditions of their connection removes them from the field of practical competition." (*Metronome* 10-1889: 8–9)

The professional musician was not only confronting the single-minded purveyors of European cultivated music and the moral guardians of American culture, but those musicians – part-time, amateur, and folk – who threatened their livelihoods and their position in performing for popular audiences. These other musicians were characterized as a threat to the emerging profession both musically and financially. Musically, non-professional musicians were characterized as not having the skilled artisanship or necessary discipline to perform "good" music, vernacular or cultivated, and a well-rounded popular performance, of course, included both traditions. Certainly, non-professional musicians with the proper training could join the fraternity of professional musicians – *Metronome* was a strong supporter of educating and disciplining the amateur musician. The non-professional musician also was viewed as threatening the livelihoods of professional musicians in providing cheap labor. The unscrupulous and miserly manager could always hire non-professional musicians to the detriment not only of professional musicians, of course, but to the listening public.

In defense of "good" music, public taste, and the livelihood of the American professional musician, there was without doubt only one course open. In tandem with the development of a professional ethos among urban musicians in the late nineteenth century was the development of professional musicians' unions. Originally developed as local mutual protection associations, these early associations became the foundations of the union locals that made up the American Federation of Musicians chartered in 1896 as part of the American Federation of Labor. The AFM was to play an important role in American music. Local unions fought hard to secure standard wages, hours, and payment for professional musicians as well as fighting to secure jobs against the encroachment of non-professional musicians, as well as foreign musicians, into the music labor market.

The importance of musicians' unions for the professional class of American musician lay not only in how unions helped over time to make music making a more sustainable profession or trade, but in how unions also helped professional musicians in their co-option of popular music making. As the American popular music market began to develop in new and more expansive ways in the early twentieth century, unions were key to professional musicians securing the best jobs in the booming market of popular music. In turn, while securing these positions, professional musicians also began the process of adopting and reinventing vernacular popular music, although initially in the controversy over ragtime the AFM issued condemnations of this pernicious music's influence on popular performance. The professional musician, however, became the dominant interpreter of vernacular popular music in the lucrative popular music market of the early twentieth century, and unions played an important role in securing this position in American music.

Unions, however, were not the only way in which professional musicians dominated local popular music performance. Band and orchestra organizations of professional musicians had the advantage over non-professional musicians in securing employment in the top "legitimate" venues of a city or region. Their reputations and connections among managers and producers in musical theater, musical revues, hotels, major dance halls, and film theaters assured their dominance of these venues. Before the rise of independent national touring management companies in the 1930s, band organizations were their own management groups. The top band and orchestra organizations included a large number of musicians in a number of different units that were employed throughout a single city and beyond. John Philip Sousa, for example, oversaw a national band organization that included more than the brass band he himself conducted.

Unions and band-orchestra organizations not only divided the professional musician from the non-professional, but also the white professional musician from the black professional musician. White union locals would not permit black professional musicians from joining their fraternity of artists. Black professional musicians had to create their own locals across the country. Black professional musicians also had to form their own band and orchestra organizations to compete in an already constrained segregated market with their white-only counterparts. White unions and band-orchestra organizations in the racially segregated market made it that much harder for black professional musicians to break the color line in American music. White unions and band-orchestra organizations not only worked against the encroachment of non-professional musicians, but also worked against the full integration of black professional musicians into the popular music market.

Of course, black unions and black band-orchestra organizations of professional musicians also co-opted popular music performance in controlling the most lucrative jobs available to black musicians.

Non-professional black musicians suffered the same fate as non-professional white musicians. As William Howland Kenny (1993) points out, black unions and band-orchestra organizations controlled the most lucrative jobs and applied quality control over the musicians to insure "good" music making and disciplined musicians. While professional black musicians controlled the major performance venues and most lucrative jobs, non-professionals populated the working class jook joints – saloons and dance halls – in the black community. With the onset of prohibition, non-professionals also were employed in the smaller speakeasies of the prohibition era, although even in the top "speakeasies" like the Cotton Club in New York City, professional musicians dominated.

In the case of both white and black professional musicians, their organizational power in conjunction with the demand for "legitimate" music in the popular entertainment market placed them in a dominant position to that of the non-professional musician. So while the American vernacular was gaining ground in the early twentieth century, the non-professional musician would only find work in the margins of the popular music market. This organizational exclusion was combined with an attitude among professional musicians of the inferiority of "illiterate" non-professionals. So while professional musicians were adopting the vernacular, and therefore moving towards more of a relationship with vernacular musicians and their music practices, they distanced themselves organizationally and ideologically from the non-professional.

This process of co-optation and control over performance helped professional musicians to "cultivate" the American vernacular. In dominating the popular music market they assured that American "popular" music until the mid-twentieth century was mediated through their professional class of musician. In terms of the racial barrier, the organizational power of white professional musicians also positioned them as the dominant mediator of American popular music during this period. Even as the black vernacular came to define in large measure American popular music as seen in the succession of popular music of the first half of the twentieth century – ragtime, syncopated dance, jazz, and swing – black professional musicians remained marginal in relation to their creative efforts and major contributions. The popular music market was structured into a status hierarchy by profession and race in which white professional musicians were on top of the status hierarchy above both black professional musicians and non-professional musicians.

Of course, another element in the status hierarchy of the professional class of musician was the subordination and segregation of female musicians. The top of this professional class was decidedly reserved for males only. While the AFM had no specific policy against female membership, union locals and band organizations assured that men dominated this profession. (Seltzer 1989) And when female musicians performed in public, they usually performed in all-female organizations, similar to the segregation of music making by race. Given the exclusion and segregation of female musicians in the profession of music performance, not surprisingly, female musicians came to occupy a special place within the music education movement in the late nineteenth century. Confronting significant obstacles as professional musicians, women found the more "domestic" role of music educator was a far more acceptable role for women. (Tick 1986) The subordination and segregation of women in the world of professional music making would continue in the twentieth century. (Ammer 1980; Neuls-Bates 1986) During World War II, for example, while "all-girl" bands performed for audiences across America as members of the AFM, no fundamental change occurred in the male domination of this profession as female musicians returned to their traditional subordinate position in the field of music following the war. (Tucker 2000)

Tin Pan Alley composers also co-opted the vernacular through their organizational power over the commercial popular music market. These composers, through their publishers, dominated popular music entertainment, which included providing financial incentives for song plugging by singers and bands. Composers, lyricists, and publishers also formed the American Society of Composers, Authors, and Publishers (ASCAP) in 1914. This association, while intended to assure financial remuneration from the performance of popular songs in addition to the sale of sheet music, also acted as a barrier to non-members. As the commercial market of popular music expanded, this organization would hold significant control over the performance of popular music in the most lucrative parts of the popular music market. As the major publishers and ASCAP co-opted the popular music market from non-professionals, they also excluded professional black composers. The initial charter of ASCAP of 170 writers only included two black composers, Henry T. Burleigh and James Weldon Johnson. (Southern 1997) Music publishers and ASCAP reproduced in popular composition the same status hierarchy by profession and race that unions and band-orchestras did in popular music performance.

In the commercial boom of the popular music market in the early twentieth century, professional musicians and composers positioned themselves as the premier artists in American popular music. In securing their positions against the non-professional artists of the American vernacular, professional musicians and composers became the mediators of the vernacular tradition in popular music. And as we have seen, from this position they applied their "cultivated" skills to the creation and performance of popular music. Yet, while musicians and composers were cultivating the American vernacular, another development was occurring in American music. A new art world of the European cultivated tradition was appearing and making its own claims to the ownership of "good" music in America.

Highbrow music: the cultivated tradition in American music

The cultivation of the fine arts in a community is always an evidence of progress toward a higher state of civilization. Nations in their primitive stages have naturally been too much engrossed with their *material* development, to pay any attention to music, painting or poetry, except as a side issue; but when, as years have rolled by, the industrial interests of the state, have become established and the people, as a result, more easy in their circumstances, the mind, freed from the fetters which bound it, has reached out beyond the prosaic and grosser pursuits of life, into the realm, where art meeting nature, joins hands for the refinement of mankind. (Editorial, *Metronome*, April 1885: 4)

In its editorial of April 1895, *Metronome* was joining other commentaries on the state of American music that appeared in the late nineteenth century and into the twentieth century. The editorial highlights the concern of many professional musicians and others at the time about the future of cultivated music in America. The concern was whether the cultivated tradition was enjoying the necessary support among cultured listeners to remain a vital part of the American musical landscape. This editorial pointed once again to the question of the place of "good" music in America. Unlike arguments about the cultivated and vernacular in popular performance, however, this editorial was addressing how a more select class "more easy in their circumstances, the mind, freed from the fetters which bound it" could enjoy and support a truly cultivated art in American music. While many professional musicians into the early years of the twentieth century adopted the American vernacular and moved towards a cultivated vernacular tradition, the cultivated tradition was moving in a separate direction towards a high art world of cultivated music in music societies, symphony orchestras, grand operas, schools, and journals.

The music historian John H. Mueller in 1951 described in less than favorable terms the state of the cultivated tradition leading into the nineteenth century. "Most of the concerts consisted of what are now deprecatingly referred to as 'tutti-frutti' programs, an admixture of vocal and instrumental solo and ensemble numbers. In contrast to the present taste, the concert programs of the pioneer period evince a heterogeneity in type and quality that seems shocking to the modern ear. Sentimental and even ribald ditties are found mated with serious Haydn symphonies." (Mueller 1951: 19) The music historians Irving Sablosky (1969) and Gilbert Chase (1987) point to how the cultivated tradition in the early nineteenth century still had yet to find sufficient support for it to be regularly performed as a refined high art music whose compositions were appreciated separately from the distractions of more popular tastes. Even among the more select audiences of the upper and middle classes, the cultivated tradition in the early part of this century was performed with the addition of "favorite airs" in the popular musical soirees of the period. These audiences preferred the virtuosity of instrumentalists or the beautiful voices of vocalists as opposed to the aesthetic appreciation of a classical composition and its refined rendition. What is commonly called the "genteel tradition" of the early nineteenth century, a music culture enjoyed by the urban elite and an emerging urban middle class, was only slowly moving to the refined performances of European cultivated music.

As the nineteenth century progressed, music societies, music clubs, and collectives of musicians began supporting the cultivated tradition as a refined high art music to be appreciated without the help of popular airs or virtuoso trickery. (Mueller 1951; Sablosky 1969) Special concerts and recitals of instrumental performances were organized for a more select audience of listeners, while choral performances common in the early nineteenth century continued. While the economics of performing a limited repertoire of the cultivated tradition were not conducive to the long-term viability of an orchestra, professional musicians still found ways to play it. These musicians could usually support themselves by combining eclectic performances for popular audiences with opportunities to perform cultivated music for a more discerning audience. The main question perplexing professional musicians, however, was the viability of permanent orchestras of the cultivated tradition, particularly ones that could perform the symphonic music that represented the best in the European classical tradition.

The professional musician, conductor, and music director, Theodore Thomas epitomized the efforts of professional musicians in the nineteenth century to establish permanent orchestras, and was recognized as the major voice in this quest to establish orchestras in America. (Sablosky 1969) "The readers of THE METRONOME are familiar with the history of the triumphs which Mr. Thomas has achieved in this country and elsewhere. He has done more than any other musician to put orchestras of the United States on the high plane which they now occupy, and it was through his instrumentality that we have been able to hear the great artists of the old country... The good results which the fine organization over which Mr. Thomas wields the baton has exerted upon the educational improvement of the United States is acknowledged by all." (*Metronome* 3-1895: 4)

Theodore Thomas was involved in several orchestra organizations that spanned the strategies of finding the miracle ingredients for successful permanent orchestras. The Theodore Thomas Orchestra was a commercial orchestra that toured the country performing symphonic music for thirty-six years beginning in 1862. Thomas was also music director of the musician cooperative Philharmonic Society of New York City and its New York Philharmonic orchestra from 1871 to 1891. Paul DiMaggio (1982) points out, however, how the commercial and cooperative efforts of professional musicians like Thomas failed as viable models for permanent symphonic orchestras. Irving Sablosky (1969) argues that Thomas was aware from the beginning of his career as an orchestra conductor that the only viable model for a permanent orchestra was patron support, and his struggle was to find it – his own orchestra was in constant financial turmoil. Thomas finally found this ideal patron in Henry L. Higginson, whose personal endowment helped establish with the aid of Thomas the Boston Symphony Orchestra in 1881.

As Paul DiMaggio (1982) and Lawrence Levine (1988) argue, the establishment of the Boston Symphony Orchestra in 1881 marked the beginning of the rise of a patron-supported high art world of European cultivated music performance. The patronage model of the Boston Symphony Orchestra proved successful in establishing permanent symphony orchestras across the country. By the end of the nineteenth century such orchestras were established in St. Louis, Pittsburgh, Cincinnati, Los Angeles, Philadelphia, New York, Chicago as well as Boston. In the first two decades of the twentieth century several additional patron-supported symphony orchestras were established in major cities including Minneapolis, San Francisco, and Houston.

Simultaneous with the efforts to support symphonic orchestras, were efforts to support the art of the "grand opera." Just like classical music, opera music was easily mixed into a variety of popular performances from large summer jubilees to musical extravaganzas. In fact, as Lawrence Levine (1988) points out, songs from European operas were popular and could be found in virtually any popular performance context, either performed straight or in parody. Operettas such as Gilbert and Sullivan's, the precursors to the American musical, were also gaining popularity among audiences in the late nineteenth century. (Chase 1987) Supporters of the cultivated tradition hoped to find ways to perform opera in the same high art context of the new permanent symphonic orchestras. European grand opera was positioned as distinct from the lowbrow popular performances of opera music and operettas.

The most successful efforts in establishing the permanent performance of grand opera was the creation of the Metropolitan Opera Company in New York City in 1883 and the Chicago Opera Company in 1889. The Boston Opera Company was formed in the late nineteenth century, but folded by 1915. As Paul DiMaggio (1991) points out, grand opera was a very expensive proposition even for urban elite and it would take several decades into the twentieth century for a patron-supported model of grand opera to evolve, even for the Metropolitan Opera Company. While the establishment of grand opera was not as successful as symphonic orchestras during the late nineteenth century and early twentieth century, grand opera performances were organized for special performances and national tours. And like symphonic orchestras, grand operas made up part of the move towards a separate European cultivated tradition during this period.

If you desire to see a higher standard of music in America; if you wish to become known as an energetic worker in the cause; if you would like to be associated with those who are in the forefront of musical matters in our country; if you care to keep abreast of this great age of musical progress, you can do so by joining the Music Teachers National Association. (*Metronome*, June 1888: 10)

The cultivated tradition also found support in the success of a music education movement in the United States in the late nineteenth century. Music education was viewed as crucial to the development of the cultured tastes necessary to support the "good" music of the European cultivated tradition. Music instruction became a regular part of public education as well as a necessary part of the cultured education of young middle class women. These were the "amateur" musicians, mostly female, appreciated by professional musicians for their taste in "good" music, but of course not sufficiently trained to be professionals. Professional musicians and others had succeeded in the nineteenth century to place cultivated music as part of a sound and moral education – this included the creation of music school settlements for orphans. The Music Teachers National Association held its first annual meeting in 1877. It was founded in 1876 as an organization dedicated to America's musical progress. The National Federation of Music Clubs, an organization of "amateur" female musicians and teachers, was established in 1899 to showcase the educational activities of women in promoting "good" music. (Sablosky 1969) Music educators and their associations not only promoted the idea of "good" music as European cultivated music, but also became major critics of the later success of the American vernacular in attracting the attention

of popular tastes, particularly the black vernacular of ragtime and syncopated dance.

In conjunction with the music education movement, music programs
in colleges and universities served as both a sign of legitimacy for the cultivated tradition and a place where music composition and music criticism
in the European cultivated tradition could be supported. Elite liberal arts
colleges such as Harvard, Yale, Princeton, Columbia, and Cornell established music courses, music chairs, and music programs during the
late nineteenth and early twentieth century. The music programs in the
Ivy League schools created an elite group of composers, educators, and
music critics, while also providing a general music appreciation among the
most elite college students in the country. As MacDonald Smith Moore
(1985) argues, these schools became a central intellectual force in music
appreciation, music criticism and music composition in the European
cultivated tradition in America. It was home for one of the most influential voices of the cultivated tradition in America in the early twentieth
century, Daniel Gregory Mason, who taught at Harvard, Princeton, and
Columbia.

Numerous conservatories of music that served to support the cultivated
tradition also appeared in the late nineteenth and early twentieth century.
Among the most influential and long lasting of these early conservatories were the Oberlin Conservatory of Music (1865), the New England
Conservatory of Music (1867), and the Chicago Musical College (1867).
Metronome was an enthusiastic supporter of the establishment, by an act
of the 51st Congress of the United States, of a National Conservatory
of Music in 1891. This conservatory's charter included the mission to
establish an American school of music in the cultivated tradition. While
conservatories trained professional musicians and composers, the less
elite conservatories focused predominantly on training the music teachers
who promoted "good" music in public education and private instruction.
Conservatories and music schools also, of course, provided performances
of the European cultivated tradition.

The growth of support for the cultivated tradition also produced new
music journals as well as the beginnings of scholarly books on music
and music history. (Sablosky 1969) In support of music education, the
journal *The Etude* was established in 1883 and for seventy-five years remained a major music education journal alongside *The Musical Courier*
established in 1880, which ended publication in 1961. Other music
journals included *Musical Record* (1878–1900), *Music* (1891–1902),
Musical America (1898–1964), and *The Musical Quarterly* (1915-present).
Metronome was a publication for professional musicians, and therefore, reflected the transformations this class of musician underwent in the early

twentieth century towards the American vernacular. These other journals retained the idea of "good" music based on its nineteenth century
conception, and remained, in the early twentieth century, supporters of
the European cultivated tradition and "good" music in America.

By the early twentieth century, a music field comprised of symphony
orchestras, grand opera, music societies, choral societies, public education, private instruction, higher education, music associations, conservatories, and journals had developed to support the European cultivated tradition. As the balance between "good" cultivated music and the
American vernacular shifted in favor of the latter in new popular music entertainment, this emerging field of cultivated music retained the
nineteenth century ideal, both aesthetic and moral, of "good" music. As
popular music entertainment boomed in the early twentieth century with
the black vernacular once again gaining greater prominence, the new music field of cultivated music became home to the most ardent critics of
this transformation in American music. As the previously pristine culture
of middle class America was moving into a more heterogeneous market
of popular music and beginning to enjoy the fruits of the American vernacular in song and dance, the field of cultivated music became a bastion
of the old ways of the nineteenth century.

As DiMaggio (1982) points out, this exclusive world of the cultivated
tradition was established outside the commercial market of music in the
United States. It was mostly a patron-supported music field that centered
on elite-supported symphony orchestras, opera houses, conservatories,
and liberal art colleges in conjunction with the broader support of music
educators, public education and private instruction. DiMaggio (1982)
and Lawrence Levine (1988) are correct in that the cultivated tradition
in music, like other high art fields during this period, became a status
symbol of distinction among urban elite in the United States. This field,
however, stretched beyond elite institutions to incorporate a middle class
that remained wedded to the values and tastes of the genteel tradition of
the nineteenth century. For many of these middle class supporters of the
new field, particularly music education, the cultivated tradition continued
to strongly resonate with a mixture of cultured and moral arguments
about American music.

While a new social world of the cultivated tradition set the boundaries for the defense of this tradition against the rise of the American
vernacular, ironically the new popular entertainment market presented
a miracle salvation for this tradition. The rise of large silent film theater
palaces in the second decade of the twentieth century suddenly presented
new opportunities for the cultivated tradition. Since these theaters were
attempting to legitimate film theater attendance, the use of orchestras

performing classical music was seen as a perfect fit. The general possibilities for promoting the cultivated tradition as high art in movie theater
concerts was not lost on the supporters of this tradition. As an article in
Musical America suggested in 1915, "when the masses hear good music
continually they will recognize it. It will then have become 'popular.'
All kinds and conditions of men, women and children patronize the
'movies.' It is there that many of them hear the only music that comes
into their lives. What a power is within our reach!" (Reprinted, *Metronome*
1-1916: 44)

Silent movie palaces provided more possibilities for professional musicians to pursue the cultivated tradition and promote "good" music.
Like populist professional musicians in the late nineteenth century, the
popular forum of movie theater palaces was acclaimed for its diversity of
audiences against the limited and elite-dominated world in which most
cultivated music as high art was performed. S. L. Rothapfel, the premier
exponent of classical music performance in movie palaces and the first
music director of the Rialto and Rivoli movie palaces in New York City,
was a strong supporter of the educational potential these venues held for
the public.

Up to two or three years ago the average man paid little attention to the better
kind of music. . .

The reason for this is obvious. Grand opera was expensive. Symphony concerts
were regarded as too "high-brow" for the average taste. Other concerts of various
sorts were given at regular intervals in scattered locations and only during a limited
season. . .

The combining of a motion picture entertainment with a high class musical program has changed this condition in a way that is amazing. Today the average
man can and does go to hear music of the most artistic quality any afternoon
or evening that he feels like it, any day in the week, any week in the year. . . The
enjoyment our patrons have experienced from the playing of our orchestra and
the singing of our soloists has done more perhaps to instill in them a love of
good music than any other one factor whose influence had been brought to bear.
(S. L. Rothapfel, *Metronome*, April 1917: 44)

Unlike the repertoire of professional musicians' performances in band
organizations like those of P. S. Gilmore and J. P. Sousa, however, the
early movie palace orchestras played strictly classical and opera music.
The "popular" attraction was the film, an art considered of lowbrow quality by professional musicians, which provided captive audiences for the
cultivated tradition. In New York City, for example, large orchestras were
performing strictly European cultivated music under the leadership of
S. L. Rothapfel and Hugo Riesenfeld in the large movie theater palaces

The Criterion, The Rialto, The Capitol, The Strand, and The Rivoli. The growing schism between the cultivated and the vernacular among professional musicians was evident in early movie palace orchestras positioning themselves as distinct from the performances of professional musicians in other popular music entertainment. Unlike musical revues and vaudeville in which the American vernacular was competing successfully against the cultivated tradition, movie palace orchestras represented the avant-garde against the fall of "good" music in America.

Any one who has taken pains to observe the character of the audiences attending the two kinds of entertainment – the movies and vaudeville – must have been impressed with the decided distinction between them in taste, emotions, and educational standard. The best class of movie theaters have risen to a standard much above that of the vaudeville show, with its coarse appeal to the lowest standard of taste... In the movie theater – if it seeks a sphere of influence in opposition to the vaudeville – the high standard conceived by the farsighted managers must not only be maintained, but adaptable, progressive features must be introduced to make this modern institute the basis for future advancement of all the allied arts which Wagner aimed to unite in his music drama. ("Musical Opportunities in the Movies," *Metronome*, September 1920: 51)

Leading into the Jazz Age of the 1920s, the cultivated tradition had found a home in both a non-commercial art world and a commercial world of movie theater palaces. The rise of the American vernacular in American music had reinvigorated the defenders of the nineteenth century ideal of "good" music. Defending against the onslaught of Tin Pan Alley song and the rhythms and sounds of ragtime and syncopated music, supporters of the old ideal of a European cultivated tradition viewed themselves as the last bastion against the victory of lowbrow tastes in American music. In this struggle, the European cultivated tradition was gradually forming a distinct music culture set against the culture of American popular music. The intermixing of the cultivated and the vernacular traditions would continue into the Jazz Age of the 1920s, but the break between these traditions was becoming more and more a reality in both the social organization of American music and the ideological struggles over "good" music in America.

A separate world: the cultivated tradition and black musicians

Eileen Southern (1997) shows how the black community leading into the twentieth century mirrored developments in the white community of an independent European cultivated tradition in American music. Since the black community, however, was segregated from these developments in the white community – exceptions being a few admissions to music conservatories and a few virtuoso artists – it had to rely on its own resources and organizations. Given limited resources, the development of a cultivated tradition within the black community was a far greater struggle that relied on the support of black colleges, black churches, and occasionally white patrons. Even given these difficulties, however, music societies, choral societies, music schools and conservatories, grand opera performances, and symphony orchestras were organized within the black community in the early twentieth century. The latter development of movie theater palaces in black communities also provided a similar venue for the cultivated tradition as those serving the white community. While these developments afforded professional black musicians and black composers someplace to be "serious" artists of the cultivated tradition, outside the black community opportunities were basically non-existent.

Like the white upper and middle class that supported the cultivated tradition, in the early twentieth century the black elite and middle class that supported the cultivated tradition retained the nineteenth century ideal of "good" music. As Samuel A. Floyd (1995) argues, the black middle class and black elite looked to white cultivated culture as a form of legitimizing their community, which included the adoption and maintenance of an unsullied European cultivated music. Unlike their white counterparts, however, promoting the cultivated tradition had larger ramifications. The black community in general faced the racist assumptions of its inferiority and its closer link to the "natural" versus the "intellectual." As Jon Michael Spencer (1997) argues, the adoption and perfection of European cultivated music was seen as one of the important ways for the black community to attack the racist ideology of the inferiority of African Americans.

While the question of the cultivated versus the vernacular for the black community created special tensions within this community over the popularity of the black vernacular, the relationship between these two traditions actually was more intertwined than among white musicians, white composers, and white audiences. This was the result of two factors affecting black artists in American music. The first factor was the limited resources and opportunities for black artists to perform and create cultivated music for either black or white audiences. These limits confronted by black artists forced them into a more immediate relationship with the American vernacular. The second factor was black professional musicians adopting a nationalist ideology at the end of the nineteenth century. This ideology promoted the incorporation of black vernacular music in both classical and popular composition.

Unlike the cultivated tradition among white professional musicians and white audiences, no venues existed in the black communities that were exclusively dedicated to this tradition outside of black churches and black colleges. The limited resources in the black community made such a development impossible. Performances of "serious" cultivated music mostly occurred in theaters that also supported popular performances – often a theater would have a single program that began with a "serious" performance of cultivated music followed by popular performances, including social dance. Given these limited opportunities, black professional musicians who performed European cultivated music in "serious" concerts also had to depend on popular performances for a stable income. In both venues and careers, black professional musicians' combination of cultivated "high art" performance and popular performance was different than for white professional musicians where the separation of high art music and popular art music was becoming more distinct in terms of venues and careers.

Many black composers, who created both classical and popular composition, also held a nationalist ideology that saw the black vernacular as core to an art form that represented the black community. These composers were initially influenced by the nationalist ideals of the Czech composer Antonín Dvořák, who became the first musical director of the National Conservatory of Music in 1892. The premier black classical composers of the early twentieth century such as Henry T. Burleigh and Robert Nathaniel Dent incorporated black "folk" music in their classical composition. Given the few opportunities for black composers and black musicians within the field of European cultivated music, however, black artists exerted a greater influence of cultivated techniques on the popular composition and performance of the black vernacular. In the early twentieth century, classically trained black composers such as William Marion Cook, John Rosamond Johnson, James Tim Brymn, and William Grant Still, composed and arranged popular music and conducted popular orchestras. W. M. Cook studied at Oberlin and the National Conservatory of Music, J. R. Johnson at the New England Conservatory of Music, James Tim Brymn at the National Conservatory of Music, and William Grant Still at Oberlin and the New England Conservatory of Music. (Roach 1992) In time, the schism between the cultivated and the vernacular in American music would manifest itself more clearly among black artists, but during this earlier period an important shared agenda of black nationalism, and the confluence of the cultivated and the vernacular, influenced this smaller and more interactive group.

The special relationship between the cultivated and the vernacular among black professional musicians in the early twentieth century is evident in the first signs of a "cultivated" vernacular high art in American music appearing among black professional musicians. In discussing "good" music and the relationship between the cultivated and vernacular traditions, my main argument is to point to how the cultivated ethos of professional musicians was slowly dividing along two paths, the high and the popular. This development over time would lead to two distinct cultivated music traditions in American music, one rooted in the European classical tradition and the other rooted in the American vernacular. Developments in the field of American music were leading not only to a "cultivated" vernacular music, however, but also towards a cultivated vernacular "high art" music. Evidence of things to come in American popular music not surprisingly appeared in the music making of one of the most successful professional black musicians' organizations of the early twentieth century, the Clef Club Orchestra in New York City. This group of musicians were to present a series of concerts beginning in 1912 that anticipated the basic elements that defined the turn to high art in American popular music during the Jazz Age of the 1920s.

The Clef Club presented a series of special concerts at Carnegie Hall in New York City between 1912 and 1915. Under the musical leadership of James Reese Europe and William H. Tyers, the Clef Club Symphony Orchestra inaugurated their "Negro Symphony Orchestra" in 1912 with 125 players performing works composed by Will Marion Cook, Harry T. Burleigh, Samuel Coleridge-Taylor, and James Reese Europe. (Southern 1997) While this orchestra was presented as performing "cultivated" music in its series of concerts, as spokesman for the Clef Club Orchestra, James Reese Europe made clear in an interview for the *New York Evening Post* on March 14, 1914, the agenda was to perform within a black vernacular idiom. "Whatever success I have had has come from the realization of the advantages of sticking to the music of my own people... We must strike out for ourselves, we must develop our own ideas, and conceive an orchestration adapted to our own abilities and instincts." (Reprint, Kimball and Bolcom 1973: 61) While Europe in his comments reproduced the racial construction of the clear distinction between black and white musicians – "our symphony orchestra never tries to play white folk's music. We should be foolish to attempt such a thing. We are no more fitted for that than a white orchestra is fitted to play our music," he emphasized the black vernacular as the positive road to a cultivated high art music among black professional musicians. This positioning of the vernacular – in music, instrumentation, and arrangement – as the basis of a cultivated high art music was a precursor to the more general movement among white and black professional musicians performing "jazz" music in the

1920s. Unfortunately, the assumed distinction between white and black musicians, promoted by Europe, would be used to white musicians' advantage during the 1920s in co-opting the cultivation of jazz.

The Clef Club Orchestra was a precursor to jazz orchestras also in how it generated controversy over claiming a cultivated vernacular high art. In a review of the 1914 Clef Club performance in Carnegie Hall in *Musical America*, the reviewer was clear in what constituted cultivated music and legitimate musicianship.

Negroes Perform Their Own Music
Annual Concert Reveals But Little Interest in Serious Composition

It is to be granted that it will take some time to imbue these negro musicians with a thorough musical appreciation, to teach them the difference between serious music and popular 'song and dance' music. There is little excuse, however, for so many songs of an obvious "vaudeville" character being heard at a concert of this kind, and what is more being sung in the manner of the variety theaters...

If the Negro Symphony Orchestra will give its attention during the coming year to a movement or two of a Haydn symphony and play it at its next concert and if the composers, who this year took obvious pleasure in conducting their marches, tangos and waltzes, will write short movements for orchestra basing them on classic models, next year's concert will inaugurate a new era for the negro musician in New York and will aid him in being appraised at his full value and in being taken seriously. It is impossible to applaud in Carnegie Hall his imitations of the vulgar dance music of Broadway originated by the tone-poets of Tin Pan Alley. (*Musical America*, March 21, 1914: 37)

As both Maud Cuney-Hare (1936) and Eileen Southern (1997) point out, a similar critique of the Clef Club Orchestra could be found among black professional musicians who believed their profession should emulate the European cultivated tradition in music, technique, and arrangement without the impurity of the vernacular tradition. Cuney-Hare cites an open letter to *Musical America* on the Clef Club performance from a black musician from Philadelphia as an example of the debate between the cultivated and the vernacular traditions among professional black musicians. Adolphus Lewis in his letter stated that "the music was typical of the light, happy-go-lucky Negro, but there are those among us who are trying to master the classics in music as well as along other lines, and to say that the program satisfied this class, would be gainsaying the truth. All the renditions of the Club were good, spicy, and catchy... All races have their folk-song and dances, but all races try to develop their art from examples set by masters of other periods; and if we expect to do anything that is lasting from an artistic standpoint, we too, must study the classics as a foundation of our work." (Cuney-Hare 1936: 138–9)

The Clef Club Orchestra's articulation of the cultivated and the vernacular traditions into a single cultivated vernacular high art was of course an exception to the rule among black professional musicians during this period. Most black professional musicians, such as Dave Peyton in Chicago, the most powerful black musician in this city, while performing eclectic popular performances, presented their occasional symphonic performances within the European cultivated tradition. On the other hand, given black professional musicians' exclusion from an emerging independent art world of cultivated music making, they in various ways applied the cultivated tradition to popular arrangement and performance. The state of the cultivated tradition in terms of the opportunities and conceptions of black professional musicians tended to bring to bear their "cultivated" talents on popular music and performance to a greater extent than white professional musicians. This was reflected not only in the early articulation of a vernacular high art music, but in the special role of black professional musicians in cultivating the vernacular in the evolution of the popular dance bands of the Jazz Age and the Swing Era.

Conclusion: American music

Yet if you raise this question of quality, you are immediately charged with being a "high-brow," "a person," in Professor Brander Matthew's already classic definition, "educated beyond his intelligence," – a charge from which a sane man naturally shrinks. "The best American music is that which the greatest number of Americans like; the greatest number of Americans like ragtime; therefore ragtime is the best American music," is a strong one, which you may oppose only at the risk of being thought a highbrow and a snob. ("Concerning Ragtime," Daniel Gregory Mason, *Metronome*, May 1918: 23)

The directions American music was taking in the early twentieth century perplexed Daniel Gregory Mason, the dean of the European cultivated tradition in America. The rise of the American vernacular was undermining the old ideal of "good" music in America. The earlier consensus among professional musicians between "good" music and the vernacular was breaking down. And as this breakdown of the old ideal continued, critics like Mason were not shy in pointing to the increasing influence of the black vernacular in American music. The class and race distinctions that determined "good" music in the nineteenth century, and the moral and aesthetic arguments that justified them, were being overwhelmed by the force of popular tastes in a booming and heterogeneous popular music market. The very question of what represented a truly American music worthy of the admiration given "good" music was appearing to split the profession of music making into two camps, the classical and the popular.

Leading into the Jazz Age of the 1920s, the professional class of musician was at a crossroads in popular performance. The clear boundaries in the nineteenth century between the cultivated populist performances of professional musicians and the vernacular performances in working class entertainment were dissolving. Changes in their relationship to the American vernacular were leading this professional class towards an important transformation. As professional musicians performed in the popular entertainment market, they incorporated the American vernacular as a core element of their ethos of performing "good" music. While many critics lamented this change, for many professional musicians the very concept of "good" music was to change by the Jazz Age. The question of "good" music among professional musicians performing popular music was shifting from a concern to include cultivated European music in popular performance to a concern to cultivate the American vernacular – the initial move towards a cultivated high art based on the vernacular tradition.

2 The Jazz Age: professional musicians and the cultivated vernacular

> The fact that jazz is our current mode of expression, has reference to our time and the way we think and talk, is interesting; but if jazz music weren't itself good the subject would be more suitable for a sociologist than for an admirer of the gay arts. Fortunately the music and the way it is played are both of great interest, both have qualities that cannot be despised; and the cry that jazz is the enthusiastic disorganization of music is as extravagant as the prophecy that if we do not stop "jazzing" we will go down, as a nation, into ruin. . . Jazz for us, isn't the last feverish excitement, a spasm of energy before death. It is the normal development of our resources, the expected, and wonderful, arrival of America at a point of creative intensity.
>
> Gilbert Seldes, "Toujours Jazz," *Dial* August 1923: 151

As an advocate of popular culture, the famous journalist Gilbert Seldes was an early defender of jazz music. In defending jazz, he pointed in particular to the symphonic jazz made famous during the 1920s by the highly successful jazz orchestras of Paul Whiteman and Vincent Lopez. Seldes was not alone in defending jazz against its numerous critics, or in posing professional jazz orchestras as testament to the legitimate, national, and artistic character of jazz music. Critics of jazz in the 1920s retained the old nineteenth century ideal of "good" music and viewed jazz as undermining moral values and behavior, or at a bare minimum corrupting musical values and techniques. For many of its defenders, however, jazz represented a true modern American music. Jazz represented a new ideal of "good" music that rejected the Euro-centric and highbrow ideals of the cultivated tradition in America – it was a lively art that was an expression of the times and the American people.

The "jazz craze" in music during the 1920s so reflected a general spirit of the times for many commentators like Seldes that this decade became known as the Jazz Age. Following World War I, jazz music certainly captured the popular imagination. The rapid popularity of jazz music led to its equally rapid spread among musicians. No other style up to this time in American popular music so quickly came to dominate popular performance. The American vernacular, which had already made significant inroads into the commercial popular music market, had captured popular tastes at an unprecedented level, seemingly sweeping aside the old "standards." And just as ragtime and syncopated dance music became part of earlier commercial popular music, the dominance of jazz in the 1920s also represented a major triumph of the black vernacular in American popular music.

The jazz craze began through the influence of non-professional musicians. While still marginal to most "legitimate" venues, non-professional musicians performing the jazz vernacular were attracting audiences to clubs, theaters, restaurants, and were popular in the speakeasies of the 1920s. They also had opportunities for their music to reach a broader audience in a booming record market following World War I. Professional musicians, however, quickly adopted jazz music in their orchestras and smaller bands. They co-opted the jazz fever while simultaneously distancing themselves from non-professionals. By occupying the most lucrative jobs in theaters, dance halls, hotels, and other venues, professional musicians positioned themselves as the premier interpreters of this new vernacular idiom in commercial popular music. The common defense of jazz as "good" music during the Jazz Age embraced the professional musicians and professional composers who performed and created jazz music, not the non-professional musicians who first introduced it.

In adopting jazz idioms, professional musicians were simply continuing the process of cultivating the American vernacular. Black professional musicians were already adopting black vernacular idioms in their music making in earlier syncopated society orchestras and simply adopted jazz idioms as well as the name in their "jazz" orchestras. White professional musicians had performed rags as part of their repertoire in the past, but with the jazz craze, many were quick to adopt syncopated dance and jazz practices in some form as the defining style of their profession. White professional musicians also quickly followed black professional musicians in transforming their bands into "jazz" orchestras, and just as quickly claimed to be the modern proponents of this new American popular music. Black and white professional jazz orchestras in the 1920s established the basic instrumentation, arrangement, and techniques of the big band dance orchestras that dominated American popular music until the 1950s.

In the 1920s, an emerging new ideal of "good" music involved a balancing of the previous cultivated practices and cultivated music of professional musicians with popular vernacular idioms. The proper balance, however, was hotly debated. Professional musicians would constantly distance themselves from the pure vernacular of non-professional musicians in defending their balance of the cultivated and the vernacular in popular performance. Popular tastes, however, were demanding jazz music and a professional musician would be remiss to ignore his patrons in the popular music market as much as stodgy critics and some professional musicians would rail against the pernicious influence of jazz. Professional musicians in mediating the popular music market had to continue to navigate the moral, aesthetic, class, and racial construction of "good" music in America.

While popular tastes in musical entertainment promoted the black vernacular in commercial popular music, the plight of the African American community in the United States continued to be dire. Some leaders in the black community had hoped that African Americans' participation during World War I in both the military and in industry, and the Great Migration out of the Jim Crow South, would change their fortunes as segregated and oppressed second class citizens. The post-war years, however, dashed most hopes of any immediate positive change. Race relations went in the opposite direction. Race riots sprung up across the nation while lynching continued to be a regular occurrence. Efforts continued to secure the legal segregation of black communities, and the labor movement continued to exclude blacks. The Ku Klux Klan reached its peak membership and popularity during the 1920s. The segregation and denigration of the black community was also reflected in the social organization of American music. Besides the segregation of audiences and most venues, black professional musicians also remained outside the artistic community of white professional musicians in terms of unions, band organizations, and this community's vision of a professional class of artist in America.

The balance of the cultivated and the vernacular among professional musicians also continued to run against elitist conceptions of popular music and popular musicians as less legitimate than the music, musicians, and composers of the European cultivated tradition of classical and opera music. Black professional musicians also continued to strive to break through the barriers erected against them in the world of European cultivated music. This continuing tension in the implied lower status of professional musicians who performed American popular music erupted during the Jazz Age into an open rebellion against the European cultivated tradition. Professional musicians in jazz orchestras attempted to counter the singular role claimed by the European cultivated tradition. These musicians asserted that jazz was a true American or African American school of *fine art* music in contrast to cultivated European music – a populist appeal for high art legitimacy.

This high art turn in American popular music, however, ultimately failed when the depression wreaked havoc on the popular music market.

With the introduction of a new popular music market of live performances, records, broadcasts, and films, the quest for legitimacy among
professional popular musicians would have to take another route. Yet, the
Jazz Age was an important moment in American music. The American
vernacular was transformed into a "cultivated" popular music and presented for the first time as "high art." The high/popular status hierarchy
between a European cultivated tradition and an American vernacular
tradition was challenged for the first time. It was a period where professional popular musicians in adopting the jazz vernacular went against the
reigning cultural hierarchy in America.

The jazz craze: popular music and the black vernacular

The Appeal of the Primitive Jazz

A strange word has gained wide-spread use in the ranks of our producers of
popular music. It is 'jazz,' used mainly as an adjective descriptive of a band. The
groups that play for dancing, when colored, seem infected with the virus that they
try to instill as a stimulus in others. They shake and jump and writhe in ways to
suggest a return of the medieval jumping mania. (*The Literary Digest*, August 25,
1917: 28)

The period following World War I was a crucial turning point in American
popular music. The American vernacular in general was storming the
ramparts of the old edifice of "good" music as Tin Pan Alley song
and dance dominated popular performance. Both professional and non-
professional musicians also were benefiting from more affluent times
and the growing importance of entertainment in the lives of most urban
Americans. To the chagrin of elite and moral defenders of nineteenth-
century cultural idealism, most urban Americans were readily joining a
Cultural Revolution in commercial popular entertainment. And at the
center of this revolution was the national craze for jazz music and jazz
dance. The jazz craze made syncopated rhythms and other black vernacular idioms central elements of American popular music making.
    While many small "jazz bands" performed a black vernacular style of
music from the Delta Region of New Orleans, jazz music in the 1920s encompassed not only this style but syncopated dance music, blues music,
piano rags, and virtually any tune "jazzed up" by musicians. The jazz craze
in essence was the craze for the black vernacular among popular audiences and the performance of this vernacular in some form by popular
musicians and popular singers both professional and non-professional.
The extent to which musicians and singers actually adopted the black
vernacular rather than a superficial imitation – a critique later jazz critics

would make of certain "sweet jazz" during the 1920s – is less important than the fact that jazz entered the consciousness of the nation and musicians as the reigning popular music.

Given the segregated music market, however, it is not surprising that a group of white artists were credited with first introducing vernacular jazz to a broader, national white audience and igniting the jazz craze in 1917. The Original Dixieland Jass Band, a group of white musicians from New Orleans, released its first recordings with the Victor Talking Machine Company in early 1917 and was an immediate sensation. Its Victor recording of "Livery Stable Blues" sold one million copies in its first year of release. The ODJB recordings in 1917 and 1918 had a great influence on the initial reception of jazz among white audiences and white musicians. Their particular style of jazz music which incorporated a heavy use of "novelty" sounds, instruments imitating anything from animals to fog horns, in addition to the collective improvisation and syncopated rhythm common to black New Orleans musicians, caught on among white popular musicians and audiences. Small "jazz" bands of white musicians quickly appeared, many directly emulating the Original Dixieland Jass Band. The novelty style of the widely popular white clarinetist Ted Lewis, crowned as the "King of Jazz" in the early years of the jazz craze, was evidence of this band's impact on popular music.

From the beginning, however, jazz was clearly viewed as originating from the black vernacular. As *Metronome* informed its readers, "according to the advice of a prominent New York musician, well-known as a composer and arranger of successful popular music, the word 'Jass' or 'Jazz' has come to mean any accidental or freak combination of instruments . . . in connection with small orchestras. The original meaning of 'Jazz' is supposed to be 'nigger' or 'negro,' and when used in connection with music is meant as a reflection of their peculiar, ragtime style of accenting the unaccented beats . . ." (*Metronome* 10-1917: 18) Even in an early advertisement for the Original Dixieland Jass Band, the publishing company Feist used the primitivism associated with the black vernacular as a marketing tool.

The Primitive "Jazz"

The word "Jazz" seems to have found a permanent place in the vocabulary of popular music. It was used originally as an adjective describing a band that in playing for dancing were so infected with their own rhythm that they themselves executed as much, if not more, contortions than the dancers. The word is purely African in origin and in New Orleans, where it is commonly interpreted as "speeding things up."

The popularity of the "raggy" music has created a demand for music with exaggerated syncopation, an attempt as it were to produce the wonderful broken rhythms of the primitive African jungle orchestra. (Advertisement, Feist News, *Metronome*, October 1917)

The jazz craze also coincided with the growth of black entertainment. During the 1920s, black entertainment districts like the South Side in Chicago and Harlem in New York City witnessed a major boom. Besides entertaining the large black populations of The Great Migration, black musicians and singers were entertaining white audiences who went "uptown" for their entertainment. The boom in the 1920s in black entertainment, as Kenny (1993) and Shaw (1986) show, was driven by the demand for the black vernacular. In musical theater, musical revues, vaudeville, dance, and speakeasies, the black vernacular and black artists were in demand. This demand was met not only in black entertainment districts, but also outside these districts as black artists performed for white audiences in musical revues, dance halls, and clubs in white entertainment districts.

The popularity of the black vernacular also increased when record producers discovered a "race" market in black music. The black vaudeville singer Mamie Smith's recording of "Crazy Blues" with the General Phonograph Company sold 100,000 copies in August 1920 and is credited with revealing the large potential for "race records." Bessie Smith's "Down Hearted Blues" released in 1923 sold over one million copies in the newly discovered race market. Jazz bands like King Oliver's Creole Jazz Band also were recorded for the race market as well as jazz orchestras of professional black musicians. Although race records were marketed to a segregated black audience – these records were only advertised in the black press and sold only to black communities – they played an important role in promoting the black vernacular.

Does Jazz Put the Sin in Syncopation?

Jazz originally was the accompaniment of the voodoo dancer, stimulating the half-crazed barbarian to the vilest deeds. The weird chant, accompanied by the syncopated rhythm of the voodoo invokers, has also been employed by other barbaric people to stimulate brutality and sensuality. That it has a demoralizing effect upon the human brain has been demonstrated by many scientists. (Ann S. Faulkner, National Music Chairman, Federation of Women's Clubs, *The Ladies Home Journal*, August 1921: 16)

The jazz craze represented a significant challenge to the defenders of the old ideal of "good" music. Like their earlier laments about ragtime and syncopated dance, the defenders of the old ideal of "good" music reacted with a fervor equal to the overwhelming enthusiasm for jazz among white and black audiences. A barrage of warnings of the moral decay and the lapse into the primitive previously associated with the black vernacular became the common parlance of critics of jazz. And as the social historian Kathy J. Ogren (1989) and the sociologist Neil Leonard (1962) show, strident critics of jazz existed in both the white and black community. Leonard refers to these critics as "traditionalists" – individuals whose conventional values were linked to the moral and aesthetic ideals of "good" music as well as to this music's racial and class implications in American culture.

In a strange form of wishful thinking, some critics of jazz simultaneously deplored the popularity of jazz while claiming its immediate demise. "Syncopation, which tends toward 'shimmying,' wriggling and hopping about dance floors as in the days of prehistoric barbarism, is disappearing and, according to those authorities who make it their business to study dancing, the demise of 'jazz' occasions more general joy than sorrow." (*Metronome* 10-1920: 44) Fenton Bott, Director of Dance Reform of the American National Association of Masters of Dancing still retained hope in 1922 that the jazz craze was seeing its last days. "The American National Association of Masters of Dancing began two years ago to work for cleaner dancing. Hundreds of welfare associations, thousands of college deans, police women everywhere and finally the public dance hall proprietors are listed in the work with us. We all feel and hope that the crest of the wave of this disgusting, wriggling 'jazz' has been reached and reports to us from every part of the country show 'clean' dancing crusades being started everywhere." (*Metronome* 2-1922: 30) The music education journal *The Etude* in its January 1925 issue, however, recognized that the crusades against jazz were failing while the jazz craze was alive and still growing. "[W]e know that on thousands of dance floors all over America tonight, any one who cares to investigate will witness in public dances of the most wanton character, dances that would have been suppressed in a low burlesque show only a few years ago. These things are inspired by Jazz and maintained by Jazz... Yet, the whole land from coast to coast is still in the throes of this form of musical epilepsy." (*The Etude* 1-1925: 5)

While fundamentally a critique based on racist ideology expressed in moral, aesthetic, and class terms, the critique of jazz was aimed at both black and white musicians as they pursued the black vernacular in popular performance. It also was aimed at the large number of consumers, particularly the young, flocking to hear and dance to jazz music. This condemnation of the black jazz vernacular, in terms of dance, rhythm, and sound – an ideology in which the black middle class was trapped as a willing accomplice – set the stage for professional musicians to present themselves as the legitimate cultivators of this music.

A question of style: vernacular jazz and professional musicians

The Jazz Band – What It Is and Isn't

The eating and dancing public has been treated for some time to the remarkable performances of so-called "Jazz Bands," unquestionably the most accomplished dispensers of nerve-racking noises and annoying rhythmic contortions the amusement-seeking world has ever experienced.

Like anything new and novel, these noise producers have gained popularity in certain quarters and considerable curiosity had been aroused as to what Jazz Bands really are, what instruments they may be composed of, where the name has come from, what kind of music they play, etc. (*Metronome*, October 1917: 18)

Professional musicians were quick to notice the craze for jazz music following World War I. No sooner had the fever hit, it seemed that popular audiences were craving "jazzy" music in theaters sporting vaudeville shows and musical revues, as well as in hotels, dance halls, nightclubs, and restaurants. Music publishers responded quickly by advertising in *Metronome* sheet music of "jazz" numbers of syncopated dance music, blues, and other popular songs. An advertisement placed by J. C. Deacon Musical Bells in the January 1918 issue of *Metronome* spread the word to professional musicians that the jazz craze was for real. "The NEW Jazz. The kind of Jazz that pleases the ear instead of torturing it. The kind of jazz that is in demand everywhere nowadays. Can YOU deliver it? If you can, you won't have to hunt jobs; THEY'LL HUNT YOU INSTEAD."

Professional white musicians quickly cashed in on the jazz craze. In an early ad for Buescher Instruments in *Metronome* in April 1921, the success of white professional musicians adopting jazz is celebrated in the success of the popular bandleader Art Hickman, "The American Emperor of Jazz." "All the fantastic and bizarre jazz effects for which Art Hickman's orchestra is famous are the melodic inventions of Art Hickman himself... And the way the younger set besiege every place Art Hickman books is evidence aplenty that Art Hickman has worked up Jazz into a fine art... with a spicing of jig-and-reel flavor, a zest of buck-and-wing – and has 'jazz' combinations and effects making every step easy and spontaneously performed." Other popular white orchestra leaders such as Ben Selvin, Paul Specht, Zez Confrey, Fred Waring, Meyer Davis, Isham Jones, Ben Bernie, Coon-Saunders, Vincent Lopez, and Paul Whiteman adopted elements of the jazz vernacular in their performances and recordings in the early 1920s.

The prominent white orchestra leaders who adopted jazz also controlled music organizations of numerous bands and orchestras. Meyer Davis, "a real champion for jazz and its lovers," for example, managed over thirty hotel, café, and society orchestras along the East Coast. (*Metronome* 9-1923: 72) Paul Specht, "Master of Rhythmic, Symphonic Syncopation," managed his own orchestra in New York City and other units including Al Epps and His Orchestra, Edward Krick's Orchestra, Hughie Barret's Rhythmodick Orchestra, and Paul Specht's Lady Syncopators, "The Valkyries of Jazz." (*Metronome* 9-1923: 82) Other popular bandleaders such as Paul Whiteman and Vincent Lopez also supervised a large number of orchestra units. As white professional musicians adopted the jazz vernacular, it quickly spread among professional units of white musicians as well as quickly being co-opted as professional white musician organizations controlled the most lucrative and legitimate performance spots. These musicians adopted in some fashion the syncopated rhythm, instrumental sounds, and short solo "breaks," that were considered the basic characteristics of the jazz vernacular that attracted jazz crazed audiences.

A Word of Warning

... the big difficulty has been the craze of jazz that has swept over the country and which has been the cause of spoiling the chances of many a promising musician of developing into anything but a jazz player of ragtime tunes. Practical examples of how disastrously this "jazz craze" works can easily be mentioned. Let us take the average young man starting to learn a brass instrument. Hardly has he commenced to master the first principles of legitimate playing, when he succumbs to the temptation to "jazz it up a bit." He catches on to the peculiar principles of syncopation and before long he is devoting his time and energies to the latest compositions from tin pan alley rather than to the study of the works of great musicians. (Theodore Dossenbach, Rochester Park Band, *Metronome* February 1921: 37)

Of course, not all white professional musicians were happy about the quick adoption of jazz by their profession. The legitimate techniques of "good" music for some were under attack, while the success of Tin Pan Alley song continued to produce rancor among the old guard of professional musicians and composers. As Robert M. Stults, a song composer from the old guard, lamented in the music education journal *The Etude*: "one cannot help comparing the dance music of thirty years ago with the travesties of the present day. Think of the stately old lancers and quadrilles, the dreamy waltzes of Waldteufel and the inspiring Strauss numbers! And then contemplate the 'rot' that we are obliged to 'hop around to' today. Recall, if you are old enough, the well-balanced dance orchestras of the old days, and then listen to the combination of fiddles, banjos, saxophones, scrub-brushes and tom-toms that are now in vogue.

Shades of Terpsichore! Happy are ye that your ears cannot hear the pande-monium that now reigns! This jazz epidemic has also had its degenerating effect on the popular songs of the day. In fact, nearly every piece of dance music we now hear is a re-hash of these often vulgar songs." (*The Etude* 9-1924: 595) Like social reformers and cultural critics who desperately hoped for the death of jazz, some white professional musicians hoped that the craze for jazz would disappear just as quickly as it appeared. For most white professional musicians, however, the question was less the rejection of the jazz vernacular than its appropriate cultivation. The role of the professional musician, once again, was to balance popular tastes and vernacular music with the cultivated techniques of "good" music of this profession.

Some Further Opinions on "Jazz" by Prominent Writers

... jazz, in the musical sense, has been undergoing a mighty metamorphosis. The strident chaos of yesterday is now the mellow harmony of sonorous strings. Horns are muted. The bizarre "blues" and maddening litanies of the old-style jazz band are dying in a vanishing diminuendo. Gymnastics and hula-hula are giving way to melody and orchestration. (*Metronome*, August 1922: 28)

White professional musicians distanced themselves from non-professionals and the pure vernacular in emphasizing their "legitimate" techniques of music making. Constantly referring to the cacophonous noise and primitive techniques of non-professionals, white professional musicians prided themselves on cultivating vernacular jazz in their or-chestras. Top professional white orchestras presented themselves as the true cultivators of the jazz vernacular. As *Metronome* in September of 1922 proclaimed "the slow state of transition from noise to melody is well nigh over, and the reign of Real Music has begun ... without conflicting in any way with the rhythm and 'pep' so desirable on a dance floor. This is best evidenced by the work of such masters of dance as Lopez, Whiteman and Specht." (*Metronome* 9-1922: 138)

To Discriminate in Music

Today we are swamped with dance music, commonly called "jazz." This is played in two distinctive methods. The method we hear the most which is also disagree-able and discordant, is the so-called "red-hot" jazz style. This method, consists in playing at random; faking, breaks, blues notes, and every kind of trick is brought into action ...

The other method of presenting this type of music is more interpretive; it is played in symphonic form of arrangement by the larger and better orchestras. They are doing a good service in presenting to the public symphonic jazz free from discordant harmony. It is not syncopation that we ridicule, but the manner in which they handle it and degrade it. (*Metronome*, June 1927: 48)

The cultivation of the vernacular was often referred to as applying "symphonic" techniques to jazz performance. The jazz orchestras of top bandleaders like Lopez, Whiteman, Specht, and others called their music "symphonic jazz" to emphasise the legitimate, cultivated music making of their orchestras. As Meyer Davis made clear, the success of white professional jazz orchestras lay in how "the special arranger has finished working up a syncopated selection for orchestral use, and inserted the numerous symphonic effects that the sophisticated public enjoys and demands." (*Metronome* 9-1923: 171) The cultivation of the vernacular was seen not only in the elimination of the "blaring discords" of vernacular jazz through the legitimate instrumental techniques of professional musicians, but also in the "symphonic" arrangement of popular songs for these society orchestras. The American vernacular and Tin Pan Alley song reached a new level of sophistication under the skilled hands of a jazz orchestra arranger. As the critic Don Knowlton in the *Harper's Monthly Magazine* article "The Anatomy of Jazz" in April of 1926 argued: "it is in the dance orchestras that the most complete transformation of a popular song is effected... The sheet-music edition of the piece bore the same relationship to the orchestration as the framework of a house bears to the completed dwelling. The man who arranges popular music for dance orchestras is rapidly becoming, in jazz fields, even more important than the composer. It is the arranger who provides life and color and contrasts and lively dissonances and blasts of indigo harmony and contrapuntal runs. He is given a bare stage, and upon it he builds a paradise." (*Harper's* 4-1926: 583) Popular jazz orchestra leader Vincent Lopez summed up the cultivation of the vernacular by white professional musicians in celebrating "the progress of the dance orchestra from small beginnings to a point where it is an organization of carefully selected instrumentation, skilled musicians, colorful arrangements and intelligently chosen programs." (*Metronome* 11-1924: 62)

While white orchestras were cultivating jazz through the application of "symphonic effects," they attempted to incorporate in some fashion the syncopated rhythm, tones, and improvisation of vernacular jazz. By the mid-1920s, top orchestras were looking for younger musicians who could provide "hot" jazz licks and jazz rhythms for their orchestras. The article "The Season's Outlook for Dance Musicians" in the September 1928 issue of *Metronome* pointed to the popularity of jazz as a powerful inducement for professional orchestras to assimilate vernacular jazz practices, particularly by hiring the younger white musicians who were caught with the hot jazz bug. "Another thing to be encouraged by leaders is individual tricks by his younger musicians. If a youngster thinks he can work out a hot break that is different, let him go to it. It may be rotten at first but undoubtedly he will make it real hot in time. All the hot boys did, and still do plenty of practicing... It goes without saying that the band who gets the money this season is the one or ones delivering the stuff. Ordinary outfits will find it tough sledding; for there is no use in fooling ourselves into believing that conditions are such that managers can hand out any kind of music to their patrons ... a musician walking into a good band, or a band walking into any kind of job with money attached must have something that sells... The strictly legitimate musician has a place in the symphony orchestra or grand opera. The dance orchestra must have a wallop and just what it is composed of nobody cares." (*Metronome* 9-1928: 57–8)

Black professional musicians, composers, and arrangers, of course, also were cultivating the jazz vernacular during the 1920s. They developed similar selected instrumentation, arrangement, and skilled musicianship as their white counterparts, but synthesized these developments far more intimately with the jazz vernacular. The music historian Samuel A. Floyd (1990) points out how black professional musicians were cultivating the jazz vernacular in popular music in orchestras like those of Fletcher Henderson and Duke Ellington, in the musicals and Tin Pan Alley songs of Noble Sissle, Eubie Blake, James P. Johnson, and Fats Waller, and in the stride-piano innovations of James P. Johnson and Charles "Luckey" Roberts. Other black orchestras experimenting in some manner with synthesizing jazz vernacular practices with the cultivated techniques of professional orchestras were under the leadership of William Marion Cook, Sam Wooding, Carroll Dickerson, Erskine Tate, Charles Elgar, Charles Cook, Bennie Moten, Alphonse Trent, and Dave Peyton. Their efforts, however, were ignored in the pages of *Metronome* and the comments of white musicians and white defenders of jazz.

The synthesis of vernacular and cultivated techniques among black musicians was distinctly different than among white musicians. As the social historian Burton W. Peretti (1992) argues, in the 1920s the emerging "jazz culture" among black musicians was the consequence of the integration of northern black professional musicians with recently arrived southern black musicians. This integration in fact began before the 1920s and influenced the earlier formation of syncopated orchestras, but in the 1920s the greater demand for the black vernacular and the greater number of southern black musicians pushed this integration to a greater extent. Many of the musicians who immigrated from the South moved quickly into the artistic world of northern professional black musicians, adopting some of the techniques and literacy skills of this professional class. Overall, as Peretti (1992) and Kenny (1993) point out, the integration of the black jazz vernacular with the cultivated tradition of professional black musicians occurred as these previously distinct sets of cultures interacted in the vibrant black entertainment market of the 1920s. The career of the famous New Orleans jazz musician Louis Armstrong follows this path of integration. In the 1920s, he moved between small jazz ensembles and the professional dance orchestras of Fletcher Henderson, Erskine Tate, and Carroll Dickerson, eventually forming his own professional jazz orchestra at the end of the decade.

Like their white counterparts, black professional musicians distinguished the playing of jazz orchestras from the uncultivated cacophonous playing of non-professional jazz bands. In the article "A Negro Explains Jazz" in the April 26, 1919 issue of *The Literary Digest*, the jazz orchestra leader James Reese Europe's comments show how northern black professional musicians, while incorporating southern jazz musicians into their orchestras, emphasized these musicians' integration into their professional culture. "The negro loves everything that is peculiar in music, and this 'jazzing' appeals to him strongly. It is accomplished in several ways. With the brass instruments we put in mutes and make a whirling motion with the tongue, at the same time blowing full pressure. With wind instruments we pinch the mouthpiece and blow hard. This produces the peculiar sound you all know. To us it is not discordant as we play the music as it is written, only that we accent strongly in this manner the notes that originally would be without accent... I have to call daily rehearsal of my band to prevent the musicians from adding to their music more than I wish them to." (*The Literary Digest* 4-26-1919: 28) Or as the top black orchestra leader in Chicago Dave Peyton advised in his music column in the *Chicago Defender* in 1928, "if you are now in a jazz band, do not give up the proper study of your instrument. You may be called upon to render real services and to play good music." (Walser 1999: 58)

Many northern professional musicians disparaged the illiteracy of recent southern immigrant musicians, even though they still integrated these musicians into their orchestras in order to "jazz up" their music making. As discussed in the previous chapter, the balancing of the black vernacular with the cultivated tradition of music making among black professional musicians elicited among certain musicians the need to emphasize the legitimacy of their music making. And as Chadwick Hansen (1960) argues in the case of Chicago musicians, this legitimacy was sometimes viewed in terms of emulating popular white jazz orchestras – in part, as a way to avoid the racial stereotyping of music making often imposed on black professional popular musicians, and in part, as a response to black middle class views of the black vernacular. Dave Peyton in his regular column in *The Chicago Defender* in 1928 noted that some black dance orchestras were succeeding in providing the same cultivated music making as white dance orchestras. These black orchestras had "the goods, they have the same quality of Lopez, Whiteman, Paul Ash, Dornberger and other prominent orchestras." (Hansen 1960: 499) Peyton applauded such efforts among black dance orchestras. "We listen to many of the famous white orchestras with their smoothness of playing, their unique attacks, their novelty arrangement of the score and other things that go to make for fine music, and we wonder why most of our own orchestras will fail to deliver music as the Nordic brothers do. There is only one answer, and that is, we must get in line, we are too satisfied with what little we know about music." The general emphasis on black jazz orchestras cultivated music making as applied to the black vernacular, including the use of symphonic effects, again appears in Dave Peyton's summary of the Jazz Age in 1928. The "style of jazz playing today requires musicianship to handle it. There is no faking, every instrument has its part to perform. The expert arrangers, theorists, as a rule put the notes down on paper in partitioned effect for the sections of the orchestra. The players must be musicians to cut the stuff. Many times you run into grand opera figurations which require technical knowledge of the musicians. The melodies, garnished with difficult eccentric figures and propelled by artful rhythms, hold grip on the world today, replacing the mushy, discordant jazz music." (Walser 1999: 58–9)

While both black and white professional musicians cultivated the jazz vernacular, white professional musicians positioned themselves as its true "modern" cultivators. White professional musicians would juxtapose their "modern" rendition of jazz compared to its "primitive" performance. Meyer Davis reminded *Metronome* readers that "modern syncopation" should not "be confused with savage syncopation. The savages syncopate without melody, while melody is preeminent in modern dance music." (*Metronome* 9-1923: 72) Percy Aldridge Grainger, a famous classical pianist and classical composer, would a few years later agree with Davis that the success of jazz consisted "mainly in a happy mixture of northern wealth of melody with the rhythmical polyphony of the negro races." (*Metronome* 7-1926: 10) Paul Whiteman, crowned the "King of Jazz" in 1923, opened his 1926 book, *Jazz*, with this common defense of jazz as the combination of the primitive with the modern. "Only just as it took centuries to produce the mango seed, so has it taken all of human life to bring forth jazz. The most primitive and the most modern combine in it. For hundreds of years, savage tribes in far places rolled out rhythms on harsh drums of home-tanned hides, rhythms that stimulated to war or soothed to peace as the need of the moment dictated. The vitality of the world's youngest nations has absorbed, added to, and carried on that rhythm, first in ragtime and blues, now in jazz." (Whiteman 1926: 15–16)

Of course, the primitive was associated with the black musician in America, and the question remained as to who was bringing "modern" cultivation to the jazz vernacular. As the popular white jazz orchestra leader Paul Specht made clear in his defense of jazz, "don't forget it is a work of art and critics have no right to confuse it with the old noisy jazz that originated with the African negro." (*Metronome* 9-1924: 34) Herbert Wiedoeft, in his article "The Development of Jazz" in 1926, distinguished white jazz orchestras like Paul Whiteman's for modernizing jazz. "They say jazz originated in the South among the negroes... Perhaps the negroes had a better conception of weird harmonies and rhythm than any one else at that time, but the real evolution of jazz music or 'the modern construction of instrumentation,' as we know it now, began with a different idea in music, just like any new discovery. 'Rhythmic jazz,' syncopation, or whatever you care to call it, came into the popularity which it has now attained through the foresight and ingenuity of those few who had the artistic idea of elevating and perfecting dance music." (*Metronome* 4-1926: 73) The popular bandleader Isham Jones went even further in disparaging the constant reference to his orchestra and music as jazz. "Many of the recent song hits were composed with no thought whatsoever of jazz as the term is used by musicians; instead, he had in mind a song with melody that would appeal to the heart – lyrics that would appeal to the mind, and with a rhythm to appeal to the feet. Because the song is successful and played by practically every dance orchestra, it is called jazz; but that is not my idea of jazz. Jazz music, to a musician, means music that appeals strictly to the feet and without much thought of melody, and is usually considered by them as the 'down South, negro type' of blues... I believe the term jazz would only be applied to its rightful type of music, and that the dance music as played to-day would be known as *American Dance Music*." (*The Etude* 8-1924: 526) For white professional musicians and their supporters, it was definitely white musicians and white Tin Pan Alley composers who were modernizing or cultivating the primitive elements of jazz – in their comments during the 1920s, professional black musicians and composers were virtually non-existent.

The lack of recognition of black professional musicians by white professional musicians is striking considering the popularity of black orchestras since the syncopated dance craze. The black professional musician Ford Dabney, for example, regularly led his successful syncopated orchestra at the New Amsterdam Theater on Broadway as part of the Ziegfeld Follies "Midnight Frolic Show" from 1913 to 1921. The absence of black professional musicians' music making in the commentary of white professional musicians cannot be accounted for by ignorance on the part of white professional musicians of their black counterparts' artistic endeavors. The two most successful white orchestra leaders and jazz spokespersons, Paul Whiteman and Vincent Lopez, for example, were quite aware of black professional musicians and composers, both actually using black professional artists talents as composers and arrangers during the 1920s. On Paul Whiteman's arrival in New York City in 1920, he began a long association with the Palais Royal a few blocks from the famous Roseland Ballroom where Fletcher Henderson's orchestra started a ten-year association in 1924. At the Roseland, Vincent Lopez performed in 1924 alternating with the Fletcher Henderson orchestra while the popular white orchestra of Jean Goldkette alternated with the Henderson orchestra in 1926. (Shaw 1987) Whiteman also attended a number of gatherings uptown in Harlem interacting with black professional musicians and other black artists. The racially segregated profession of musician, however, led to a complete absence of black professional musicians in white professional popular musicians' acclamations on jazz music.

Gilbert Seldes in his 1923 article "Toujours Jazz" in *Dial* made clear in his defense of jazz and acclamation of white professional musicians like Paul Whiteman and Vincent Lopez that black professional musicians were not part of the modernizing and cultivating of jazz music. There "will always be wayward, instinctive, and primitive geniuses who will affect us directly, without interposition of the intellect . . . the greatest art is likely to be that in which an uncorrupted sensibility is *worked* by a creative intelligence. So far in their music the negroes have given their response to the world with an exceptional naïveté, a directness of expression which has interested *our* minds as well as touched our emotions; they have shown comparatively little evidence of the functioning of *their* intelligence. . . Nowhere is the failure of the negro to exploit his gifts more obvious than in the use he has made of the jazz orchestra; for although nearly every negro jazz band is better than nearly every white band, no negro band has yet come up to the level of the best white ones, and the leader of the best of all, by a little joke, is called Whiteman." (*The Dial* 8-1923: 160) Seldes did acknowledge the compositional accomplishments of the black professional musicians and composers Eubie Blake, Noble Sissle, and W. C. Handy. Yet, he claimed that "the negro is not our salvation because with all my feeling for what he instinctively offers, for his desirable indifference to our set of conventions about emotional decency, I am on the side of civilization" (*The Dial* 8-1923: 159–60). For Seldes, on the side of civilization and cultivating jazz were white Tin Pan Alley composers like Zez Confrey, Irving Berlin, George Gershwin, Cole Porter, and

Walter Donaldson. For white defenders of popular jazz music in the 1920s like Seldes, Osgood, and Knowlton, it was white professional musicians, arrangers, and composers that represented the legitimate cultivation of the black jazz vernacular.

As both white and black professional musicians cultivated the jazz vernacular, they navigated the moral, aesthetic, racial, and class distinctions articulated in the concept of "good" music. Cultivation for these artists involved a distancing from the negative distinctions imposed on the jazz vernacular by the old ideal of "good" music. For white professional musicians, this included not only the articulation of middle class morals and tastes through their music making and statements, but a clear distinction between themselves and the pure jazz vernacular and black musicians. Black professional musicians also articulated middle class morals and tastes in their music making as they cultivated the jazz vernacular. These musicians, however, had to deal with the racist construction of themselves as black artists. In distancing themselves from the black vernacular, they were grappling with their lower status, seeking through assimilation to the music making of white orchestras to break the racial barrier to their efforts to be recognized as a legitimate professional class of musician. Caught between popular tastes and the market, and the old ideal of "good" music and its defenders, both white and black professional musicians mediated this conflict while assimilating the black jazz vernacular into their music making. In the process, these artists created a third stream between the vernacular and the cultivated traditions, a "cultivated vernacular" commercial popular music – the big band style of popular music.

One hundred percent American: white professional musicians and the vernacular as high art

ARE AMERICAN HOTELS SPONSORING A TRULY NATIONAL MUSIC?

The managers of our leading metropolitan hotels and amusement gardens who engage high price dance orchestras for the entertainment of their patrons are indirectly doing more to promote the cause of American music than any other class . . .

We are present developing a popular music that is fully as characteristic as that of any other nation and through the efforts of those who engage these high-grade organizations, it is gradually assuming the proportions of an entirely new art form. One could easily trace its evolution from the days of our first home ballads and country dances with the later influences of ragtime and "Jazz," until at the present time when musicians of symphonic caliber are lending their art to blend the whole into a truly National music . . .

Here we have the nucleus of a real American School of Music, Music for Americans played by Americans in a thoroughly characteristic manner and like nothing else under the sun. . .

. . . our National music of the Future will owe more to the Hotel Man that unconsciously laid its foundations, than to the Societies that subscribe large sums to send our promising young composers to Rome. (*Metronome*, May 1923: 34, 60)

When Carleton L. Colby in the May 1923 issue of *Metronome* suggested that in hiring jazz orchestras the hotel man was unwittingly aiding in the development of a true American school of music, he was joining a growing chorus of white professional musicians. These musicians positioned jazz orchestras and jazz music as an alternative to the symphony orchestras and opera companies performing in the European cultivated tradition. They, as well as their supporters, proclaimed jazz as an art form of equal merit to that of European cultivated music. Infected with a jingoistic populism, they even argued for the superior merit of jazz music since it was an authentic American art form based on the American vernacular and enjoyed by the American public. White professional musicians performing popular music claimed a more legitimate status than their brethren trapped in what they claimed was an elitist and Eurocentric world of classical and operatic music.

In claiming jazz orchestras, jazz musicians, and jazz music deserved the same, if not more, respect than symphony orchestras, symphony musicians, and European cultivated music, professional musicians in the 1920s made a crucial step in transforming the ideal of "good" music in America. Not only was commercial popular music performed by professional musicians acclaimed as "good" music in relation to uncultivated vernacular music, but these musicians were no longer content to accept it as a second rate art form in relation to the status accorded classical and opera music. And at the core of this transformation were the various ways commercial popular music was denigrated and classical music venerated, and therefore, how professional musicians' own status was constantly challenged by the old ideals of "good" music and the European cultivated tradition. Underlying this conflict, of course, was the way the social organization of music production in America led most professional musicians into careers as popular musicians. In other words, to claim jazz music as the American school of music was to position popular musicians as the premier professional musicians in the United States.

Since the late nineteenth century, patron-supported symphony orchestras presented one of the few opportunities for a career in performing the cultivated tradition as a refined high art for professional musicians. A position in one of these symphony orchestras was viewed as one of the most prestigious positions available in the profession. American musicians looking for a prestigious career faced not only the limited opportunities in the few permanent orchestras in the United States, but also these new elite institutions' predilection for importing European conductors and musicians. When the German-born Walter Damrosch, conductor of the New York Symphony, suggested in 1893 that no suitable cellist for his organization could be found in the United States, *Metronome* vehemently disagreed, and hoped the "fad" among symphony orchestras for European musicians would soon pass. (*Metronome* 12-1893: 1) While musicians' unions fought to provide their members' positions in symphony orchestras, the preference among elite symphony orchestras for foreign-trained classical musicians remained into the early twentieth century. Such a preference among these organizations remained a constant reminder to American professional musicians of their lower status in the field of European cultivated music – a lower status amplified by the elitist attitudes in this field towards the commercial popular music many of these musicians performed for a livelihood.

This early tension between established symphony orchestras and American professional musicians led to several attempts in the late nineteenth and early twentieth century to create symphony orchestras made up of only American-born professionals. At the birth of the Jazz Age in 1919, conductor and composer Mortimer Wilson in New York City made a call for the formation of an "All American Symphony Orchestra." This call to arms, like previous ones, was heralded by *Metronome*. In March 1919, an editorial quoted Wilson's lament about the low position of American musicians over the last fifty years in which "during this time he has been slowly but surely shaking off the shackles which were placed upon him for his sin, the unpardonable sin of *being an American*." *Metronome* in the same editorial also quoted the *New York Review's* comments in support of Wilson's efforts that given the "discrimination against the native-born musician... It then would seem first necessary to demonstrate to the Americans that the native musician is the equal of the foreign-born artist. This can never be done through musical organizations which are foreign in sympathy, policy and personal [sic], as are all our so-called American orchestras." (*Metronome* 3-1919: 21) While Mortimer Wilson's efforts failed, *Metronome* continued to support efforts in opening opportunities for American musicians. In an article in August 1924, "How American Orchestra Players are Being Developed," *Metronome* commended the valiant efforts since 1922 of the American Orchestral Society in New York City as a "training school in symphonic routine" for American artists. (*Metronome* 8-1924: 27)

The complaints of American musicians about the use of European musicians in American symphony orchestras gained additional fervor with the advent of nationalist propaganda during World War I. The historian Barbara L. Tischler (1986) points to the surge in nationalism during World War I and the pressures experienced by symphony orchestras given the prominence of German compositions, conductors, and musicians in these orchestras in the early twentieth century. American professional musicians' more general complaints of Euro-centrist hiring practices by symphony orchestras resonated with this "100% Americanism" campaign during the war. Ultimately, no significant changes in the world of symphony orchestras occurred as a result of nationalist propaganda during the war, however, such "made in America" jingoism would continue among American professional musicians. As contributor Francis L. York made clear in *Metronome* in 1920, a rebellion among professional musicians was mounting: "America has at last broken away from the leading strings of Europe, and has begun to think and act for itself in matters industrial, financial, artistic, and literary. Recent utterances of prominent men in all walks of life . . . all point to greater independence of thought, greater self-confidence, and a clearer vision of Americas position in the world of art and letters. . . Many musicians have now subscribed to a musical Declaration of Independence, have cast aside their former disbelief in our own creative ability and their excessive admiration for all music that comes to us from across the sea." (*Metronome* 5-1920: 60)

For most professional musicians in the 1920s, their revolutionary declaration of independence would occur outside the hallowed halls of the European cultivated tradition. In the early 1920s, professional musicians began to position jazz orchestras, where the vast majority of them plied their trade, and jazz music, as an alternative to symphonic orchestras and European cultivated music. As an advertisement for Buescher Instruments with Paul Whiteman argued, "America – the United States of America – has symphony orchestras ranking with the world's finest. Most of these devote their time and talent to playing the music of every country in the world except America. In personnel, most of them are predominantly European. All this may be as it should be, for America has needed and still needs to know the best music of the entire world. But America has its own music! And to this Paul Whiteman and His Orchestra devote their serious attention." (*Metronome* 3-1922: 29) The sentiments expressed by Carleton L. Colby about the patronage of hotel men "indirectly doing more to promote the cause of American music" was becoming a battle cry for professional musicians. Frank J. Gibbons in his *Metronome* article in September of 1923, "A Survey of America's Music," made clear that American "rhapsodies and symphonies" were to be found in "hotels, cafes, vaudeville houses and phonograph companies." Jazz orchestras in these live venues and on record were "regaling us with symphonic, contrapuntal, fantastic, intricately rhythmcd dance music, quite new in treatment and effect..." and "in at least a score of orchestras the execution is up to the best symphonic standards." (*Metronome* 9-1923: 81) As the professional drummer William Ludwig in *Metronome* in May 1922 argued, "as the final step we now have the new syncopated melody orchestra, developed partly by the composers and arrangers of the music they play... The next step is already determined. It is the syncopated Concert Orchestra. And as a matter of course there will be European Tours not for Symphony Orchestras but for the modern American Syncopating Concert Orchestra. These compositions will not be revamped European music, but real American creations and Europe will welcome them." (*Metronome* 5-1922: 78)

Outside the legitimate world of symphony and opera orchestras, professional musicians felt compelled to stress their status as highly skilled artists. As bandleader Paul Specht complained, "many people today seem to be surprised when I tell them that members of the top notch dance orchestras of today must be schooled musicians, conservatory trained in every respect, technic, who have taste to phrase and color their own parts." (*Metronome* 9-1924: 34) Vincent Lopez, himself a classically trained pianist, was even more specific in arguing that following the jazz craze "the field of jazz was then opened to legitimate and trained musicians and dance bands were shortly composed of artists, for the pay is higher than on most musical engagements. It is common now in the best dance organizations to find performers of the highest calibre, men who can, and often do, in season, play in the finest concert ensembles." (*Metronome* 11-1924: 63) Or as orchestra leader Paul Whiteman, former member of the Denver and San Francisco Symphonies, argued "men taken from symphonies are the easiest to train. They have good discipline and they usually leave the symphony because they are interested in jazz and want to experiment along a new line." (*Metronome* 6-1926: 14) The jazz orchestra leader Meyer Davis also noted three years before Whiteman that "the new complicated, symphonic arrangements of jazz selections present difficulties equal to those of the classics... Jazz musicians, too, are specialists that cannot be easily replaced. Many persons have the notion that any person who can play good standard music could step right into a jazz orchestra and do the work without difficulty. Such is not the case." (*Metronome* 9-1923: 171)

Growing Pains

Every day or so, somebody emphasizes my horrible jazz present by referring to my honorable symphony and string-quartet past... The point I am trying to make is that we believe in jazz. We didn't chuck our honorable places among honorable musicians just to go after the filthy lucre, not by several tinker's dams. We claim we're still musicians, perhaps even better musicians than we would have been if we hadn't strayed off the straight and narrow paths allotted by convention to first-rate members of our profession. (Paul Whiteman, *Jazz*, 1926: 48–9)

The comments by professional musicians on their unrecognized cultivated skills underscored how these musicians felt a need to work against the lower status accorded them as popular musicians. Like their predecessors, many of these musicians in some fashion were schooled in the cultivated tradition but found their livelihood in popular performance. As Whiteman's comments make clear, however, certain highbrows of the cultivated tradition viewed popular music making as less than legitimate and certainly not an artistic endeavor. Of course, part of the highbrow disdain for professional musicians and their popular music making was in the "crass" commercial demand underlying their success, set against the "pure" aesthetic tastes of well-educated audiences in the European cultivated tradition. So while the music critic H. O. Osgood, editor of the *Musical Courier*, in a 1925 *American Mercury* article acknowledged that "the technical standard required of the player in a good jazz band is higher than that demanded from the same kind of instrumentalist in a symphony orchestra," others would be less kind. (*American Mercury* 11-1925: 329) In an earlier article in the *American Mercury*, the voice of the European cultivated tradition, Daniel Gregory Mason, was clear about his view of the technical standards of jazz orchestra musicians in his comments on the Paul Whiteman Orchestra. "Like all primitive forms of art it is so poverty-stricken in interest for the mind (whatever its luxury of appeal to the senses through mere mass of noise or through odd effects of muted trumpets, squeaking clarinets, or flatulent trombones) that it kills its victims by sheer boredom." (*American Mercury* 4-1925: 466)

Classical or Jazz?

Many musical societies have been organized to tell us what *is* music; what musical fare we shall partake of – what Mr. Average American Citizen *must be made to swallow*. We must swallow and *like* everything these self-constituted authorities prescribe as long as they stamp it *classical*.

Are we justified in branding Mr. Average American Citizen an uncouth ignoramus because he prefers a well-defined *melody* of home manufacture to a *meaningless* composition from overseas? (Randall Welles, Staff Sgt. Assistant Bandleader, Camp Travis, Texas, *Metronome*, May 1922: 34)

Many professional musicians framed the denigration of jazz orchestras, jazz musicians, and jazz music by upholders of the old ideal of "good" music as an elitist condemnation of popular tastes. Resonating with earlier

populist professional musicians, professional musicians in the 1920s condemned the elitism of the defenders of European cultivated music. These
musicians in the 1920s also pointed to their role as educators of public
taste in their "jazzy" renditions of classical music. As Meyer Davis argued,
the "better type of jazz, too, cultivates an appreciation of all good music.
It is well known that much of the most popular syncopation consists in
adaptations from the classics. In hearing and liking these selections, you
are unconsciously appreciating the great composers. Thus a musical theft
from a great composer may react to the benefit of the general public."
(*Metronome* 9-1923: 171)

Professional musicians in the 1920s, however, went further in actually
defending popular tastes and using the commercial success of jazz as testament to its validity as a true expression of the American people. Meyer
Davis did not limit "good" music to only the classics, and he was clear
that "jazz is certainly, however, the American music of the future. Nothing can dislodge it from the popular affections..." As Paul Whiteman
in his 1926 book *Jazz*, claimed in his defense of jazz "the test of art is
its appeal to great masses of humanity. The artist must say something
that is intelligible to all the people." (Whiteman 1926: 126) In an earlier
interview with the *New York Times* in 1924, Whiteman made a similar
populist appeal in noting that "the progress made in this field in the past
few years is conclusive evidence that the future of jazz is assured. The
fact that a small orchestra playing popular music can outdraw by far a
huge symphony organization clearly shows the verdict of the American
people." Vincent Lopez argued that when "you hear the performance of
one of the prominent jazz bands today you hear the musical language
of the common people." (*Metronome* 11-1924: 62) Such popular appeal
of course did not appease the ardent defenders of European cultivated
music. As Meyer Davis pointedly remarked, "if one dares to express a
liking for jazz among devotees to the 'classics,' the results are similar to
pitching a lighted match into a gasoline tank, conversationally speaking."
(*Metronome* 9-1923: 72) Vincent Lopez, however, was more hopeful that
while "there only remains to be obtained the indorsement of those cav-
illers who, steeped in the obstinacy of ancient prejudices, refuse to admit
virtue in new things until forced to do so by current opinion. They will
come to it soon for their captious arguments are unprevailing against
proven excellence." (*Metronome* 11-1924: 62)

Selvin's Orchestra, of the Moulin Rouge, New York
One of the Finest American Plan Orchestras

...when the waltz and two-step went out and the trot came in, a lot of talented chaps began concocting lively, unclassifiable stuff full of rhythm and noise.

Someone styled it rag-time, probably because they couldn't count its measures... Here and there an incorrigible Europeite tried to pin it down to five-quarter count. The rag-timers paid no attention to the scholars, and American rhythms invaded all parts of the world, followed by execrations and cheers.

Then the great war and "jazz" the tone-picture of a world in chaos. The jazz wave held over for a while after the war. It has grown to the stature and class of real music... In less than ten years a distinct American plan of instrumentation has been worked out, keeping pace with American music, with its intricately rhymed fantastic contrapuntal effects. It's made in the U. S. A., nowhere else and heard in every part of the world. (Advertisement, Buescher Band Instrument Company, *Metronome*, August 1922: 23)

The populist appeal made by professional musicians was also linked to a jingoism that emphasized jazz as "made in America" and presented a genealogy of jazz as an American school of music linked to American popular music of the past. Frank J. Gibbons in his ad copy written for the Buescher Company in August 1922 offered this anti-European revisionist history of an American school of music. In celebrating the success of the Ben Selvin Orchestra, this ad argued that the true school of American music began with nineteenth-century professional musicians and popular music of the past and ended with the success of jazz orchestras and jazz music. As Doron K. Antrim acclaimed in *Metronome* in 1923, "jazz has been called 'The National Anthem,' and it is probably the most unique and original music to which America had yet given birth." (*Metronome* 1-1923: 59) In his discussion of jazz bands in a 1924 issue of *Metronome*, Vincent Lopez positioned jazz as the culmination of a true American school of music. "Jazz, or the fox trot music, is the real American music. Since the founding of the United States as an independent nation there has been a constantly broadening inquiry as to what constitutes the true American literature and the genuine American music. The literature may be still in the making but the quest for American music is ended... Jazz is an amalgam, a blend, of all the musical forms which have been introduced to us and is indigenous to the United States." (*Metronome* 11-1924: 62) Paul Whiteman also celebrated the true national character of jazz in his 1926 book *Jazz*. "Jazz is the spirit of a new country. It catches up the underlying life motif of a continent and period, molding it into a form which expresses the fundamental emotion of the people, the place and time so authentically that it is immediately recognizable... At the same time, it evolves new forms, new colors, new technical methods, just as America constantly throws aside old machines for newer and more efficient ones." (Whiteman 1926: 130)

While jazz orchestras were regaling popular audiences in hotels, cafes, dance halls, and vaudeville theaters with "American" music, another major test of legitimacy for professional musicians was to invade the sacred concert halls of America with jazz music. Leading the way was the most successful bandleader of the 1920s, Paul Whiteman. On February 12, 1924, Paul Whiteman, with arrangements by Ferdie Grofe, had the first of his many special concerts in the 1920s with a "Concert of Modern Music" in Aeolian Hall in New York City. Whiteman's concert at Aeolian Hall started with a "true form of jazz" in the performance of "Livery Stable Blues." The concert then presented a series of performances showcasing the "modern embellishments" of jazz performance in jazz tunes, popular Broadway songs, old standards, and the contrasting of legitimate scoring versus jazz scoring. The concert also included a dance suite by the famous composer of popular songs, American musicals, and classical compositions Victor Herbert. The most famous performance in the concert, however, was the premiere of the young Tin Pan Alley composer George Gershwin's "Rhapsody in Blue," performed on piano by George Gershwin with the Paul Whiteman Orchestra.

Whiteman later remarked in his book *Jazz* in 1926 on this "experiment" at Aeolian Hall. "But here I saw the common people of America taking all the jazz they could get and mad to get more, yet not having the courage to admit that they took it seriously. I believe that jazz was beginning a new movement in the world's art of music. I wanted it to be recognized as such. I knew it never would be in my lifetime until the recognized authorities on music gave it their approval." For Whiteman, the concert was a success as he "trembled at our temerity when we made out the lists of patrons and patronesses for the concert. But in a few days, I exulted at our daring, for the acceptances began to come in." (Whiteman 1926: 93, 95) Whiteman was not alone in celebrating the success of his concert. *The Musical Digest*, which covered Whiteman's concert, excerpted reviews from the New York papers the *Herald*, the *Tribune*, the *World*, the *Post*, the *Sun*, and the *New York Times*. W. J. Henderson in the *Herald* exclaimed that if "this way lies the path toward the upper development of American modern music into a high art form, then one can heartily congratulate Mr. Gershwin on his disclosure of some of the possibilities... Paul Whiteman, himself, a born conductor and a musical personality of force and courage who is to be congratulated on his adventure and admirable results he obtained in proving the euphony of the jazz orchestra." The music critic Olin Downes of the *New York Times* believed the concert showed "remarkably beautiful examples of scoring for a few instruments; scoring of singular economy, balance, color and effectiveness; music at times vulgar, cheap, in poor taste, elsewhere of irresistible swing and insouciance and recklessness and life; music played as only such players as these may play it – like the melomaniacs that they are,

bitten by rhythms that would have twiddled the toes of St. Anthony...
Mr. Gershwin's composition shows extraordinary talent... This is fresh
and new and full of promise." (*The Musical Digest* 2-19-1924: 3) Following the concert, *Metronome* provided its own review and celebrated
Whiteman's concert of modern music and the recognition this would
accord jazz orchestras.

Paul Whiteman and His Orchestra Make Their Debut on the Concert Stage

The orchestra appeared on its merits as an American Plan Orchestra, making
no apologies for its 100 per cent American Plan of instrumentation... without
begging pardon or craving indulgence, but with a very serious intent to prove
that American music has idioms, melodic concepts, rhythmatics and dynamics
that entitle it to a respectful hearing and a just appraisal and a place of no little
importance among the Music of Nations.

. . .

The most renowned critics on the most renowned of New York dailies took the
Recital very seriously, and its freely predicted that Paul Whiteman, "The Mae-
stro Who Symphonized Syncopation," sometimes appropriately referred to as
"America's Berlioz," has opened the way for an era of Concerts and Recitals of
distinctly American Music in the greatest auditoriums of the nation. (*Metronome*,
April 1924: 92)

Whiteman immediately followed his Aeolian concert with another performance at Carnegie Hall in New York City. The two concerts were
then followed by a six-week tour in May and June of 1924 covering
fifteen cities as far west as St. Louis and including three cities in Canada.
Presenting a similar program as the first concerts in New York City, the
Whiteman orchestra performed "American pieces of varied type calculated to show American music just as it is, from rag-time to blues and
symphonized syncopation." (*Metronome* 6-1924: 23) In preparing for another transcontinental tour in September 1924, Whiteman's major sponsor, The Buescher Instrument Company, again celebrated his triumph
in an advertisement in *Metronome*. "Americans will have a glorious opportunity to hear American Music 'put on' with all the wealth of esthetic
detail that heretofore has been reserved exclusively for foreign music in
America! Every number programmed will be an American number –
100% American! Every number will be especially arranged and scored
with as much thought and ingenuity and feeling for orchestral effect as
has ever been given to the great symphonies." (*Metronome* 8-1924: 22)
In reaching Chicago on his transcontinental tour, *Metronome* noted the
great success of the Whiteman orchestra at the Studebaker Theatre with
1,000 ardent fans turned away at the box office and equally assured

readers that "music critics took Whiteman seriously." (*Metronome* 12-1924: 79) Glenn Dillard Gunn in *The Herald and Examiner* in Chicago noticed that all "the musical highbrows of Chicago and as many of the lowbrows as could find a place in the theater seemed to be agreed on this point: Whiteman unquestionably directs a band of virtuosi who have refined and perfected the musical idiom to which they have devoted themselves... The harshness, blatancy and vulgarity of early 'jazz' have disappeared. In their place are heard suavity, an astonishing refinement of dynamic contrasts, warm, rich and many-colored tones and rhythms that are insistent and varied." (*The Musical Digest* 11-25-1924: 13)

Vincent Lopez also began performing special jazz concerts in New York City in 1924 in such respected concert halls as the Metropolitan Opera House and Carnegie Hall. Besides these concerts, Vincent Lopez did a concert tour of the East Coast. His jazz concert on November 23, 1924 at the Metropolitan Opera House showed an eclectic range of performances from classical standards, to Tin Pan Alley song, to a special composition by the black composer W. C. Handy called "The Evolution of the 'Blues'." Olin Downes in *The New York Times* again supported the efforts in symphonic jazz in stating that Lopez' effort "demonstrates the real promise in American music!" (Shaw 1987: 152) The *Mail Telegram* was convinced that the East Coast tour of Lopez was "certain of success if the reception at his first concert is to be taken as a criterion." (*The Musical Digest* 12-2-1924: 15)

The populist appeal of symphonic jazz was also evident in the celebration of the ascendancy of jazz from its "lowbrow" origins to mix with "highbrow" culture. *The New York Times* on the future of jazz celebrated jazz as making "the world safe for democracy. It is going to seat the highbrow beside the lowbrow at concerts. There will be endowed chairs for the dissemination of knowledge of jazz at the fore-most conservatories of music. In that bright future, syncopation will doff its informal attire and don evening clothes, even to the high hat and the cape." (*Metronome* 2-1924: 103) In reviewing the Whiteman concert at Aeolian Hall, Henrietta Strauss, a critic at *The Nation*, was less sure that music, "from an educational standpoint, is not entirely a democratizing force, for there will always be the ultimate mental division of the 'high-brow' from the 'low-brow.'" She still, however, admitted that "here one had the unique experience of being shoved into a concert hall by a cabaret player from Fourteenth Street, and of being shoved out again by some smug musician from the studio, his smugness for once demoralized by the naked allurement of rhythm." And resonating with the jingoism of professional musicians, Strauss also argued that "to the musician trained in other schools there was something very new and exciting and moving in this utter abandonment of all emotional reserve. And there was also, perhaps, a secret and overwhelming realization that he had been caught napping, that a distinctive and well-developed art having obvious kinship with the world-thought of to-day had grown up, unheeded, under his very ears while he had been straining his auditory nerves to catch the echoes of sound three thousand miles away." (*The Literary Digest*, 3-22-1924: 30)

The reception and success of the jazz concerts by Whiteman and Lopez led to greater hope among professional musicians that jazz was finally receiving the full respect it deserved. Vincent Lopez himself hoped that "we may expect jazz to gain a high place in the regard of serious music lovers and students with the result that it will be refined and polished to such an extent that we will be proud of it instead of feeling apologetic when it is credited to us... It is possible and very probable that in the near future our conservatories as well as those colleges having music departments will add jazz to their curriculums, and many of us are working to that end." (*Metronome*, 11-1924: 67) The jazz orchestra leader Harry A. Yerkes also expressed the future hopes of this profession in his article in the December 1924 issue of *Metronome*. "Who'd ever have thought of that boisterous enfant terrible of music, learning manners, submitting to discipline, absorbing science, reveling in work, and developing into the graceful Prince Charming who now wins the world which first jeered and execrated him... Jazz now attends lectures, gives lectures, studies and teaches; listens and talks; analyzes and is analyzed; awaits calmly at the portals of high art until the day when he will be unanimously carried in on the shoulders of those who have shed their gloom through joyous harmony." Yerkes himself entered the hallowed portals of Aeolian Hall on December 6, 1925 with a jazz concert "with a program selected to give the listener a birdseye view of jazz music and the probable development of American popular music in the future." (*Metronome* 12-1925: 16)

While symphonic jazz concerts represented the emulation of the high art aesthetic of symphony orchestras, white professional musicians claimed that jazz orchestras in general, whether in concert halls, movie theaters, vaudeville theaters, hotels, or dance halls, were performing a popular national art form rivaling the European cultivated tradition. The populist and nationalist ideology to which jazz musicians turned to claim their legitimacy served to undermine the Euro-centrism and elitism these musicians experienced. Of course, whether the audiences in theaters, hotels, and dance halls thought they were appreciating a high art music was a question white professional musicians conveniently left unanswered, although in their symphonic jazz concerts, where highbrow met lowbrow, audiences expectations were oriented to high art performance.

The equating of jazz orchestras and jazz music with symphony orchestras and European cultivated music was mostly the work of professional musicians. These musicians had a few supporters outside the profession promoting jazz as an American art. The famous journalist Gilbert Seldes argued in his 1923 article in *Dial*, the "reason jazz is worth writing about is that it is worth listening to. I have heard it said by those who have suffered much that it is about the only native music worth listening to in America." (*The Dial* 8-1923: 152) The music critic Henry Osbourne Osgood also defended jazz music and jazz orchestras, but was less inclined to equate this American art form with the best of the European cultivated tradition. As Osgood argued in a 1925 article in *The American Mercury*, there was "just as much chance of the jazz rhapsody displacing the symphony as the cornerstone of musical architecture as there is of the roast being supplanted by the cocktail." Although there was "plenty of room for both – and the musical epicure will enjoy both, each in its own way and at its own time." (*American Mercury* 11-1925: 129) While not equal to a classical symphony, Osgood would explain later in a 1926 article that jazz orchestration "meets the highest test of any art – the accomplishments of large effects with small means. . . Jazz orchestration, it thus appears, has become a genuine art. Unknown seven or eight years ago, it has developed even more quickly than the aeroplane. And whether or not jazz itself remains, the lessons to be learned from it will not be forgotten by orchestrators of more serious music." (*American Mercury* 4-1926: 578, 585)

Other supporters of jazz music were less magnanimous than Seldes and Osgood in comparing jazz with classical music. Don Knowlton in *Harper's Monthly Magazine* in 1926 defended the merits of jazz music and jazz orchestras, but rejected professional musicians' claim that jazz was high art worthy of the same appreciation as classical music. "Five years ago it was proper to loathe jazz. To-day it is the smart thing to hail it as the only truly American contribution to music, and to acclaim it as Art. Either attitude is ridiculous. Jazz bears much the same relationship to music as does the limerick to poetry." Knowlton, however, did support the claim of many professional musicians that their work at least aided the development of an appreciation among popular audiences for European cultivated music. "Snort if you will, but the fact remains that the shop girl who has heard Paul Whiteman has taken a step toward appreciation of Beethoven's Seventh Symphony." (*Harper's* 4-1926: 578)

Despite resistance to their strident claims, white professional musicians in their role as mediators of the American vernacular had significantly shifted the concept of "good" music and "high art" music within their profession. As populists, these musicians defended the legitimacy of popular music making and its potential as an American fine art music. As elitist professionals, they laid claim against the non-professional musician, and the unacknowledged black professional musician, in having transformed the American vernacular into "good" music. Empowered by their professional ethos, these musicians were the first "popular" artists to claim not only the basic legitimacy of their popular art, but to suggest its equal status to the European cultivated music tradition. As white professional musicians were fomenting their own cultural revolution, however, black professional musicians also were grappling with the question of the vernacular as high art within their own segregated professional class – a struggle absent during this decade from the pages of *Metronome* and the proclamations of white professional musicians on American jazz music.

Uplifting the race: the black vernacular as high art and the harlem renaissance

I have come back from France more firmly convinced than ever that negroes should write negro music. We have our own racial feeling and if we try to copy whites we will make bad copies... We won France by playing music which was ours and not a pale imitation of others, and if we are to develop in America we must develop along our own lines. Our musicians do their best work when using negro material. (James Reese Europe, "A Negro Explains 'Jazz'," *The Literary Digest*, April 26, 1919: 28)

Lieutenant James Reese Europe returned from Europe in 1919 as bandleader of the highly acclaimed black military band of the 369th US Infantry. The *St. Louis Post-Dispatch* in covering the regiment band overseas in June 1918 claimed that "the first and foremost Afro-American contribution to the French fighting line is its band...the dusky band is fast becoming celebrated throughout France." Sergeant Noble Sissle, the regimental drum major, commented that "when our country was dance-mad a few years ago, we quite agreed with the popular Broadway song composer who wrote: 'Syncopation rules the nation, You can't get away from it.' But if you see the effect our good, old 'jazz' melodies have on the people of every race and creed you would change the word 'Nation' quoted above to 'World'... Having been associated with Lieut. Europe in civil life during his 'jazz bombardment' on the delicate, classical, musical ears of New York's critics, and having watched 'the walls of Jericho' come tumbling down, I was naturally curious to see what would be the effect of a 'real American tune,' as Victor Herbert calls our Southern syncopated tunes, as played by a real American band." (Kimball and Bolcom 1973: 68) For Sissle, the 369th was another testament to black professional musicians' legitimate role as the purveyors of a uniquely American music – syncopated jazz music.

Europe and Sissle on their return to the United States embarked on a national tour with the 369th "jazz band" – "the band that set all France JAZZ MAD!" The band was composed of sixty-five "battling musicians" and "masters of jazz" – "the greatest bunch of musicians and jazz artists in the world." (Kimball and Bolcom 1973: 74) The band performed a series of syncopated concerts presenting an eclectic repertoire of music from spirituals, blues, popular song, classical, and opera music articulated through the black vernacular – "a gorgeous racket of syncopation and jazzing" according to the *New York Sun*. (Southern 1997: 356) Like the pre-war Clef Club Orchestra concerts and Clef Club syncopated dance orchestras, Europe once again was positioning black professional musicians as the premier artists of the cultivated black vernacular, and in his concert performances presenting this cultivated vernacular music making as high art. He also took the opportunity, following his success across the Atlantic, to once again assert that the future of black professional musicians lay in their cultivation of the black vernacular. On his triumphant return tour, however, James Reese Europe met an untimely death at the hands of one of his own band members in Boston in May 1919.

Europe, however, was not alone in seeking to combine the black vernacular and cultivated music making into a unique high art expression of African American musicians. William Marion Cook, for example, also attempted to bridge the black vernacular and the cultivated tradition in fine art performance in his formation of the New York Syncopated Orchestra in December 1918. This orchestra, with Cook as conductor and William Tyers as assistant conductor, performed syncopated concerts on a four-month tour of the United States in 1919. These concerts were followed by a successful European tour as the American Syncopated Orchestra or Southern Syncopated Orchestra that included the New Orleans clarinetist Sidney Bechet. This orchestra performed an eclectic repertoire of African American folk music, both popular and classical music by black composers, as well as standard concert works. (Southern 1997) The acclaim that followed this orchestra around Europe was evident as the famous French classical conductor, Ernest Ansermet, comments in *Revue Romande* in October 1919. "The first thing which strikes one about the Southern Syncopated Orchestra is the astonishing perfection, the superb taste, and the fervor of its playing... The musician who directs them and to whom the constitution of the ensemble is due, Mr. Will Marion Cook, is moreover a master in every respect, and there is no orchestra leader I delight as much in seeing conduct." Ansermet, however, while praising this orchestra and William Marion Cook still questioned whether

these musicians were similarly as cultivated as European classical musicians. "I couldn't say if these artists make it a duty to be sincere, if they
are penetrated by the idea that they have a 'mission' to fulfill, if they are
convinced of the 'nobility' of their task, if they have that holy 'audacity'
and that sacred 'valor' which our code of musical morals requires of our
European musicians, nor indeed if they are animated by an 'idea' whatsoever. But I can see they have a very keen sense of the music they love,
and a pleasure in making which they communicate to the hearer with
irresistible force, – a pleasure which pushes them to outdo themselves
all the time, to constantly enrich and refine their medium." (*Jazz Hot*
11/12-1938: 5)

These early efforts at symphonic jazz concerts, however, were over-
shadowed by the new commercial success of "black" entertainment in
musical revues, social dance, and race recordings. On the one hand, the
white producers and club owners who controlled the most lucrative live
venues for black professional musicians supported the demand of white
audiences for popular "black" entertainment. (Kenny 1993) On the other
hand, black middle class audiences, and the older generation of black professional musicians, continued to view the commercial black vernacular
as inferior or denigrating to the "race," and therefore, preferred the emulation of the cultivated tradition as a high art expression of the African
American community. The early efforts of the cultivated black jazz vernacular as high art were easily eclipsed in 1924 by white professional
musicians in their own efforts to legitimize their professional community of artists. The black writer J. A. Rogers in his contribution "Jazz at
Home" in the book *The New Negro* in 1925 pointed to this shift from black
professional musicians to white professional musicians as practitioners of
jazz as high art. "The pioneer work in the artistic development of jazz
was done by Negro artists; it was the lead of the so-called 'syncopated
orchestras' of Tyers and Will Marion Cook, the former playing for the
Castles of dancing fame, and the latter touring as a concertizing orchestra
in the great American centers and abroad. Because of the difficulties of
financial backing, these expert combinations have had to yield ground
to white orchestras of the type of Paul Whiteman and Vincent Lopez,
organizations that are now demonstrating the finer possibilities of jazz
music." (Rogers 1968: 221) Dave Peyton, a strong proponent of emulating white professional musicians as a path to legitimating the professional
class of black musician, however, applauded the success of such efforts
by white jazz orchestras. In 1928, Peyton wrote in the *Chicago Defender*
that to "know Paul Whiteman is to understand at last the phenomenon of
American jazz. Whiteman did not invent jazz – he specifically disclaims
this – but, he was the first to write an orchestral score for jazz, and from its

inception ten years ago right to the present he has been its acknowledged exponent all over the world." (Hansen 1960: 499)

The music historian Samuel A. Floyd (1990, 1995) argues that the black vernacular as part of a high art music expression in the work of black professional musicians during the 1920s remained wedded more to the old ideal of "good" music. Such efforts by Europe and Cook were rare in comparison to those efforts, and their support among the elite community of black artists and black middle class, to translate the black vernacular more directly into classical composition and classical perfor- mance. William Grant Still, whose *Afro-American Symphony* (1930) epit- omized the classical efforts of black artists, believed that the agenda was "to elevate Negro musical idioms to a position of dignity and effectiveness in the field of symphonic and operatic music." (Floyd 1990: 13) As Floyd argues, black professional musicians were cultivating the black vernacu- lar in popular music, but the question of claiming a *high art* expression of the black vernacular in the 1920s among black professional musicians and other black artists remained more within the European cultivated tradition.

The Jazz Age coincided with the *Harlem Renaissance* of the 1920s. This artistic movement centered in New York City envisioned the arts as a vehicle for undermining racist stereotyping in images of black culture – a transformation from the Old Negro to the New Negro – and thereby becoming an important force in overcoming the subordination of the African American community. Given the worsening state of race relations in America, Renaissance thinkers hoped that their community's artistic accomplishments could help in overcoming the stereotypes that ratio- nalized their economic, political, and social oppression. From the same generation as William Marion Cook, James Weldon Johnson articulated this vision in the preface to his *Book of American Negro Poetry* published in 1922. "The final measure of the greatness of all peoples is the amount and standard of the literature and art that they have produced... No peo- ple that has produced great literature and art has ever been looked upon by the world as distinctly inferior. The status of the Negro in the United States is more a question of national mental attitude toward the race than of actual conditions. And nothing will do more to change that mental atti- tude and raise his status than a demonstration of intellectual parity by the Negro through the production of literature and art." (Johnson 1931: 9) As Alain Locke wrote in his introduction to *The New Negro* in 1925, "for the present, more immediate hope rests in the revaluation by white and black alike of the Negro in terms of his artistic endowments and cultural contributions, past and prospective." For the black artist, the "cultural recognition they win should in turn prove the key to that reevaluation of the Negro which must precede or accompany any considerable further betterment of race relationships." (Locke 1925: 15)

The historians Nathan Irvin Huggins (1971) and David Levering Lewis (1979) both point to how the Harlem Renaissance vision focused on high culture as the artistic vehicle for uplifting the race. The historians Kathy J. Ogren (1989) and Jon Michael Spencer (1997) show how during the Renaissance commercial jazz remained suspect among the black middle class and black artists in its perceived reproduction of denigrating stereotypes of black culture – Hansen (1960) makes a similar case for Chicago during this period. Spencer argues that racist images imposed on black popular entertainment led many black professional musicians to distance themselves from commercial popular music in their attempts to articulate the black vernacular in high art music. Both Ogren and Spencer point to how the commercialized black vernacular was viewed as suspect in relation to the "folk" black vernacular, the latter being a legitimate source for black artists to use in the creation of high art music, literature, theater, and painting. Ogren (1989: 116–7) summarizes the position of the commercial black vernacular in which "Harlem Renaissance leaders generally devalued blues and jazz, at least as usually performed, and preferred the transformation of blues and jazz themes into symphonic arrangements patterned after European art music. Some leaders disdained jazz because of its identification with vice, crime, and migrant 'backwardness.' When jazz was eventually revalued as part of the rise of a cult of primitivism, some community spokesmen objected to it for reinforcing the negative stereotypes primitivism seemed to encourage." As Samuel A. Floyd points out "it was in the realm of concert music that Renaissance thinkers hoped for great achievement, expecting that black folk music would serve as the basis for great symphonic compositions that would be performed by accomplished black musicians." (Floyd 1990: 12)

The importance of the earlier efforts of Europe and Cook, however, were not completely ignored within the black community of artists and writers of the Renaissance. J. A. Rogers in his contribution on jazz in the book *The New Negro* in 1925 highlighted the central role of black professional musicians in elevating jazz to high art. "Musically jazz has a great future. It is rapidly being sublimated. In the more famous jazz orchestras like those of Will Marion Cook, Paul Whiteman, Sissle and Blake, Sam Stewart, Fletcher Henderson, Vincent Lopez and the Clef Club units, there are none of the vulgarities and crudities of the lowly origin or the only too cheap imitations." Rogers hoped that jazz while "at present it vulgarizes, with more wholesome growth in the future, it may on the contrary truly democratize ... and they are wise, who instead of protesting against it, try to lift and divert it into nobler channels." (Rogers

1968: 221, 224) As Ogren (1989) argues, however, Rogers, like his Renaissance compatriots Alain Locke and James Weldon Johnson, defended the beauty and traditions of the black vernacular, even certain commercial expression of this vernacular, but still viewed the general commercialization of the black vernacular as compromising the goal of the New Negro. The question was not whether the fruits of the black vernacular, which as Johnson argued in 1922 were "the only things artistic that have yet sprung from American soil and been universally acknowledged as distinctive American products," could form the foundation of a unique high art expression of black artists. The question was the balance between this vernacular and cultivated art making. During the Renaissance, the balance remained on the side of cultivated art.

However, just as a younger generation of Renaissance writers including Claude McKay, Langston Hughes, and Zora Neale Hurston were to embrace the commercial jazz vernacular more openly, a younger generation of black professional musicians like Fletcher Henderson, Don Redman, and Duke Ellington were moving the cultivated jazz vernacular along a path independent of the European cultivated tradition. The coming shift among black professional musicians can be seen in the special symphonic jazz concert given at Carnegie Hall in New York City in 1928 featuring the W. C. Handy Orchestra and Jubilee Singers. The concert was framed around jazz with the program prologue beginning with "The Birth of Jazz" and ending in a "Jazz Finale" and W. C. Handy's famous "St. Louis Blues." The concert included popular works by Handy, James A. Bland, Bert Williams, Hogan Jordan, William Marion Cook, Scott Joplin, and Clarence Williams. The concert also included spirituals arranged by J. Rosamond Johnson and classical compositions by Samuel Coleridge-Taylor, Nathaniel Dett, William Marion Cook, and Henry T. Burleigh. The concert also premiered the musical songsmith and stride pianist James P. Johnson's *Yamekraw Rhapsody* performed by Fats Waller with the Handy Orchestra and arranged by William Grant Still. While the concert represented a "symphonic" strategy, it represented a movement back to the earlier efforts of Europe and Cook, and those of Whiteman and Lopez, in balancing the vernacular and the cultivated in a high art expression.

As was the case in general for symphonic jazz, this crisscrossing of the commercial black vernacular with the European cultivated tradition in the Carnegie Hall concert would not extend beyond the 1920s. Instead, black professional musicians would focus on developing a cultivated vernacular high art within the music making of swing big band performance and small swing ensembles – a shift away from the European cultivated tradition. The most prominent advocate of this new strategy was Duke

Ellington, who by the end of the 1920s took on the agenda articulated by the late James Reese Europe at the beginning of the Jazz Age – to develop a music that uniquely expresses African American music idioms. In his efforts, Ellington would continue the general vision of the Renaissance to uplift the race through art. And in general, black professional musicians over the next four decades would develop a high art tradition based on the black vernacular idiom unimagined by the visionaries of the 1920s' Renaissance.

As the Jazz Age ended, James Weldon Johnson, who since the turn of the century had participated in efforts to change the image, status, and lives of African Americans in the United States, continued to have hope for the emancipation of his community through the power of its artistic voice.

Forces are going out that are reshaping public sentiment and opinion; forces that are going far towards smashing the stereotype that the Negro is nothing more than a beggar at the gates of the nation, waiting to be thrown the crumbs of civilization. Through his artistic efforts the Negro is smashing this immemorial stereotype faster than he has ever done through any method he has been able to use. He is making it realized that he is the possessor of a wealth of natural endowments and that he has long been a generous giver to America. He is impressing upon the national mind the conviction that he is an active and important force in American life; that he is a creator as well as a creature; that he has given as well as received; that his gifts have been not only obvious and material, but also spiritual and aesthetic; that he is a contributor to the nation's common cultural store; in fine, he is helping to form American civilization. (James Weldon Johnson, *Black Manhattan*, 1930: 283–4)

This dream would continue to resonate among black professional musicians as they moved along a different path than their predecessors. Along this new path of the cultivated vernacular, however, black artists would still have to contend with the racist assumptions that continued to exclude them from the pantheon of "creators" of legitimate art in America. They continued to struggle to gain recognition that the music tradition called jazz in its cultivated expression stemmed from the spiritual and aesthetic gifts of black artists in America.

Defending "good" music: jazz and the cultivated tradition

That the majority of what we are pleased to call our musical public are still in this childish or savage stage of taste is shown by the popularity of jazz. Jazz is the doggerel of music. It is the sing-song that the school-boy repeats mechanically before he becomes sensitive to refined cadence... For precisely this reason is it popular with listless, inattentive, easily distracted people, incapable of the effort required to grasp the more complex symmetries of real music.

. . .

As we look about a concert hall at the faces of the audience, so little concentrated, so easily distracted, so incapable apparently of sequacious thought or feeling, can we wonder at the popularity of the most banal and obvious sing-song in the "hits" of the day in musical comedy, rag-time, and jazz, at the eager response, on a somewhat higher plane, to primitives like Stravinsky and decadents like Debussy, at the long indifference to anything more subtle or powerful, making it take decades for Brahams to get the ear of the general public, if indeed he ever gets it? (Daniel Gregory Mason, *The American Mercury*, April 1925: 465–7)

As pleased with the jazz craze as he was with the earlier craze for ragtime, Daniel Gregory Mason was a vocal opponent of jazz. He particularly was opposed to any suggestion that jazz music had a place in "serious" music – the preserve of the cultivated tradition of which he was a self-appointed guardian. The historian MacDonald Smith Moore (1985) shows how composers and critics in the cultivated tradition in the United States debated the merits of jazz music. Most members of the New England School of cultivated music like Mason, and other defenders of the old ideal of "good" music, were stridently against the influence of jazz in both popular music and classical music. Repeating the moral, aesthetic, class, and racial epithets used to condemn the popularization of vernacular jazz, the guardians of the old ideal ridiculed any idea of jazz meriting the status of high art or even having an influence on serious music composition and performance. As David Stanley Smith, Professor of Music at Yale University, argued in *The Musician* of August 1926, jazz music's "monotonous rhythm, as unvaried as the chug-chug of a steam engine, enslaves its practitioners within a formula, and induces in composer, performer, and listener a stupor of mind and emotion." On the other hand, many of those individuals who embraced "modernism" in cultivated music were sympathetic to jazz music. These modernists emphasized jazz as the legitimate expression of the times and a nation. As the European modernist Leopold Stokowski, conductor of the Philadelphia Orchestra, enthusiastically exclaimed in 1924, jazz had "come to stay. It is an expression of the times, of the breathless, energetic, super-active times in which we are living, and it is useless to fight against it." (*The Etude* 9-1924: 595)

The debate within the cultivated tradition between old idealists and modernists on the influence of jazz revolved mainly around the influence of "popular" jazz on "serious" music composition and performance. That the question would be posed in such a manner spoke to how, by the 1920s, the European cultivated tradition had organizationally and ideologically broken from the world of commercial popular music. Crossover between popular music and cultivated music occurred during the 1920s, but organizational and ideological barriers left little chance that jazz musicians would transform the cultivated tradition. The very formation of a separate world of cultivated music in the United States was predicated on its distinction from commercial popular music, popular musicians, and popular tastes – a distinction further exacerbated by jazz music being an expression of the black vernacular. The influence of jazz within the cultivated tradition, however, was debated during the 1920s as professional musicians laid claim to a truly American art form and modernists promoted the incorporation of jazz in serious music composition and performance.

The jazz debate was underscored by the question of the formation of an American School of cultivated music that had occupied critics and composers within the cultivated tradition in the United States since the nineteenth century. The jazz debate within the cultivated tradition, therefore, involved the issue of "good" music as well as national identity. The debate brought to light the connection made by old idealists between aesthetic, moral, class, and racial constructions of "good" music and national identity. As MacDonald Smith Moore (1985) argues, the search for an American identity in classical music in the United States in the late nineteenth and early twentieth centuries was dominated by an idealism predicated on a middle class Anglo-American identity. This idealism also involved a moral purity and uplift that viewed multi-ethnic urban culture and the American vernacular as an abomination. What Moore refers to as the "redemptive culture" of old idealists like Mason juxtaposed an idealized Anglo American culture to the "cosmopolitan culture" of large American cities. As *Musical America* commented, jazz certainly "represents very faithfully the tiny segment of America who lies between Forty-second and Fiftieth Streets, Broadway. Yet that is not precisely the whole of America, or its better part." (*Musical America*, 2-23-1924: 32) David Stanley Smith certainly agreed that jazz was not representative of America or American idealism:

The unfortunate thing about jazz is that its allurements have led many people (thoughtful and thoughtless alike) to herald it as a great American contribution to musical art, indeed the only real contribution. . . But the fallacy in the argument lies in the incompleteness of the jazz artist's vision of America. To him America is Forty-second street, glittering, expensive hotels, cabarets, musical comedies, fine clothes, taxis, banquets, and all the show and pomp of money and money getting. All this finds its faithful portraiture in jazz. But the jazz artist is rarely found roaming among the hills of Vermont, he is not often discovered absorbed in a view of golden wheat stretching for miles over a prairie. The quiet idealistic, religious America, the America of good books, of great pictures – his America is blank to him, or at the most an unspeakable bore. (David Stanley Smith, *The Musician*, August 1926)

While Mason, Smith, and others in the field of European cultivated music rejected jazz as representative of America and warned against any influence of jazz over high art music, others in this field had a more open mind about jazz and cultivated music. These supporters of jazz were mostly modernists, artists allied with the "New Music" movement in Europe that had moved away from nineteenth century classical composition and idealism – the composition and idealism that the New England School continued to view as the essence of the cultivated tradition. Mason's earlier comment on the decadence and primitivism of modernist composers Debussy and Stravinsky is a reference to their compositional use of ragtime and jazz and their prominence as purveyors of modernism in classical composition. A new generation of American composers in the 1920s, however, adopted the modernism of the European New Music movement as well as European modernist's fascination with jazz as the sound of modernity. The American composer Aaron Copland, for example, was a modernist who became one of the most prominent and outspoken proponents of jazz in serious composition in the 1920s. For defenders of the old idealism, therefore, both a lowbrow vernacular and a highbrow avant-garde were assaulting "good" music. Daniel Gregory Mason deplored "how the indifference of the plain people, the central mass of intelligent Americans, divides our public disastrously into a thick layer of musical 'lowbrows' or hoodlums at the bottom, who support the trivialities and inanities of jazz and other 'popular' trash, and a thin but equally injurious layer of 'high brows' or snobs at the top, who cultivate eccentricity and fads, thereby dangerously artificializing our concert life... this lack of a middle body of sound taste between the erratic extremes retards the development of our native music." (Mason 1930: 10–11)

While modernists in the cultivated tradition welcomed jazz music and its influence on "serious" music, few of these defenders of jazz suggested that popular jazz music and popular jazz orchestras, while encapsulating the modern spirit of the times, were part of the world of serious music. *Metronome* in December 1925 noted the rare exception. In a translated article from the music journal *Die Musik*, the French modernist composer Daruis Milhaud applauded jazz as "serious" music. "In the Jazz

Band the North Americans have actually found a form of artistic expression that is absolutely their own, and their leading Jazz Bands attain such perfection in their performances that they are worthy to share the fame of the well-known symphonic organizations. . ." (*Metronome*, 12-15-1925: 15) Milhaud, like other European modernists, also provided the rare recognition of black professional musicians as purveyors of modern jazz. "Even though with the American Jazz Bands everything may be at the highest point of perfection and no slightest part be lacking in careful study, yet with the negroes the proportion of improvisational element is considerably greater. But what stupendous musical means and what imagination are requisite in order to render all this flawlessly! From the technical standpoint one finds they have greater facility in playing; each instrument follows its own melodic line and improvises along the line of the harmonic thread which runs through the number performed." Milhaud, however, continued to place even these highly skilled techniques within the primitivism associated with African American culture. "With the negroes the dance has retained its African, savage character; the intensity and impressiveness of its rhythms and melodies give it the tragic nature of despair." (*Metronome*, 12-15-1925: 16) The European modernist Leopold Stokowski in the September 1924 issue of *The Etude* was even more direct in placing black professional popular musicians in the forefront of modern jazz. "The Negro musicians in America are playing a great part in this change. They have an open mind, and unbiased outlook. They are not hampered by traditions or conventions, and with their new ideas, their constant experiments, they are causing new blood to flow in the veins of music. In America, I think, there lies perhaps the greatest hope in the whole musical world." (*The Etude* 9-1924: 595)

Stokowski's comments on jazz appeared in the second of two special issues of the music education journal *The Etude* in the summer of 1924 on "The Jazz Problem: Where Is Jazz Leading America?" (*The Etude* 8-1924, 9-1924) The symphonic jazz concerts of Paul Whiteman and Vincent Lopez in 1924 had attracted the attention of educators, critics, and artists in the cultivated tradition and temporarily placed center stage the question of jazz as high art. Following Paul Whiteman's Aeolian Hall jazz concert in February 1924, for example, the cultivated music journal *Musical America* was quick to respond. Whiteman drew compliments in the journal's regular column "Mephisto's Musings" in February 1924. The column noted that the concert "attracted the biggest audience to Aeolian Hall of the season." The column complimented the progress made by Paul Whiteman and white professional musicians. And unlike

European modernists' adulation of black musicians, the columnist was relieved that this concert "certainly managed to show that we must no longer consider syncopated music in terms of vulgar, noisy, blatant cacophony produced by Negroes at cabarets or vaudeville shows, that it has evolved from that and is now worthy of consideration as a distinct feature of our future musical life." In a feature article on the concert in the same issue of *Musical America*, similar comments on the "popular" success of the concert, and the racial construction of the advances in jazz presented by these white professional popular musicians, were made. The article, however, viewed comparisons of symphonic jazz to the classical cultivated tradition in a far less positive light.

Capacity House Fervently Applauds as Jazz Invades Realm of Serious Music

The program and an elaborate program-book described the event as "an experiment in modern music," and to judge by the thunders of applause which met the brilliant efforts of the bandsmen and their master, the experiment can be counted a complete success in the popular sense...

The concert proved, if it proved anything, that jazz is definitely out of the jungle stage; that it can make, and has made, a signally important contribution to the art of scoring for small ensembles; that it is easy and even fascinating to listen to – in homeopathic doses; that its attraction resides in qualities almost exclusively external. For there is nothing noble, moving, or dignified about this particular form of music. It is simply immensely clever, effervescent, and for the moment stimulating. But of it all, so far as this present writer is able to discern, its nothing of significance, nothing eloquent and fine, nothing that nourishes the imagination... (*Musical America*, February 23, 1924: 32)

The special series on jazz in *The Etude* also addressed the debate over jazz as legitimate art. *The Etude* gathered the comments of professional musicians, composers, and conductors in the cultivated tradition, and a few jazz orchestra leaders and popular song composers, to address the problem of jazz. Of course, except for some comments by jazz bandleaders, the question for most commentators was whether jazz music had a place in the compositions and performances *within* the European cultivated tradition. The question was far less related to the challenge of professional musicians of whether jazz music and jazz orchestras merited entrance into the vaulted halls of serious high art music in the United States. Yet even the answers to the question of the place of jazz in "serious" music composition was mostly an emphatic no.

The special investigation into jazz started with *The Etude* making clear that it had "no illusions on Jazz" and as "a mirror of contemporary musical education effort. We, therefore, do most emphatically *not endorse*

Jazz, merely by *discussing it...* In its original form it has no place in musical education and deserves none. It will have to be transmogrified many times before it can present its credentials for the Walhalla of music." *The Etude,* however, recognized that "the melodic and rhythmic inventive skill of many of the composers of Jazz, such men as Berlin, Confrey, Gershwin and Cohan, is extraordinary. Passing through the skilled hands of such orchestral leaders of high-class Jazz orchestras conducted by Paul Whiteman, Isham Jones, Waring, and others, the effects have been such that serious musicians such as John Alden Carpenter, Percy Grainger and Leopold Stokowski, have predicted that Jazz will have an immense influence upon musical composition, not only of America, but also the world." (*The Etude* 8-1924: 515) As these editorial comments in *The Etude* underscored, however, the question among critics and artists of the European cultivated tradition was whether jazz music had a place in the compositions and techniques of this tradition. The comments by contributor Will Earhart, for example, left little doubt as to the potential of jazz orchestras and jazz musicians to attain a level of artistry warranting the same respect as symphony orchestras and classical music.

I do not approve of "jazz" because it represents, in its convulsive, twitching, hiccoughing rhythms, the abdication of control by the central nervous system – the brain...

"Jazz" is defended sometimes because, in its later manifestations, well trained musicians have put some real interest of musical thought and design into it. Such bright spots of the kind that I have noticed are merely intermittent. They usually appear as oases with a desert of drivel before and another following. Their effect, to me, is that of a voo-doo dancer suddenly shouting out some witty epigram and then relapsing to his primitive nature.

Perhaps everything must be judged by the company it keeps – and attracts. Bach fugues, Beethoven symphonies, works by Debussy and Ravel are heard in certain places and received by a certain clientele gathered there. They seem to be appropriate to the places in which they are heard, and to the people who gather there to hear them. So does "Jazz." (Will Earhart, Director of Music, Pittsburgh, *The Etude,* August 1924: 520)

Frank Damrosch, Director of the Institute of Musical Art in New York City, was of a similar mind as Earhart. Jazz merited little respect since it "is to real music what the caricature is to the portrait. The caricature may be clever, but it aims at distortion of line and feature in order to make its point; similarly, jazz may be clever but its effects are made by exaggeration, distortion, and vulgarisms." The vulgarity of jazz for Damrosch, as in Earhart's earlier comments, was constructed around racist allusions to primitivism and the savage. "If jazz originated in the dance rhythms of the negro, it was at least interesting as the self-expression of a primitive race. When jazz was adopted by the 'highly civilized' white race, it tended to degenerate it towards primitivity. When a savage distorts his features and paints his face so as to produce startling effects, we smile at his childishness; but when a civilized man imitates him, not as a joke but in all seriousness, we turn away in disgust." (*The Etude* 8-1924: 518)

Other commentaries were less critical of jazz music and jazz orchestras. American classical composer, John Alden Carpenter, from the same New England School generation as Mason and Smith, reiterated the populist appeal of defenders of jazz. "All music that has significance must necessarily be the product of its time; and whether, we believe that the world to-day is headed toward Heaven or Elsewhere, there is no profit in any attempt to induce the creative musician to alter his spontaneous mode of expression in order that he may thus affect the contemporary social conditions. Nor shall we make any better progress by attempting to legislate contemporary American music out of popularity by resolution of clubs and civic bodies. I am convinced that our contemporary popular music (please note that I avoid labeling it 'jazz') is by far the most spontaneous, the most personal, the most characteristic, and by virtue of these qualities, the most important musical expression that America has achieved. I am strongly inclined to believe that the musical historian of the year two thousand will find the birthday of American music and that of Irving Berlin to have been the same." (*The Etude* 8-1924: 518) The classical composer Percy Grainger more directly defended jazz music and jazz orchestras whose "orchestral arrangements are often made by musicians with unusual experience. To my mind, this form of Jazz is the finest popular music known to me in any country of to-day or even of the past. Its excellence rests on its combination of Nordic melodiousness with Negro tribal, rhythmic polyphony plus the great musical refinement and sophistication that has come through the vast army of highly trained cosmopolitan musicians who play in Jazz. There never was a popular music so classical. . ." Grainger even as a defender of jazz, however, was less supportive of the idea of jazz as an important influence on the serious high art music of the European cultivated tradition. "Apart from its influence on orchestration, Jazz will not form any basis for classical music of the future, to my mind. . . Therefore, the laws which govern Jazz and other popular music can never govern music of the greatest depth or the greatest importance. I do not wish to belittle Jazz or other popular music. . . But there will always exist between the best popular music and classical music that same distinction that there is between a perfect farmhouse and a perfect cathedral." (*The Etude* 9-1924: 593)

The comments by Carpenter and Grainger, however, were the minority voice among artists and critics in the cultivated tradition contributing to the series. Walter Spalding, Professor of Music at Harvard University, for example, argued that "some of us only take umbrage when we hear the extreme devotees of Jazz say that it is the greatest modern contribution to music and is destined to supercede all other music... But good music must surely have many other qualities, such as melodic outline, deep emotional appeal, sublimity and ideality; and if the best we can say of Jazz is that it is exciting, it seems to me that many of the highest attributes of music are left out." (*The Etude* 9-1924: 595) The American classical composer, Henry F. Gilbert, commented that he found "almost all pieces of so-called Jazz music, when stripped of their instrumentation... Have almost nothing new to offer in the way of strictly musical interest..." (*The Etude* 8-1924: 518). Another contributor, Clay Smith, also saw little value in jazz as "even the best of this entertaining and popular music has no place with the great classics or even with fine concert numbers, except perhaps in a few cases where musicians of the highest standing such as Stravinsky, Carpenter, Cadman, Guion, Grainger, Huertez, and others with real musical training, have playfully taken 'Jazz' idioms and made them into modernistic pieces of the super-jazz type." (*The Etude* 9-1924: 595)

Certainly the editors of *The Etude* were left unconvinced by the defenders of jazz music and jazz orchestras that this popular music would have an influence on "serious" music in America. In the January 1925 issue, the editors continued their lament on the effects of jazz and reaffirmed their beliefs in the redemptive culture that defined the cultivated tradition and "good" music. "Tap America anywhere in the air and nine times out of ten, Jazz will burst forth. A great deal of this may, of course, be a background of entirely innocent fun. It may bring great and enlivening stimulation to hard workers who need just that thing. On the other hand, we know that in its sinister aspects, Jazz is doing a vast amount of harm to young minds and bodies yet developed to resist evil temptations. This is no mere editorial bias. Fortune has cast us into deep life channels and we have come to regard these problems in their relation to the cosmic scheme of things. We know that good music, allied with good morals and ethics, has an edifying and purifying value..." Luckily for *The Etude*, most of the magazine's readers were in agreement. In response to the special issues on jazz, the editors "received a large number of opinions upon the subject from our readers. Some wrote excellent little articles but we think that the subject has been sufficiently aired in THE ETUDE... The result showed that about *twenty-five per cent.* were in favor of the 'better kind of Jazz,' while *seventy-five per cent.* were emphatically opposed to jazz. One reader drew this picture. On the one side was a desolate old back yard, filled with rubbish, tin cans and weeds, representing Jazz, with a beautiful sunflower growing out of the heap representing 'the better kind of Jazz.' On the other side was a glorious garden representing good music, beautiful music. We admit that the comparison was a powerful and fairly accurate one." (*The Etude* 1-1925: 5–6)

While professional musicians had their supporters within the cultivated tradition, the old ideal of "good" music would remain steadfast against any change in the world of European cultivated music. In fact, except for the major two-issue series on jazz in *The Etude* in 1924, the question of jazz as either a unique American art form or as an influence in "serious" music was basically absent in the journals supporting European cultivated music. In such journals as *Musical America*, *Musical Quarterly*, *The Etude*, and *Musical Digest*, the question of jazz music as art was rarely discussed. Even the journal *Modern Music*, established by the League of Composers, an organization of modernist classical composers, only had three articles on jazz in the 1920s. Although in its first season of performances and lectures, this organization did sponsor a "Jazz Symposium" with Vincent Lopez supplying examples for the edification of the audience. Also, while Walter Damrosch of the New York Symphony would commission jazz compositions in 1925 from George Gershwin and Victor Herbert, this was a rare moment of crossover. Paul Whiteman and Vincent Lopez would perform "jazz" works by classical composers like John Alden Carpenter and Deems Taylor, but these performances too were a rare exception.

As Lawrence Levine (1989) argues, the concept of Culture – the moral, aesthetic, class and racial construction of redemptive culture as well as the reification of European culture – positioned jazz as outside its legitimate boundaries. Ironically, as both Levine (1989) and Moore (1985) point out, the very outsider status of jazz was both celebrated by its defenders and condemned by its critics. Unfortunately for professional musicians, the avant-garde modernists support of jazz only emphasized the deviant nature of jazz to old idealists of "good" music. And as the sociologist Catherine M. Cameron (1996) points out, even modernists were in retreat by the 1930s. Many modernist American composers like Aaron Copland abandoned jazz as well as modernism moving towards "neo-classical" composition, and those who remained committed to modernism remained marginal in the field of cultivated music in the United States. What little discussion there had been of American popular music influencing "serious" music, or its actual use in classical composition, disappeared after the Jazz Age. In general, jazz music fundamentally challenged the precepts on which a separate world of European cultivated music was established, and therefore, professional musicians had little hope of gaining the acceptance of those committed to this music tradition in the United States.

There was one place, however, where jazz and popular music did successfully share a performance venue with the European cultivated tradition, the commercial movie theater. While promoters of the European cultivated tradition in the 1920s continued to find a place in movie palaces across the country to expose popular audiences to "serious" music, movie palaces also had begun complementing these orchestras with musical revues of dancers, singers, and musicians performing popular music as well as "standards." Most movie theaters in general employed orchestras and bands of differing sizes similar to those employed in vaudeville, or in the smallest theaters, organists or pianists. Overall, the AFM listed a peak of 26,000 musicians employed in movie theaters in the 1920s, approximately one-sixth of their membership. (*Metronome* 3-1930) In the 1920s, both larger and smaller theaters also began to use jazz bands and orchestras; some movie theaters also began adopting jazz policies to attract audiences. "Following the war there was an epidemic of stage bands in the flickers. Some of the chains kept 100 bands on the move booking a different one each week. Nearly every de luxer featured one stage band and sometimes two on the weekly bill. Theatre orchestras began adopting these instruments. Some theatres tried a jazz band in the pit. In 1925 Ben Bernie was engaged by Riesenfeld for eight weeks at the Rivoli. In 1927, Bennie Krueger was circulating around three B and K Chicago houses." (*Metronome* 5-1932: 12) Vincent Lopez brought his orchestra to a musical extravaganza produced by Joseph Plunkett at the Mark Strand Theater in New York City in January 1926, balancing the performances of the Mark Strand Symphony Orchestra directed by Carl Edouarde. That same month besides the symphony orchestra at the Rivoli Theater in New York City, "the jazz orchestra, billed as Eddie Elkins and His Melody Mixers played four popular numbers and were received with the general approval that is always accorded anything as sure-fire as a good jazz unit in a picture theatre." (*Metronome* 2-15-1926: 22–3) Jazz certainly was invading movie theaters.

Promoters of the cultivated tradition, however, still viewed movie palaces as important venues for educating the general public to the better type of music. *Metronome* continued to support these efforts and the men behind them like S. L. Rothapfel, or Carl Edouarde who, according to *Metronome*, Walter Damrosch of the New York Symphony credited as having "done more to educate the masses to better music than any other individual I know." (*Metronome* 2-15-1926: 19) Movie theaters and palaces, however, were moving more towards a popular music policy. As sound film began replacing silent film in the late 1920s, the need for full orchestras to perform film music also no longer existed, so theaters began reducing or eliminating their large orchestras and viewing live performances on their own merits in attracting audiences, all leading to greater use of popular orchestras. The Roxy Theater in New York City, the "Cathedral of the Motion Picture," the original home of S. L. Rothapfel, eventually succumbed to these changes in 1932. Eliminating its seventy-five member symphony orchestra, which had peaked to 112 members during the 1920s, the Roxy hired the popular big band, Fred Waring and His Pennsylvanians. L. K. Sidney, an executive of the De Luxe chain of motion picture theaters on the Loew Circuit, expressed the attitudes of theater owners by the late 1920s on the appropriate music for their patrons in the January 1928 issue of *Metronome*.

What Modern Music Has Done to the Motion Picture Theaters

Who would have dreamt that the popular form of music would chase the classics out of all picture theatres insofar as feature orchestral numbers are concerned? No one, but unfortunately or fortunately, that is exactly what has happened...

It is probably done in fine musicianly style, but, it becomes tiresome and draggy and asks a long waiting audience a good deal to sit thru a number of this type – and expect them to enjoy it. Just glance around at your next door neighbors and see how they are doing. For at least ten minutes you hear a mumble of conversation and finally the orchestra outplays their talk and beats them into submission, winning the battle against conversation only because the audience has run out of breadth and conversation. Then the orchestra with a majestic fanfare and blare of brass climaxes itself into a big ovation, not in appreciation of the splendid artistic phrasing or musical technical work, but because they are glad it is over.

The stage band with its jazz instrumentation has served a splendid purpose in bringing to the theatre audiences who patronize motion pictures a fine conception of rhythm and popular music... The public attending theatres or any amusement place love to hear the music they know and I can assure you from observation that they know more about popular music than they do about the classics." (L. K. Sidney, *Metronome*, January 1928: 26)

The changes in movie theaters, both the increased use of popular music and the eventual decline in employment of musicians with the advent of sound film, highlighted the culmination of the high/popular split in both American music and the profession of musician in the United States. Advocates of the European cultivated tradition had hoped to maintain a foothold in popular performance, and reach a broader popular audience, in large movie palaces across the country. These venues also provided significant employment for professional musicians performing within the cultivated tradition, and therefore, helped to maintain the shared music-making culture of professional musicians. With the collapse of this commercial market, the patron-supported world of European cultivated music was more than ever a distinct world of music making and music appreciation; although music education and early commercial radio provided a link to a broader part of the American public. This change also significantly changed the employment opportunities of professional musicians within this tradition. Along with the revolt of professional popular musicians and their development of an alternative ideal of "good" music, the loss of movie theater palaces was a final step in a general break within the profession of music making. Now American music would be more than ever divided between those musicians and audiences who practiced and enjoyed popular music making and those musicians and audiences who practiced and enjoyed European cultivated music making.

Conclusion: the end of the jazz age

A New Era Dawns

There appears to be a growing conviction among present day writers and editors that we are soon to enter another era in our historical development, if indeed we have not already entered it. That feverish decade following the world war, has come to an end, and many things that characterized that decade are being discarded. People are tired of raucous jazz, hysteria, stark reality and other concomitants of the post war age and are turning longing eyes toward the flowering and shady paths down which our forefathers strolled.

There are other indications of a change of heart. Blaring jazz music – consisting mostly of noise – is being replaced more and more by soft and subdued melody. (Editorial, *Metronome*, March 1931: 12)

The swan song for jazz was sung many times during the Jazz Age, but as the "Crash of '29" led America into the Great Depression, it seemed that the vibrant, optimistic decade in which jazz music became a national sensation was definitely at an end. For defenders of the old ideal of "good" music, these changes were hopeful harbingers of the waning of jazz. E. C. Mills, former chairman of the American Society of Composers, Authors, and Publishers, expressed the optimism among traditionalists still critical of popular jazz. "Out of the war-time travail came jazz as we know it now. It expresses a musical motif born of fear, excitement, and hurry... To a large extent the life of a nation reflects its music, no less than the music itself is a reflection of the temper of the people. Is it not time for a return to sanity? I think we should go back to melody and let it serve instead of noise to give us the inspiration which we expect from music." (*Metronome* 1-1930: 42) Traditionalists, of course, had reason to be optimistic as the economic depression following the 1929 stock market crash wreaked havoc on the commercial market of popular jazz music. Defenders of the European cultivated tradition also had reason to celebrate as the confident proclamations of professional musicians on jazz as America's first authentic art receded to the background as these musicians adjusted to changed economic circumstances and a new popular music market.

Professional musicians' struggle for legitimacy during the Jazz Age, however, laid the ideological and musical foundation upon which the next generation of professional musicians would construct a modern jazz paradigm. In their quest for legitimacy as professional artists, they were the first popular artists to attempt to transform the moral, aesthetic, class, and racial constructions of the old ideal of "good" music in America. While their efforts contained their own complicity in manners of distinction, the contradictions of an elite populism embedded in a racist culture, they did struggle to create an alternative understanding of art and society in America. As the self-appointed mediators of the American vernacular, professional musicians and composers ardently worked to construct an alternative form of "good" music to that of the European cultivated music tradition – a music reflecting in some fashion the world of popular audiences and popular tastes. In this process of syncretism, the reinvention and reinterpretation of musical idioms and practices, these artists created the American big band dance orchestra and the Tin Pan Alley song that dominated American popular music until the middle of the twentieth century. While jazz did not become a universally recognized American high art form during the Jazz Age, professional musicians and composers transformed it into a "legitimate" popular art music, although at the expense of those non-professional vernacular musicians who did not assimilate into their profession. The need for professional musicians to legitimate popular dance orchestras disappeared after the 1920s, and the old ideal of "good" music no longer occupied this professional class of musician.

The emergence of an alternative ideal of "good" music among professional musicians signaled a final separation between popular music making and the cultivated tradition in American music. This break was both ideological and practical; a reflection of both a new professional ethos among professional musicians and the culmination of the division in the social organization of American music between the world of popular music and the world of European cultivated music. A new generation of professional musician would be trained in the art of the "cultivated vernacular" and from this lively art they would develop a high art tradition distinct from the European cultivated tradition. The previously shared ethos of cultivated music making in the first three decades of the twentieth century among professional musicians now split along two paths, the popular and the classical. The previous crisscrossing professionally between the cultivated tradition and popular music making was no longer part of this profession. The future big band leaders and musicians of the Swing Era began their professional careers not in symphonies, but in the small jazz ensembles and jazz orchestras of the Jazz Age.

3   The swing craze: professional musicians, swing music, and the art of improvisation

> If I should be asked to advise one of these young men what to do to become a front-rank swing player, I would urge him to learn to read expertly and be just as *able* to play to score as any "regular" musician. Then I would tell him never to forget for one minute of his life that the true spirit of swing music lies in free playing and that he must always keep his own musical feeling free. He must try always to originate and not just imitate.
>
> Louis Armstrong, Swing That Music, 1936: 121

Louis Armstrong's autobiography was published at the beginning of a "swing craze" that hit the nation in the summer of 1935. The publication of Armstrong's autobiography demonstrated a new status accorded the jazz vernacular as well as a new status gained by black musicians. To suggest that the literate skill of reading a musical score was insufficient for a professional musician to be a top swing artist seemed radical advice given the obsession with the cultivated skills of music making just a decade earlier. By the 1930s, however, many professional musicians viewed the vernacular art of jazz improvisation as one of the most skilled expressions in American popular music and Louis Armstrong as its greatest practitioner. At the same time, black musicians like Louis Armstrong, Duke Ellington and Teddy Wilson also gained recognition among white musicians and white music critics as premier artists in American popular music. This was a significant change from the Jazz Age when black professional musicians were denigrated or completely absent in the written commentary of top white musicians and critics acclaiming the cultivated jazz vernacular.

Just before the swing craze, however, the future of jazz actually looked bleak. The song composer Hoagy Carmichael expressed a common feeling in the early 1930s that "jazz was dying and at a fast clip. The stock market crash had sent millions of jazzbos to the ranks of the unemployed." (*Metronome* 8-1933: 23) In these early years of the Great Depression, traditionalist values seemed to have gained the upper hand as a consolidated music industry promoted the smooth sounds of "sweet" big band music.

96

The fate of jazz was not only in jeopardy due to hard economic times, but also seemed threatened by the power over popular music of a new mass media industry of broadcasts, recordings, and film. Just when the fortunes of jazz seemed dead and buried, however, the swing craze re-ignited popular interest in the cultivated jazz vernacular.

The promotion of sweet music and the subsequent swing craze, how-ever, set in motion a new distinction within the profession of musician. No longer singularly obsessed with the world of European cultivated music, professional musicians who assimilated the black jazz vernacu-lar now viewed sweet music as their more direct nemesis. The previous distinction between a patron-supported European cultivated music and an open market of commercial popular music now shifted to a perceived battle within the popular music market. The race and class boundaries articulated in the old ideal of "good" music were now articulated more directly for professional musicians in the distinction between the popular music cultures of sweet and swing.

These transformations within the profession of popular musician also reflected changes in the reception of jazz outside this profession. As Monroe Berger (1947) and Neil Leonard (1962) argue, the previous tra-ditionalist fear of jazz had gradually been dissipated by the swing craze. In the early 1930s, the cultural pendulum momentarily swung away from the black vernacular influence in popular music; yet when the swing craze hit the nation it actually faced less resistance than the jazz craze in the 1920s. Berger and Leonard suggest this change came about by a process of as-similation and acceptance in which the efforts of professional musicians and changes in the production of popular music made cultivated jazz into a less threatening cultural expression. The more defensive posturing of professional musicians during the Jazz Age, therefore, was unnecessary by the time of the swing craze, although the dominance of sweet music for some swing musicians and critics continued to position swing as out-side the mainstream – a "hep" swing culture against a conventional sweet culture.

Besides no longer facing strident opposition from traditionalists, swing music also was more widely embraced and celebrated in America than jazz nearly two decades earlier. The historians David Stowe (1994) and Lewis A. Erenberg (1998) argue that swing music and swing culture benefited from the more general change in the cultural and political landscape of the New Deal Era. During the New Deal, America was captured by a populist ideology that rejected in some fashion the previous class, racial and ethnic boundaries in American culture. This populism was reflected in the reception of swing in that the "way in which people thought about swing revealed new patterns of thinking about history, about racial and cultural difference, and about the nature of American society." (Stowe 1994: 1) Of course, not all Americans embraced this new populism let alone swing music. The greater acceptance of swing certainly reflected a transformation in American culture in relation to distinctions of class and race, but popular music as well as American culture still retained class and race distinctions.

While new patterns of thinking about race and cultural difference emerged during this period, racial segregation in its various manifestations remained a reality for the African American community. The movement towards change in race relations in America was only in its early stages during the New Deal and resistance to such change remained strong, including lynching and race riots. This situation in race relations was reflected in the profession of musician and in the popular music industry – in most ways race relations barely changed even given the new democratic vision of the jazz culture. While white and black professional musicians interacted as artists in swing concerts, dance halls, and clubs, the profession remained segregated in terms of unions, regular band organizations, performance spaces, and even audiences.

As distinctions of class, ethnicity, and race played out in the meaning associated with the swing craze, underlying these various associations was the final culmination of the role of professional musicians in mediating the popular music market. The jazz culture of professional swing musicians as we will see was the final resolution of their balancing of the cultivated and vernacular traditions in performing for popular audiences from minstrelsy, to ragtime, to syncopated dance, to jazz, finally to swing. Swing music was a unique syncretism of the cultivated practices of musicians and composers with the practices and musical forms of the black vernacular. The most important transformation among professional musicians was their development of an artistic ethos and identity around the vernacular art of improvisation.

After the crash: the new popular music industry and sweet music

The Jazz Pioneers Are Passing
Where Do We Go From Here?

Everybody was talking about Guy Lombardo and Rudy Vallee. I listened to their radio programs and tore my hair when people told me this was wonderful music. It was good, simple music, but that was all. Rudy Vallee and Guy Lombardo had found the key to the public's heart... Radio programs turned to entertainment for the people who sat at home and grieved over their financial loss... It was the day of the crooner. Rudy Vallee was at the top of his ladder, and Bing Crosby and

Morton Downey were to follow soon. Rhapsody in Blue had been written and jazz was dying. (Hoagy Carmichael, *Metronome* August 1933: 23)

In the early years of the Great Depression, both the vernacular and cultivated styles of jazz that were fashionable during the Jazz Age suddenly receded from the music market. White musicians who had used "hot" jazz practices in their music making in the 1920s and were rewarded with positions in the top jazz orchestras and recording dates now faced few job prospects. Meanwhile, black orchestras faced a devastated race market with only a few finding a lucrative niche in a new constricted market. The new music market in the early 1930s led to a shift to "sweet" music performed by white big bands such as the highly successful bands of Wayne King and Guy Lombardo. The song writer, singer, and pianist Hoagy Carmichael, like many members of his generation of young white musicians who caught the jazz bug in the 1920s, viewed the fortunes of jazz as spent by the early 1930s. Trumpeter Max Kaminsky in his later autobiography remembered those days. "The reverberations of the stock market crash faded away and the country found itself sunk in a paralysis of fear, unemployment, and want . . . in the main, jazz took a nose-dive along with the blithe spirit of the twenties. The public didn't have the heart for the never-say-die attitude of hot jazz, and the sweet, soothing strains of Wayne King, Guy Lombardo, Rudy Vallee and Fred Waring bands took over the scene." (Kaminsky 1963: 55–6) The fall of jazz music and the rise of sweet music became a regular refrain among white musicians and critics. The future of jazz did seem bleak at the time. As Dorin K. Antrim, editor of *Metronome*, commented in December 1933, it "can be set down as a certainty, however, that the jazz exemplified by the Dixieland boys, who initiated the idea, is now as passe as grand-pap's shaving mug." (*Metronome* 12-1933: 22)

Of course, the fortunes of musicians and music in general looked uniformly desperate in the early 1930s. The introduction of sound film and network radio in the 1920s as well as the economic collapse of the music market in live performance and records devastated the employment opportunities for musicians. As Lewis A. Erenberg (1998: 13) argues, "as the nervous energy of the 1920s gave way to shock and despair, the new pleasure institutions of the first two decades of the century – movies, cabarets, ballrooms, records, bands – collapsed. . . Live entertainment everywhere plunged into an abyss." In 1932, Joseph N. Weber, President of the AFM, admitted that "professional music is in higher favor with the American public today than ever before, and yet the professional musician was never in worse plight economically . . . musical employment conditions remain about as bad as ever. . . Dance halls, clubs, restaurants, private and public parties and celebrations – all human activities for which music is customarily engaged – have felt the cold grasp of hard times." (*Metronome* 4-1932: 21) Even patron-supported symphony orchestras and opera companies were hit hard by the depression. For the approximately 140,000 union members, the general employment conditions looked dreadful. I. A. Hirschman in "The Musician and the Depression" in *The Nation* confirmed the poor state of the profession of musician in 1933, reporting that two-thirds of musicians were unemployed nationally. (*The Nation* 11-15-1933: 565)

While the depression affected all musicians, nonprofessional musicians were hit the hardest as what steady employment was available in the top venues and well-paying jobs went to union musicians. In addition, only union musicians could benefit from the various efforts of the AFM to provide temporary aid and employment to musicians. Even the New Deal Federal Music Project under the directorship of Nikolai Sokoloff, previously director and conductor of the Cleveland Orchestra, set standards under which professional musicians almost exclusively received consideration. (McDonald 1969) This general situation affected nonprofessional musicians formerly active in the jazz, race, and hillbilly markets. Professional black musicians, however, were hit much harder than their white colleagues – although nonprofessional black musicians were hit even harder still – as black music entertainment both live and recorded collapsed and most remaining employment opportunities and major booking agencies were the exclusive reserve of white professional musicians. Black entertainment districts suffered across the country. The major black touring circuit of the Theater Owners Booking Association which covered 80 black theaters across the country during the 1920s folded by 1932 with most theaters converting to sound movie houses. (Kenny 1993; Southern 1997; NGDJ 1994) Only a few black professional orchestras like Duke Ellington's and Cab Calloway's survived these hard times while once successful black entertainers like Bessie Smith and Jelly Roll Morton who created and performed classic blues and classic jazz were left behind. In general, the vernacular music that had reached a peak of influence in the commercial music market during the 1920s was receding to this market's margins.

As musicians struggled in these early years of the depression, the popular music market also was reshaping towards a more consolidated form of social organization. The industry in the early 1930s moved towards a more centralized organization in radio, recording, publishing, film, and live performance, which included a greater concentration in booking and management of musicians. This new music industry certainly was not monolithic, but the concentration within each form of production within the industry, and the mutual interests and ownership across these forms, were unique in building the mainstream of the music market around a narrower set of music conventions. At the same time, the role of mass media in the form of radio, film, phonographs, and jukeboxes, was playing a greater part than ever in the exposure of commercial popular music to a national audience. The new industry focused its energies on conventional Tin Pan Alley song and the big band dance conventions of earlier professional society orchestras. So while the American vernacular receded to the margins of the music market due to hard economic times, it also saw its fortunes turn for the worse due to changes in the popular music industry. Nonprofessional musicians were to find themselves more or less excluded from this new industry while professional musicians had to adjust to its new conventions and new decision-makers.

The new popular music industry centered on the power of national booking and management agencies, national radio networks, major record companies, the Hollywood studio system, and Tin Pan Alley song publishers. Booking and management of musicians was dominated in the 1930s and 1940s by the power house agency MCA, formed in Chicago in 1924, representing over half of professional orchestras, next were the William Morris Agency and the General Amusements Corporation. The record industry was dominated by the major record companies RCA, Columbia, Decca, and the American Recording Company-Brunswick – the latter company merged with Columbia in 1938. Capitol Records would become an important record company beginning with its establishment in 1942. The rise of national networks began with the National Broadcasting Company and the Columbia Broadcasting System in the late 1920s with the addition of the Mutual Network in 1934 and the American Broadcasting Company in 1942. The Hollywood studio system and movie exposition was dominated by five fully-integrated film companies, Loew's-MGM, Paramount, RKO, 20th Century Fox, and Warners, with three other film companies Columbia, United Artists, and Universal. Both the broadcast industry and film industry included popular music as a major part of their industries. These industries along with the record industry also were integrated through cross-ownership. Radio broadcasting relied on music programming to attract audiences, while film companies acquired music publishing companies, benefiting from the synergy of profits gained from royalties plus the mutual publicity between films and popular songs. Finally, ASCAP became the arbiter of the music produced in radio and film, while music-publishing companies were integrated with radio, record, and film companies. Of course, the AFM would play an important role in guaranteeing the use of union musicians in radio, film, and live performance. All the different players in this new popular music industry, of course, shared one basic interest: to garner profits from the popular music market. The AFM worked to assure that a fair share of this profit landed in the hands of professional musicians.

Of course, professional musicians always had to confront the vagaries of commercial markets and the commercial interests of the producers of live, written, and recorded music. In the 1930s, however, the greater role of large national industries in mediating between musicians and audiences in the production of music affected how professional musicians understood the world of commercial popular music. Major players in the new consolidating industry turned out not to be big lovers of jazz, and instead were looking to reintroduce "good" music to the American public. Some professional musicians would welcome these changes, as they preferred sweet music over jazz music, but other professional musicians would resent the new conditions in the industry until the swing craze in 1935 reopened the popular music market to the cultivated jazz vernacular.

The formation of The Radio Music Company in 1930 exemplified changes in the industry in the early 1930s and their immediate effect on jazz. This company was formed incorporating the National Broadcasting Company with the large music publishing firms of Carl Fischer and Leo Feist. The new Chairman of the RMC Board, M. H. Aylesworth, President of NBC, stated that the "policy of the Radio Music Company will be dedicated to the improvement of music in general, the advancement of American culture and the promotion of education of young people to the art of music." Board member E. C. Mills was more direct. "We have had, perhaps, too much jazz... In the popular field, therefore, the Radio Music Company will have the definite objective of a finer product." (*Metronome* 1-1930: 42) To accomplish this mission Erno Rapee was appointed the following year as music director of NBC. In the 1920s, Rapee was a famous symphony conductor and music director at the movie palaces the Rivoli, Capitol, and Roxy in New York City. Just a year earlier, while working in Hollywood on the production of sound film, Rapee had voiced his hopes about the new role of film and radio in American music. "Mr. Rapee believes we will educate the song writers to compose better lyrics, and we will teach the public musical appreciation via radio and pictures... 'The thing one constantly hears comes to be tolerated, then endured, then liked,' Rapee explained. 'In such pictures as *Viennese Nights*, written by Romberg and Hammerstein, being given to the public, they will soon forget the jazzy tunes they thought they liked, and come to look for better things." (*Metronome* 7-1930: 30)

In the early years of radio networks and radio programming, music directors preferred classical music and popular standards for primetime music programs. (Sanjek 1988) Dance orchestras did have prime time shows as well as sustaining programs, although most were relegated to the post-primetime hours. An editorial in *Metronome* in September of 1931 criticized this trend. "The N.B.C., particularly, since Erno Rapee became music director, has sought to foster the idea that the public is demanding better music. Fine. But back of all this is the old reference that popular music is trash and classical music wonderful. In short, music of the past must be good, music of the present must be lowbrow. Music is not to be classified in any such manner. There is good and bad jazz like anything else, and the good deserves consideration without prejudice." (*Metronome* 9-1931: 21) Erno Rapee soon left NBC as music director, but continued in broadcasting as conductor of the Radio City Music Hall Symphony and its program *Music Hall on the Air* from 1933 to 1944. NBC general music director Frank Black, however, continued to emphasize the education of the radio audience through the careful introduction of classical music. "When you have radio listeners writing in and asking for little known compositions of Bach and Beethoven, it makes you feel that the venture is worth while... Radio has made more people music conscious than anything that has happened before. The reason is that more people hear it today. The ordinary symphony orchestra may play four times a week to three thousand people, whereas one radio broadcast can play to ten million people. Certainly the public is demanding a better type of music." In terms of popular music, Black was looking equally for a refinement in the rendition of popular music to the old ideals of "good" music. He admitted, "I do not mean classics predominate in the public appreciation, but that when a listener wants dance music, he wants good dance music." (*Metronome* 9-1933: 35, 45) Black in a later interview clarified that jazz did not fall in the category of good dance music. (*Metronome* 12-1933: 31)

As Frank Black suggested, if dance music was to be part of primetime programming it would be of the wholesome kind. The orchestra leader B. A. Rolfe, one of the first professional musicians to present dance music in a primetime program, made clear the preferences of radio networks. "If I were to be bold, may I remark that ten years ago I forecast the disappearance of the jangling blues and the weird admixture most people call jazz. I feel that it is truly dead today and in its place is rising a newer and more warm melodic strain in the popular music of the nation." (*Metronome* 12-1933: 31) The anti-jazz attitude was not confined solely to radio music directors and radio orchestra leaders. Victor Young, musical director of the American Brunswick Record Company, also was not a lover of jazz. "Melody will hold sway as they bury what most people call jazz. It will not be music that is sweet and simple like the old time ballads, it will be more involved than the ragtime of ten years ago, and more melodic than the simple early tunes which made Americans dance."

(*Metronome* 12-1933: 31) Young also was music director for a number of radio programs as well as an important contributor to film music in his association with Paramount Studios.

There were professional musicians in radio and recording who were less prejudiced against jazz music, at least cultivated jazz music. A popular jazz orchestra leader of the 1920s, Nat Skilkret directed a number of radio programs and recordings while working primarily for the RCA-Victor Company. "Why talk about jazz as something different from other musical materials? After sane analysis one must admit that there are fundamentally three qualities of music: good, bad, and indifferent. There is not exact artistic demarcation between classical music and jazz." Skilkret, however, in discussing program sponsors admitted, "naturally, then, there must be a tieup between the advertising and the music. The various ways in which this is to be done is opening up an entirely unique field of great importance to the program builder. He answers the demands for smoother programs by a great deal of original headwork and research... to enter the radio field profitably, one must first sell his ideas to a program sponsor." Skilkret's interviewer, Irving R. Sussman, agreed that "Skilkret has taken part in the tendency to do away with blare and syncopated bombast. The jazz he plays is performed artistically, with nuances, style, all the serious musicianship befitting a musical gentleman who is thoroughly acquainted with his Bach and Beethoven. And how the people go for it!" (*Metronome* 10-1930: 20–1)

Professional musicians entering the new system obviously had to respond to the views of network music directors, program sponsors, and record company music directors as well as what seemed to be a shift in the tastes of music audiences in the early 1930s. Regardless of the popularity of jazz during the 1920s, many middle-class Americans still preferred classical music as well as popular standards in song and dance. The upscale *Literary Digest* in 1933 had a poll on the likes and dislikes of their readers on radio programming. The big winner was classical music where symphony orchestras received the largest approval with 5,458 positive responses while the famous symphony conductor Walter Damrosch and his *Music Appreciation Hour* received the largest approval for a radio program with 1,370 positive responses – only fourteen respondents expressed a dislike for the program. The sweet sounds of the radio programs of Rudy Vallee and Wayne King did well with positive responses of 1,330 and 684, although Vallee also received 756 negative responses while King only received 54. On the other hand, jazz fared the worst with 10,876 respondents disliking jazz and only 518 liking this type of music – 9,636 respondents were not pleased with crooners like Bing Crosby either. Blues fared poorly too with 1,352 respondents disliking it and only 38 expressing a liking for this music. The editors chose a letter from A. N. Rognstad, Secretary of the Clarkston Chamber of Commerce in the state of Washington, as representative of the comments of respondents dislikes in radio music. "I only hope that when you have tabulated this straw ballot the program directors will take a tip and give us better programs. The modern jazz orchestra, radio crooners and harmony busters are simply terrible. There is absolutely no music in it." In the following issue, the editors chose the letter of Francis S. Scherr of Homestead, Florida as another "typical" letter. "The results of your radio poll are most heartening. Is it really possible that the sickening jazz and crooning is over. . . ? You have shown the way to all music lovers of good music and decent entertainment." (*Literary Digest* 12-16-1933: 9, 12-23-1933: 8 and 1-6-1934: 12) Certainly in the early outset of the depression, American middle class tastes seemed to be moving away from any interest in the American vernacular of the Jazz Age. These tastes were aided by decision-makers in the music industry who hoped to bring American tastes back to the old ideals of "good" music. The traditionalist forces that condemned the jazz craze during the 1920s seemed to have gained the upper hand in the early 1930s.

In smoothing out the already cultivated vernacular of jazz orchestras from the 1920s, many white professional musicians moved back towards the old "legitimate" techniques of professional popular orchestras dropping the "hot" breaks, tones, and syncopation that were just slowly being integrated into dance orchestra performance in the 1920s. Jacques Renard, for example, was the bandleader of the Coconut Grove Orchestra in the late 1920s and early 1930s, a major orchestra that was broadcast by remote over the national airwaves. In an interview in *Metronome* in 1931, Renard stated a familiar refrain in the early 1930s. "Jazz today is, for the most part, a different thing from what it was seven or eight years ago. The old jazz – noisy, boisterous, full of discords, has largely given way to a more suave, a smoother and a truer playing. Of course, you will hear the noisy type of jazz in some clubs. For instance when I was in New York a few days ago I heard a Negro orchestra playing pretty much as they used to play several years ago. There was the abrupt, jerky rhythm and much blasting of trumpets that some people still seem to like a lot. . . But as a rule the interest is now more in the less violent, the less sensational playing both for dinner and for dancing." As for the hot breaks used by jazz orchestras in the late 1920s, Renard commented that another "striking difference in the jazz today over that of a few years ago is the precision with which all the parts are written out for the players. The old way was to furnish only a skeleton of the piece and to allow the players not carrying the melody to fill in – what we call ad libbing. This gave the individual performers a chance to roam all over the lot but it hardly led to the qualities that are now giving jazz its strong appeal." (*Metronome* 11-1931: 29) In the early 1930s, even Paul Whiteman distanced himself from jazz. "Jazz is rhythm in its wildest form, more suitable to bizarre, boisterous savage dances than the suave stepping of the sophisticates of today." (*Metronome* 12-1933: 23) Of course, the suave dance moves of sophisticated middle class dancers were new versions of the "lilting waltzes, rhythmic fox trots, and tangos" that predated the jazz craze and the boisterous jazz dances like the stomp, black bottom, and Charleston. Such dancing could be found in the "clean, wholesome atmosphere in the ballrooms" dotting America. (*Metronome* 11-1932: 11) Wayne King, "The Waltz King," for example, was bringing the old standard dances back in vogue along with other successful sweet dance orchestras, and his efforts in 1932 "to champion the cause of the waltz . . . played to record-breaking business everywhere." (*Metronome* 11-1932: 11) King believed that his responsibility was in "creating a beautiful ideal" for his dancers, "sweet, clean and wholesome." (Greene 1995)

The comments in the early 1930s about the "smoothing" out of jazz in white dance orchestras were not radically different than comments during the 1920s about cultivating the jazz vernacular. Prominent professional musicians once again were emphasizing the cultivated techniques associated with the old ideal of "good" music. The balancing of the jazz vernacular and cultivated techniques in the 1920s, however, momentarily disappeared as sweet orchestras shifted towards music practices that eliminated the breaks, rhythm, and tones of the jazz vernacular. Guy Lombardo and His Royal Canadians epitomized this new style and his 1934 hit "The Sweetest Music This Side of Heaven" inspired this music's label among those remaining jazz enthusiasts. Just when the craze for jazz during the previous decade seemed to have positioned the cultivated jazz vernacular as the premier American popular music, the smooth sounds of sweet cultivated music returned to the forefront in the early 1930s.

The swing craze: the return of the cultivated jazz vernacular

We're Coming Out of the Depresh

It's going to be a great swing year, take it from old Uncle MET. There are plenty of indications at present to the effect that tempos will be much more torrid this season than last. To all intents and purposes, the new season will probably show a decided swerve from sweet to swing stuff, and bring forth possibly something entirely new in dance tempos, but in any event something that sets a livelier pace...people are more in a celebrating mood and naturally will want to pep things up. (*Metronome* September 1935)

With the smooth sounds of sweet big bands lulling audiences away from jazz, suddenly a swing craze hit the nation in 1935. The beginning of the national craze for swing was linked to the enthusiastic response in the Palomar Ballroom in Los Angeles to the touring Benny Goodman Orchestra in August 1935. Like the earlier jazz craze, a white band led this new craze for swing music. Benny Goodman was part of a young generation of white musicians like Bix Biederbeck, Bunny Berigan, Frank Trumbauer, Artie Shaw, Red Nichols, Red Norvo, Tommy Dorsey, and Jimmy Dorsey that adopted the jazz vernacular during their early years of apprenticeship in music in the 1920s. These musicians in the 1920s performed in jazz orchestras led by such bandleaders as Paul Whiteman, Vincent Lopez, Jean Goldkette, and Ben Pollack as "hot" musicians and they recorded in small jazz ensembles. Demonstrating the power of network radio, the Goodman Orchestra had a third spot on the nationally broadcast radio program *Let's Dance* on NBC in late 1934 which allowed young listeners in Los Angeles to hear the sound of swing and flock to the Palomar Ballroom. Led by the soon crowned "King of Swing" Benny Goodman, swing music invaded the popular music market just as jazz music had nearly two decades earlier. Swing musician Max Kaminsky later remembered the sudden craze for swing. "Almost overnight the jitterbugs, with their shoulder-length page boy bobs, fashionably grimy saddle shoes, and their peg-leg, sharpie zoot suits began pouring out of their homes in every town, city, and hamlet in the nation streaming into the dance halls to dance to the exciting new sound of swing." (Kaminsky 1963: 79) Unlike the jazz craze, however, the swing craze was instigated not by non-professional musicians performing the jazz vernacular, but by professional musicians performing a cultivated jazz vernacular under a new name – swing.

Swing bands were viewed as a strike against the brief dominance of sweet bands in the early 1930s. While *Metronome* celebrated the swing craze, the major cheerleader for swing was a new musician magazine *Down Beat* that started publication in 1934 under the editorial direction of two jazz enthusiasts Carl Cons and Glenn Burrs. This more tabloid-like magazine quickly rivaled *Metronome* as the major voice for professional musicians eventually surpassing the older magazine's circulation in the 1940s. During Goodman's successful national tour, for example, a report from Chicago in *Down Beat* voiced the renewed hopes people placed with "Benny Goodman's band. A group of men that literally eat and sleep and think in the same groove. A group of musicians so closely attuned, so imbued with 'that correct feeling' that they have built up a confidence in each other, and 'a complete rhythmic assurance in the band,' that leaves each man free to play and improvise with all the skill and feeling he is capable of... Let's hope that their success will make it possible for other musicians to make a living playing the kind of music that they enjoy, in an atmosphere that will extend them to their best efforts." (*Down Beat* 11-1935: 1, 9) Carl Cons was quite clear about the ramifications of the swing craze for jazz in his article "What Is Swing" in 1936. " 'Swing' has been called many names but it has been alive and kicking since 1916. It has developed, changed face, lost favor, and now returns in sophisticated and polished arrangements: suave, well-poised, and superbly disciplined." Jazz was back and was "once more respectable and desirable, and is successfully weaning Joe Public from the saccharine diet of lollypop bands." (*Down Beat* 4-1936: 1)

Since the editors at both *Down Beat* and *Metronome* were strong swing supporters, the battle between swing and sweet became a rather acrimonious affair in the pages of these magazines. The battle line was most clearly set when the annual readers' polls in both magazines designated two basic categories of swing and sweet for big bands and professional musicians. While editors and critics certainly set the tone in these magazines, the distinction between swing and sweet was generally recognized among musicians as well. *Metronome* in May 1936 of course immediately celebrated the swing fever among professional musicians in the results of its annual readers' poll. "The most significant aspect of the entire contest is that hep American musicians (readers of METRONOME) have definitely swung to swing. Numbers (especially when they're not written out) speak louder than words, so look, for yourself, at what METRONOME'S METICULOUS MATHEMATICIAN is slinging at you... Modern, hep musicians throughout the country have voted 55% of their points for the nineteen swing bands and only 45% of their points for the thirty-eight sweet bands... Statistics prove that American musicians are definitely swing minded and swing preferring." (*Metronome* 5-1936) *Down Beat* in July 1936 announced the results of its swing and "corn" band contest in which the latter sweet category "was started in a spirit of 'jive' and good humor, and we hope no musician lost his perspective and got offended." The results were "a fair indication of what the average American musician thinks, and what HIS ideas of who are fine artists and who are not... the results are startling and carry a moral to the hungry swing man. Almost to a man – THEY ARE TREMENDOUSLY POPULAR WITH THE PUBLIC and very successful commercially!" (*Down Beat* 7-1936: 1, 12)

In the same July 1936 issue of *Down Beat*, Guy Lombardo responded to the recent swing craze in a front-page interview "So My Band Is Corny? Lombardo Says 'Average Musician Is Swing Crazy'." Given that

Lombardo had been "criticized severely many times by different writers in the columns of this and other professional music papers for playing a too-simple and monotonous type [of] music," the editors wanted him to have the opportunity to respond. Lombardo, like many sweet defenders, laid claim to satisfying the sweet tastes demanded by the commercial market as well as remaining committed to performing music of "tonal quality" and "melodic charm." "Well, boys, let me tell you something. I don't mind anybody's opinion and musicians can talk about my band until they're exhausted but – MUSIC IS MY LIVELIHOOD, and like any other business, the product has to be in demand and commercial, or the producer will be eliminated. It's a survival of the fittest. AND MUSICIANS DON'T PAY THE CHECKS! You can say all you like about art, but no man can live on admiration and the applause of his fellow players. The average musician is swing crazy. He criticizes other musicians who do not play as he does, but who chooses to make a good living playing the kind of music the public wants and WILL PAY FOR." (*Down Beat* 7-1936: 1) In a later letter to the editor, musician Ray Gross from Niles, Michigan defended Lombardo and sweet big bands against swing critics, again emphasizing the demands of audiences. "Why are they forever 'running down' Lombardo, Wayne King, and now starting on Horace Heidt? Do they think that Lombardo falls asleep every night on the job because he gets a kick out of hearing his sax section play dreamy music?... No – they haven't sense enough to realize that Joe Public demands those things; after all, isn't Joe Public buying our meal tickets? I say give 'em what they want." Another letter sent by musician Whitey Myrick from Detroit, Michigan disagreed with Lombardo's arguments about the quality and appeal of swing music, also reminding the bandleader of the commercial advantages given sweet big bands in the 1930s. "Us little guys that strive for bread and butter shouldn't disagree with you big boys but, when you stated that hot music takes away tone quality I can't stand it any longer... I'll grant you that the people still like your brand of music but, after all it's only the name, yours was one of the first to be built up over the air. Don't try to kid us Guy, we have sense enough to know that any band that gets on the big chains often enough can draw plenty... No Guy, you can't white robe your band to musicians. I'll give you all the credit in the world from a business standpoint, but musically, GOOD-BYE." (*Down Beat* 9-1936: 4)

The battle between swing and sweet continued as a mostly older generation of white professional musicians defended sweet music against what they considered the less cultivated style of swing music. In "The Swing Mania Annoys Me" in 1936, Fred Waring felt it was "high time some voice is raised against the current revival of swing music. I feel that it's being overdone to the point where it will quickly die out." (*Metronome*

9-1936: 35) Sweet bandleader Eddy Duchin also reminded *Down Beat* readers that sweet was still the most successful style in the commercial market. "Swing is great, but if you will notice a swing song is seldom listed as one of the first fifteen popular songs in the country. I play it occasionally myself and get a big kick out of doing so. But, for my listeners and for the best vehicle to interpret oneself to the public I will take the everlasting effect of Romance Music." (*Down Beat* 1-1938: 1) In *Newsweek* in July 1938, the bickering between sweet and swing musicians was evident in the article " 'Swing' Is On the Way, But Up or Down? Embattled Experts Can't Agree." The sweet bandleader Key Keyser knew the answer was definitely down. "Even during the height of the so-called 'swing era,' the supremacy of bands like those of Guy Lombardo and Hal Kemp was never seriously threatened. Today these [sweet] bands are more popular than ever. The wise maestri admit seeing the handwriting on the wall, and are toning down their efforts considerably. That in itself is a thorough indication that swing will soon be put back on the record shelf." Of course, not all sweet musicians were so anti-swing, the sweet bandleader Hal Kemp in the *Newsweek* article explained "swing has always been here and will always stay." (*Newsweek* 7-25-1938: 26) Some of the older generation of white professional musicians defended swing. Paul Whiteman, for example, following the swing craze returned to defend the cultivated jazz vernacular after its brief fall from grace in the early 1930s. In the 1938 *Newsweek* article on the future prospect of swing, Whiteman explained that the "disappearance of swing is a prospect too far in the future to justify any exulting by its enemies. I think swing is here for a pretty long encampment." (*Newsweek* 7-25-1938: 26)

Sweet musicians were not wrong in pointing to the continued popularity of their music following the swing craze. *Down Beat* admitted in January 1938 that even with the continued upturn in the music market, "sugar-music such as Lombardo, Olson and Hal Kemp and such ace dispensers of corn as Shep Fields (rippling rhythm) and Kay Keyser still outnumber the ace swing units such as Benny Goodman, Tommy Dorsey and Bob Crosby." Rudy Vallee was the largest money-maker among professional musicians in 1937. Sweet bands also continued to dominate radio network programming. While the swing bands of Glenn Gray, Benny Goodman, the Dorsey Brothers, Bob Crosby, Artie Shaw, and Glenn Miller appeared on network-sponsored programs, most sponsored bands were sweet. Of course, black swing bands like Duke Ellington's received no network sponsorship. The top white sweet bands of Guy Lombardo, Fred Martin, Wayne King, Horace Heidt, Andre Kostelnetz, Will Osborne, George Olson, Russ Morgan, Fred Waring, and Eddy Duchin among others dominated sponsored network programs.

While losing the battle for sponsored network programming, swing did reach audiences through live remote broadcasts as well as local and national radio DJs who played recorded music. Martin Block and his *Make Believe Ballroom* broadcast from New York City, for example, was an enthusiastic supporter of swing – he was master of ceremony at the largest swing concert in this city on Randalls Island in 1936. The rising importance of jukeboxes also helped swing bands reach audiences. A new generation of young "jitterbugs" and "ickies" did flock to swing music and the live performances of swing big bands, but sweet music remained an important part of the popular music market. This music's ensconced position in the more conservative radio network programming also fed the battle between swing and sweet since these programs were considered the premier spots for the profession providing the greatest exposure for professional big bands. So while swing music was garnering large audiences in live, broadcast, and recorded performances, the victory remained for some bittersweet as old anti-jazz and "good" music sentiments shaped network programming.

The rejection of jazz in the early consolidation of the new music industry signaled a basic conservatism that would characterize the industry over the next two decades. Even while a cultivated jazz vernacular would reemerge with the swing craze of 1935, the conservatism of the industry succeeded over the long term maintaining sweet music as the most lucrative style in the national circulation of popular music. In the late 1940s, with the collapse of the touring market for big bands this bias was even more evident as major record companies used in-house orchestras and singers performing a smoother big band music often with the addition of "cultivated" strings. Of course, this was a commercial industry, so it did respond to the swing craze catapulting to national stardom professional swing musicians like Benny Goodman, Artie Shaw, Tommy Dorsey, Jimmy Dorsey, Glenn Miller, Harry James, and Gene Krupa. But sweet and swing remained a basic distinction among popular big bands. Sweet music articulated through popular music the old ideals of the professional class of popular musician, while swing music articulated a new vision among professional musicians that positioned the cultivated black jazz vernacular center stage in their music making.

Getting respect: the status of black professional musicians and the swing market

Swing's Black Royalty

Modern Swing came out with two trumpeters, "King" Oliver and "Prince" Armstrong who, like the most royal of Swing's personages, were Negroes.

The late Joe "King" Oliver took the rough, street-corner jazz of New Orleans, cleaned it up and gave it form. "Prince" Louis ("Satchelmouth") Armstrong, who had learned to play trumpet in a waif's home, learned to play Swing in Oliver's band, perfected his style under Fletcher Henderson. Blessed with unbelievable technique and a rich imagination, Armstrong became the greatest of all Swing musicians.

Quieter, more studious than the rampant Armstrong is Edward Kennedy "Duke" Ellington. Only a fair pianist but an extraordinary leader-composer-arranger, Ellington has taught his superb band to play the subtlest and most varied kind of jazz. Bill "Count" Basie, a top-notch pianist, has written a major Swing classic, *One O'Clock Jump*. ("Swing: The Hottest and Best Kind of Jazz Reaches Its Golden Age," *Life*, August 8, 1938: 52)

While white swing musicians rode the crest of the swing craze to the top of their profession and national acclaim, black orchestras and black musicians also received greater national attention than ever before. More importantly, black professional musicians by the advent of the Swing Era gained recognition and legitimacy for the first time among white professional musicians. Invisible up through the Jazz Age and just gracing its pages in the early 1930s, black professional musicians by the swing craze received regular coverage by *Metronome* as acknowledged co-participants in American popular music. *Down Beat* from its inception in 1934 gave black professional musicians regular coverage and introduced a number of jazz critics who strongly promoted black musicians past and present. *Metronome*, for example, elected Teddy Wilson as the first black professional musician in its series "Musicians Hall of Fame" in September 1936, although the next black professional musicians would not win this honor again until Benny Carter, Cootie Williams, and Roy Eldridge all did in 1941. Benny Goodman was quoted as saying "Teddy Wilson is the greatest musician in dance music today, irrespective of instrument," while *Metronome* noted "his colossal technique; the rapid thought transference from brain to fingers; his conception of single finger figures; his solid and tasty bass work." (*Metronome* 9-1936: 39) Given the status of black professional musicians before the 1930s, this was a striking transformation. Unfortunately, the new status of black professional musicians failed to change the basic workings of the segregated world of music making in America, including the persistence of separate musician union locals. And in the end, white swing musicians retained the greater recognition both within their profession and outside it, while reaping the greater financial rewards. Yet the change in status of black professional musicians was an important transformation in American music. For the first time, white professional musicians acknowledged black professional musicians in general as *artistic* equals, and some as the best artists, in the field of American music.

The change in status for black professional musicians began in the early years when sweet music reigned in the mainstream of American music. Duke Ellington, Louis Armstrong, Cab Calloway, and Jimmie Lunceford among a few black professional musicians and their orchestras achieved national recognition before the swing craze, although the craze did consolidate this new status and visibility for black professional musicians. *Metronome*, for example, noted in 1931 that "recognized as such by everyone, everywhere, Duke Ellington stands alone today as leader of the greatest colored orchestra in the world. Critics on low-brow tabloids and intellectual quarterlies have analyzed his technique and given him the check and double check." (*Metronome* 3-1931: 34) In reporting on Ellington's tour of England and the European continent in 1933, H. A. Overstreet was emphatic that "here is real American music. It stems from jazz, but it is not jazz – it is more. It is the only American music that has been accepted in England and the Continent with something like awe and reverence and by musicians themselves. It is music that touches the frontiers of tomorrow." (*Metronome* 10-1933: 31) Of course, earlier black professional musicians such as Scott Joplin, William Marion Cook, and James Reese Europe among others had received wide acclaim across the Atlantic, although to little affect on the general attitudes of white professional musicians in the United States. Ellington in performing cultivated jazz, however, was the first black professional musician to attain national stature among white professional musicians as a premier leader in the field of American popular music – he was selected as the most popular dance bandleader in 1931 in a poll by *Orchestra World*. (Cuney-Hare 1936)

The historian Thomas J. Hennessey (1994) notes that a crucial change during the depression was the emergence of management companies that replaced the role of black musicians managing their own organizations. With white management, a few select black professional musicians gained the contacts and influence in the music industry unavailable to African Americans in general whether musicians, publishers, producers, or managers. As mentioned previously, however, the major national management agencies for big bands were not interested in black orchestras in the early 1930s. Black orchestras relied on a few smaller agencies to manage their careers with the most important agency being Mills Music. Following the crash, this company was the premier management company for black professional musicians including the Duke Ellington Orchestra, Cab Calloway Orchestra, McKinney's Cotton Pickers, and the Mills Blue Rhythm Band. *Metronome* hailed Irving Mills as "one of the world's most astute judges and developers of musical talent." In discussing Mills and his management of Ellington and Calloway, *Metronome* was clear that as "a result of Irving Mills' perspicacity in recognizing talent when he meets it, coupled with his skill in bringing out and developing that talent, and, finally, in making it commercial, Cab Calloway is well up on the list of the top ten orchestras." (*Metronome* 1-1933: 19) Except for Louis Armstrong, Mills Music managed the few successful black orchestras in terms of national recognition and financial rewards.

Mills Music was an all-in-one outfit that since 1926 managed publicity, live performances, recording, and publishing of music for black professional musicians while taking a large commission of up to fifty percent of earnings; the typical percentage in the big agencies for white name bands was ten percent. Mills was certainly astute at more than just recognizing talent, but exploiting it too – most managers of black big bands charged much higher commissions than managers of white big bands. While extracting a larger percentage than usual for management, Mills did succeed in gaining his black orchestras national attention and financial success. *Fortune* magazine in August 1933 featured an article on Duke Ellington's success including the 250,000 dollar annual gross of his orchestra. Of course, Ellington's contract retained forty-five percent of gross earnings for Mills. (Hennessey 1994) The importance of Mills in the early 1930s also was evident with the presence of black professional musicians in the pages of *Metronome* dependent mostly on their association with this famous white manager – the first time black professional musicians regularly appeared in this magazine. The appearance of these musicians included advertising. In 1933, Con Band Instruments placed the first full-page ad in *Metronome* featuring black professional musicians. The ad was titled COLORED ARTISTS WIN WORLD FAME and featured the Duke Ellington Orchestra, Cab Calloway Orchestra, and Mills Blue Rhythm Band. Con Instruments acclaimed that "colored artists of America have won a warm place in the hearts of music lovers the world over. Theirs is a distinctive type of modern music, blending a peculiar plaintive quality with life and fire and red-hot rhythm. It sets pulses throbbing and feet tapping wherever youth holds sway." (*Metronome* 12-1933: 7)

As the Con Instrument advertisement suggests black professional orchestras were still marketed in the early 1930s as "hot" jazz bands. So while white orchestras and the mainstream market went sweet, the racial construction of the popular music market still maintained a small niche market for jazz performed by black professional musicians that was exploited by Irving Mills, other managers, as well as black jazz orchestras. The *Fortune* magazine article celebrating Ellington's success pointed to this distinct position of black jazz orchestras against white sweet orchestras. "The curly-headed Vallee has made a fortune dispensing popular ballads to the vast public which always adores them. In this respect he resembles Guy Lombardo, Russ Columbo, Bing Crosby, and various other radio and tea-dancing idols. On the other hand, Mr. Ellington and his orchestra offer rich, original music, music of pulse and gusto, stemming out of the lyricism of the Negro and played with great virtuosity. Ellington's music is jazz; it is the best jazz." (*Fortune* 8-1933) The black jazz niche still placed black professional musicians in danger of falling into racial stereotypes – an accusation made against Cab Calloway singing and dancing "hi-di-hi" and "ho-de-ho." Cab Calloway's performance persona was part of a calculated strategy of his manager Irving Mills who "just as he encouraged Ellington to exercise his natural talent for composing and arranging . . . developed Calloway and his orchestra as an entertaining combination." (*Metronome* 1-1933: 19) While stereotyping remained, black jazz orchestras in the early 1930s ran the gamut of performance persona from the "sophisticated" Ellington and Lunceford Orchestras to the "hep" Cab Calloway and Louis Armstrong Orchestras. The contradictory status of black professional musicians – respected in new ways, yet still segregated and stereotyped – was most evident in Louis Armstrong who attained a wide following as the greatest trumpeter in American popular music yet was eventually criticized by some within the black community for conforming his entertainment persona to white "Uncle Tom" stereotypes.

In the early 1930s, black professional musicians were just gaining general recognition among their white peers. The Harlem jazz scene, for example, was being covered for the first time in *Metronome*. In articles like "Baton Beaters of Harlem: How Some of Them Swing Into Their Stride" *Metronome* reviewed black professional big bands performing in New York City. (*Metronome* 7-1934: 12) The magazine reviewed performances and recordings of black bands including the Duke Ellington Orchestra, Cab Calloway Orchestra, McKinney Cotton Pickers, Fletcher Henderson Orchestra, Teddy Hill Orchestra, Jimmie Lunceford Orchestra, Luis Russell Orchestra, and the Chick Webb Orchestra. In December 1933, *Metronome* for the first time asked a black professional musician to comment on the state of American music. With the "death" of jazz still fresh on the minds of professional musicians, editor Doron K. Antrim thought it best to ask the question "After Jazz – What?" of "the men best qualified to speak on the subject," which included Duke Ellington as well as Paul Whiteman. Ellington claimed that "it is my honest belief that the musical rhythm known as jazz will never bow out for a full exit. I do feel though, that its accepted forms are due for radical changes." (*Metronome* 12-1933: 23) The new coverage of black professional musicians, however, was not always flattering. In what would become an intermittent critique of black professional big bands in *Metronome* and *Down Beat*, a review of Luis Russell and His Harlemites concluded that there was "very little to distinguish this band, unless it is the rhythm. Playing modern music with an abandon that is Harlem, Luis Russell apparently neither cares nor knows tone quality." (*Metronome* 5-1933: 20) Harlem orchestras, of course, were performing with rhythmic abandon the swing style that across the Atlantic brought hoards of admirers to sold-out performances and eventually carried white swing big bands to the top of their profession following the swing craze in 1935.

The occasional unflattering commentaries of Harlem orchestras in the early 1930s, of course, fit in well with some of the old guard of the profession and their prevailing anti-jazz and sweet sentiments. Such less than flattering comments persisted in the late 1930s, usually focusing on the poor "tone" of some black big bands and musicians, but were minor compared to the mostly positive commentary on black swing musicians and big bands. By the swing craze, a new generation of white professional musicians and their supporters led the profession down a different path. The swing craze represented a generational change where, particularly at the top of the white swing fraternity that included Benny Goodman, Artie Shaw, Gene Krupa, and Tommy Dorsey, white professional swing musicians admired and emulated black professional musicians. The new generation of editors at *Metronome* and *Down Beat* – George Simon, Glenn Burrs, and Carl Cons – also were swing supporters. George Simon in 1938, for example, noted the rise to national fame of the Chick Webb Orchestra and made "a humble prayer that this truly great Chick Webb band, which can cut just about any swing outfit in the world, won't turn into one of those stiff, stagey aggregations... The band is too great, both personally and musically, to allow itself to tumble into such listless doldrums." In the same column Simon praised the playing of Roy Eldridge at the Three Deuces in Chicago where "literally blowing his head and the place's roof off. The man's conceptions and execution are as hair-raising as ever, and, on top of that, he's combined those brilliant qualities with a vastly improved tone." (*Metronome* 1-1938: 20) In general, by 1935 a significant change had occurred in the major journals for professional musicians in the United States where black professional musicians now received regular coverage, criticism, reviews, and feature articles in both *Metronome* and *Down Beat* magazines. *Down Beat* specifically claimed to adhere to a colorblind policy in an editorial in October 1936. "Down Beat does not subscribe to racial prejudice and has never drawn the color line in any of its reporting or criticism of personalities in the music world, preferring to judge musicians strictly on their ability and not on any basis of the complexion of their skin!" (*Down Beat* 10-1936: 2) This magazine, however, did feature a few cartoons with racist imagery. A few months earlier *Down Beat* applauded the new status of black professional musicians in a 1936 readers' poll for the best all-time swing band. In a front-page article headlined "8 Whites & 6 Negroes Win Places in All Time Swing Band" *Down Beat* noted that "almost half of the men in the swing band selection are colored is indication of the genuine musician's respect for superior talent, regardless of color... The first swing band is made up of creative artists to the nth degree." (*Down Beat* 7-1936: 1, 12)

Letters sent by readers to *Metronome* and *Down Beat* also demonstrated that many professional musicians were avid fans of black swing big bands and their stellar musicians. G. B. M. of Naugatuck, Connecticut wrote, "I consider Jimmie Lunceford's great band to be astride them all. He can play anything and make it sound heavenly. No white band yet has come anywhere near that wonderful Lunceford harmony and weird muted effects of the brass section... Jimmie Lunceford can not be surpassed. His whole personnel is high rated – all being conservatory men, I believe – and what expert musicians." J. H. F. in Bennington, Vermont lauded the Fletcher Henderson Orchestra since "Henderson achieved a freedom and standard of ensemble work as well as of individual brilliance that the Goodman boys seldom, if ever, attain." (*Metronome* 5-1936: 16) Of course, other readers expressed preferences for white musicians and big bands. Readers' letters, however, revealed a significant transformation as black artists were recognized as co-participants in the field of American music making.

Successful white professional musicians also praised black professional musicians including the former "King of Jazz" Paul Whiteman. In his *Colliers* article in 1938, "The All-American Swing Band," Whiteman selected six black swing musicians – Benny Carter, Chu Berry, Roy Eldridge, Louis Armstrong, Art Tatum, and Eddie South for a twenty-six-member swing band. "Every man I'm picking on my All-American team, except one, is a fine reader of music, a man who has mastered the fundamentals of music and who has gone beyond that technique to add something of his own. I am not only presenting the greatest swing band in the country; I am presenting a group of the best musicians in the country." (*Colliers* 9-10-1939: 9) Rudy Vallee wrote the introduction to Louis Armstrong's 1936 autobiography, and although admitting that "in so many ways Louis and I are direct opposites," he praised Armstrong. "Armstrong's amazing mastery of the trumpet has brought him world-wide fame and today he is generally regarded as one of the greatest, if not the very greatest, of all living trumpeters, particularly, of course, in the high register." (Armstrong 1936: xv) As Benny Goodman wrote in his 1939 autobiography, "nobody cares much what colors or races are represented just as long as we play good music. . . I know for example, that our concert in Carnegie Hall would have lost a lot if we didn't have the cooperation of fellows like Johnny Hodges, who is by far the greatest man on alto sax that I ever heard, or Harry Carney, who is just about the same on baritone, or 'Cootie' Williams, whose trumpet playing is like nobody else's. Then in the jam session we had such other great colored players as Lester Young, who is one of my favorite musicians, that swell guitar player Freddie Green, Count Basie on piano and Buck Clayton to play his own particular kind of trumpet, with Walter Page doing wonderful things on bass." (Goodman 1939: 231)

The general shift in the status of black professional musicians among white professional musicians became evident when both *Metronome* and *Down Beat* magazines introduced their readers' polls in 1936. While the annual readers' polls in the late 1930s almost consistently positioned white professional musicians and big bands at number one in the swing division, from the beginning of these polls in 1936 black professional musicians regularly appeared near the top of the lists of instrumentalists and bands. The 1936 readers' poll for the best all-time swing band in *Down Beat* indicated the shifting status of black musicians. The band included the black musicians Louis Armstrong, Roy Eldridge, Coleman Hawkins, Chu Berry, Pops Foster, and Teddy Wilson with white musicians Bix Beiderbecke, Tommy Dorsey, Jack Teargarden, Benny Goodman, Jimmy Dorsey, Gene Krupa, Eddie Lang, and Joe Venuti. Of course, of the eight categories that made up this fourteen piece all-time swing band six white professional musicians won the number one spot including the deceased Bix Beiderbecke over Louis Armstrong. The Benny Goodman and Casa Loma Orchestras also won the top honors for best swing big bands, while the next three winners in this poll were the Jimmie Lunceford, Fletcher Henderson, and Duke Ellington Orchestras. The *Metronome* readers' poll that same year placed the Goodman, Casa Loma, and Jimmy Dorsey Orchestras in the top swing big band list with the Lunceford and Ellington Orchestras rounding the top five bands.

That white swing musicians and white swing bands almost consistently won top honors in the *Metronome* and *Down Beat* readers' poll revealed that black professional musicians still confronted a status conflict with white musicians who identified more strongly with white swing musicians. Black artists did occasionally win top honors, like black tenor saxophonist Chu Berry and singer Ella Fitzgerald in *Down Beats* readers' poll for 1937, but such top honors remained rare for black professional musicians. The status discrepancy between white and black musicians left *Down Beat* celebrating Duke Ellington's second place finish in their 1940 readers' poll. "Duke Ellington's feat of placing second to

Goodman in the swing division is considered the outstanding feature of the poll. For 10 years a favorite with musicians, Ellington nevertheless has been unable to show better than fifth in any poll." (*Down Beat* 1-1941: 1) Ellington finally won top honors in the 1942 *Down Beat* readers' poll. It is interesting to note that the status of black swing musicians among musicians across the Atlantic seemed to differ from their fellow musicians in the United States. *Metronome* noted the striking difference in 1938 in an article on the readers' poll of the musicians' magazine *Melody Maker* in Great Britain: " 'Duke Greatest Band of All!' Votes Britishers: Ellington's Boys Easy Winners as English Musicians Ballot... All Star Band Differs Radically From Americans." "Duke gained a convincing two hundred point victory over America's favorite (as evinced by a recent METRONOME poll), Benny Goodman... Britishers picked their favorite instrumentalists, jibing with the Metronome poll on only four men." All the different winners in Britain noted by *Metronome* were black artists in contrast to the white artists who won the *Metronome* poll, although *Metronome* did not explicitly note the obvious race disparity. Louis Armstrong beat out Bunny Berigan while "another overwhelming victory went to tenorman Coleman Hawkins, who gathered seven times as many votes as Bud Freeman." Johnny Hodges and Benny Carter won the top hot alto positions, while Israel Crosby beat Bob Haggart and Ella Fitzgerald beat Helen Ward. *Metronome* assured its readers, however, that "at first glance these varied discrepancies might seem very alarming. They shouldn't be, though, when you stop to consider that the Britishers are forced to decide upon various merits via varied phonograph records only, hardly ever having the opportunity to hear our instrumentalists and bands in person or over the air. Conditions being as they are, England is to be congratulated upon its highly intelligent voting!" (*Metronome* 1-1938: 13, 33)

Of course, conditions being as they were in the United States, white swing big bands had far greater access than black swing big bands to live performance venues, radio, as well as recordings. Given the popular music market in the United States, when white professional musicians in the swing craze reentered the "jazz" market, where black professional musicians were gaining recognition and status, these fellow white swing musicians took the top spots in the national market as well as the attention of popular musicians. The discrepancy between the black originators of swing music and their white followers in the voting of professional musicians certainly seemed to reflect the overall condition of the popular swing market and the profession of music making. And while *Down Beat* claimed "most white musicians do not recognize color lines in music," Jim Crow color lines persisted in the field of American music little changed from the Jazz Age. (*Down Beat* 10-1936: 2) While black musicians certainly attained a greater status and visibility within the profession of popular music making, such advances did little to transform the racist structure of the industry or profession. White professional musicians would acclaim the talents of many black professional musicians and the quality of black swing big bands, but again, white professional musicians made little effort to change the support given to their black brethren.

While black orchestras managed by smaller booking agencies and supported by music recordings were part of a national circuit for popular music, they remained segregated from the mainstream of the circuit. By 1938, a few black orchestras were picked up by larger agencies as Mills Music brought its artists to Consolidated Radio Artists and MCA signed its first black artist, Count Basie, in 1939. The national touring circuit as well as local venues, however, still remained segregated across the country. This segregated circuit included the South where touring was often a dangerous affair – even outside the South strict rules of racial segregation remained the rule rather than the exception. Black swing musicians had to abide to all the strict rules of racial segregation as well as harassment that made touring even harder than it certainly was for white swing musicians. The swing trombonist Dickie Wells remembered his days touring the South. "There weren't any big agencies then, and very few white bands played those territories. It was very seldom white bands played colored ballrooms, although we used to play white ball rooms. . . No, the Swing Era didn't open up any new ground for colored bands." (Wells 1991: 49) The swing saxophonist Garvin Bushell remembered the general state of touring for black musicians. "In those days on the road, all you had to do was be black and you'd get accused of doing something. Once we were driving between gigs in Massachusetts, and they stopped us because someone had turned in a false alarm and they thought we did it. They handcuffed us and put us in jail, so we missed our gig." (Bushell 1990: 83) Hotels across the country and network radio programs also showed no interest in black orchestras: the usual excuse was that these orchestras would offend southern hotel guests or southern radio listeners.

The AFM also remained segregated during the big band era with only two integrated locals in the United States in New York City and Detroit. Union board member William Everett Samuels remembered the state of race relations in the AFM during the 1930s including the first national convention attended by Chicago black local 208. "This was a meeting of all locals in the United States and Canada. But, then, they just had their thumbs down on Negroes – that's all. . . That's the way it was. Very few of the AF of M leaders – none of 'em hardly – would stand up against the discrimination in the 30s, 40s, 50s, and on." (Spivey 1984: 56, 58) The result was that black orchestras and black musicians were excluded from the most lucrative positions in the big band business. These orchestras did find exposure in remote broadcasts from black performance venues; some broadcast nationally in the late post-primetime hours. Black orchestras recorded on labels specializing in swing and race music. Even the integrated local in New York City did little to change basic racial discrimination in music. Bandleader and famous swing saxophonist Benny Carter, later a major union activist in Los Angeles, remembered the working situation for black musicians in New York City in the 1930s. "We felt the difference strongly. The 'downtown' white world was largely unavailable to us. It not only offered better pay for our sort of work but provided opportunities in shows, for example. The difference was especially noticeable in radio, which was becoming increasingly important. Radio staff and studio orchestras were closed to us and these were the steadier jobs paying hundreds of dollars weekly at a time when the union scale at places like the Savoy was thirty-three dollars. Scale was higher downtown because the American Federation of Musicians followed a system of rating clubs, halls and other places according to certain criteria and accepted a corresponding difference in scale of pay to musicians. Harlem had fewer locations with higher ratings. Of course, many white musicians, making more than we did, came to listen to us and play with us. We welcomed them and enjoyed the jamming. But we couldn't go downtown to join them." (Berger *et al.* 1982: 45)

The social organization of music production, where large national industries were mediating the popular music market, also continued and reinforced racial segregation in American music. While swing was a national phenomenon, recording companies and the music industry in general still viewed black bands as catering to a "race" market. In the process, white swing musicians garnered the bulk of the financial rewards and national recognition. Irving Kolodin pointed out the situation of black professional musicians to readers of *Harper's Magazine* in 1941. "It is rather more curious that another group of names has been even less conspicuous in this inquiry... They are names with a familiar echo even to a public unfamiliar with this subject; but almost never to be encountered in a prominent hotel, and never on a commercial radio program. They are of course all Negro musicians – and rigorously excluded, as if by Congressional decree, from these two principal sources of prestige and financial reward. Thus, though each enjoys a serious repute among students of jazz music, and substantial income from records and theater engagements and dance hall appearances, they can never hope to equal the fabulous earnings of Goodman, Shaw, or Glen Miller." (*Harper's Magazine* 6-1941: 79) Most of the top white swing big bands either had black arrangers or regularly bought popular arrangements from black swing big bands. Benny Goodman initiated the practice of hiring black arrangers or regularly buying their arrangements in his use of Fletcher Henderson, Edgar Simpson, Horace Henderson, Sy Oliver and Jimmy Mundy. His success using black arrangers was repeated by other top swing big bands including Tommy Dorsey hiring the famous black arranger Sy Oliver in 1939 after Oliver's longtime association with the Jimmie Lunceford Orchestra. The disparity in rewards between black and white big bands was most evident when white swing big bands made bigger hit recordings of songs previously recorded by black big bands. Goodman made Count Basie's "One O'clock Jump" a bigger hit in 1938 than an earlier recording by the Basie band while Glenn Miller made "Tuxedo Junction" a bigger hit in 1940 than an earlier recording by Erskine Hawkins.

The assimilation of the black jazz vernacular into the professional class of musician in the United States did bring together white and black professional musicians around a shared jazz culture. Within this jazz culture, black professional musicians had attained a status as legitimate artists unprecedented in America up to that time. Yet, even given this change, white swing musicians reaped the vast majority of rewards from swing's popularity. The conditions of Jim Crow during the Swing Era, regardless of the new status of black professional musicians, generated a deep resentment on the part of many black professional musicians. As we will see in the next chapter, such resentment would express itself in a new musical movement called bebop in which black professional musicians would express open hostility to Jim Crow and attempt to reassert the central role of black musicians in jazz.

Swing populism: music, class, and race

Swing Is Here to Stay

I refer, of course, to the absurd statements that were made periodically by Professor Pastypuss or Professor Bigotted that 'Jazz is on its way out! The people of America are sick and tired of the cacophonous bleatings and moanings of the typical jazz-band. They will not last another two years.' Fortunately the people of America paid no attention to the worthy prof., but instead demanded more and better jazz. And now, shades of Pastypuss, ten years later I hear the same thing with the slight change of the word "Jazz" to "Swing." (Scotty Lawrence, *Metronome*, August 1937: 13)

The swing musician Scotty Lawrence in the August 1937 issue of *Metronome* presented a common view of swing as a populist triumph. In line with the progressive and radical spirits of the New Deal Era, David Stowe (1994) and Lewis A. Erenberg (1998) argue that swing music was viewed by many as the truly popular music of America. Unlike the culture of sweet music that articulated class, race, and ethnic distinctions of exclusion, swing music was seen by many swing enthusiasts as an inclusive democratic art. Swing populism found expression not only in the pages of *Metronome* and *Down Beat*. It found expression in the general press and black press as well as in progressive and radical politics. Eventually swing populism even was co-opted by the music industry and the American government to help fight the war against fascism. Part of swing populism also included the fight against racial discrimination, which included critiques of the segregated world of music making. Benny Goodman expressed this swing populism in *Colliers* in 1939. "Swing means a lot to every musician – and to everybody else, including jitterbugs. Swing is the food and drink and the relaxation and the music of the times." (*Colliers* 2-25-1939: 60)

Down Beat editor Carl Cons in 1936 was clear about swing music as a populist art. Cons informed readers that "we can with safety return to the business in hand – that of swinging. A burned child dreads the fire, but during adolescence it learns to handle matches and so control the fire (most of the time). Here we have the art of handling matches almost learned and now we hear that there is to be no more fire – no more roasted venison – roasted on a spit beside a fire in the open – but now nothing but the civilized fillet mignons of sweet music – done to a turn on a modernistic, chromium-plated grill. I'll have mine rare, please!" (*Down Beat* 4-1936: 6) Scotty Lawrence also pointed to the class victory of the swing craze. "Perhaps the social 400 (who do pay off nicely – I am told) are still by preference gracefully stepping on each others' toes with a 'Pahdom me' to the strains of *Love in Bloom* with muted brass and sax vibrato like a brand new permanent wave. But if you would care to spend an hour or so in a twenty-cent dance hall in any city, any night, there you will see dancing that really represents young America." (*Metronome* 8-1937: 13) Irving Kolodin in *Harper's Magazine* even placed the class conflict within the profession of popular musician. "Despite the enthusiasm for swing music among college boys for a good part of the past decade, a scant few swing musicians of account, and scarcely even a minor hot band, have emerged from that back ground... The real sturdy stuff of jazz is produced by the men who have been gutter rats in their time, out on their own at seventeen, clubbing round in night spots, honky-tonks, and gin-mills before they were old enough to vote... It is the smoother, relatively more cultivated boy (and, alas, the cultivation is only relative) with four years in a State university who provides the more stable 'commercial' stuff." (*Harper's Magazine* 6-1941: 81–2)

Otis Ferguson in the "Spirit of Swing" in *The New Republic* celebrated the popular roots of swing in his description of the Benny Goodman Orchestra at the Pennsylvania Hotel in New York City in 1936. "And if you leave at the end, before the 'Good-Bye' signature, you will seem to hear this great rattling march of the hobos through the taxis, lights and people, ringing under the low sky over Manhattan as if it were a strange high thing after all (which it is) and as if it came from the American ground under these buildings, roads, and motor cars (which it did)." (*The New Republic* 12-30-1936: 271) A *New York Times* editorial applauded the populism of swing in its comments on a swing concert on Randalls Island in New York City in 1938. "Music is 23,000 jitterbugs and alligators swarming into, and at times all over, the Randalls Island Stadium to listen to twenty-five swing bands... But there was not a mite of harm in them. They were of all races, all colors, all walks – or rather all swings and shags – of life." (*New York Times* 5-31-38: 18) *Life Magazine* in "Swing: The Hottest and Best Kind of Jazz Reaches Its Golden Age" in 1938 claimed that it "was the fashion two years ago, and a year ago, and six months ago to say that the form of jazz called 'Swing' was on the way out. It is still the fashion to say that Swing is on the way out. Maybe so – but the fact is that, as of August 1938, Swing is the most popular kind of popular music." (*Life* 8-8-1938: 51) Benny Goodman, interviewed by music critic Howard Taubman in 1940, again pointed to swing as a truly populist music. "As for the music that makes these youngsters behave as they do, Benny Goodman makes no apologies for it. What is more, he staunchly defends it as the true American spirit in music. He regards it as something that has emerged out of our habits, climate, institutions, and people." (*New York Times Magazine* 12-29-1940: 15)

Of course the expression of swing populism in musicians' magazines and the general press occurred against the backdrop of progressive and radical politics during the New Deal Era. Both progressive New Dealers and the American Left adopted a stance against racial discrimination. The Roosevelt administration adopted a policy of racial equality with many New Deal programs aiding African Americans. Black political organizations and spokespersons, however, had to apply pressure to ensure more aggressive efforts by the Roosevelt Administration to transform institutionalized racism in the United States. The radical left attempted to work with more mainstream black organizations fighting race discrimination, participating mostly through the newly formed National Negro Congress organized in 1936 to centralize the efforts of these organizations. The radical legal organization International Labor Defense worked to help blacks in the Jim Crow justice system in the South including the infamous Scottsboro Case in Alabama. The radical labor union, the Congress of Industrial Organizations, led by John Lewis, adopted a colorblind policy, while A. Philip Randolph, President of the Brotherhood of Sleeping Car Porters and the National Negro Congress, led efforts to end racial discrimination. The American Federation of Labor in 1942 rejected a resolution introduced by Randolph to study race discrimination in unions. (Franklin and Moss 1994; Christian 1999)

Erenberg (1998) details the interrelationship between swing and New Deal progressive and radical politics. Swing as a racially integrated world of music making as well as music created by African Americans meshed with this new political agenda among progressives and radicals. The democratic and populist culture of swing also was seen as a weapon in the United Front Against Fascism. With the advent of the Popular Front in 1936, communists embraced popular American culture including swing as a culture of the people. As Erenberg argues, the "rise of a broad left-democratic commitment to swing as part of an authentic 'people's culture' placed the music at the forefront of challenges to the music industry and to American society." (Erenberg 1998: 122) Progressive swing enthusiasts like John Hammond, Charles E. Smith, Dale Curran, and Louis Harap among others wrote in radical journals about jazz and swing as an authentic expression of African Americans and against the discrimination black artists faced in Jim Crow America. They also critiqued the general commercial exploitation of musicians within the music industry. While Hammond wrote for the radical journal *New Masses*, Charles Edward Smith, Louis Harap and Dale Curran wrote for the communist *Daily Worker*. Harap also wrote for the radical journal *Science and Society*. (Berger 1947) The music critic B. H. Higgins in the progressive journal *The Nation* also was a jazz and swing supporter. Swing concerts in the 1930s were organized to support progressive causes such as the Scottsborro Case in Alabama and the Republicans and American Lincoln Brigade in the Spanish Civil War. Concerts were organized to attract youth to the communist party. The American Left also sponsored several swing concerts celebrating this music as a true American art created by African Americans. John Hammond organized two "From Spirituals to Swing" concerts in Carnegie Hall in 1938 and 1939 sponsored by *The New Masses*. The program written by Hammond and James Dugan "The Music Nobody Knows" for the first concert highlighted both the artistry of African Americans as well as their subordination. "American Negro music has thrived in an atmosphere of detraction, oppression, distortion, and unreflective enthusiasm... In this hot jazz style the music is uniquely American, the most important cultural exhibit we have given the world." (Dugan and Hammond 1974: 191)

Stowe (1994) and Erenberg (1998) also show how with the advent of America's entrance to World War II swing culture was enlisted by the entertainment industry and the New Deal government to help fight the war. Obviously, as the preferred music of young jitterbugs swing music was a perfect vehicle for linking Americanism with the fight against fascism – an ideological conjoining already established by progressives and radicals before 1941. Swing big bands including the bands of Goodman, Calloway, and Ellington performed for the USO and special concerts were organized for Russian War Relief. While the swing bandleader Captain Glen Miller became an icon when he enlisted in 1943, other swing bandleaders also joined the armed forces. The Andrew Sisters sang the popular hit "Boogie Woogie Bugle Boy" for the swingsters fighting across the Atlantic and Pacific Oceans. The film *Stage Door Canteen* featured the Benny Goodman and Count Basie Orchestras entertaining an interracial audience of soldiers. Erenberg also shows some efforts on the part of progressive entertainers to have integrated canteens in Los Angeles, New York, and Washington DC. As David Stowe (1994: 143) points out, while swing music was only a small part of the cultural mobilization to support the war, "the distinctive ideology that had accrued to swing during the 1930s – a belief in American exceptionalism, in ethnic pluralism and democratic equality – was ideally suited to the collective needs of a nation battling fascism."

Unfortunately, there was one slight problem with swing propaganda for the war effort. America remained a Jim Crow country regardless of the New Deal ideals of the Roosevelt Years. Even within the war effort Jim Crow remained with segregated troops, war facilities, war factories, defense workers housing, and soldiers' canteens. Threatened with a March on Washington in 1940, organized by A. Philip Randolph and other black leaders, Roosevelt issued Executive Order 8802 to end discrimination in defense industries to be implemented through the Fair Employment Practices Committee. Race discrimination, however, continued in defense employment and housing leading to continued pressure on the Roosevelt administration. World War II like World War I brought the race problem in America to the forefront as any change in Jim Crow America engendered racial hostility. While swing populism was supporting the war effort, race riots erupted across the country in the early 1940s. As sociologist Winifred Raushenbush warned in 1943, "for many months, the heat lightning of racial trouble had flickered ominously in the American sky, lighting up Fort Bragg, North Carolina; Mobile, Alabama; Beaumont, Texas; Los Angeles, and scores of other defense towns and Army camps. Then... the lightning struck hard. For thirty hours 100,000 people fought pitched battles in the heart of our production centers. Detroit hospitals took in casualties at the rate of one a minute." (*American Mercury* 9-1943: 302) With the riot in Detroit and riots in other major cities across the country, the *American Mercury* featured an article "The Negro Problem Reaches a Crisis." "The Detroit and Harlem race riots of recent memory have only dramatized a situation in American race relations that has been festering for years and now threatens to shake the nation." (*American Mercury* 12-1944: 680) While Stowe and Erenberg are correct in pointing to how swing represented a more racially tolerant culture and efforts to end race discrimination, there was another America equally powerful rejecting and fighting against racial tolerance and equality. And this other America's response to changes in race relations as we will see was to have a direct effect on the world of music making.

Given the anti-racism ideology in progressive and radical swing populism, the question remains how this ideal of racial equality played out among swing musicians and in the pages of *Metronome* and *Down Beat*. The question of racism rarely appeared in *Metronome* and *Down Beat* during the 1930s – a more direct commentary only appeared with the increased race problems in the early 1940s. We have seen already how these magazines celebrated the rise in status of black professional musicians during the 1930s and included these artists in their regular coverage of the professional world of music making. *Metronome*, however, ignored the issue of racism in the music industry during the 1930s except for one article on a Jimmie Lunceford performance that pointed to why so many good black big bands remained unknown. "The reason for the undeserved obscurity of these swell colored bands has a lot to do with the time-worn racial barrier. We are becoming more liberal, but there still remains prejudice against the black man." (*Metronome* 5-1936: 26) From the beginning of its publication *Down Beat* editors Glenn Burrs and Carl Cons expressed progressive New Deal ideals. After six months of publication, this magazine presented its progressive labor ideals in its editorial "The Down Beat Marks Tempo and Explains Its Aims." "The tremendous growth of Radio, the Talkies, the return to power and influence of huge monopolies and trusts, and the ever increasing complexity and mechanization of civilized living, has left the musician with an inadequate voice in his own affairs. . . So, among the objectives and ambitions of the Down Beat one stands out in bold relief, and that is to give an adequate voice to the musician and his problems." (*Down Beat* 1-1935: 2) *Down Beat* in 1936 also announced a colorblind editorial policy. "Down Beat does not subscribe to racial prejudice and has never drawn a color line in any of its reporting or criticism of personalities in the music world, preferring to judge musicians strictly on their ability and not on any basis of the complexion of their skin. And we are glad to say most white musicians do not recognize color lines in music." (*Down Beat* 10-1936: 4) While *Down Beat* claimed a colorblind policy in its coverage and its editors were against racism in music, during the 1930s like *Metronome* it rarely addressed racism in the music industry or the question of race relations within the profession of music making.

In the *Down Beat* series "History of Swing" written by Marshal Stearns a few comments appeared about race relations in American music. "In evaluating the contribution of the American Negro to swing music, a contribution which is the most important single element of the phenomenon, it should be remembered that for many years, due to racial prejudices which still exist in part today, recognition was only given to white musicians, no matter what kind of music they played." (*Down Beat* 6-1936: 4) Stearns later informed readers that in the history of jazz "each time a great white band emerged to fame in the past, great colored bands had preceded it without attracting as much attention." (*Down Beat* 3-1937: 5) In 1938, George Frazier made clear that there was "more racial prejudice within the profession than anyone would care to believe ... there is no room in art for prejudice. Talent alone should be the requirement and not the color of one's skin." (*Down Beat* 6-1937: 4) R. L. Larkin made a more forceful remark in "Are White Bands Stealing Ideas From the Negro?" "Many a white band, by hiring Negro arrangers, has utilized colored tricks to excellent advantage... Today the top bands, Goodman, Miller, the Dorseys, Krupa, Herman, James, Barnet and most all the rest use nothing but Negroid music. Most of all of them have Negro arrangers. Thus the colored bands are no longer distinctive as they once were. The whites are successfully stealing their stuff ... colored bands don't get location spots as white groups do. The cold facts are that *prejudice* still exists, not only in the south, but throughout the United States. So a colored orchestra cannot soak up airtime and then hit the road all the time. It's tough. Many a Negro musician's health cracks. And the pay isn't high." (*Down Beat* 12-5-1940: 5) Outside of these comments, *Down Beat* did not infuse politics in its coverage of American music, although for its time, just covering and celebrating black music and black musicians was a radical change for American music journals. Progressives Carl Cons, John Hammond, and Dave Dexter in the early 1940s purchased *Music and Rhythm* hoping to compensate for what they felt was the lack of coverage of Jim Crow in *Down Beat* and *Metronome*. (Hammond 1977) Unfortunately, *Music and Rhythm* folded in 1942.

One question on racial equality covered by *Down Beat* during the 1930s was the question of racially integrated "name" bands brought about by Benny Goodman's hiring of the black pianist Teddy Wilson. During the 1930s, black and white musicians did occasionally perform together in recording studios, special concerts, special jam sessions, and a few nightclubs, but as we've seen the commercial market of live swing remained segregated. The question for *Down Beat* was the possibility of integrated bands in the mainstream swing market. In an editorial in 1936, *Down Beat* commended Wilson's regular performances with the Goodman ensembles "in a world sick with carbuncles of hate" and "ravished with fevers of race discrimination." "Conditions in the music world are not as discouragingly bad as they are in some other worlds, but there are plenty of instances of talent suffering because of race and color, and plenty more because of unjust and disgusting exploitation... It is with a great deal of pleasure that we noted a colored boy of great talent employed with a group of white musicians and playing to generous applause night after night on the sole basis of his merit as a musician. We still like to believe that regardless of race, creed, or color we are all Americans, and that as Americans we are all free and equal deserving of the respect and admiration of our fellow men according to the extent of our abilities and talents." (*Down Beat* 5-1936: 2) While *Down Beat* commended Benny Goodman's hiring of Teddy Wilson and Lionel Hampton, editorially it maintained an ambiguous position on the viability of integrated bands at the time given the difficulties inherent in breaking the rules of Jim Crow. In "Can a Negro Play His Best in a White Band," *Down Beat* again commended Goodman's integrated ensembles as well as expressed relief in the lack of anticipated riots in Dallas during his tour, but expressed reservations about whether it was a "good idea." Making reference to the common view of the different stylistic qualities between black and white swing musicians and the pressures of performing in an integrated band, *Down Beat* preferred a separate but equal policy in live swing performances even though "there have been many interesting and good records made by mixed groups of black and white musicians." "But if a man cannot possibly play his best with a group of musicians with different taste, he is a fool to limit himself by holding it up as a desirable ideal. The fact that there are social implications beyond their talent is enough to place either white or black musicians at a nervous disadvantage that spoils their ease and flow of ideas and is manifestly unfair to each other's musical talents." (*Down Beat* 10-1937: 3)

The question of integrated name bands came up again when Goodman later hired Charlie Christian and Fletcher Henderson as performers in 1939. *Down Beat* maintained a neutral position. "Whether it is good or bad, in its final analysis the editors of DOWN BEAT frankly do not know." Woody Herman, who would hire black musicians in the 1940s, argued that "no orchestra has greater respect for Negro musicians and their music than ours... But in spite of the tremendous debt we owe Negro musicians and composers for our style we would not consider that the addition of one or more Negroes would enhance that style, anymore than the addition of a white musician would improve Duke Ellington's orchestra. . . We have too much respect for the vitality and imagination of Negro musicians to ask any one of them to sacrifice his integrity." Jimmy Dorsey was quoted as believing that "Benny should be congratulated for his courage in adding Negro musicians to his orchestra. . . To my mind, the question resolves itself to one of style. I feel my present instrumentation, without Negro talent, expresses my style best." Artie Shaw exclaimed "I'd put colored boys in the band in a minute if they had the talent – and a great deal of them have." Teddy Wilson believed "the hiring of colored musicians to play in white bands is an excellent idea," while Ella Fitzgerald believed such hiring practices were "mutually beneficial. Both races have a lot to offer each other. It would be hard to understand the advisability of racial distinction where artistry in musical advancement is concerned." *Down Beat*'s remark that "several leaders, in fact, said they believed that within two more years, use of colored musicians in white bands will be accepted everywhere in the States," however, was rather over optimistic. (*Down Beat* 10-15-1939: 1, 10, 23)

While many white and black swing musicians supported the idea of integration and equality between swing musicians, little effort was made to change the segregated world of big band music during the Swing Era. Lionel Hampton noted in his later memoir that it was "sad to think about all those black and white musicians going around admiring each other, playing off each other, jamming privately together, and yet knowing they couldn't be seen together in public. But they just accepted that that was the way things were, and got together privately as often as they could." (Hampton 1989: 24–5) Hampton remembered his days with Goodman. "With Benny, touring with two black musicians was a pioneering effort. Nobody had ever traveled with an integrated band before, and even though Teddy Wilson and I were only part of the Benny Goodman Quartet, not the whole orchestra, that was still too much for some white folks. . . Goodman was no civil rights activist. He didn't talk much about racism. His whole concentration was on music, but it galled him that something as petty as race prejudice could mess up the music he wanted to hear and play. He realized that America was poorer in music than it should be, because of racism." (Hampton 1989: 63, 65) Goodman himself celebrated the opportunity for black and white musicians to play together in his 1939 autobiography. "It was during these months, around the end of 1933 and the beginning of 1934, that I first began to make records with colored musicians. . . I think that one of the most important things that has happened in the last few years is the number of times good musicians have gotten together and played in mixed bands on records – something they don't get a chance to do in public. Some of the things that have given me the greatest pleasure as a musician would not have come about otherwise." (Goodman 1939: 129–30) For some black professional musicians, the question was one of an overarching racial system in music making, which of course included racist white musicians, but supportive white swing musicians were not necessarily seen as collaborators. As Benny Carter remembered, "we learned from each other and we didn't much blame the white musicians – we did envy them, though. What was holding us back was not just individual differences but a whole system of discrimination and segregation involving musicians, audiences, bookings, productions and so on." (Berger *et al.* 1982: 45–6)

Some black professional musicians, however, were not as sympathetic. Dizzy Gillespie, part of a younger generation than Carter and Hampton, was less forgiving of white musicians in his later remarks about the 1930s when he was playing with Cab Calloway. "At that time, there was less discrimination in the field of jazz than in any other part of American life. But it still existed, because they had only one major white band that hired black musicians on a permanent basis, and that band was Benny Goodman's. Of course, the white bands got most of the jobs that paid best, and the black musicians, the major creators, as a rule were frozen out. They used all kinds of excuses to justify this evil, such as the trouble mixed bands might provoke among racist customers and employers, the problems of finding restaurants, hotels . . . and other public accommodations for the black members of the troupe. But the main reason those forms of discrimination persisted was because the bands themselves accepted it, and profited from the injustice, because they were insulated from competition with black bands and musicians." (Gillespie 1986: 157) Hampton also noted how some black intellectuals and musicians perceived Goodman's racially integrated band as just another form of exploitation. "Meanwhile, he was getting flack from some critics in the black community who accused him of using blacks. That was non-sense." (Hampton 1989: 63) John Hammond remembered Duke Ellington's position regarding integrated bands. "I can remember arguing with Duke about my efforts to create mixed bands. His point was: Why help the white bands by filling them with black players, thereby threatening the survival of Negro bands? I know that Ellington felt that white bandleaders were trying to steal the Negro's music, as well he might have, for not only were his musicians stolen, but also his tunes and even the sound of his band, to the extent that was possible. . . I feel that jazz always has had a duty to promote racial understanding and interracial cooperation." (Hammond 1977: 136–7)

The United States entrance into World War II led to an even worse state of race relations in American music. The conditions for black swing bands

only worsened. The war had a devastating effect on the big band business. Bandleaders and musicians enlisted at the same time that domestic
resources were focused on supporting the war effort. Of course, some
professional black musicians like Dizzy Gillespie and Buck Clayton were
not interested in fighting to defend a Jim Crow America and employed
various strategies to avoid conscription. (Gillespie 1979; Clayton 1987)
The rationing of gasoline, material for tires, and the need for buses for the
military effort made touring a daunting task. While white big bands had to
deal with changed circumstances, black big bands had an even more difficult time. *Down Beat* noted the severe situation for black bands in 1942.
"The situation for colored bands is nothing short of desperate ... colored
bands economically couldn't afford trains, hadn't cars, faced Jim Crow
regulations on the trains in the south, and since there were only a handful of location dates that they could play, during a year, and not many
more theaters, must travel... Life is going to be tough enough for the
white bands. It's going to cease for the colored bands unless an effort is
made immediately by all offices to breakdown the non-saleability of these
bands at the usual locations, and the government does something about
rail transportation in the south. This is more than the loss of some bands –
it will mean the breaking-up of some of the best sources of musical ideas
in the country." (*Down Beat* 8-1-42: 23)

In addition to wartime touring difficulties, race relations further
eroded. Set in the context of race riots occurring across the country, racial
disturbances became regular occurrences in clubs and dance halls. Black
bands eventually were banned in a few cities from previous nightspots
where they performed for white patrons or integrated audiences due to
possible racial violence. Other black clubs were closed for similar reasons
or raided by police for anti-drug enforcement with black musicians rou-
tinely arrested for drug possession or alleged possession. *Down Beat* in
"Coast Ops Nix on Colored Bands" covered the recent change in booking
policy of major clubs in Los Angeles. "Due to a marked increase result-
ing from racial friction, nitery operators in this territory are definitely
averse to booking Negro bands. The Zucca Brothers, who featured Negro bands and entertainers almost exclusively at their niteries ... now have
white combos exclusively, and they are not planning to use negro bands
in the future... All of them fear that some minor case of racial prejudice
on the part of some misguided white patron may cause a disturbance that
will become serious." *Down Beat*'s editorial in the same issue noted the
terrible changes. "Operators of nightclubs and ballrooms in California
have established a new policy which precludes the future booking of colored bands, undoubtedly bars mixed orchestras, too... It is too bad that
musicians who, in meeting their fellows from all classes and races upon

the common plane of their art, have done as much as any group toward breaking down archaic class or race consciousness, should suffer from the very evil they are helping to correct. Most of them know that intellect has no identifying color. It is neither black, nor brown, nor yellow, nor red – nor white!" (*Down Beat* 10-1-1943: 6,10) In Philadelphia that same year the local white union banned the broadcast of a mixed band from a military canteen. (*Down Beat* 12-1-1943) In New York City, *Down Beat* noted the new tensions with the war in "Racial Hatred Rears Ugly Mug in Music." "High persons in the music business, managers of entertainment spots and civilian and military authorities are taking extra precautions to prevent outcroppings of fights and brawls, especially inter-racial settos. They fear one little spark may set off that dynamite dreaded by all – a race riot." (*Down Beat* 8-1944)

In 1943, a *Metronome* editorial came out against racism in music. "The bigotry, the prejudice, the anti-Negro feeling in this country is still enormous, in spite of amendments to the Constitution, in spite of blood shed in the cause of freedom and tolerance, in spite of all the sanctimonious repetition of the words 'without regard to race or creed or color... the music business cannot justify the existence of the evil in its own ranks because of its widespread existence outside the business. Musicians are artists and artists are traditionally above bigotry and prejudice... The rank and file of white musicians have long ago thrown aside prejudice and taken up their horns and sticks and music and sat down to play side by side with their colored brothers... Break up jimcrowism in the union. Merge all colored locals with the white locals into decent, American representative bodies." (*Metronome* 4-1943: 4) But racial tensions continued in the music world. In New York City, the major nightclub scene on 52nd Street had recently opened its doors to interracial audiences – this scene had both white and black musicians since the early 1930s. The clubs and street, however, were troubled by racial tension and police harassment. *Metronome* feared the problems developing in this premier swing district in "Tension Mounts on 52nd Street." "Democracy is having difficulties along 52nd Street. The apparent interracial harmony that existed in the nightclub fraternity has been disturbed by several alarming events in the past few weeks. White and colored musicians have been working in each other's bands, and colored patrons have been treated with decent respect... Suddenly last month, the police swooped down on the White Rose and ordered a midnight curfew there, as a result of the alleged picking up of two plainclothesmen by girls who were said to be hanging out at the bar... One evening Johnny Guarnieri was walking peacefully along the street with two musician friends who happened to be colored. The group was approached by a policeman brandishing a club, who told them to 'get off the sidewalk,' and added 'We don't want you niggers on the streets." (*Metronome* 8-1944: 7) Arnold Shaw remembered the racial tension on Swing Street during the early 1940s. "As the 52nd St. joints filled with men in khaki and Navy whites, black musicians suddenly found themselves facing nightly hazards. Many of the military were from the South. They were not accustomed to the easy mixing of colors among musicians and audiences. And they particularly resented the attention that white chicks showered on black performers. Dizzy Gillespie, Billy Taylor, and many other musicians carry unforgettable memories of the dangers involved in going home after the clubs closed. They felt lucky if they could make the Sixth Avenue subway station without an encounter." (Shaw 1971: 255)

While swing populism held the hope for a democracy based on racial equality, by the end of the war race relations were in a terrible state. Jim-Crowism was deeply ingrained in American culture and American institutions. No better evidence was in the lack of significant change in the world of music making. At the end of the war, black professional musicians faced the same Jim Crow music industry, while grappling with racial hostility in newly racially integrated entertainment districts across the country. While many white swing musicians considered their black brethren as equals and rejected racism, the Jim Crow conditions of music making remained intact. A new generation of black professional musician, however, would take the radical politics of the 1930s and transform them into a radical jazz ethos incorporating anti-commercialism and anti-racist militancy. They would claim "bebop" as a "progressive" black jazz style that rejected the complacency and commercialism of mainstream black swing music. In this radical move, beboppers also articulated an anti-commercialism and anti-establishment ethos that already had taken hold of white "hepcat" musicians during the 1920s and 1930s. These white hepcats also saw themselves as rebels against mainstream American culture, although a somewhat admittedly different radical politics than the Popular Front.

Romantic outsiders: white hepcat musicians as rebels

The Dilemma of Jazz

Speaking historically, jazz was born in conflict with middle class values, boiling out of the fields, streets and sporting houses as a segregated, defiant music of poor people... During World War I and the prohibition era, jazz pursued a purple existence outside the pale of middle class society, including even the Negro middle class. Raucous, ebullient, exhibitionist, it was the music of the "speaks," played occasionally as counterpoint to sub-machine gun fire... It was pointedly an expression of rebellion against the mores and strictures of a 'boobosie' (as Mencken dubbed it), whose spokesmen filled magazines and newspapers with virulent attacks on this worthless 'corrupter' of youth. (Artie Shaw, *Jazz*, April 1965: 8)

Artie Shaw in 1965 remembered early jazz and its conflict in the 1920s with traditionalist values. For "hepcat" white musicians like Shaw who made the black jazz vernacular their own during that decade, the swing-sweet divide in the 1930s represented a cultural schism between a hep urban culture and a conservative middle class culture. The swing-sweet divide reminded white swing musicians of earlier anti-jazz sentiments with the "commercial" sweet culture of big band music articulating a similar sentiment. Even the old guard "jazz" orchestras of the 1920s like those led by Paul Whiteman and Vincent Lopez were seen as promulgators of a cultivated sweet jazz. The sociologist Neil Leonard (1962) argues that these hepcat white musicians were "romantic outsiders" – adopting the black vernacular in order to rebel against mainstream American culture. Black swing musicians obviously faced a segregated society and culture, but they were "permanent outsiders" – the designated Other in American culture. Whether white musicians adopted the black jazz vernacular in order to rebel, or in identifying with and adopting this vernacular they became rebels, the end result was their becoming outsiders to the domi-nant culture of the 1920s and early 1930s – particularly within the music profession. Even as the black jazz vernacular invaded the popular music market of white jitterbugging fans and white swing big bands, the early rebellion by hepcats against sweet commercial culture would continue to resonate with white swing musicians. This hepcat ethos against "commer-cial" popular music and middle-class conventional culture became an en-during jazz ideology that informed future "rebellions" among professional musicians as well as the self-image and cultural trope of jazz musicians as "hip" urban artists living and creating outside the American mainstream.

Young white musicians who adopted the black jazz vernacular during the 1920s constantly confronted the ire of traditionalists. Swing musi-cian Scotty Lawrence in "Swing is Here to Stay" in 1937 remembered the anti-jazz sentiments of the 1920s, including secretly practicing jazz "licks" behind his father's back since "you know how Army bandsmen felt about jazz ten years ago." (*Metronome* 8-1937: 13) Among young jazz-crazed white musicians, a special cohort of musicians became the most vocal and successful hepcat musicians. This cohort of young white musicians formed the core of the white swing fraternity in New York City in the 1930s. Benny Goodman described his cohort of hot jazz musicians in the early 1930s as "pretty much of a clique by themselves. They hung around the same places, made the same spots after work, drank together and worked together whenever they had a chance." (Goodman 1939: 101) Neil Leonard's (1962) argument on hepcat white musicians in the 1920s as romantic outsiders is based on this cohort of musicians that included Hoagie Carmichael, Bix Beiderbecke, Frank Teschemacher, Frankie Trumbauer, Benny Goodman, Artie Shaw, Mezz Mezzrow, Bud Freeman, and Eddie Condon. For Leonard, these hepcats were representative of the new generation of white musicians who were attracted to the black jazz vernacular. Their attraction according to Leonard was as white middle class youth seeking to rebel against the constraints of mainstream American culture. The hepcat musician Mezz Mezzrow, himself working class, described in his memoir *Really the Blues* in 1946 this rejection of middle class culture in his celebration of the middle class hepcats Bud Freeman, Frankie Teschemacher, Dave Tough, and Jimmy MacPartland. They were from what Mezzrow called "a well-to-do suburb where all the days were Sabbaths. A sleepy-time neighborhood big as a yawn and just about as lively, loaded with shade-tress and clipped lawns and a groggy-eyed population that never came out of its coma except to turn over. In all their schemes these kids aimed to run out of town the sloppy, insipid, yes-we-have-no-bananas music of the day, which seemed to echo the knocked-out spirit of their sleepwalking neighbors." (Mezzrow 1946: 103–4)

Leonard, however, was wrong in positioning the romantic outsider ethos as simply a middle class youth rebellion. Hepcat musicians were from diverse class and ethnic backgrounds. In fact, as Irving Kolodin suggested in 1941, most jazz and swing musicians in the 1920s and 1930s were working class. (*Harper's Magazine* 6-1941) The special cohort of hepcats included working class youth like Mezz Mezzrow, Benny Goodman, Artie Shaw, Max Kaminsky, and Eddie Condon. Many hepcat white musicians already were "outsiders" by class and ethnicity to mainstream middle class Anglo culture, and the black vernacular came to articulate their sense of alienation or difference. The strongest identification was expressed in writing by the working class Jewish Americans Mezz Mezzrow (Milton Mesirow) and Artie Shaw (Arthur Arshawsky) who viewed themselves as sharing a similar outsider status in America as African Americans. (Mezzrow 1946; Shaw 1952) Artie Shaw wrote of his deep identification with black musicians in Harlem in the late 1920s and early 1930s. "For the most part I was actually living the life of a Negro musician, adopting Negro values and attitudes, and accepting the Negro out-group point of view not only about music but life in general... Since I could find no way to break into the white world, I was willing to forget it and go on about the business of trying to make a place for myself in this colored world into which I accidentally stumbled and in which I now felt I belonged in a way I had never felt in any other milieu I had ever been part of." (Shaw 1952: 228–9) White hepcat musicians regardless of class or ethnicity shared a general romantic outsider view of themselves – a distinction expressed through their identification with and adoption of the black vernacular in music and in language. In this sense, all hepcats rejected the traditionalist sensibility that defined middle class culture.

For the special cohort of hepcats, their journey to rebellion began with their excursions to the black entertainment districts in the South Side of Chicago and in Harlem in New York City. The black bandleader William Everett Samuels remembered Chicago in the 1920s when young white musicians, known as alligators, would come to learn and copy black professional musicians. "Yeah, the white musicians would come out there all the time and try and copy what the Negroes were doing. You could see 'em at the Grand Terrace Theater. They were copying stuff down on the cuffs of their shirts and things – little riffs and things that they had." (Spivey 1984: 39) The black swing xylophonist Lionel Hampton remembered that as a young musician in Chicago he attended parties with black musicians like Jelly Roll Morton, Jimmy Noone, King Oliver, and Louis Armstrong where "from time to time, white musicians came to Uncle Richard's parties and jammed with the black musicians. I remember Mugsy Spanier and Frank Teschemacher and Bix Beiderbecke. They would jam until my grandmother put breakfast on the table." (Hampton 1989: 24) Benny Goodman in his 1939 autobiography remembered a foray to the South Side he made with Bix Beiderbecke when "after work we went over to the Sunset to hear Louis and Earl Hines, who was in a class by himself on piano. From there we went to the Nest to hear Jimmy Noone, and we made a night of it." (Goodman 1939: 75) Artie Shaw also remembered those early days in Chicago in his 1952 memoir *The Trouble with Cinderella*. "In those days the South Side of Chicago was one of the foremost conservatories in the world. There was Earl Hines' big band playing nightly at the Grand Terrace Cafe; Louis Armstrong and his small combination playing at the Sunset Cafe; Jimmy Noone playing clarinet in front of his own little Appex Club outfit. And hanging around in these smoke-filled, dimly lit joints – some of them no more than dingy cellars loosely converted into all-night speakeasies with postage-stamp dance floors and dime-sized tables – were guys like Bix Beiderbecke and Bud Freeman, Red McKenzie and Jimmy MacPartland... Gene Krupa... George Wettling... Eddie Condon... Muggsy Spanier... Ben Pollack... Benny Goodman... Frank Teschemacher... Dick McDonough, Bunny Berigan, Don Murray, and so many others. They were all there, listening and soaking up by osmosis this new idiom in American music. . . " (Shaw 1952: 196–7)

With a declining music scene in Chicago in the late 1920s, musicians migrated to New York City. Just as before, white hepcat musicians continued taking late night forays into the black community. In the early 1930s during the reign of sweet music, jazz-crazed white musicians would take freelance work in the radio and recording studios then go off to Harlem to jam. *Metronome* noted in the early 1930s that in New York City the Dorsey Brothers were "free lance and the radio and records keep them plenty busy. They have appeared on their own and with Vallee, Rubinoff, Skilkret, B. A. Rolfe, Lennie Hayton." But "the boys like to hear good colored bands and usually wind up by sitting in." (*Metronome* 5-1933: 29) 52nd Street outside Harlem was a major hangout for the special cohort of young white musicians who "played hot" due to its close proximity to several theaters, radio broadcasts, and recording studios. "The Street" was to play an important role in the emergence of a jazz art world with the first important jazz clubs and their featuring of black professional musicians from Harlem. Yet, the importance for hepcat musicians of black clubs in Harlem remained. In Arnold Shaw's memoir and oral history of 52nd Street, the swing saxophonist Bud Freeman a member of Goodman's clique remembered the early 1930s. The "guys would crowd into cabs and chase up to Harlem – there to continue jamming and drinking at Dickie Wells' on East 136th St., Yeah Man, Smalls Paradise, Clarence Robinson's, Clam House, Ye Old Nest, Ubangi Club, Breakfast Club, Pod's and Jerry's on West 133d – and other joints where you sometimes had to go down a flight of stone steps into a tenement basement and clamber over a pile of coal." (Shaw 1971: 62)

With their identification with black musicians and vernacular jazz, hepcat musicians in the 1920s viewed white professional jazz orchestras as pale imitators of jazz. Irving Kolodin, a collaborator in Benny Goodman's 1939 autobiography, pointed to how young hepcat white musicians in listening to black musicians rejected their white elders' scorn of vernacular jazz and their elders' attempts to cultivate it. "What these youngsters heard as they travelled from place to place was a tremendous capacity for improvisation, an endless fertility and invention, a breathtaking range of rhythm patterns, plus an interplay of all these elements that was simply unheard of in the organized, paper-written jazz of the day. They could not fail to contrast it with what passed for 'jazz' in the playing of the large white bands, and their preference was established with hardly a struggle." Benny Goodman himself expressed the new orientation of young white professional musicians away from white orchestras towards the black jazz vernacular performed by black musicians. "The big white bands, like

Whiteman, Isham Jones and the rest didn't play what musicians considered real jazz. They used 'symphonic' arrangements, with fiddles, and all sorts of effects, the musicians rarely having the opportunity to stand up and play a chorus out of their own heads. One of the first big bands which combined arrangement with some leeway for the soloists was Fletcher Henderson's, around 1924. For a while it had such men as Armstrong, Charlie Green, on trombone, Buster Bailey, Don Redman and Coleman Hawkins in the reeds, and Kaiser Marshall on drums." (Goodman 1939: 55–6, 62–3) Hepcat musicians considered the Ben Pollack, Jean Goldkette, and Glenn Gray orchestras in which many of them performed as the only promulgators of white big band jazz in the 1920s and early 1930s. In general, professional white jazz orchestras were viewed with disdain as pseudo jazz. (Goodman 1939; Kaminsky 1963; Condon 1947)

Hepcat musicians represented the avant-garde in the assimilation of the black jazz vernacular by a new generation of white professional musicians. Not only did hepcats disdain the pseudo jazz of white jazz orchestras in the 1920s, but also held black musicians as their artistic mentors. Max Kaminsky in his later memoir remembers the impact of hearing Louis Armstrong for the first time and reveals the romanticism and respect hepcat musicians held for black jazz musicians. "I was just unprepared for the full impact of his playing too . . . the combination of Louis's dazzling virtuosity and sensational brilliance of tone so overwhelmed me that I felt as if I had stared into the sun's eye. All I could think of doing was to run away and hide until the blindness left me. Louis is *the* great creative jazz genius." (Kaminsky 1963: 40) Bix Beiderbecke, who became the tragic romantic hero of hepcat musicians after his death in 1931, came to epitomize the new orientation of young white musicians. *Life Magazine*'s photo series on swing in 1938 was influenced by the advising of Eddie Condon, a friend of Beiderbecke and part of the clique of hepcat musicians. In a separate piece on Bix, the new orientation of hepcats was made clear. "A promising 19-year-old white trumpeter named 'Bix' Beiderbecke heard him and realized immediately that Armstrong's music was true hot style, that by comparison his own playing was faltering and 'corny' (i.e. stale and outdated). Bix Beiderbecke was too fine a musician to be simply an imitator. But he boldly decided to absorb Negro style, which white musicians scorned to play. The decision was momentous. It made Bix the greatest of white trumpeters (he actually played cornet) and the most important of all white jazz influences." (*Life* 8-8-1938: 54)

With the advent of the reign of sweet music, hepcat white musicians felt even more alienated from the popular music market. At least in the late 1920s they were able to side as "hot" players in orchestras and record as small jazz ensembles in the still booming jazz market. Following the

depression, however, their fortunes seemed bleak. This period solidified
a disdain for, or alienation from, "commercial" music as white big bands
went sweet and "hot" musicians had to conform to the new market for
the best paying jobs. As Hoagy Carmichael admitted in 1933, "the boys
were losing their enthusiasm for hot stuff, and many of them, such as the
Dorsey Boys, Miff Mole, Carl Kress and Phil Napoleon joined radio staff
orchestras to play programs of every description. No more hot licks – no
more thrills – into the pits! . . . most of the jazz aggregations, throughout
the country developed a bad case of 'clanks'. . . Such capable band leaders as Ben Bernie, George Olsen, Nat Skilkret, Paul Whiteman, Rudy
Valley and a host of others will give the public what they want, so why
bother . . ." (*Metronome* 8-1933: 23) Benny Goodman remembered the
sad state of affairs in the early 1930s when "for my part, it meant playing
more commercial programs." Goodman performed in a number of radio
bands and orchestras including Harry Reser's corny band the Clicquot
Club Eskimos on NBC. "The saddest thing, always, was a recognized hot
man who went in for that sort of work because he made good dough and
got steady work around the studios. But whenever you met him you could
tell that the work bored the pants off him, and I have seen more than a
few fellows crack up for this one reason." (Goodman 1939: 121, 101)

With the swing craze, the earlier rebellion of hepcat musicians was
now part of a popular swing culture including jitterbugs – defined in *Life*
magazine in 1938 as the "extreme swing addicts who get so excited by its
music that they cannot stand or be still while it is being played." Sporting
urban attire as zootsuiters and bobbysockers, jitterbugs adopted the black
vernacular not only in music and dance but like their hepcat predecessors
also in argot when in "their quieter moments, they discuss Swing with
weird words like *jive, gut-bucket, dog-house, push-pipe, agony-pipe*." And for
hepcat musicians, jitterbugs were "the people who pay to get into dance
halls, nightclubs, and big outdoor arenas to hear him play, who buy his
phonograph records and who listen to swing radio programs." (*Life* 8-8-
1938: 56) The victory of swing certainly seemed a vindication of earlier
hepcat musicians' rejection of middle class traditionalist culture. While
the swing craze was celebrated as a victory over the traditionalist culture
of sweet music, however, many white swing musicians would still retain
a sense of the romantic outsider.

The power of the romantic outsider ideal among white swing musicians
during the swing craze was evident in Bix Beiderbecke, the mythic hepcat white musician, five years after his death winning top trumpet honors
over Louis Armstrong in the all-time swing band contest in *Metronome*
in 1936. A certain disdain for commercial music and the dance market still remained among white swing musicians who romanticized the
early days of hepcat musicians performing hot jazz. Many young white

musicians also had to perform in big bands led by older professional musicians less enamored with the craze for swing. Some among the initial cohort of white hepcat musicians even viewed swing big band music as a compromise to the authentic black jazz vernacular they adopted during the 1920s. Eddie Condon became the vanguard of this group of hepcat musicians. His influence on the *Life Magazine* photo series on swing was evident in the section "Jitterbugs are Poison and Bread & Butter." "Bix Beiderbecke, an earnest artist, would turn sadly over in his grave if he knew that the art for which he died had been take over by the jitterbugs... To the hot musician, jitterbugs are plain poison. But they must be humored because they have brought prosperity to Swing." (*Life* 8-8-1938: 56) Even those hepcat musicians who enjoyed unbounded success in the new swing market expressed reservations. Artie Shaw who led a top swing big band proclaimed in an exclusive to *Metronome* in 1939 "I Still Don't Like Litterbugs." " 'Sure, I don't like jitterbugs! I don't like the business angles connected with music'... Shaw explained that he was still an idealist, that when he first started his band he had pictured getting to the top and playing the kind of music he wanted to. 'But it's not like that at all,' he said... 'I want everybody to know that all I'm interested in is making good music.' " (*Metronome* 11-1939: 10, 26) Benny Goodman was more diplomatic in his 1939 *Collier's* article "Now Take the Jitterbug." "In other words, jitterbugs helped us drag jazz out of the old saloon mechanical piano and give it a new life and dignity... So far so good. Unfortunately jitterbugs began to take on certain mannerisms not exactly listed in the code of true musical appreciation." (*Colliers* 2-25-1939: 12) In *Down Beat* in 1938, the young swing musician Leslie Leiber expressed his frustration with the commercial dance market.

Tonight, I might mention, is the apogee of my career. Whatever I may aspire to as a saxophone player and whatever respect and glory I can ever reap should be mine this evening.

And yet in front of me, people are obliviously milling around, dancing with their eyes shut, bumping into acquaintances and stepping on their partners. Although I have already taken two solo choruses, no one at the party is yet aware that I am alive, except the pair who knocked my music stand over. And all they did was laugh and dance away...

Bach might be playing the contrapuntal accompaniment on the piano, and still nobody would listen to the music. To hell with pure tones, exquisite improvisations, the pristine voice of angels! Cut out the music, give these people what they want... (Leslie Leiber, *Down Beat*, 1-38: 7)

It seemed that while the swing craze reintroduced the black jazz vernacular to popular audiences around the nation, the romantic outsider ethos of early hepcats actually spread among white swing musicians. This hep culture of white swing musicians maintained a sense of alienation from the popular music market as well as popular audiences. The sociologist Carl Lastrucci did a study of white big band musicians in San Francisco in the late 1930s and discovered the romantic outsider ethos among these musicians. He found that the dance musician "believes that what he calls 'pure jazz' is a serious and highly creative art form which, not understood and hence unappreciated, is perverted for commercial ends into the type of popular music which he is required to play for a livelihood. This attitude leads him, first, to regard himself as a creative artist rather than as a commercial entertainer... Second, it imbues him with a deep scorn for most laymen for he blames them for demanding the (to him) innocuous music commonly referred to as jazz or swing." (Lastrucci 1941: 170) Not all white swing musicians necessarily held an outsider ethos, but it remained a significant and prevalent ethos. More importantly, while the romantic outsider ethos was at first a rebellion against conventional middle class culture, particularly its anti-jazz sentiments, by the 1930s it came to also articulate a romantic ideal of artists struggling to perform an authentic and creative art form. This positioning of the art of jazz against "commercial" popular music became an important construct articulated in future "rebellions" among professional jazz musicians.

MUSICIANS DESERT GIN & WEED TO SWING AGAIN

It is remarkable what a slight improvement in economic status can do for thwarted and disillusioned artists who have been driven to drink and weed by their inability to find a place of employment in which they might adequately express themselves. Since the public's acceptance – almost amounting to insistence – of rhythmic improvisation it is not an unusual sight to see once hopeless drunkards emerge as sober and world beating trumpeters, percussionists and guitarists. In the old days there was every reason for the inspired player to find refuge in stimulants, deprived as he was of the natural appreciation the artistic temperament must have if it is to survive. But now, the fad of swing has at least brought back into their natural place in society countless souls who had long since been given up as lost souls. (John Hammond, *Down Beat* July 1936: 1)

Hepcat romantic outsiders, in their alienation from conventional values also transgressed conventional moral boundaries. The jazz enthusiast John Hammond expressed the romantic link between musical alienation, cultural rebellion, and deviancy that would become a common myth of jazz. Irving Kolodin's reference to hepcats as "gutter rats" and Artie Shaw's reference to the "speaks" and "machine-gun fire" of the hepcat life speak to this romanticism associated with the deviant life-style of hepcat musicians. The 1938 *Life Magazine* essay on Bix Beiderbecke also presented the romantic portrayal of hepcat swing musicians' lifestyle as deviant. His dogged pursuit of the black jazz vernacular "brought him early death and posthumous fame... His only interest was music. After quitting work in the early morning, he would round up other musicians, go off on long, exhausting, drunken 'jam' sessions. He led the irregular, dissipated life that swing players have always led." (*Life* 8-8-1938: 54) That same month *The New York Times* described the romantic deviant swing musician who "physically exhausted, his nerves at edge, he finishes his stint sometime before dawn, packs his instrument, fortifies himself with the bottle, and repairs to a favored joint for a jam-session... The physical and nervous toll of such fanatic pace is extreme, and many swingsters require some artificial stimulus of immediate effect. They find it in the cup and the 'weed'.... The swingster will smoke his 'reefer' so long as he needs it and he will need it so long as the demands of his job and his material rewards remain incompatible with human physical resources." (*New York Times* 8-14-1938: 7/19) Carl Lastrucci (1941: 169) also noted the general deviance of the hepcat white musician, although denied his reefer madness, who is "characteristically plagued by domestic troubles, has a high rate of divorce and separation, gambles freely, associates most often with semipromiscuous women... Although he drinks hard liquors inordinately and has a comparatively high rate of venereal disease, he is not – as popular rumor would have it – a marihuana addict." The publication of *Young Man With a Horn* in 1938, a novel based on the romantic outsider hero Bix Beiderbecke, even codified the hepcat deviant rebel as a literary figure.

Of course, the image of the hepcat swing musician as deviant, whether romantic or defamatory, was not well received by those musicians and others working to legitimize swing music as a populist American art. *Metronome* responded to the popular image of the deviant hepcat in the article "They're Killing Our Swing!" The press seemed to have "done a very fine job of giving the general public a vivid picture of what swing is NOT, of the kind of lives musicians DON'T lead, of the kind of morals and personal habits they DON'T have, of the kind of language they DON'T speak... And in so doing, they've handed every intelligent, self-respecting musician a pain more intense than that caused by any conceivable klinker, and an almost uncontrollable urge to hunt up each of the writers and to squeeze his head into the welcome bell of a tuba... Such publicity on the subject of marijuana is far more prevalent than is the amount of reefing that's actually done among musicians." (*Metronome* 9-1938: 11, 40) Of course, *Down Beat* presented a two part series "Death Is My Partner... I Shall Not Want" in November 1937 "because of the widespread use of marijuana among musicians and the almost unbelievable ignorance concerning its origin, effects, etc... Musicians who as a class burn it in astonishing quantities and must accept responsibility for hastening the advance of this narcotic phenomenon, find it aids them in swinging a tune (or so they rationalize). No jam session is worthy of that exalted title without a stick or two of 'tea' to pass around." *Down Beat* noted the popularity of songs referring to "weed," "vipers," "mellow," and of course, "La Cucaracha . . . marihuana que fumar." (*Down Beat* 11-1937: 8) Paul Whiteman felt compelled in his essay "All American Swing Band" to address the question of the hepcat deviant. "First of all I want to correct one erroneous impression that has sprung up about swing music. A great many people think that a swing musician has to fight his way through a fog of marijuana smoke before he can play a hot lick. . . A reefer man or a man whose technique comes out of a bottle couldn't last two nights with one of our first-rate swing bands." (*Colliers* 9-10-1938: 9) *Down Beat* was equally displeased with the hepcat image and was quick to voice its views of Lastrucci's portrayal of swing musicians when he presented his research at an academic conference which was reported in the general press. "Two Pacific coast sociologists, bent on sticking their noses into something they knew nothing about, recently investigated the life and habits of 100 successful band leaders. . . College profs sometimes are funny ducks. In this case their observations are, frankly, humorous even tho absurd. A lot of us once spent time in college classrooms could do a fair-to-middling job of 'analyzing' some of the people we met there, too. And those people wouldn't be students." (*Down Beat* 3-15-1940: 2) Lionel Hampton voiced his anger with the reefer image of swing musicians in 1940. "ALL musicians do NOT smoke weeds, nor do ALL musicians drink! I know that's going to get a lot of yokels back on their heels, but they need it. Why the profession has to keep taking black eyes because a few cats here and there believe in living their lives, is a little beyond me. . . We're pretty much a level-headed bunch of people, and damned if I, for one, don't resent the popular conception that all we do is get high off our tea, and use grog for chasers. . . Weed and pint bottles didn't originate in Harlem, either." (*Down Beat* 6-1940: 2, 11) Hampton's last remark referred to the not uncommon comments on reefer madness emanating from Harlem and infecting white swing musicians and white jitterbugs.

Defenders of jazz, however, also were aware that the reefer image of swing was leading to police harassment of swing musicians. *Down Beat* in 1938 noted the increased attention law enforcement was giving reefer swingsters, while also presenting the common view that the origin of this deviant behavior was in the black community. "The idea that weed which is supposed to have first taken hold of the low-down musicians playing in Harlem dives is now spreading to the bigger bands where instrumentalists now use it to emit the wild abandoned rhythms which comprise swing music is said to be arousing intense interest at J. Edgar Hoover's headquarters. Whether it is true or not the FBI is convinced that there is a good deal to the rumors which they have heard and they are planning an investigation." (*Down Beat* 8-1938: 2) Early police action against swing musicians usually focused on black swing musicians and black clubs, particularly integrated clubs. *Down Beat* later reported the raiding of a popular club in Minneapolis by police in "Jam Spot Raided as 'Thrill Club For Jazz-Struck Young Girls." "More than 50 Minneapolis musicians and their friends were snatched by detectives from a jam session at the Harlem Breakfast Club last month and thrown in jail to languish there until the following noon. The charge: the club is a 'thrill' place for jazz-struck girls and their 'reefer smoking' musicians friends!" *Down Beat* noted that several local top black musicians were thrown into jail as well as "many other jobbing white and negro musicians." The Breakfast club was "the last and only place white and colored musicians could get together for 'sessions' . . . and always has been a common meeting place for musicians of all classes and races to express their feelings without interruption from those who neither care for nor understand this type of music." (*Down Beat* 9-1-1940: 1) The fears of the reefer image leading to police harassment of swing musicians and audiences proved to be entirely warranted.

The jazz musician as social deviant, whether romantic or derogatory, remained part of the jazz mystique of romantic outsider regardless of the efforts of some musicians and others. By the early 1940s, police surveillance at jazz clubs led to a drug crisis in jazz. Jazz musicians did use narcotics and its use increased during the 1940s. In addition, many professional musicians did live "asocial" lives in relation to middle class conventional values and life-styles. As Lastrucci, and later sociologists, would point out, jazz musicians spent a large amount of their time in the "deviant" world of late-night popular entertainment, and for many, the life of a popular musician was not conducive to middle class domestic bliss. For some defenders of jazz, of course, this image of the swing musician harkened back to the derogatory moral condemnation of jazz by traditionalists during the Jazz Age.

If hepcat white swing musicians adopted a romantic outsider ethos; the obvious question is whether black swing musicians adopted a similar ethos. While black swing musicians in the 1930s were certainly hep and certainly outsiders, they did not express the same disdain for popular audiences and the popular market. Like their white swing compatriots, of course, black swing musicians participated in a late-night urban entertainment scene that involved "asocial" behavior like drinking and drug use. But no romantic ideal was associated with this life-style among professional black musicians as it was with hepcat white musicians. The problem for black musicians in the 1920s and 1930s was not to escape mainstream white culture. Black musicians were permanent outsiders. Their interest, if any, was to gain respect as musicians and individuals. Nor was their problem the inability to perform jazz. The expectations of white audiences and white producers were that black musicians performed jazz! Regardless of anti-jazz sentiments, even within the black community, jazz and swing were the path for a successful and lucrative career as a professional black musician. Also, as the music historian Scott DeVeaux (1997) points out, while white musicians viewed themselves as "romantic outsiders" against middle class values, top black musicians status within their own community placed them squarely within the middle class. Many of the top black professional musicians were from the middle class in terms of the class structure of their own community. Several of the top black bandleaders as well as musicians had college educations including Fletcher Henderson, Don Redman, Coleman Hawkins, Jimmie Lunceford, and Andy Kirk with Cab Calloway dropping his pursuit of a law degree in order to pursue a career in music. This is not to suggest that black swing musicians did not feel alienated from a society that relegated them to second class citizens and artists. Such alienation, however, had yet to be overtly expressed in their ethos as musicians, except in the case of Duke Ellington who consistently called his music "Negro Music" to distinguish it from white swing musicians and their co-optation of jazz. A new generation of young black bebop musicians, however, would adopt a new "hip" outsider ethos articulating sentiments of their white hepcat contemporaries but expressing a different social alienation than their white swing compatriots.

The art of swing: improvisation and jam sessions

The answer is improvisation – free, inspired improvisation. This is the foremost salient element of swing, whose lure is in the unexpected, the unpremeditated. Independent of printed notes, each variation is an adventure, unique and ephemeral. It is composing as one plays; the gap between conception and realization is welded in the fleeting moment's inspiration... it is a creative process necessarily engendered in a state of highest emotional excitement. (Gama Gilbert, "SWING: WHAT IS IT," *The New York Times*, September 5, 1937: 5)

Gama Gilbert of the *New York Times*, in explaining the music that caused yet another "craze" in American popular music, not surprisingly pointed to improvisation as this music's foremost practice. Gilbert was simply reiterating what many musicians and critics were saying about swing music – they viewed improvisation as its definitive craft. As Louis Armstrong in his autobiography *Swing that Music* in 1936 claimed, the "very soul and spirit of swing is free improvisation." (Armstrong 1936: 73) In addition, while rhythm, tone, and special arranging distinguished swing big bands from sweet big bands, improvisation stood out as a distinct practice since it was both showcased in swing big band performances and rarely practiced by sweet big bands. Besides swing big bands, small swing ensembles, some as smaller units of a big band, showcased improvisation even more, being more direct descendants of the vernacular jazz ensembles of the 1920s. Improvisation, therefore, was an integral part of swing performances whether in a dance hall, hotel, theater, club, or outdoor concert. Commercial swing performances featuring improvisation ranged from solo swing pianists like Fats Waller and Art Tatum, to swing ensembles like the Benny Goodman Quartet and the John Kirby Sextet, to swing big bands when musicians took a chorus and "stretched it out." As Benny Goodman in his 1939 autobiography *Kingdom of Swing* explained, while swing altered jazz "somewhat by the use of bigger bands with more instruments, playing arrangements instead of jamming all the time . . . the most important element is still improvisation, the liberty a soloist has to stand up and play a chorus in the way he feels – sometimes good, sometimes bad, but still an expression of *himself*, rather than somebody else who wrote something for him." (Goodman 1939: 237)

As the different articulations of jazz from hepcat rebels, to swing populism, to the rise of professional black musicians' status as premier swing artists shaped the meaning of jazz during the 1930s, a radical transformation was occurring within the ethos of professional musicians. While swing music represented the general assimilation of the black jazz vernacular into the music practices of professional musicians, this synthesis between cultivated and vernacular traditions in American music found its most profound realization in the adoption of jazz improvisation by a new generation of professional musician. This "illiterate" vernacular practice became the most valued skill among professional swing musicians. The previous "cultivated" ethos that emphasized musical literacy was replaced by a new professional "jazz" ethos in which improvisation became the premier craft of swing musicians and the primary skill defining a swing musician's status. Of course, the tonal and rhythmic elements of legitimate technique emphasized by the old cultivated ethos also were expanded, incorporating the tonal and rhythmic elements of the black jazz vernacular, but it was the use of these different elements in improvisation that determined a swing musician's status. The annual polls of both *Metronome* and *Down Beat* beginning in 1936 attested to the new value given improvisation and the status given its best practitioners. The instrumentalist winners of the polls' swing division were renowned for their improvisational skills – unlike the instrumentalist winners in the sweet division. Goodman revealed the new orientation of swing musicians in his remarks on purely literate musicians who were labeled by swing musicians, often in a less than complimentary way, as "legitimate," "straight," or "regular" musicians. "None of us had much use for what was known then and probably always will be, as 'commercial' musicians. If a fellow happened to be a good legitimate trumpet man or a swell straight clarinet player, he might get credit for being a fine musician who could read a part upside down at sight, but we didn't pay much attention to them." (Goodman 1939: 101)

Many straight musicians, however, still remained suspicious of younger musicians better practiced in improvisation than reading. Max Kaminsky remembered in the 1930s while doing a job at Radio City Hall the "highly uncomplimentary" comments he received "about illiterate and undependable jazz musicians." (Kaminsky 1963: 90) Of course, Kaminsky admitted "it took a little time at first to adjust to playing in the big swing bands. All the years before, we had just played songs as we felt them, but now a whole new era of arranged section playing was starting, and reading the parts and counting the rests was a completely different feeling from the free-swinging improvisation I had been use to." (Kaminsky 1963: 80) The veteran bandleader Hughie Barrett while "relishing the freedom of improvisation as much as the next fellow" warned young musicians against the lure of improvisation and expressed a fear reminiscent of the 1920s that jazz would undermine their playing. "The current swing vogue is having a decided effect on the young musician... He neglects tone practice, scales, technical exercises for a carefree festival of ad lib playing for his own amusement. Within six months he may have mastered a few tricks on his instrument, learned a few melodies. He then considers himself a swing musician. What he does not realize is that to be a good swing instrumentalist one must first build a solid foundation in musicianship in order to be a thorough master of his instrument... Too often, the youngster is fascinated by some colorful character in the annals of jazz who is reputed unable to read music. Let that lad realize that the best swingsters are those who are capable of filling an important seat in any of the highly reputed bands." (*Metronome* 10-1937: 65) Or as a saxophone columnist in *Metronome* explained, swing musicians "must learn to play the instrument properly in all its mechanical and physical aspects before you attempt to add any individual touches of your own. All prominent musicians, 'hot' or legitimate, have to have absolute command of the elementary factors." (*Metronome* 2-1936: 33) Obviously being musically literate and technically proficient was an important and essential skill among professional swing musicians regardless of some musicians who feared a lapse in technique among younger musicians. For swing musicians, however, improvisation clearly had become the more respected skill that defined their status among their fellow swing peers and the tonal and rhythmic qualities of the black vernacular were preferred over the "sweet" sound of old legitimate techniques. And with the swing craze, just like the earlier jazz craze, improvisation once again captured the imagination of young musicians interested in joining the profession of popular musician.

The original incorporation of improvisation into professional arrangements and performances for big bands and ensembles was driven by the wholesale adoption of this practice by professional black musicians. While some black professional musicians during the 1920s distanced themselves from this vernacular practice, improvisation spread rapidly among this professional class of musician, particularly among a younger generation. Duke Ellington, for example, remembered Harlem in the early 1920s when "at nights everybody used to carry their horns round with them and wherever there was a piano you'd find hornblowers sitting in and jamming. There'd be maybe a piano player, and a drummer, and about six different cornet players; everybody trying to outblow everybody else... Nobody went to bed at nights, and round three and four in the mornings you'd find everyone making the rounds bringing their horns with them." (Shapiro and Hentoff 1955: 168) The practice of improvisation also spread through recordings with the introduction of a race market for jazz and blues. Swing trombonist Dicky Wells remembered how for black professional musicians in the 1920s "everybody was trying to play something like Louis Armstrong. His records influenced all jazz musicians, not only trumpet players." (Wells 1991: 37) The swing xylophonist Lionel Hampton also remembered his younger days in the 1920s when he "was listening to jazz records by Louis Armstrong and Coleman Hawkins – I got so that I could take their solos off those records and play them note for note on my xylophone." (Hampton 1989: 23) Count Basie in his 1985 autobiography *Good Morning Blues* provided a description of the improvising jazz culture that developed among black professional musicians in the 1920s. His portrait of the Rhythm Club in Harlem is typical of comments by other black musicians on famous jamming spots across the country. "There was a good house band in there, but the thing about the Rhythm Club was that somebody was always sitting in... So there were always some of them around, and then in the late morning and after midnight, when the other joints were closing, you'd see all cats dropping in there on their way home from work, and most of them would be carrying their instruments too. Sometimes those battles used to last until the middle of the next morning. The Rhythm Club sessions were a good way for a new musician to get himself some quick recognition if you were

somebody with something special. And if you didn't and didn't have any
better sense than to go in there and tangle with them cats, that was the
quickest way to get yourself embarrassed. They didn't have any mercy on
upstarts in there." (Basie 1985: 78)

The value and status accorded improvisation was reflected in how this
practice became an integral part of black professional musicians' artistic
lives. The practice of jamming – groups of musicians improvising outside
regular commercial jobs – represented the extent to which this practice defined these musicians' artistry. As Basie's comments suggest, by the 1920s
black professional musicians constantly jammed among themselves during their off hours competing against one another while honing down this
specialized skill of music making. Certain venues like the Rhythm Club
were well known for their "cutting sessions" where professional musicians dropped by to "sit-in" with the resident band, and by "after-hours"
larger numbers of musicians appeared ready to demonstrate their skills
at improvisation. Of course, aside from the more well known venues for
professional musicians to jam, as Ellington's portrait of Harlem suggests,
jamming occurred in many other commercial venues as well as informal
sessions. In his jazz history and memoir, *Jazz Masters of the Thirties*, the
swing trumpeter Rex Stewart pointed out the continued importance of
improvisation and jamming in the 1930s "when a musician had to prove
himself to other musicians in a cutting session. Whether a fellow hailed
from New Orleans, San Francisco, Chicago, or wherever, he had to come
to the center – New York City – before he could get on the road to (relatively speaking) fame and fortune . . . his skill was tested in competition
with the established ones. If he couldn't cut the mustard, he became
part of the anonymous mob; capable, perhaps, but not of star quality.
However, if the critical, hardblowing jazzmen conceded him recognition,
that acclaim would carry him on to bigger and better jobs. This musical
action on the New York battlefield was the cutting session, and the expression was an appropriate one. When a musician picked up his instrument,
his intention was to outperform the other man. No quarter was given or
expected, and the wound to a musician's ego and reputation could be as
deep as a cut." (Stewart 1982: 143)

New York City was the center for establishing "name" big bands in
the 1930s, so big bands and musicians from across the country arrived in this city to make their reputation. The Count Basie Orchestra
and Andy Kirk's Clouds of Joy, for example, while highly successful regional big bands only established national reputations once visiting and
recording in New York City. While New York City held a special position
in the national circulation of swing music, oral histories and autobiogra-
phies of black professional musicians in the 1920s and 1930s attest to

the widespread adoption of jamming in major cities across the country such as Chicago, Philadelphia, Detroit, St. Louis, Kansas City, and
Los Angeles. They show the jamming culture in the 1930s and 1940s
as a ubiquitous and competitive affair where black musicians developed
their skills in competing against other musicians, established their status
among peers, and played their way into commercial paying jobs. Kansas
City, for example, attained a special reputation in the early 1930s for its
black musicians' improvisational skills and hot jam sessions. The swing
drummer Jo Jones remembered the early 1930s when "some places in
Kansas City never closed. You could be sleeping one morning at six A.M.,
and a traveling band would come into town for a few hours, and they
would wake you up to make a couple of hours' session with them until
eight in the morning." (Shapiro and Hentoff 1955: 284) As black swing
big bands and ensembles performed for the commercial market during
the Swing Era, black musicians across the country continually jammed
to compete for jobs, develop their skills, establish their reputations, and
to simply enjoy the pleasure as well as the competition of improvising
among fellow musicians.

While the core of the jazz culture of jamming remained within the community of black musicians, white musicians gradually adopted the practice of improvisation within their own professional community. Of course,
white musicians in the early years of the jazz craze, mostly unfamiliar with
the jazz vernacular practiced by black musicians, listened to the recordings and performances of the Original Dixieland Jass Band, Ted Lewis,
and other similar white jazz bands. They adopted what Max Kaminsky
referred to as "the little flutings and corny licks that were regarded
as 'hot' in those days." (Kaminsky 1963: 33) Even Benny Goodman
admitted being initially influenced by Ted Lewis recordings until he
heard the jazz performed by black musicians in Chicago. (Goodman
1939) Young hepcat white musicians like Benny Goodman adopted the
black jazz vernacular of improvisation in their initial excursions to black
entertainment districts in the 1920s as well as listening to the recordings of black musicians for the new race market. Goodman remembered how hepcat white musicians picked up the practice of jamming
among themselves in the 1920s. "The room down stairs, where they
jammed, was a dismal, unpainted place, with wooden walls, and no covering on the floor... If the boys were going good, you'd be just as apt
as not to see the other fellows beating the rhythm on the wall with their
hands when somebody took a chorus... I remember one session there
that began about two in the morning and lasted well into the bright
daylight hours, when Ben Pollack sat in on drums, and I played clarinet."
(Goodman 1939: 74)

While sweet music reigned in the early 1930s, the assimilation of improvisation by a new generation of white professional musician seemed to be little hampered by anti-jazz sentiments. By the swing craze jamming and improvisation had spread widely among white musicians. In November 1936, for example, the Chicago column in *Down Beat* revealed the extent to which white professional musicians adopted jamming and improvisation. Local 10 was the white-only local of the AFM in Chicago. "A few nights ago we attended the closing session of Johnnie Parker's band at The Stables and musicians poured in all during the course of the evening and after hours to wish the boys well on their new engagement, and last evening the same kind of a crowd gathered at the Winona Gardens to give Frank Snyder and his boys a send-off. A gala barrel-house affair we staggered into; Paul Mares, Mel Henki... this list would read like the roster of Local 10 should we continue. As we woke up at our corner table they were carrying the last of the boys off the bandstand to conclude what was probably the largest jam of musicians in Chicago records." (*Down Beat* 11-1936: 32) With the success of a new swing market and the rise to stardom of white swing musicians, the community of white musicians had even more incentive to hone down the improvisational practices of the jazz culture. The study mentioned previously by the sociologist Carl Lastrucci (1941) on dance band musicians in San Francisco in the late 1930s provided evidence of the widespread adoption of improvisation and jamming among white musicians from coast to coast. In his study, he noted the ethos of improvisation and the central role of jamming among white musicians. "He even scorns the legitimate musician, for he regards the 'legit man' as merely an instrumental technician whose musicianship is limited to printed notes... Jamming (improvisation) with a small group... of fellow musicians, invariably in a small café after closing hours while the drinks flow freely, provides not only an outlet for his artistic and social frustrations but also permits him to speak fluently in the language he knows best: that of instrumental dexterity and creative improvisation." (Lastrucci 1941: 170)

By the Swing Era, the originally vernacular practice of improvisation became undeniably a defining skill for swing musicians. These musicians engaged in jamming and gauged the status of their peers by their improvisational skills. The new swing market also assured that jamming had very practical implications. In general, however, it must be emphasized that while black and white musicians shared this jazz culture of improvisation, as artists they lived and performed in distinctly separate communities. The jamming culture was one place where black and white musicians could more freely interact as well as in recording studios where integrated small ensembles recorded music highlighting improvisation. The importance of the shared jazz culture is evident in Lionel Hampton's description of how Benny Goodman hired him as a member of his small swing ensemble – the only successful commercial integrated band during the Swing Era. "After the break, he got up on the bandstand with me, pulled his clarinet out of his case, and we started to jam. We jammed all night and into the morning – it must have been six o'clock when he finally said, 'Pleased to meet ya,' and left. . . The next night was even more exciting. I'm up on stage playing as usual, and I hear this clarinet player next to me, and I turn and there is Benny Goodman, playing right next to me. He had brought Gene Krupa and Teddy Wilson along, and the four of us got on the bandstand together, and man, we started wailing." (Hampton 1989: 53)

Both Neil Leonard (1987) and Scott DeVeaux (1997) argue that jamming became a ritualized activity for swing musicians where they performed among themselves outside the demands of commercial performances and dancing audiences. Rex Stewart's earlier comments on cutting sessions in New York City in the 1930s pointed to the ritualized nature of jamming. Artie Shaw also remembered the ritual as well as romanticism of jamming in the 1930s where to "participate, the cats had to cut into their sleep, hours of rest, the time they spent with their families and friends. It was an indulgence practiced after men finished blowing their regular jobs. . . The jam session was a non-commercial, in-group institution. For the starting musician, it provided a chance to be heard, and, on occasion, a challenging and stimulating opportunity to play with the big, established names. The fat cats jammed for the sheer love of playing, for the excitement of communicating with the exuberant audiences of the day, or, compulsively, because nothing seemed to matter as much as blowing." (*Jazz* 4-1965: 8) Jamming was music performed for musicians who had a deep appreciation and critical ear for the art of improvisation. It was a performance space in which musicians could articulate an ethos independent of commercial popular performance conventions. This separate cultural space as ritual became the locus for various transformations in the ethos of professional musicians. The first transformation, of course, was improvisation becoming the defining skill of this professional class of musician. Eventually, however, this autonomous cultural space was where professional musicians developed the ethos of improvisational jazz as a distinct "art" separate from commercial popular music.

The development of an ethos of improvisational jazz as "art" was already evident in the 1930s. The alienation or disdain towards popular audiences and the music industry among some hepcat white swing musicians centered on the practice of improvisation and the perceived lack of appreciation and respect it received. As the earlier comments by the white swing musician Leslie Leiber and the study of white west coast musicians by Carl Lastrucci show, white swing musicians viewed improvisation as an unappreciated "art." With frantic ickies "reaching over and grabbing the trombone when it shot towards them" or risking "an eye by goggling their worshipful heads about two inches from the business end of my waggling clarinet," Benny Goodman could hardly blame his drummer "Gene Krupa's sticks from slipping one night and conking a sycophant." For Goodman, "the bugs form of applauding most everything at the wrong time" might have been "petty matters, I'm sorry to report, began to be a little tough to take and, I repeat, hurt swing." (*Colliers* 2-25-1938: 12) Many white swing musicians perceived improvisation as an under-appreciated art and felt alienated from audiences who lacked the same appreciation they felt about this practice. The white swing musician Dick Rogers in 1941 expressed the romantic view of jamming and the anti-commercial ethos of white hepcat musicians. "Jam sessions are the real stuff. They reflect the true spirit of jazz music... I like to get away from all the 'commercial' inhibitions which jazz music puts on players, and cut loose with some music that's just my own. A lot of other musicians like it too, and that's why we have sessions. Nobody asks us to play. We just do... Many a big-time commercial sideman likes to get away from all the phony music he plays for a living, and get down to earth with genuine jazz." (*Music and Rhythm* 1-1941: 24) By the late 1930s and early 1940s, a special cohort of black musicians in New York City also would articulate this view of improvisation as an underappreciated art, along with the view of black musicians as unappreciated artists. Gathering in late-nightclubs to jam these musicians created the first modern jazz style called bebop.

Conclusion: swing as an American art

Is Swing Dead?

Those who really "feel" swing, those who love it for its own sake even before the fashionable word, "swing," made it acceptable to the public, will never let it die. They cannot conceive of an American Democracy without it. If swing dies, it will die over the dead body of American freedom... A man who improvises with a musical instrument, is using the same liberty exercised by an editorial writer who spouts his own opinions or an architect who throws over past ideas and builds the world a skyscraper. Improvisation is the application of an unhandcuffed-feeling to music. The same conditions that pioneered its birth, will see to its continuation in this country. (Benny Goodman, *Music and Rhythm* August 1941: 10)

Benny Goodman once again pointed to swing as a truly populist music, while pointing to improvisation as swing's most democratic expression.

Once again, the old traditionalist ideal of "good" music that attempted to shape American popular music to its own image fell victim to the attraction of vernacular idioms to American audiences. Of course, professional musicians and composers remained the mediators of the popular music market, but during the Swing Era this mediation involved a far greater integration of the vernacular as a new generation of professional popular musician assimilated the black jazz vernacular. Unlike their elders, professional swing musicians' ethos focused on the elaboration of the rhythms, tones, and improvisational techniques of vernacular music. This new ethos, of course, melded with the earlier skills that defined their profession, but swing music represented a far greater syncretism between the cultivated and vernacular traditions in American music.

The swing culture was an interaction of class, ethnic, and race distinctions centered in urban America – a heterogeneous urban culture articulating an alternative vision of American culture. The new urban hep culture of swing music stood in contrast to the more conventional culture of sweet music. Of course, while class and ethnicity were articulated in American music and the swing-sweet divide, race was the determining distinction as black idioms and artists centrally defined swing music and culture. Black musicians performed exclusively in the jazz/swing market articulating the black jazz vernacular from the "sophisticated" music making of Duke Ellington and Jimmie Lunceford to the "hot" music making of Count Basie and Chick Webb. Their emulation of black big bands and the use of black swing arrangements distinguished white swing big bands like Benny Goodman's and Woody Herman's from sweet big bands. Hepcat white musicians adopted the black vernacular as rebels against a dominant middle class culture. Meanwhile jitterbugs across the country adopted black vernacular dance, dress, and language while swinging to the Lindy Hop developed in the Savoy Ballroom in Harlem. The cultivated jazz vernacular of swing even came to symbolize a New Deal American populism that eventually rose to fight fascist forces threatening to destroy democratic ideals and promulgating an ideology of race superiority. Racism, unfortunately, still pervaded American swing culture. Jim-Crowism continued to position black swing musicians in the margins of the popular music market even as they gained greater status within their profession. White hepcat musicians like Artie Shaw and Benny Goodman who identified with the black vernacular as class and ethnic outsiders were still able to "pass" into mainstream American culture, entering the popular music market and becoming two of the most popular swing musicians of the era.

The Swing Era did not see the same obsessive positioning of jazz as high art done by professional musicians during the previous Jazz Age.

Professional musicians in the 1930s were preoccupied with surviving the depression and regaining a foothold in the popular music market. This is not to suggest that professional swing musicians did not consider swing legitimate music, or that they were unaware of the views of certain "straight" musicians and highbrows towards their music. The agenda of jazz as high art, however, only slowly reasserted itself beginning in the late 1930s, including the requisite invasion of Carnegie Hall. Hepcat white musicians viewed improvisational jazz as an unappreciated art, while a young cohort of hip black musicians just began to develop a new modern jazz ethos. The new transformation of jazz to high art, however, would travel down a distinctly different path both musically and organizationally. Professional musicians as they articulated a new jazz ethos would find themselves serving a niche "jazz" market supported by an emerging art world of critics, producers, and audiences. The mediation of the popular music market by professional musicians gave way by the mid-twentieth century to their serving a new independent jazz art world and establishing jazz as a unique high art tradition in American music.

4 The rise of a jazz art world: jazz enthusiasts, professional musicians, and the modernist revolt

> Have you ever heard the average devotee of classical music talk about jazz? A patronizing attitude of condescension hangs on him like a cigar-butt on the face of a politician. The fire is out and something smells. He speaks of classical music as "good" music and he means that all other music is bad. Jazz is the worst of all... Why the public seems to hear and enjoy jazz more than classical music is a horrible mystery. The majority of people are stupid, ignorant, and all wrong. And so the long-haired devotee throws his scores over his head and takes off with mental bumps of bewildered disapproval. He can't play or understand jazz but he knows it's terrible.
>
> Marshall Stearns, "Bessie Versus Beethoven," *Music and Rhythm* 2-1941: 5

Marshall Stearns in 1941 sounded the all too familiar lament since the Jazz Age about the less than positive attitudes classical "longhairs" held about jazz. Stearns, along with a growing community of jazz enthusiasts in the 1930s, considered jazz a serious American art suffering from various forms of resistance and corruption. These enthusiasts viewed this music as under siege not only from the lack of recognition from classical long-hairs, but also from the demands of the commercial music industry, the ignorance of popular audiences, and worse yet, the capitulation of swing musicians. Jazz enthusiasts were "righteous" aficionados who were avid supporters of what they called genuine or real jazz. Captivated by the hot jazz of the 1920s, these enthusiasts in the 1930s began a collective effort to revitalize and preserve what they viewed as an authentic jazz tradition.

The efforts of jazz enthusiasts, as well as their demand for genuine jazz, led to the beginning of a jazz art world. In this art world, enthusiasts enjoyed what they believed was a unique music genre distinct from commercial popular music whether swing or sweet. They were self-proclaimed "connoisseurs" who believed jazz deserved serious appreciation and patronage. In performances and recordings, enthusiasts patronized jazz whether performed by small ensembles, solo pianists, or the rare commercial big band that for enthusiasts truly incorporated real jazz. Enthusiasts also began writing about jazz. A new jazz criticism emerged that legitimized jazz as a distinct music tradition as well as constructed a social history of this authentic American music. By the 1940s, the jazz art world expanded into a national commercial market for jazz patronized not only by early jazz connoisseurs, but also by an expanding and diverse audience who enjoyed jazz performed in clubs and concert halls across the country as well as jazz recorded by a growing number of independent record labels.

The taste of most of the early jazz connoisseurs, however, was not for the cultivated jazz of professional swing musicians. They preferred the black jazz vernacular popular during the Jazz Age. This new community of connoisseurs reversed the previous relationship between the cultivated and vernacular traditions – they championed vernacular music practices against the cultivated techniques and attitudes of professional musicians that they believed destroyed the vitality and true art of jazz. While swing musicians themselves held a high regard for jazz, they also applied their professional ethos to its further cultivation. Jazz enthusiasts, however, dedicated themselves to a jazz tradition often at odds with the choices and ethos of professional musicians. They were both avid supporters and at times harsh critics of swing musicians, providing important support in criticism and production of jazz music while sometimes aggravating musicians with their rigid views and somewhat haughty attitudes about genuine jazz. Professional musicians were confronting a new community of gatekeepers, ideologues, and audiences in American music. Professional swing musicians were no longer simply battling the forces of sweet music, but a new opponent who championed vernacular jazz against "modern" swing music.

Professional swing musicians, however, performed and recorded for the new jazz art world even as many continued to perform in more commercial swing big bands. These musicians continued to apply their professional ethos to jazz in technique, harmony, and rhythm, regardless of the protests of many jazz enthusiasts. The new jazz art world, unfortunately, quickly became divided between jazz traditionalists and jazz modernists. Jazz traditionalists supported vernacular jazz, while jazz modernists supported the continued cultivation of jazz by professional musicians. This conflict continued to plague the jazz art world into the late 1940s even while a new generation of professional musician made the great leap forward to the radical modernist jazz style called bebop. By the end of the 1940s, modernist professional musicians and their supporters had gained the upper hand against jazz traditionalists setting a course towards a modern jazz renaissance in the 1950s and 1960s.

While swing was enjoying wide popularity as dance music during the Swing Era, jazz music underwent a significant reconfiguration both in

meaning and in practice. Outside the world of popular swing music and
dancing jitterbugs, jazz enthusiasts and professional musicians were transforming jazz as an art form. The one shared value of all enthusiasts and
musicians was their view of jazz as a unique and serious American art: the
lack of consensus was on what constituted real jazz. During this period
of the late 1930s and the 1940s, the various distinctions that accompanied jazz from the initial craze of the 1920s through the swing craze of
the 1930s were to take new and unexpected configurations. This process
of reconfiguration by enthusiasts and musicians was to articulate distinctions of class, race, aesthetics, and conventional values in equally new and
unexpected ways. In the process, what was once celebrated as the popular art of America was transformed into a celebrated marginal music
distinct from commercial popular music. With the foundations of a jazz
art world in place, professional musicians would occupy a new position
in American music.

Hot jazz: jazz enthusiasts and the rise of a jazz art world

Don't Talk About Collectors – I Married One with a Wax Head

All of his thinking is done in terms of jazz music. All of his actions are accompanied by it. It permeates to the innermost reaches of his soul... The collecting
bug once having bitten him, a man is powerless to escape its effects. He collects
every available record in every available spare moment ... he can make the necessary excursions to the darkest parts of the city and countryside, canvass the
basements of second hand stores, and Salvation Army outlets... He goes about
with a haggard, hazy look, a copy of *Downbeat* in one hand, and a record catalog
in the other. (Harriet Hershé, *Music and Rhythm* 11-1940: 33-4)

In one of a number of hot jazz magazines that appeared during the late
1930s, Mrs. Harriet Hershé was lamenting her lot in life being married to
a hot jazz collector. Hot jazz collecting had reached a point by 1940 that
music magazines sported cartoons as well as articles like Mrs. Hershé's
lampooning the fanaticism of this new participant in the world of jazz.
Sharing a cult-like devotion to jazz, most of these collectors viewed hot
jazz as an authentic American art. The most popular hot jazz was the
old 1920s recordings of such black artists as Bessie Smith, King Oliver,
Jelly Roll Morton and Louis Armstrong as well as old 1920s recordings
by early hepcat white musicians like Bix Beiderbecke and Red Nichols.
The new records of professional black orchestras were popular like the orchestras of Lunceford, Henderson, and Ellington. Most collectors, however, preferred the black jazz vernacular as performed before its cultivation by professional musicians. These self-proclaimed "jazz enthusiasts"

in the 1930s and 1940s became the first critics, producers, and consumers of an emerging jazz art world that ran parallel to the popular swing market and its jitterbugging fans. The first vanguard of jazz aficionados in the 1930s and 1940s were part of a growing community of like-minded white jazz enthusiasts across the country. This new community of enthusiasts would attend jazz concerts, jazz nightclubs, and jam sessions, join hot jazz clubs, buy and trade jazz records, and read about jazz in hot jazz sheets as well as in *Down Beat* and *Metronome*.

Collecting hot became popular during the early 1930s among young white male jazz enthusiasts. Their interest in the jazz vernacular, whether performed by black or white artists, meant finding old jazz recordings mostly recorded during the 1920s for the "race" market. The "death" of jazz in the early 1930s also meant that new jazz recordings were rare except for those recorded by black professional orchestras. Collecting hot, therefore, meant generally rummaging for jazz records in remainder bins at furniture shops, junkyards or Salvation Army depots located mostly in black neighborhoods. More committed collectors would roam black neighborhoods door to door, or take autos, buses, and trains to different parts of the country searching for jazz records. Hot collector George Hoefer, for example, remembered the South Side of Chicago as a gold mine for white collectors of jazz records in the early 1930s as this black community struggled to survive the depression. "Cottage Grove Avenue from 35th to 47th streets was one solid mass of junk shops door to door. These shops had victrola records stowed away in every corner... It was depression and south siders were selling their machines crammed full of wax for a few necessary pennies." (*Miller* 1944: 76) Hot collector Dick Reiber roamed the black community of Philadelphia to find hot records. "It happened one morning in the Negro section of Philadelphia... I had the colored kids running at my heels. 'Mr. Record Man,' they said, 'that lady standin' on the steps over there says she wants to see you'... At the end of the street, Beulah led me through a hole in a wooden fence where a board had been torn out. That took us into the alley where she lived... I went from one house to another by invitation. I had the colored kids running at my heels begging 'Mr. Record Man' to come to their house ... when colored people beg you to buy Armstrong's and Bessie's and Jabbo's and Oliver's for a nickel apiece – well, that's some kind of a discophiles's paradise, too." (*H.R.S. Rag* 7-1938: 9–11) While Hoefer pointed to collectors as a group "identical in its lack of race discrimination," the greatest source of hot records during the early 1930s was from African Americans selling their phonographs and records to junk shops or directly to collectors due to the terrible hardships of the depression. Their "passion to hear jazz regardless of circumstances," unfortunately, seemed to circumvent white enthusiasts' acknowledgement of this terrible irony, even as some of them openly condemned racism. (Miller 1944: 71) And their passion for collecting was indeed a single-minded mission. Hot collector William Russell while "touring the country" had "penetrated into every obscure corner of the land where hot records could possibly be found." (*H.R.S. Rag* 8-40: 4) As Jerry Wexler remembered, "we were record hunters, fierce and indefatigable. To discover, in the back of some basement in Far Rockaway, a carton of unopened, still-in-original-wrapper sets of black swans – a label owned by W. C. Handy and responsible for Ethel Water's first recordings – was an experience second only to orgasm." (Wexler 1993: 35)

Collectors in the 1930s prided themselves on their arcane knowledge of jazz recordings. This knowledge encompassed knowing the various jazz labels and their recording artists, the personnel for specific recordings, the serial numbers of records, and even "covert variations of initial recordings" and "recordings different in content but identical both in title and serial number." (Miller 1944: 25) As a hot collector from San Francisco remarked in 1938, "I've been listening to records for four solid years and know the catalogs backwards and forwards and the good points in all the discs released." (*H.R.S. Rag* 7-1938: 13) With their obsession for detail, some collectors would question jazz musicians about old recordings dates and their entire personnel as well as other arcane information. Many collectors cataloged their records and arcane data in notebooks while building vast collections of records neatly organized where a jazz recording could be easily found "on shelf L album 75 waxing 7." (Miller 1944: 70) Most collectors also were avid enthusiasts for particular styles or jazz musicians. Hot collector Stephen W. Smith, for example, differentiated Princeton and Yale enthusiasts by the former's preference for black vernacular jazz ensembles and blues singers and the latter's preference for cultivated black jazz orchestras. (Ramsey and Smith 1939) Their obsession with detail and style also made hot collectors extremely partisan in their views about hot jazz. Jazz enthusiast Paul Eduard Miller complained of the extreme partisan tastes of collectors in 1941. "With a fanaticism reminiscent of the frenzied pulpit-pounder, hot jazz fans have cultivated a strictly esoteric approach to the subject of hot music." (*Music and Rhythm* 2-1941: 70) George Hoefer in "Collectors: Personalities and Anecdotes" euphemistically described the hot collector as "not necessarily eccentric, but he is most certainly colorful." (Miller 1944: 72)

With their fever for hot collecting, hot collectors gradually developed a trading and selling network both at the local and national level. This network included hot record shops and dealers, record catalogs, hot jazz magazines, hot jazz organizations, and eventually hot jazz record labels. American hot collectors also communicated with European hot collectors. Several well-known jazz enthusiasts living in the United States also were foreign born. The first hot collector magazine *Jazz Hot: Revue Internationale de la Musique de Jazz* of the Hot Club de France began publication in 1935 in both French and English. *Jazz Hot* included contributions by American enthusiasts John Hammond, George Frazier, Stanley Dance and Canadian enthusiast Helen Oakley, who was the lone woman among the vanguard. The American publication of French hot collector Charles Delaunay's *Hot Discography* in 1936 was enthusiastically received by collectors and was quickly followed by a new revised edition in 1938. Jazz enthusiasts in America also published their own catalogs such as the *Hot Record Exchange*, while hot collector William Love in Nashville edited *Who's Who of Jazz Collecting* to aid collectors along. Enthusiasts published hot jazz magazines specifically for collectors: *H.R.S Rag* (1938), *Jazz Information* (1939), *The Record Changer* (1942), *Jazz* (1942), *The Jazz Quarterly* (1942), *The Jazz Record* (1943), *The Needle: Record Collector's Guide* (1944), *The Jazz Session* (1944), *American Jazz Review* (1944), *Index to Jazz* (1945), and *Jazzfinder* (1948). These American magazines, except for the *Record Changer*, were short-lived ventures often published at irregular intervals. Jazz enthusiasts Bob Thiele and Dan Priest published *Jazz* magazine from 1939 to 1943. "Around 1939, we decided to publish a magazine ... having secured an ancient linotype machine. The first issue was really interesting as we were just two teenage jazz fanatics who, in the zealous belief that nothing was impossible, somehow obtained enough articles and pictures to fill up a magazine, and persuaded the finest writers and photographers in the business to contribute their efforts. They weren't interested in money (not that we had any to pay them) as much as they wanted their work published in some fashion." (Thiele 1995: 16) These small magazines reflected the views of their jazz collecting publishers and the community of jazz enthusiasts in general. *Jazz Information* announced in its first issue that it was "devoted exclusively to the weekly coverage of the latest news and records in the hot jazz field... Jazz Information depends entirely on what support it receives from those whose interest in jazz goes beyond Tin Pan Alley and the sensationalism of the swing fad." (*Jazz Information* 9-8-1939: 1) Collectors and specialty shops also occasionally placed classified ads in both *Down Beat* and *Metronome*. George Hoefer in 1940 also started a hot record collectors' column "The Hot Box" in *Down Beat*. The central role of record collecting in an emerging jazz art world was evident when the editors of *Down Beat* in 1940 acclaimed Delaunay's *Hot Discography* as "the greatest jazz work ever published." (*Down Beat* 11-1940: 5)

At the local level, jazz enthusiasts congregated at hot record specialty shops such as the Hot Record Shop and Record Rendezvous in New York City, Session Record Shop and Grove Record Shop in Chicago, Jazz Man Record Shop in Hollywood, and Pop's Record Shop in Dearborn, Michigan. The hot magazine *H.R.S. Rag* in 1940 listed twenty-five record shops where hot records could be bought in New York City, Boston, Worcester, Cambridge, Providence, New Haven, Philadelphia, Baltimore, Washington DC, Nashville, Columbus, Cleveland, Chicago, Minneapolis, Denver, Berkeley, San Francisco, and Hollywood. Some of the specialty shops also published jazz catalogs and hot record rags. The owners of these shops produced some of the first jazz labels as well as making up a national network of shop owners for new jazz labels to sell their records. The most famous and influential hot record shop was the Commodore Music Shop run by hot collector Milt Gabler located at East 42nd Street in New York City. Gabler's shop published *Jazz Information* as well as a reissue of *Hot Discography* in 1940. Like most jazz shops, the Commodore Shop was not a huge money making machine. Jazz enthusiasts were in it for other reasons. As Gabler remembered, the "major thing was you met people there that loved music and jazz in particular, and you could always find someone you could talk to about your hobby, including my salesmen, myself, my brothers or brothers-in-law. It became a hangout for the critics, artists, record collectors. We struggled... I was satisfied with it being the most important jazz store." (Fox 1986: 75)

Their passion for jazz eventually led jazz enthusiasts into other activities besides collecting, selling, and trading old jazz recordings and publishing small magazines and catalogs. For jazz enthusiasts, "righteous" jazz had become the poor stepchild in American music left behind after the crash by the commercialism of the music industry and unappreciative American consumers. Their passion led to adopting a missionary zeal in resurrecting righteous jazz in America. Inspired by hot jazz clubs in Europe, jazz enthusiasts in the United States established similar clubs or societies in several cities as well as college campuses to promote hot jazz. The United Hot Clubs of America was organized in 1935 by enthusiasts Milt Gabler, John Hammond and Marshall Stearns as a national network for hot jazz clubs including at the time New York City, Yale University, Chicago, Cleveland, Boston, and Los Angeles. To join a local club one paid a membership fee of two dollars, while local clubs paid five dollars to be part of UHCA. (*Jazz Hot* 9/10,11/12-1935) UHCA was affiliated with the International Federation of Hot Clubs that included organizations in France, England, Germany, Italy, Poland, Denmark, Spain, and Belgium. Marshall Stearns envisioned a worldwide jazz movement centered on activities in the United States and expressed the missionary zeal of jazz enthusiasts. "At last the numerous organizations of the western hemisphere, composed of truly appreciative hot-fans, will have the opportunity to unite and make their convictions felt as one all-powerful man. Such an organization will have tremendous power, and justly so, for there is much to be done. With the launching of the United Hot Clubs of America, a great and rapidly growing organization composed of musicians as well as the increasingly numerous swing fans ... the logical center of world-wide activity has been found. From America, where the first strains of jazz originated, comes a new and vital interest in the phenomenon of jazz." (*Jazz Hot* 9/10-1935: 1) Other hot jazz clubs or jazz societies were formed in the late 1930s and early 1940s in Trenton, Philadelphia, Detroit, San Francisco, and a number of college campuses. Besides providing a network for hot collectors, hot clubs organized jam sessions, concerts, and produced hot jazz records. Most activities in the early jazz art world, however, were done on the individual initiative of jazz enthusiasts outside "official" association with a hot club. Jazz enthusiasts would organize their own jam sessions and concerts, and produce their own records. Whether the efforts of a hot club or the efforts of individual jazz enthusiasts, these activities were guided by the same general mission: to support the appreciation of righteous jazz.

A major activity of hot clubs and jazz enthusiasts was organizing jam sessions. Jam sessions were popular among jazz enthusiasts because they viewed them as the most authentic expression of hot jazz since they centered on improvisation. These sessions occurred in recording studios, hotels, clubs, inns, restaurants, and even enthusiasts' homes. Usually weekend afternoon affairs musicians were invited to perform in improvisational jam sessions for a nominal union scale fee. The first and most successful of the hot club jam sessions was initiated by Milt Gabler in New York City starting at the Master Recording Studios in 1935 and moving in 1937 to the nightclub Famous Door and later to the nightclub Jimmy Ryan's. "Squirrel" Ashcroft of the Chicago Rhythm Club ran jam sessions in his own home. The San Francisco Hot Jazz Society started jam sessions in 1939. At its second jam session "nearly four hundred hot music fans packed El Jardin Restaurant" where "more than twenty musicians took the stand during a six hour session." (*Jazz Information* 2-2-1940: 1) This society later held regular sessions at the Dawn Club, while jam sessions were also regularly held at the Big Bear Tavern across the bay in Oakland. The hepcat musician Eddie Condon, beginning in the late 1930s, ran a popular jam session at Nick's in New York City, while hot collector Teddy Reig organized a regular jam session at Kelly's Stables beginning in 1941. Jam sessions were also held during the 1930s at the Café Society in New York City. Meanwhile, jazz enthusiasts organized jam sessions at the Green Haven Inn in Mamaroneck in upscale Westchester County, New York. Thai hot collector Harry Lim, in the late 1930s, financed jam sessions at the folk music club Village Vanguard in New York City then moved to Chicago in 1940 and organized jam sessions at the Sherman Hotel. The disc jockey and swing enthusiast Al Jarvis organized jam sessions in Los Angeles in the late 1930s. The attraction of jam sessions for jazz enthusiasts led to constant efforts on their part to organize sessions during the 1930s and early 1940s.

Hot clubs and jazz enthusiasts also organized jazz concerts and smaller recitals. Concerts and recitals presented a variety of programs, but generally followed two basic forms. One concert form featured swing big bands as their main attraction while presenting smaller jazz ensembles and jam sessions to introduce audiences to righteous jazz. The Chicago Rhythm Club organized "Rhythm Concerts" starting in 1935 in the Congress Hotel featuring a name swing big band followed by a jam session. The second Rhythm Concert featured the Fletcher Henderson Orchestra with members of the Benny Goodman Orchestra joining in for a jam session. In 1937, *Down Beat* editors Glenn Burrs and Carl Cons also organized two swing concerts at the Congress Hotel Casino. The second concert featured, "to the delight of the 800 folks who jammed the Congress Hotel," the Jimmy Dorsey big band with small ensemble work by members of the big band and a quartet led by black trumpeter Roy Eldridge. (*Down Beat* 1-1938: 2) The big event of 1938 was a Benny Goodman concert in Carnegie Hall. Besides the performance of the Goodman big band, the concert featured the Goodman Quartet with Teddy Wilson, Lionel Hampton and Gene Krupa, and a final jam session with members of the Count Basie Orchestra. Even larger swing concerts were organized using popular swing big bands to attract "average" fans and introducing them to less well-known jazz musicians. The jazz enthusiast and jazz club owner Joe Helbock organized a swing concert in New York City in 1936. "The Big Town got its first official Swing Concert, and healthy portion of 'ride' and 'sock' music with a lot of 'jive' and 'truckin'' thrown in for good measure, as the city's leading jam-men paraded across the stage of the Imperial Theater in a 3 hour session. From nine o'clock till past midnight 17 bands laid-in-the-grove as one after the other in rapid succession improvised to the delight of the packed auditorium." (*Down Beat* 6-1936: 1) In 1938, the popular disc jockey Martin Block organized *The Carnival of Swing*, an outdoor concert of twenty-five bands on Randalls Island Stadium in New York City.

The other form of concert or recital programming was designed to be a more programmatic presentation of jazz. By the end of the 1930s, programmatic concerts became the common jazz concert format. These concerts often had printed programs that elucidated the significance of the event to audiences and sometimes included brief lectures. The jazz enthusiast John Hammond, for example, organized two jazz concerts "From Spirituals to Swing" in Carnegie Hall in New York City in 1938 and 1939. These concerts were designed to show "Negro music from its raw beginnings to the latest jazz ... all the music of the blacks in which jazz is rooted." (Hammond 1977: 199) Both concerts were accompanied with program notes and brief lectures between performances. The initial meeting of the Metropolitan Hot Club in New York City in 1940 featured a lecture by Ralph Berton entitled "Blues: Their Origin and Development" as well as performances by black artists Sam Price, Leadbelly, Meade Lux Lewis, and white hepcat pianist Art Hodes. (*H.R.S. Rag* 11-1940: 18) In 1943, the jazz enthusiast Rudi Blesh was invited to the San Francisco Museum of Art to present a series of lectures on jazz and invited the New Orleans trumpeter Bunk Johnson to perform. The jazz critics Barry Ulanov and Leonard Feather organized several "New Jazz" concerts in New York City in 1944 and 1945 in conjunction with their formation of The New Jazz Foundation. Leonard Feather noted the "intelligent notes in the leaflet and lucid announcements on the stage." (*Metronome* 1-1945: 9) The most successful of these early programmatic jazz concerts were organized by hepcat musician and jazz enthusiast Eddie Condon running from 1942 until 1946 in Town Hall and Carnegie Hall in New York City. The first concert in Carnegie Hall featured Fats Waller with a small ensemble and program notes by John Hammond. The second concert at Town Hall in 1942 established a more jam session format for these concerts. Condon's skills as jazz promoter eventually led to sold out audiences and coverage of this new phenomenon in the national media. *Newsweek* covered a Town Hall concert in 1944 in "Eddie Condon's Le Jazz Intellectual." "After nearly two years of missionary work Eddie Condon's Jazz Concerts had at last drawn a full house of converts. Last minute box-office sales had so clogged up the lobby that regular ticket-holders had to come in from the street... For the men who made these concerts possible, the afternoon's sellout was proof of their theory that 'it is about time that lovers of hot music have a chance to listen in comfortable seats, without getting sinus trouble, and free from the compulsion to get woozy with cut whiskey at speakeasy prices...'" (*Newsweek* 1-24-1944: 62)

Jazz concerts not only presented jazz as a serious art form, but when located in concert halls usually reserved for European cultivated music also represented for jazz enthusiasts and musicians the new legitimate status of this music. Beginning with Benny Goodman's swing concert at Carnegie Hall in 1938, the jazz press always celebrated swing musicians' entrance into concert halls usually reserved for classical performance. *Metronome* announced the Goodman concert in "Benny Goodman Crashes Sedate Carnegie Hall." "The King shall swing amid the ancient rafters of New York's Carnegie Hall this coming January 16th! Benjamin Goodman, virtuoso of the clarinet, and his veritable virile vipers are scheduled for a one-night stand . . . the Goodman swing concert will be the first ever to infest the atrabilious atmosphere of the staid, old hall." (*Metronome* 1-1938: 13) Following Goodman, professional musicians began to have regular concerts at Carnegie Hall to the delight of jazz critics. Paul Eduard Miller noted the new development in "The Deceased of Carnegie Hall Turn Over in Their Graves As Jazz Lifts the Roof." "If the Benny Goodman concert at Carnegie Hall caused the deceased members of its past Board of Directors to turn in their graves, they must have been spinning like whirling tops during November. . . On Nov. 21 W. C. Handy was feted beneath Carnegie's rafters on his 65th birthday, saluted by a galaxy of swingsters including Cab Calloway, Teddy Wilson, Jimmy Lunceford, Lionel Hampton, Maxine Sullivan and many more. . . With other jazzists slated to entrench themselves within Carnegie Hall during the next few weeks . . . wags are predicting that the N.Y. Philharmonic Orchestra may soon be billed as a novelty band." (*Down Beat* 12-1938: 3)

While hot clubs and jazz enthusiasts organized their own jam sessions, concerts, and recitals, jazz enthusiasts also went to commercial nightclubs that featured small jazz ensembles. Early jazz enthusiasts during the 1930s frequented certain jazz clubs that gained reputations among the jazz cognoscenti. New York City had the largest number of special jazz clubs including the Onyx, Café Society, Kelly's Stables, Famous Door, Nick's, and Jimmy Ryan's. Chicago's Three Deuces and Paul Mares Barbecue were special clubs for jazz enthusiasts during the 1930s, while in Los Angeles jazz enthusiast Billy Berg ran the Trouville and Waldorf clubs until opening the famous Billy Berg's in 1941. These clubs were located in white entertainment districts, and except for the Café Society, into the early 1940s were white-only establishments where white and black jazz artists performed to white jazz enthusiasts. The most active districts in the 1930s were 52nd Street and Greenwich Village in New York City. Hot collector Bob Thiele remembered the jazz scene in Greenwich Village in the late 1930s. "The Village was phenomenal as a center of around-the-clock activity . . . with so much classic jazz as well as many other kinds of great music available at the numerous clubs you could walk into just about any time of the day and night. It had the best possible introduction to jazz in Greenwich Village when it seemed that those few square miles were the true epicenter of musical energy in the world." (Thiele 1995: 12–13) The more ambitious jazz enthusiasts also would visit clubs in the black entertainment districts of Harlem in New York City, the South Side in Chicago, Central Avenue in Los Angeles, and "Little Harlem" in San Fransicso.

Hot clubs and jazz enthusiasts also were involved in producing reissues of old jazz recordings as well as producing new recordings. In the early 1930s, jazz enthusiast John Hammond produced hot jazz recordings for English Columbia for the European market. The UHCA under Milt Gabler formed the Hot Record Society in 1937 with an advisory board of eighteen hot collectors that produced the first reissues of old jazz recordings for the new jazz art world. "The aim of the Hot Record Society is to choose rare and out-of-print records that are already known to connoisseurs by hearsay or so good as to recommend themselves." (*Jazz Hot* 5/6-1937: 12) Most old jazz recordings were owned by the major record companies, so jazz enthusiasts like Milt Gabler leased the masters in order to produce reissues. As *Time* magazine pointed out in "Hot Society," jazz, "blowiest of the arts, has been disgracefully lax about keeping her barrelhouse in order. The master recordings of hundreds of notable numbers, played by inspired but informal groups of musicians in obscure studios, have been lost or destroyed . . . commercial record companies are chiefly interested in making and selling new records, and the hot clubs are composed of amateurs uninterested in administrative detail. Wide open, therefore, was the place which a brand new Hot Record Society undertook last week to fill." (*Time* 5-1937: 50) As a hot jazz enthusiast from San Francisco put it, the "subscribers in this club want a 'wow' disc that will send 'em and one that can be played over and over for want of hearing the old jazz pour out." (*H.R.S. Rag* 7-1938: 13) Irving Mills recognized the new fad for hot jazz and recorded some of his contracted black artists in small ensembles on the Master and Variety labels in 1937 – the latter labels recordings were supervised by jazz enthusiast Helen Oakley. Jazz enthusiasts in the late 1930s also started a number of labels like Commodore, General, Jazzman, Signature, Blue Note, and Solo Art producing new recordings of hot jazz. Bob Thiele remembered at age seventeen starting the Signature label in 1938 which made new recordings of jazz musicians. "I began to hear so many musicians who weren't being recorded, and me on my white horse was determined to document their stuff. It was sort of perseverance and aberrant dedication to collect and make records. . . I was always impressed and envious there were small labels around that made jazz records. They probably weren't selling too many of them, but at least they were recording jazz. . . I would then hit the record stores in Manhattan on Broadway and on Madison Avenue and actually sell the shellacs out of the back of my father's car directly to the dealers. Advertising was a couple of small ads in music magazines, and I would have one or two record store owners in each of the major cities. At that time, those dealers would buy perhaps two copies of almost every record that came out, especially for their collector customers." (Thiele 1995: 25–6) These initial efforts, as Thiele suggested, involved mostly limited pressings and short-lived enterprises, only Blue Note remained a major independent jazz label. The difficulties of producing records, particularly with the advent of World War II, delayed the growth of jazz labels until the post-war period.

In their missionary zeal, jazz enthusiasts took every advantage of spreading the appreciation of jazz. In the late 1930s, enthusiasts took to the airwaves to reach a broader audience. Most efforts by enthusiasts were through local public radio stations or late hours on small commercial stations. In New York City, WNYC was a municipal station used by jazz enthusiasts. Jazz enthusiast Ralph Berton, and later enthusiast Ralph Gleason, ran a regular series "Metropolitan Reviewer" in the late 1930s and early 1940s on WNYC. In a *Jazz Information* interview, Gleason expressed his satisfaction with "increasing the audience for hot jazz by convincing previously allergic people that the music is not something alien to good taste." (*Jazz Information* 8-9-1940: 13) The Philadelphia Hot Club began two weekly shows on WHAT in 1939. George Hoefer in 1940 had a jazz program "Jazz in Review" in Chicago using a question and answer format illustrated with recordings. Hoefer's program was designed "with the fundamental psychology that a large number of people are prospective Jazz enthusiasts" and was intended "to educate those people." (*H.R.S. Rag* 1-1941: 20)

Jazz enthusiasts, however, were aware that live, recorded, or broadcast music sometimes accompanied by brief commentary was insufficient to elevate jazz from its low status and terrible neglect. The small collectors' magazines also only reached the already converted. Jazz enthusiasts, therefore, reached beyond the core of their community as jazz critics preaching the gospel of righteous jazz. One significant audience for jazz enthusiasts turned jazz critics was professional musicians who read *Down Beat* and *Metronome*. Their large circulation and position as the top professional musicians' magazines placed them center stage in an emerging jazz art world. *Down Beat* jazz critics included George Avakian, Charles Delaunay, Dave Dexter, Reed Dickerson, George Frazier, Leonard Feather, Marvin Freedman, Ted Hallock, George Hoefer, John Hammond, Mike Levin, Ted Locke, John Lucas, Paul Eduard Miller, Helen Oakley, Hughes Panassié, Charles Edward Smith, Frank Stacy, Marshall Stearns, Dan Swinton, Ted Toll, and Bob White. *Metronome* also had extensive jazz criticism, but most was written in-house by George Simon, Barry Ulanov, and Leonard Feather. Jazz criticism appeared in a number of ways addressing a variety of topics. Jazz critics provided a regular commentary on the new jazz art world in their regular reviews of records, concerts, clubs, and jam sessions. Most articles in these two magazines, however, were on professional musicians with occasional articles by jazz critics on older jazz musicians and jazz styles enjoyed by hot jazz record collectors. Marshall Stearns series "History of Swing" in *Down Beat*, which ran from August 1936 to April 1938, was a rare exception in attempting a detailed history of jazz. This series presented the basic history of jazz as constructed by early jazz critics linking swing with a jazz lineage beginning in New Orleans, spreading to Chicago, and then to New York where Harlem jazz would become the model for both black and white big band swing. While jazz enthusiasts read both magazines, the greater importance of these magazines was in the communication between critics and musicians.

Metronome, *Down Beat* and small collectors' magazines, of course, were for a select readership of musicians and jazz enthusiasts. Jazz critics also reached out to a broader public through articles and record reviews in other publications. *Harper's*, *Esquire*, and the *New Republic* featured jazz articles, while *Town and Country*, *Mademoiselle*, and *American Music Lover* featured mostly record reviews. Progressive jazz critics also wrote for the radical journals *New Masses* and *The Daily Worker*. Jazz critics also published jazz books for the general public as well as for jazz enthusiasts. Hughes Panassié's *Jazz Hot* was published in English translation in 1936. "In it the entire subject is studied thoroughly in every phrase, making it invaluable to professional musicians and amateur swing fans alike... The appendix of hot records, old and new, foreign and domestic, is sixty pages long." (*Metronome* 9-1936: 55) American jazz critic Wilder Hobson's *American Jazz Music* and an anthology of articles by early jazz critics, *Jazzmen*, were both published in 1939. Several American jazz critics edited *The Jazz Record Book* for hot collectors in 1942. "Here, at last, is the all-inclusive, all-informative guide to swing music, or hot jazz. Now you can follow jazz and its players from the beginning in New Orleans to the big-name bands of today... A complete up-to-date listing of all the important jazz records is a valuable feature of this greatly needed book." (*Music and Rhythm* 4-1942: 41) Panassié's second jazz book *The Real Jazz* was published in English translation in 1942. The Belgian jazz critic Robert Goffin's *Jazz: From the Congo to the Metropolitan* was published in English translation in 1944. When major record companies began producing jazz boxed-sets in the early 1940s, jazz critics were selected to write introductions and short descriptions of each recording discussing the music and musicians. Certain jazz enthusiasts also became important "sources" for music critics and journalists writing about jazz and swing in newspapers and magazines. The most influential sources were enthusiasts John Hammond and Eddie Condon. This jazz criticism was intended to expand the community of jazz enthusiasts as well as combat those unconvinced that jazz was an art form worthy of appreciation.

Jazz enthusiasts were intent on building an audience for hot jazz music and jazz musicians through jam sessions, concerts, clubs, recordings, radio, and criticism. While the dreams of jazz enthusiasts in building a large hot jazz movement did not materialize as they had hoped, they did lay the initial foundations of a jazz art world. More importantly, this vanguard of jazz enthusiasts was instrumental in establishing the beginnings of a new jazz market. This new jazz market, of course, also was helped by the popular swing craze that paralleled the efforts of jazz enthusiasts and brought audiences to swing concerts and jazz clubs. The new commercial jazz market by the early 1940s involved enthusiasts personally committed to the jazz art world as well as individuals seeing the opportunity to cash in on the new market. As DeVeaux (1997) points out, even the specialized world of jam sessions by the late 1930s was picked up by commercial clubs and bars as an attraction for paying customers. In 1945, *Ebony* magazine noted the commercial market for jam sessions. "[T]o the confirmed jazz addict. Mecca is any smoke-filled, crowded, hole-in-the wall nightspot where tired musicians gather to shoot the 'jive' and join in a jam session. Time was when these jam sessions were small exclusive gatherings in a Harlem basement over some needled bear. Today the jam session has become public property. . . The old-time musicians bemoan the popularity of the jam session today, long for the day when a couple of the boys could relax in anonymity. But those days are gone forever because the dividends of a jam session today are too lofty to skip." (*Ebony* 11-1945: 6) Besides jam sessions, the jazz club scene continued to grow in the 1940s. *The New Grove Dictionary of Jazz* (1988) lists approximately 120 clubs in the United States in the 1940s that had small jazz ensembles or jazz pianists. As the jazz club scene grew in the 1940s, Los Angeles joined New York and Chicago as a major center for jazz clubs. Other jazz clubs appeared in cities around the country with Boston, Detroit, Philadelphia, San Francisco, and St. Louis having a number of jazz clubs. The major districts sporting jazz clubs became popular entertainment districts attracting a diversity of audiences, although mostly segregated audiences as most of the top special jazz clubs were white-only establishments up to the early 1940s. By the middle 1940s musicians were moving regularly between major cities to perform in a new jazz club circuit. (Chilton 1972)

By the end of World War II, booking agents and promoters saw the potential in the national jazz market. Willard Alexander, an agent in the large MCA agency, announced in 1945 that this agency was ready to manage artists for the new jazz market. Alexander eventually formed his own special agency for jazz artists. Smaller agencies also managed artists for the new market, the two most important agencies were run by Joe Glazer and Moe Gale with Billy Shaw, formerly of William Morris and the Gale Agency, forming his own agency by the end of the 1940s. The most successful promoter of jazz for the new market was Norman Granz. Granz began his successful career as a jazz promoter with the concert series "Jazz at the Philharmonic" that premiered in 1944 at the Philharmonic Auditorium in Los Angeles. Granz eventually established a touring concert group of jazz musicians under this banner. "Jazz at the Philharmonic" toured numerous cities in the United States and Canada during the 1940s. In 1949, this program appeared in twenty-nine cities across the United States and Canada. (*Down Beat* 10-7-1949: 7) By the 1950s this concert program also toured Europe, Japan, and Australia. Granz also produced other jazz concerts in the late 1940s and began recording his artists for the jazz record market. In 1949, Granz released a limited edition box set of jazz recordings, "The Jazz Scene," especially for jazz connoisseurs at the unprecedented price of $25. Jazz enthusiast Michael Levin celebrated this new achievement in the jazz art world while inadvertently revealing Granz's savvy commercial instincts when it came to jazz enthusiasts. "*The Jazz Scene*, probably the most remarkable record album ever issued, even to its price ($25), is now out, the slightly delayed love child of *JATP* promoter Norman Granz... The six 12-inch vinylite records are packaged in a fashion that will really pop your eyes... Is it worth the $25? I think so. I'd pay it myself. With only 5,000 copies, it will certainly be a collector's item very shortly." (*Down Beat* 1-13-1950: 14)

With "The Jazz Scene" Granz was tapping into the growing market for recorded jazz served mostly by small independent labels. In 1945, *Metronome* listed over forty independent labels recording jazz for the new market. Joining older labels like Commodore, Signature, and Blue Note, were newer labels like Apollo, Comet, Continental, Guild, Jump, Keynote, Manor, Musicraft, Savoy, and Sunset. As Leonard Feather noted, while the jazz record market was "limited to a five or six figure audience of fans, the fact that they could record most of these musicians cheaply" – musicians were paid a flat scale – "and that the discs could be sold for 75c or a dollar, instead of the usual 35c or 50c, brought a swarm of new companies into the recording field. Most of them wanted to cut jazz discs featuring small bands, trios, quartets and sextets specially assembled for the occasion, with never a color line." (Miller 1945: 23) George Hoefer in 1947 noted the growth in jazz recordings since "the momentum in jazz interest has been surprisingly strong since the war ended" with the "indies carrying the ball." "Many of the small independent labels are making a living from jazz records. They specialize and seem to have the know-how to record better jazz than the majors are currently waxing." Major record companies were recording jazz box sets for the new market mostly of reissues but also including new recordings. But the independent labels were the backbone of the new market. (*Down Beat* 3-26-1947: 13) In the listing of new jazz recordings in *Esquire's Jazz Book 1946*, of the eighty-seven recordings of small jazz units seventy-six were produced by small independents while another twelve were produced by the newly formed Capitol Records with its jazz recording under the stewardship of jazz enthusiast Dave Dexter. (Miller 1946)

Whether concerts, clubs, or recordings, the new jazz market expanded in the 1940s into a national commercial market. This market, however, remained quite unstable. Clubs disappeared as quickly as they appeared. During the 1940s, 52nd Street was repeatedly designated "dead" by *Metronome* and *Down Beat* only to be resurrected with the opening of new jazz clubs – although by the end of the decade this famous Swing Street finally succumbed to the unstable jazz market. Labels always faced difficult times. As jazz enthusiast Bill Gottlieb informed *Down Beat* readers, independent labels in general had a difficult time without the advantages of the majors. "Meantime, the 300 independents you're always reading about have had rough sledding... Musiccraft, despite a fine roster of talent, has been wobbling, Keynote, Signature, Four Star, and a dozen others have been forced to refinance... But most of the owners do something else for a living, too, or operate on a low level with the boss man also being recording director, publicity manager and wrapper. Only a handful of indies . . . have their heads above water..." (*Down Beat* 5-7-1947: 1) The instability of the jazz market would continue even as the audience for recorded and live jazz continued to grow into the 1950s.

While the jazz art world and jazz market grew from the late 1930s into the 1940s, enthusiasts were looking for more than just audiences for jazz. They were looking to elevate this music as an art form deserving of "serious" appreciation. Replicating in many ways the classical "enthusiasts" a century earlier who through societies, concerts, recitals, journals, and books attempted to elevate the cultivated tradition as a distinct world of music performance and appreciation, jazz enthusiasts shared a similar vision for jazz. This resonance with an earlier movement to establish an American art world in music certainly should not be surprising when it's revealed that early jazz enthusiasts were predominately white, middle and upper class, and college educated. Unfortunately, this new class of jazz enthusiast felt embattled against commercialism, ignorant audiences, over-cultivated professional musicians, all of which hindered the true appreciation of righteous jazz and its artists.

The righteous elite: jazz connoisseurs, longhairs, and jitterbugs

The status of *hot* today is quite different from that of its early days, i.e., little more than a decade ago. Today a check-up reveals collectors of *hot* in almost every college and preparatory school in the country. The substantial following enjoyed by Louis Armstrong is due largely to jazz enthusiasts at prominent universities – Yale, Princeton, etc. – who began collecting his records five or six years ago. That the popularity of *hot* jazz is not even more widespread may be attributed to the lack of any literature treating *hot* as a special field, and also to the deadening effect of the shallow emotionalism of sweet (popular) jazz upon the public ear. (Charles Edward Smith, *Esquire*, February 1934: 96)

As jazz enthusiasts worked to build a hot jazz movement, they were looking to create jazz connoisseurs who could appreciate jazz as a serious American art form. This righteous elite of a rising jazz art world were mostly white, male, college educated, and middle to upper class enthusiasts, many who pursued the sacred mission of jazz appreciation and jazz criticism. It also included some white, male, and working class enthusiasts who mostly pursued the more practical mission of producing jazz. Of course, the enthusiasts who fashioned themselves as jazz critics and jazz producers all viewed themselves as premier jazz connoisseurs. Early jazz enthusiasts were looking for jazz connoisseurs whose impeccable and unquestionable taste could distinguish genuine jazz from commercialized derivatives as well as help elevate genuine jazz from its lowbrow status. They lectured audiences at jazz concerts, recitals, and art museums. They wrote for *Harper's Magazine*, *The New Republic*, *Esquire*, *Town and Country*, and *Mademoiselle*. They wrote for the upscale classical record guide *American Music Lover*, and even, the women's needlepoint magazine *The Delineator*. They published jazz books and jazz magazines. All these efforts were made to nurture a new class of jazz connoisseur.

Most of the first white jazz enthusiasts, as Charles Edward Smith suggested in 1934, caught the hot jazz fever during their preparatory school or college days. While the national market went sweet in the early 1930s, hot jazz became popular on prep school and college campuses around the country. Hot collector Blair Kinsman in 1940 recalled catching the jazz bug while attending preparatory school in the early 1930s. "During the last two years of prep school, some ten years ago, I had the privilege of having for a friend an instructor who knew, intimately, Beiderbecke, Armstrong, Hines and the rest of the group of musicians playing hot jazz in Chicago between 1926 and 1929... I have collected hot jazz records since 1930." (*Jazz Information* 4-26-1940: 4) The bandleader Sammy Kaye remembered that "the craze for hot music seemed to hit the colleges in the early 30's, or at least it hit Ohio University... The names of Louis

Armstrong, Duke Ellington, and Fats Waller were becoming household words . . . fraternity, dormitory and college-hangout phonographs blared night and day with the latest hot releases." (*Music and Rhythm* 2-1941: 14) The hot collector Jerry Wexler remembered catching the jazz bug in the mid-1930s while listening to old race records at Kansas State College. "My most important teacher was a fraternity boy, Dale Shrof. . . As an undergraduate, he possessed a wide knowledge of jazz and the willingness to share good news . . . he filled in gaps in my education, introducing me to the glories of an older pre-swing music that was love on first hearing." (Wexler 1993: 30) As Holman Harvey noted about the swing craze while introducing needlepoint women readers to the special world of jam sessions, the "boy next door, home from college, can babble of nothing else." (*The Delineator* 11-1936: 10)

Jazz enthusiasts and musicians were aware of the growing audience for hot jazz among more affluent and educated whites. The hepcat musician Max Kaminsky, for example, noted the type of class that made up early jazz enthusiasts in his later comments on the 1930s jazz scene in New York City. "Jazz was only barely beginning to catch on. . . At that time, in the late thirties, the only people who went to nightclubs were people with money, mostly society people and celebrities of the sports and show-business worlds, not the general public. . . The first Saturday that I worked at the Famous Door, the society people I played for in Bar Harbor just the weekend before came in and there I was again." (Kaminsky 1963: 89) When *Down Beat* celebrated the success of the second concert presented by the Chicago Rhythm Club in 1936 in "2nd Rhythm Concert Delights Local 'Cats' & '400'" it highlighted the attendance by Chicago's elite and the strategic location of the event in the Congress Hotel. "And Harlem's sons of swing lifted their horns to the cool sophisticated ceiling of the swanky Urban room and poured out their melodic heat and afrie cadenzas to some 800 enthusiastic, stomping, applauding white folks. . . Benny's terrific drummer 'sat in' for a few numbers and not only 'Sent' (elated to youse high brows) the customers but the jigs as well. . . Debutantes and musicians alike filled the air with 'Swing it – Pops!' and 'Yeah Man!'" (*Down Beat* 4-1936: 1) John Hammond in the following issue expressed delight while attending this concert in Chicago while noting the type of audience. "I was literally overwhelmed at the mob which attempted to jam its way into the Urban Room. . . My eye could spot only a small minority of musicians and all the faddists and would-be-society folk which could be collected on an Easter day." (*Down Beat* 5-1936: 2) Hot collector Stephen W. Smith in 1940 recognized that the "prodigious efforts" of "the people who have liked jazz music have brought it out of the dark ages into polite society." (*H.R.S. Rag* 9-1940: 31)

David Rosenbaum, reporting from San Francisco, noted the continued importance of affluent whites in the early 1940s. "The amazed visitor can now drop by into the Club Alabam and witness socialite couples in formal attire mingle with the residents of little Harlem, both crowding around the tables to enjoy the stomp music of the Wilbur Barranco crew." (*Down Beat* 1-15-1942: 9) The demand for jazz among affluent white enthusiasts was evident enough that by the early 1940s major record companies began producing expensive boxed sets of old and new jazz recordings. The upscale *Esquire* also began publishing an annual jazz book in 1944 that featured extensive discographies as well as hot jazz criticism.

Given their own social class and that of the growing community of jazz enthusiasts, many jazz critics hoped the new class of enthusiast would elevate the status of jazz music. Paul Eduard Miller in brushing aside past anti-jazz critics was hopeful that "we have seen the last of the days when such critics were brave enough to insist that jazz was music fit only for morons." (*Down Beat* 2-1939: 20) The new audience for jazz music was not made-up of lowbrow morons, but highbrow jazz connoisseurs. Jazz critic George Hoefer pointed to the growth of jazz connoisseurship during the 1930s in *Jazz Information* in 1940. "Out of the musical meles of the thirties has emerged a coterie of jazz connoisseurs made up to a large extent of hot record collectors and critical followers outside of the professional music field." (*Jazz Information* 7-26-1940: 11) Jazz critic Roger Pryor Dodge discussed the broader significance of the new jazz art world and its affluent white jazz connoisseurs. "This is not jazz moving ahead under its own impetus. It is connoisseurship on a grand scale making the ball roll. Jazz in the 1920s was on its own; it was hot and rare stuff responsible for jazz history. But only connoisseurship, improved and distilled through jazz centers, provides what we have today. And only connoisseurship will take care of the future." (*H.R.S. Society Rag* 1-1941: 15) While Dodge was focusing on the patronage of jazz musicians by jazz connoisseurs, jazz critic George Frazier in "Record Collectors Are Not 'Jerks'" defended fanatic hot collectors as patrons of the historical art-archives of hot jazz. "Any art form must be preserved somehow in order to be apprehended and appreciated... Record collectors, whether they realize it or not (many of the serious-minded ones do) are helping to preserve the fine art of hot jazz... Like Andrew Carnegie and the doctrine of financial stewardship, collectors must assume the salvation of original hot records." (*Music and Rhythm* 3-1941: 60–2) Paul Eduard Miller made clear that the future of jazz required that the new jazz consumer was a connoisseur with taste in his article "Judging and Appreciating the Best in Hot Music" in 1941. "Artistic taste, which includes taste in hot music, is almost exclusively dependent upon the faculty to draw distinctions... taste is a quality of knowing where, when, and how things 'belong,' the placing of one thing in harmonious relation to another. It is closely allied to sensitivity and vividness of imagination. To a considerable extent, it is not a cultivated characteristic, but rather an instinctive, intuitive reaching forth for beauty – beauty in every phrase and form. But allowing that the listener, in hot music, has a natural predisposition toward drawing distinctions, he can consciously cultivate his taste." (*Music and Rhythm* 2-1941: 68) Many jazz enthusiasts agreed that connoisseurship was essential to any appreciation of jazz. Hot collector Merrill Hammond of Worcester, Massachusetts, wrote in 1939 that "most of the boys haven't been at it long, but their ears are excellent. In fact I believe as a general rule the younger collectors, once initiated, develop impeccable taste." (*Jazz Information* 12-22-1939: 7) As Miller would later remark in *Esquire*'s 1944 *Jazz Book*, for jazz connoisseurs there must be "a personal predisposition towards the spirit of the music, a positive desire to respond to it, a willingness to comprehend and feel its basic messages. Such an attitude is not unique; it forms the basis of an approach to any art." (Miller 1944: 17–18)

As connoisseurs with impeccable taste, many jazz enthusiasts viewed jazz as an art equivalent to other consecrated high art forms whether literature, painting, or music. Jazz critic Reed Dickerson, for example, argued in his *Harper's* article "Hot Music" in 1936 that "simple in its essence, jazz has now become an intensely complex, highly developed art. . . [T]his much can be said of the best jazz: that it possesses all the elements found in any valid work of art, whether a poem by Keats or a canvas of Manet." (*Harper's* 4-1936: 573-4) In an introduction to Panassié's *Hot Jazz* in 1936, the translators Lyle and Eleanor Dowling also pointed out that "hot jazz has now become, in its own right, a classic art exhibiting all the formal rigors and economy associated with classicism." (Panassié 1936: vii) Paul Eduard Miller argued in *Down Beat* that the time was "ripe for jazz music to be judged according to the standards of all legitimate music and for it to be put on an equal basis of comparison with the best classical selections. . . The genuine artistic level of music, regardless of form, can be recognized solely by the application of the test of all superior music." (*Down Beat* 9-1936: 2) Critics also pointed to the common links between jazz and classical music. In 1936, Reed Dickerson explained hot jazz to the readers of *Harper's* and pointed to the link between jazz improvisation and the tradition of European cultivated music. "Handel, Bach, and Beethoven were all great improvisers. . . Improvisation continued from Mendelssohn and Hummel to César Franck and Saint-Saëns, although by the end of the 19th century it had dwindled to such an extent that even cadenzas were written down. There is ample justification for improvisation, both historically and artistically. Emotionally, it is the most natural way of composing and performing music, and when ably done perhaps the most vital. This gives us the key to jazz." (*Harper's* 4-1936: 571) Paul Eduard Miller made clear the relation between jazz as a serious art form and the tastes of jazz connoisseurs in pointing to the qualities of good jazz appreciation. "It must be remembered that such a test is valid only when made by one whose musical background is adequate and whose appreciation of all art forms is continuously undergoing development." (*Down Beat* 9-1936: 2)

Consider the Critics

We now approach the era of the Jazz Critic – he who is to jazz, what the concert critic is to classical, academic music. It is no longer the exception to find a jazz critic on familiar ground when discussing his subject. He knows all of the here-to-fore anonymous players by name and handles the subject turned over to him in the same sublimated shop *talk* manner as his established, classical confrères handle the Academy! Just as the concert critic, well acquainted with the seventeenth and eighteenth century music and full of well-bred enthusiasm ... so will the jazz critic talk seriously on Boogie Woogie piano and then proceed with obvious satisfaction to consider a Teddy Wilson. (Roger Pryor Dodge (Ramsey and Smith 1939: 328))

   Since the new jazz art world was to be built on connoisseurship, jazz criticism as the domain of special connoisseurs was a regular refrain among early jazz critics. While writing as jazz experts, however, few jazz critics were trained academics, music critics, or journalists. As Ronald G. Welburn (1983) points out, they were white jazz enthusiasts with a college education attempting to create a "serious" discourse on jazz outside such legitimate, institutionalized professions. Early jazz critics, therefore, not only promoted a new jazz connoisseurship, but also worked to legitimate their special role. Jazz critics' explicit claims of legitimacy were a response to being both outside legitimate channels of cultural consecration, particularly those in the world of European cultivated music, and as connoisseurs of a low status art. As Roger Pryor Dodge "Consider the Critics" in *Jazzmen* shows, critics sought to claim the same legitimate status as music critics of the cultivated tradition. In the introduction to *Jazzmen*, the editors also assured readers that the book was "written by men selected for outstanding knowledge of particular subjects. Each man brings to his subject a thorough acquaintance with the music, and, generally speaking, with the men who enjoy it. He brings to the writing of his material an enthusiasm born of a conviction that *Jazzmen* is a book that had to be written." (Ramsey and Smith 1939: xvi)

   Their concern with their own legitimacy led sometimes to pretentious claims on the part of critics. Paul Eduard Miller pointed to the unique position of critics as premier connoisseurs of jazz. "To many the superiority of one piece of music over another is mainly a matter of personal taste, but here, as in all art, the judgment of an artistically critical mind must be taken as the only sound judgment. The overwhelming choice of a majority which has so often proved itself incapable of recognizing achievement cannot possibly be considered seriously." (*Down Beat* 9-1936: 2) As critic George Frazier argued, "the guys who write the brave, true stuff realize that a mere handful of readers will know what it's all about, and the guys who write the brave, true stuff don't give a damn for appealing to any but the handful. When a man becomes imbued with the notion that he's an oracle to the masses his output is bound to suffer little by little and in the end become absolutely worthless." (*Jazz Hot* 6-1936:3) *Metronome* invited French critic Hughes Panassié to comment on the role of critics in 1937. "A good critic is a man whose judgement is working in a synthetic way, whose taste is sure enough to distinguish, through the interpretation, the profound nature of the musician-creator expressing himself, and bringing light what there is in him." (*Metronome* 9-1937: 24) Critic Ted Locke, in responding to the increasing tension between critics and musicians, later reiterated the essential role, and elitist pretensions, of connoisseur critics. "Of course a musical education is helpful to a certain degree but of more importance is good taste, discrimination, a philosophical background ... in short, intellect. Critics must necessarily be far more cultured than the people whose work they review. To quote Oscar Wilde: '... criticism demands infinitely more cultivation than creation does.' Intelligence is not a requirement of artistic endeavor. Anyone who has much contact with musicians finds that as a group they belong to the moron class ... many of the men who produce our beautiful music are mentally below par ... we must conclude that intelligence isn't necessary to produce great art, but it can't be denied that intelligence is necessary to appreciate it. We cannot dispense with criticism. Jazz musicians must be brought to realize that. Perhaps if they were able to read and understand Wilde's excellent treatise "The Critic and the Artist" they would sooner become resigned to the truth." (*Down Beat* 2-15-1941: 8)

Critics' self conception as specialists was buttressed by their universal belief that outside the community of jazz enthusiasts the true nature of jazz music was yet to be discovered in both its musical and social significance. Of course, for jazz critics this lack of appreciation and understanding was what made jazz an endangered music susceptible to neglect and commercialism. The missionary zeal of early jazz critics reflected this mentality of an art and its practitioners under siege. The combination of their pretension to connoisseurship and their sense of being radical spokespersons for a neglected and disdained art led to a sometimes highly partisan and harshly critical criticism. This self-conception, of course, resonated in general with hot jazz collectors who felt equally impassioned and equally endowed with special gifts of appreciation.

Jazz connoisseurs were not pleased by what they perceived as the continued disdain for jazz among classical music lovers. The translators of Panassié's *Hot Jazz* Lyle & Eleanor Dowling expressed the common complaint of jazz enthusiasts. "This cycle of birth, growth and blossoming has been rehearsed without so much as a word of intelligent comment from the prominent music critics in the United States. Now music critics, over the decades since there have been such things, have established so flawless a record for overlooking or combatting everything of any contemporary cultural importance that it is perhaps over-naïve to expect sudden improvement in these quarters. Nevertheless, their ignorance and indifference to hot jazz have constituted so enormous a missing-of-the-point that no one can fail to be appalled." (Panassié 1936: viii) James Higgins in 1938 attempted to explain "Why Jazz Is Held in Contempt by Classicists & Why It Should Not Be." "There is no doubt that hot jazz is in considerable disrepute among those who know or pretend to know classical music... And the great body of listeners, some intelligent, others nursed on a diet of pretty melodies, look on swing as something amusing, fantastic or horrible. They refuse to see in it any element which might validly connect it with the arts... What I want to treat here is the general attitude of disgust or amusement, the inevitable comparison with classical music, in short, the refusal of those not interested in jazz to grant its claim to art." (*Down Beat* 8-1938: 7) Jazz enthusiast Louis Harap in writing "The Case for Hot Jazz" in *The Musical Quarterly* pointed to the poor regard classical musicians held for jazz. "Classical musicians may smile at the notion of good taste in jazz, for many of them regard the whole genre as an undifferentiated mass of bad taste. Yet a careful study will reveal great differences within jazz and in the artistic integrity of its creators." (*The Musical Quarterly* 1-1941: 50) Paul Eduard Miller in *Esquire's Jazz Book* in 1944 informed his readers that the legitimate status of jazz was still under question among certain highbrows. "Even more important, perhaps, is to regard as totally untrustworthy the quasi-academic criticism and apologies originating with classical musicologists and commentators who prefer to remain unsympathetic and oblivious to everything beyond the pale of 'serious' music." (Miller 1944: 17)

Is Jazz Music?

The answer, I think, will be found by clearing away the pseudo-classical verbiage of the jazz critic and looking at the aesthetic nature of jazz itself. Jazz, for all the enthusiasms of its intellectual fans, is not music in the sense that an opera or a symphony is music. It is a variety of folk music and art music is profound and nearly absolute. The former grows like a weed or a wild flower, exhibits no intellectual complexities, makes a simple, direct emotional appeal that may be felt by people who are not even remotely interested in music as an art... [I]t is not subject to intellectual criticism, for it lacks the main element toward which such criticism would be directed: the creative ingenuity and technique of an unusual, trained musical mind. (Winthrop Sargeant, *American Mercury* October 1943: 405)

Winthrop Sargeant took a lesson from the book of his venerable fore-father Daniel Gregory Mason in his searing remarks on the claims of jazz critics. Sargeant had expressed a similar sentiment in his 1938 book *Jazz: Hot and Hybrid*. For Sargeant, the issue was not jazz as popular music, but whether jazz was an art form equal to the European cultivated tradition. While Sargeant aggressively rejected the claims of jazz critics, the world of European cultivated music basically ignored the protests of jazz critics as well as the new jazz art world. Monroe Berger (1947) in his review of four journals dedicated to the cultivated tradition noted a shift towards a basic benign neglect towards jazz on the part of the European classical establishment during the Swing Era. While swing music performed by professional musicians did not elicit heated criticism, it did not elicit much in the way of acclaim. Given that its institutions, artists, repertoire, and music practices were quite distinct from the world of swing musicians and jazz music such neglect was not surprising. The music education journal *The Musician*, however, did invite jazz critic Leonard Feather in 1941 to write a swing column "Tempo di Jazz," in "keeping with its policy to give voice to all phases of music." (*The Musician* 5-1941: 97) Neil Leonard (1962) noted that some previous anti-jazz critics like Virgil Thompson and Fritz Kreisler actually came to accept jazz. Thompson in 1934 commended Louis Armstrong whose "style of improvisation would seem to have combined the highest reaches of instrumental virtuosity with the most tensely disciplined melodic structure and the most sponta-neous emotional expression." (*Modern Music* 5/6-1936: 16–17) Previous supporters of jazz like Aaron Copland, Igor Stravinsky, and Leopold Stokowski continued commenting on jazz as well as writing classical com-positions in the jazz idiom. Stokowski in 1943 once again heralded jazz as a great American art. "Jazz is a vitally important part of our folk music and folk lore. It has no traditions, no limitations, so it will go on forever developing so long as musicians give free rein to their imaginations. Jazz is unique – there has never been anything like it in Art. In this kind of music the United States is second to none in the whole world." Stokowski also praised Duke Ellington. "Ellington never imitates the symphony. His music seems simple, but really is art music of great subtlety. He began fairly early in jazz and is still growing to greater heights. In my opinion Duke Ellington is one of America's outstanding artists." (*Metronome* 8-1943: 29) In general, however, the criticism and performances of the new jazz art world made little impact, nor received much commentary, in the world of classical and opera music.

Considering the perceived classical longhairs' disdain or ignoring of jazz, one would imagine that jazz connoisseurs considered the swing craze in 1935 a welcome godsend. For many enthusiasts, however, this rejuvenation of interest in cultivated jazz was part miracle and part curse. The swing craze created a new and larger audience for swing music which most jazz enthusiasts appreciated, but unfortunately, the average swing fan seemed to lack the personal "predisposition" for the jazz appreciation coveted by jazz critics and other jazz connoisseurs. This might have had some relationship to the new fans' class and education. Not that critics noted that social fact directly, they preferred to see new swing fans as simply lacking taste. Critic Wilder Hobson in *American Jazz Music* was disgusted with the average swing fan. It was "obvious to anyone who has followed this music over a considerable period of time, that while the amount of public jazz playing has increased considerably during the 'swing' fad, a great deal of it has been very routine or exhibitionistic, or both... Many audiences give their loudest applause to florid technical exhibitionism, screaming top notes or sheer power, no matter how mechanical these may be." Of course, the new swing fans were not completely to blame for their attraction to exhibitionism. Hobson reminded readers that the commercialism of jazz was a major obstacle for new fans to know and learn to appreciate genuine jazz. He "intended to help the reader who is unfamiliar with the field to distinguish between genuine jazz and the mass popular 'jazz' or 'swing' – which the players call 'commercial' – surrounding it." Unfortunately, Hobson noted that "the 'swing' fad, which still continues as this is written, has largely built on the commercially salable mixture of a certain amount of jazz playing... As for jazz, sometimes it is talented and spirited, but it is more likely to be routine and exhibitionist, with a heavy emphasis on the rhythm-blasting and technical display which delights many audiences." (Hobson 1939: 87, 74, 152–3) For Hobson and all other jazz critics, the development of a true appreciation of genuine jazz confronted a combination of the ignorance of many swing fans with the commercialism of most swing music. As George Hoefer argued in 1940 in *Jazz Information*, "hot jazz has attained an evolutionary phase denoted by the acquisition of a 'public.' The term 'public' being used to identify a following consisting of a swing faddist majority plus a minority made up of those who have captured for themselves a sincere appreciation of jazz music. For the most part, the former group can be left out of this discussion, as of little value to the growth of jazz as an art. In fact, the average swing fan's solicitude has been responsible for the malignant aspects in modern commercial swing music." (*Jazz Information* 7-26-1940: 11) Hot collector Blair Kinsmen in his letter to *Jazz Information* was representative of many collectors' views on the average swing fan. "The swing addict today may now and then acquire a good record, but he never understands it and it soon passes into the junkpile." (*Jazz Information* 4-26-1940: 4)

Besides the tendency for the average swing fan to lack any true jazz appreciation, enjoying exhibitionism instead of artistry, the swing fan also had the terrible tendency to dance rather than listen to a band. Reed Dickerson in "Hot Music" welcomed the rejection of dancing jitterbugs at a Chicago Rhythm Club concert. "The recent booing of several persons who attempted to dance at a Sunday afternoon concert held in a Chicago hotel may be attributed to the tastes of an audience that preferred to listen to a music whose appeal was quite as much to the head as it was to the feet... So far as jazz is concerned there has been little in our vocabulary to honor this distinction... the current word 'swing' is the latest attempt to name an art which is struggling to emancipate itself from the narrow limitations of a mechanical and banal ballroom music." (*Harper's* 4-1936: 567) *Metronome* informed its readers that on his first visit to the United States the French jazz critic Hughes Panassié was shocked at seeing dancing jitterbugs and suggested a quick remedy, "Chloroform 'Jeeter Bogs,' Says Panassié." (*Metronome* 11-1938: 13) In the program for "From Spirituals to Swing" in 1938 Hammond and Dugan noted that "the jitterbug millions, lurching along on their new Children's Crusade, have scared a lot of people away from hot jazz. Jitterbug taste is not the arbiter of hot jazz." (Dugan and Hammond 1974: 194) *Metronome* in 1939 did note hopeful changes to a classier form of jazz appreciation in "Swing's for Listeners – Not Dancers! Jitterbug Antics Are Now Corny Even with Public, Which Begins to Appreciate Real Swing". "More and more people are enjoying their swing these days. This can be traced to the fact that the public is listening to true swing music rather than dancing to it... real fans are beginning to realize that swing is appreciated more by those who listen and watch than the ones who attempt to dance to its music." (*Metronome* 10-1939: 19) As *Newsweek* pointed out in its coverage of an Eddie Condon Jazz Concert, the new jazz enthusiast was certainly a high-class connoisseur. "These people, then, might be said to represent a group of the longhairs of jazz. Harry James or Benny Goodman fever at the Paramount leave them cold – and jitterbugging in the aisles is not even considered at the Town Hall concerts...

Eddie Condon has had an enormous influence on Le Jazz Intellectuel. . ."
(*Newsweek* 1-24-1944: 62)

The article "Swings for Listeners – Not Dancers" also took heart in the fact that on college campuses "the greater proportion of young collegians would rather watch the instrumentalists than dance to their music." (*Metronome* 10-1939: 19) This supposed move to a better form of jazz appreciation among college students was aided by young collegians in hot clubs working to insure better-educated jazz audiences on their campuses. Jazz enthusiasts and jazz musicians disparagingly called supposedly clueless collegian swing fans "ickies". Young jazz critic George Avakian as a member of the Yale Hot Club complained of the unformed taste of most collegian swing fans in a letter to *Metronome* in 1938. "Here's one swing cat that is plenty tired of what his favorite pastime is turning into. For a while, few people knew anything about swing and things were fine. Then swing became a household word, but the ickies (analogous to the Park Avenue nouveau riche) were disregarded. Now they're catered to and the stuff that's being handed out to them is passed off as some of the best swing there is! . . . Most of them may be those crew-cutted, gabardine-jacketed, bow-tied cats (so they think!) from Yale, Princeton, Harvard, Choate, or Lawrenceville." (*Metronome* 1-1938: 9) *Metronome* in November 1938, however, noted a promising development with the reorganization of the United Hot Clubs of America and election of a national board spearheaded by the Ohio State Swing Club. In that same issue, the recent activity of the Brooklyn College hot club was celebrated in "Jitterbugs Banned on Campus: Brooklyn College Campaign for Real Swing." "A campaign of education on real swing music, including banning of the jitterbugs, is sweeping over the campus of Brooklyn College. In this campaign jitterbugs are classed as rodents which must be eliminated... A group of students have organized under the banner of the 'United Hot Clubs of America' in an effort to promote a love for 'genuine swing music.' Already several hundred followers have been recruited and the organization is swiftly swelling. The organization hopes to spread the movement to other campuses." (*Metronome*, November 1938: 43) It seemed to the chosen connoisseurs of the jazz vanguard that even collegians needed a proper education to direct them to the right form of appreciation of jazz.

While young collegians apparently needed a proper jazz education, a new class of fan also was discovering jazz and seemed to threaten the sacrosanct art world being built by affluent white jazz enthusiasts. Of course, working class blacks were listening to swing big bands and ensembles throughout this period, just not in the special clubs of the new jazz art world. And with the swing craze, working class whites were listening to swing big bands and ensembles too, like the small band the *New York Times* reported at the cabaret Chez Callahan in Queens in New York City in 1939. At one in the morning it was "packed with shouting laughing people taking their fling at night life. The boys in the five-piece band have been grinding out blaring swing since 8:30. Their shirts cling wetly to their ribs under their crumpled dress suits. The trumpet and sax men puff out flushed, shining cheeks and blow hard on their instruments. The pianist plays rhythm with his left hand while he gulps a long draught of beer. The drummer draws on the cigarette dangling from his lips as he beats on the taut skins." (*New York Times Magazine* 9-10-1939: 12) Obviously, working class audiences were enjoying jazz, but just not like jazz connoisseurs in the newly forming jazz art world.

The early exclusivity of the jazz art world, however, began to diversify by the 1940s, even as it continued to attract affluent college-educated whites who would remain important as a financial base and status marker for this art world. But as Lewis A. Erenberg (1998: 59) argues, working class swing fans also developed an appreciation for jazz, what he calls a "democratization of artistic connoisseurship." Not necessarily the same appreciation hoped for by early jazz connoisseurs, or the same implied distinctions of taste and class. Eventually jazz enthusiasts included working class hot collectors like an avid collector of Louis Armstrong who was a retired mail clerk living in Cincinnati. As hot collector George Hoefer noted in his 1944 contribution "Collectors: Personalities and Anecdotes" in *Esquire* magazine's first of several annual jazz books, collectors had become "as variegated a group as there are walks of life." (Miller 1944: 71) Meanwhile, working class audiences were enjoying listening to small swing ensembles. The national scene of special jazz clubs, like 52nd Street in New York City, by the early 1940s was growing and many local jazz scenes became popular entertainment districts sporting diverse crowds including their eventual racial integration. The war also effected the future community of jazz enthusiasts. Some working class male veterans of the war would catch the jazz bug through V-Disks produced fortuitously by jazz enthusiasts, while returning home and eventually entering college through the GI Bill. Finally, the jazz art world, and more importantly jazz musicians, remained dependent on nightclubs as performance venues. Unlike the few more exclusive hot club concerts and jam sessions, these cultural spaces were part of urban popular nightlife and urban popular culture. A strange reverse process of cultivation was occurring where the original more exclusive and elitist jazz art world was being occupied by a more heterogeneous community. Max Kaminsky noticed these changes in jam sessions at Ryan's in New York City in the early 1940s. "The fans who included specimens of all the varieties – the earnest jazz purist;

the jivey hep cat; the intense intellectual; extroverts from the advertising
world; Broadway types; sentimental drunks; dedicated drinkers; plain
people; and plain characters – were all members of the same fraternity...
The Ryan's regulars were the most sincere and discriminating group of
fans I ever played for anywhere, and you could hear a swizzlestick drop
as they listened to musicians." (Kaminsky 1963: 122, 123)

While there was a gradual "democratization" of jazz connoisseurship
in the 1940s and 1950s, the early jazz art world and new jazz market
was driven by a community of mostly upper or middle class, college educated, white male enthusiasts. This community was distinctly different
from most jazz musicians by race, class and/or education. Enthusiasts
and musicians came together through the music of the black jazz vernacular. As we will see, however, how they appreciated and viewed this music
tradition was not necessarily the same. Some hepcat white musicians did
share the same disdain for commercialism and the average swing fan as
jazz connoisseurs, although not expressing the same pretension to some
special predisposition for aesthetic refinement. Jazz connoisseurs through
listening, writing, and producing were transforming the nature of jazz's
reception as an art form. With their preference for small jazz ensembles
they also were creating a new market for performances using the vernacular practice of improvisation adopted by professional musicians as their
defining art. A new market appeared where hepcat jazz musicians and
black jazz musicians could find paying audiences who appreciated the
art of improvisation. In the 1930s parallel to the commercial market for
swing music, was a distinctly different market for a new jazz art world of
jazz connoisseurs. Unfortunately for professional swing musicians, many
of these early jazz connoisseurs were to have rather clearly defined tastes
for the black jazz vernacular and strong opinions about what constituted
genuine jazz.

Genuine jazz: jazz romanticism and the black vernacular

The esoteric hot jazz fan waxes so emotional over his beliefs that he has hardened
them into unshakable faith. This faith is imbedded in a deep, narrow groove,
from which point he can see or hear nothing save *his* kind of jazz. (Paul Eduard
Miller, *Music and Rhythm*, February 1941: 70)

The question of "genuine" jazz was a central concern within the new
jazz art world. It ran through jazz discourse in a variety of ways as it
articulated this art world's attempt to construct the aesthetic, cultural
and social significance of jazz music. As music created by black musicians and singers and originally performed in the commercial market of

honky-tonks, speakeasies, nightclubs, and black Vaudeville theaters, jazz
music remained an exotic, or at least unfamiliar, culture to the white
jazz enthusiasts who embraced it. Even the social world of white hepcat
musicians was alien to affluent white enthusiasts. Early jazz discourse,
therefore, dealt extensively in describing the social world of jazz before
it reached the ears of enthusiasts in special clubs, jam sessions, concerts,
and recordings. It was a highly romanticized narrative of the struggle,
as well as the ribald nightlife, of jazz musicians and the communities in
which they created and performed their music. In some ways, the early
jazz narrative borrowed from the romanticism of white hepcat musicians,
many of whom regularly interacted with jazz critics and other enthusiasts. The romantic view of jazz for some also retained this music's position against the conventional culture and values of white middle and
upper class Americans – jazz connoisseurs were rebelling against their
strait-laced class. The romanticism of the jazz narrative combined with
the connoisseurship of jazz collectors to create a battle line within the
new jazz art world over what was genuine or righteous jazz. The question
was not whether genuine jazz was the creation of African Americans,
or whether black musicians were the major exponents of genuine jazz,
critics and enthusiasts alike agreed on this basic premise. As Paul Eduard Miller made clear in 1936, "we might even go so far as to say that
swing music has been the one artistic creation of the Aframerican...
Not a few have achieved artistic success, for among the countless
Negro musicians who thus found normal and genuinely creative outlet in swing music, a considerable portion was gifted with inherent talent. These are the soloists and composers of high distinction, the torch-
bearers in the true jazz tradition." (*Down Beat* October 1936: 5) The
question was who performed genuine jazz or authentic black music and
who performed a derivative form of jazz emptied of its vitality and authenticity through either a capitulation to commercialism or a misguided
professionalism.

Hughes Panassié's *Jazz Hot* revealed the parameters of genuine jazz
that occupied jazz critics and enthusiasts. Panassié distinguished "hot"
jazz from "straight" jazz. Small ensembles using the collective improvisation and intonation of the black jazz vernacular performed hot jazz. Large
or small bands using written arrangements, more legitimate intonation,
but still utilizing improvisation, performed straight jazz. Panassié's example of the Duke Ellington Orchestra as a straight jazz proponent revealed
the distinction he was making. Of course, already aware of the debates
about genuine jazz, Panassié made clear that hot interpretation was not
"more 'authentic' than straight interpretation... Straight interpretation
is authentic jazz just as long as it keeps its swing." (Panassié 1936: 24)

Panassié, however, also clearly expressed the jazz connoisseurs' preference for genuine "hot" jazz when he informed readers that "hot jazz differs more from 'classical' music than does straight jazz... it is more spontaneous, more dynamic, and infinitely more baffling. That is why listeners accustomed to classical music will prefer 'straight' performances." Hot jazz when "performed by the very best musicians, these collective improvisations surpass the best written ensembles, from the hot point of view." (Panassié 1936: 24, 35) Panassié was making a basic distinction between the early practices of the black jazz vernacular with those of professional swing musicians that other jazz critics and jazz enthusiasts would make in articles, reviews, album booklets, and letters. "Genuine" jazz as defined by its most avid followers was the black jazz vernacular – early blues, early jazz, and boogie-woogie piano – untainted by the commercial market and the cultivated techniques of professional musicians.

For avid jazz enthusiasts and many early jazz critics, genuine jazz was the folk music of a romanticized black folk culture and black folk musicians. Charles Edward Smith in his 1934 *Esquire* article expressed the common view of jazz as folk music. "From its inception the term hot differentiated what was genuine and had the quality of folk music – whether slow Blues or fast stomp – from what was imitative or blatantly derivative..." (*Esquire* 2-1934: 96) Walter Sidney argued that "like any other folk music, these melodies were hammered out by countless people, passed down from one singer or player to another, come out simple in form yet carry a profound weight of emotion. They form what might be called the musical language of jazz." (*Jazz Information* 12-8-1939: 3) Or as he later remarked on New Orleans jazz, "these forms of jazz were not the invention of any one man, or group of men. They were the product and picture of the life of the community, especially the Negro community." (*H.R.S. Rag* 3-1941: 13) The romanticized narrative of jazz as folk music revolved around the idea of jazz as authentic and untainted. Jazz's authenticity resided in its direct expression of the social life of lower class blacks. It reflected their oppressive conditions as well as their exciting and ribald nightlife. "Genuine" jazz was a vital folk art, not a monotonous cultivated music.

The romantic view of early jazz asserted black folk music as expressive of the stark reality of racial oppression. William Russell and Stephen W. Smith wrote on the early origins of jazz in *Jazzmen*. "By nature the Negroes were no less happy than other people. But mirth and laughter find little expression in the song of a people long depressed with thoughts of exile, slavery, and oppression. Music born under such conditions can only express a spirit of resignation touched with yearnings." (Ramsey and Smith 1939: 8–9) Such oppressive conditions were seen as responsible for the unique qualities of black folk music. As Hughes Panassié argued, it was the "expression of sadness, of the melancholy of the soul of the oppressed Negro, which gives swing music its intensely moving accent. This poetic quality is another thing peculiar to swing music, deeply comprehended only after long experience..." (Panassié 1936: 294) E. Simms Campbell in his 1938 *Esquire* article "Jam in the Nineties" noted the important emotional support jazz provided African Americans during the 1920s. "They were a solace to Negro domestics, who, after working for hours over laundry tubs, mopping floors and shining brass, would go to the dingy comfort of a one-room flat in the Negro tenements and there put these records on their victrolas. It was a release from things white – they could hum – pat their feet – and be colored." (*Esquire* 12-1938: 202)

The romantic view of jazz also included how segregation, poverty, and musical illiteracy led to the unique musical form called jazz. The segregation of black musicians led to the central role of African music idioms in jazz and the unique musical syncretism created by illiterate black folk artists in blues and jazz. Russell and Smith in *Jazzmen* noted that "the young New Orleans aspirant, having no teacher to show him the supposed limitations of his instrument, went ahead by himself and frequently hit upon new paths and opened up undreamed-of possibilities... But the freedom of the New Orleans musician from any restraining tradition and supervision enabled him to develop on most of the instruments not only new technical resources but an appropriate and unique jazz style." (Ramsey and Smith 1939: 10) Campbell presented a similar argument in "Jam in the Nineties." "True, many a white musician shared the same fate, but he was not continually relegated to the bottom as were these early-day Negro pioneers. This shunting aside naturally made the Negro draw into himself. With no outlet to exchange ideas on music other than with members of his own race, he became more and more essentially Negroid in musical feeling and in interpretation." (*Esquire* 12-1938: 102, 202) Jazz enthusiast Merrill M. Hammond, Jr. noted how the hard times of early jazz musicians led to their creative music making. "When jazz was coming up the river, a man played primarily because he loved the music, and not because he was going to become wealthy by playing it... because in those days jazz was not patronized in any way. Therefore he must have played the music to express his ideas, and for no other reason... He was truly a creative artist." (*Jazz Information* 3-15-1940: 4) As Hughes Panassié noted in *The Real Jazz* in 1942, early "jazz musicians had played as much for their own pleasure as to make a living. They enjoyed playing at dances and provoking the enthusiasm of the dancers and any musicians who came to hear them. They played by instinct, without thought of technique..." (Panassié 1942: 53–4)

Portrayals of the exciting and eccentric lives of jazz musicians in lo-
cales never visited by critics' readers also were part of the romantic view
of jazz. Whether honky-tonks and barrelhouses in New Orleans or the
speakeasies and rent parties in Chicago and New York, jazz critics wanted
to convey the exciting life of the lower class world of jazz. William Russell
and Stephen W. Smith wrote about New Orleans and the first jazz cor-
netist Buddy Bolden in *Jazzmen*. "More often Bolden played at one of
the dance halls in the Negro district... The hustlers, gamblers, and race
track followers were often hard-working musicians in their off seasons,
or when luck turned and they needed a little ready cash. At night, however, the Tin Type trembled with life and activity, especially when Bolden
was 'socking it out.' The 'high class' or 'dicty' people didn't go to such
low-down affairs as the Tin Type dances. At about twelve o'clock, when
the ball was getting right, the more respectable Negroes who did attend
went home... When the orchestra settled down to the slow blues, the
music was mean and dirty, as Tin Type roared full blast." (Ramsey and
Smith 1939: 12–13) Campbell in "Jam in the Nineties" also described
the deviant life of New Orleans musicians. "At this time New Orleans
was steeped in wickedness, bawdy houses running full blast, faro games
on most street corners and voluptuous creole beauties soliciting trade
among the welter of gamblers, steamboat men and hustlers of every
nationality." (*Esquire* 12-1938: 102) In *Jazzmen*, Russell described the
nightlife of boogie-woogie pianists Albert Amons and Meade Lux Lewis
in Chicago when "they began to make money playing for club parties
and house 'kados.' Those were the big Prohibition days, and with several jugs on hand, everyone, including the pianist, got stewed. When
the house party was raided, Albert and Lux hid outside on the window
sill; after the Law had cleared out the mob they climbed back inside
and finished the unemptied jugs." (Ramsey and Smith 1939: 190) Then
there were the rough parties in Harlem during the 1920s frequented by
black stride pianists like James P. Johnson after performing for more respectable affairs. "Outside the regular parlor socials which went on week
nights and Saturday nights, there was also the weekend social, starting
on Sunday afternoon and breaking up Monday morning. This somewhat wilder party was an indication of the increasing roughness of the
affairs. As the parties grew in size and popularity gangs moved in and
took over the collection from the landlady's assistant. The Harlem Rats,
Harlem Pink Roses, Murphy's Gang, and the Jolly Fellows, among others, placed their men on the door, handled the money and searched
the patrons for razors, switch blade knives, and lead pipes wrapped in
newspaper, exacting a percentage for their services." (*H.R.S. Rag* 9-
1940: 18)

How jazz critics framed the art of improvisation also reflected a deep romanticism. James W. Poling in "Music After Midnight" in *Esquire* in 1936 presented the romantic view of improvisation and jazz. "When, in this article, I refer to jazz music I mean, unless otherwise stated, the *real* jazz and not the synthetic stuff which is customarily passed out to today's unsuspecting and gullible public... *Hot* music is a music of the soul. No musician, no matter how accomplished technically, can play *hot* unless it is in him, unless it is in his blood, his heart, his soul. The *Hot* man, when he goes into one of those spontaneous, highly syncopated solos, is as intoxicated with his music as is his appreciative auditor." (*Esquire* 6-1936: 92) B. S. Rogers in "Swing is From the Heart" in *Esquire* in 1939 presented a similar view. "Improvisation is the soul of jazz. Without it there is a body but no personality. Listen to a performance which hasn't got it (and what you're listening to is probably routine dance music), and you take nothing away; no emotion, no feeling of energy, no impression of character... No matter how it's done, the music called jazz – its surprising, shocking rhythms, its color and fascinating contrapuntal effects – is produced by improvisation. Without it the music is dull, flat, nerveless. It isn't jazz." (*Esquire* 4-1939: 118) As critic Eugene Williams wrote in the booklet for a boxed set of old recordings by Louis Armstrong reissued by Columbia Records for the new market of jazz connoisseurs, "jazz is a medium through which a natural, uninhibited spirit can express itself with the utmost freedom; all Louis Armstrong needs to do is play from the heart." (Brunswick Collectors Series, 1944, No.B-1016)

The final part of the romantic narrative was the obscurity of early black jazz artists during the 1930s. That early jazz musicians were forced into other jobs or trades other than music making, like the boogie-woogie pianist Meade Lux Lewis working at a garage in Chicago or the clarinetist Sidney Bechet as a tailor in New York City, demonstrated the terrible state of neglect of this vibrant folk music. (*Esquire* 4-1936) As an editorial in *H.R.S. Rag* pointedly remarked, buying old records and going to cheap jam sessions was not helping destitute jazz musicians. "The recent deaths of Dodds, Ladnier and others, all in straitened circumstances should serve as a reminder to hot clubs that it is not enough to talk about how neglected these men are... Hot music is not in such good financial shape today that Hot Clubs can shut themselves into their clubrooms with a bunch of rare old records." (*H.R.S. Rag* 9-1940: 19) This narrative also included the trials and tribulations of hepcat white jazz musicians forced to turn "legit" or suffer the consequences and end up performing in small dives to inebriated patrons, most of whom were other hepcat white musicians. As Wilder Hobson made clear in *American Jazz Music* in 1939, true jazz musicians were "men who either *cannot* or *will not* take the trouble to develop the 'legitimate' technical proficiency required for the commercial bands. They started as jazz improvisers, and that is where they have remained. It is of course hard to say in any given case whether such a man is unable or unwilling. But there are a certain number of widely recognized jazz players who, in language which would get a laugh from any of them, might be said to have artistic conscience. Genuine jazz is the only music they want." (Hobson 1939: 173) Critic Dave Dexter for the Capitol boxed-set *New American Jazz* celebrated that jazz "has outgrown its infancy. Gone are the days when musicians were forced to hide away in the back rooms of saloons in order to express themselves, and display their talents, naturally and spontaneously. The American public accepts good jazz now. And while jazz is an art which, because of its youth, still has yet acquired the mass following which it deserves and someday will have, it nevertheless has made phenomenal progress since the first notes of le hot filled the warm, invigorating night air of New Orleans some four decades ago." (Capitol Album, 1944, R-3) Eugene Williams also noted the obscurity of jazz musicians in the booklet accompanying Columbia Records' boxed-set *Boogie Woogie Piano*, "Boogie woogie music, until a few years ago, was the exclusive property of the obscure Negro pianists who created it. Then a handful of record collectors and musicians began to talk it up; and today, by courtesy of radio, phonograph and film, 'boogie woogie' is almost a household word all over the United States." (Brunswick Collector Series, 1943, No.B-1005)

The romantic jazz narrative was not a completely false portrayal, but a highly delineated and idyllic narrative about genuine jazz and genuine jazz musicians. It certainly was true that many early jazz artists like Sidney Bechet and Bessie Smith following the Crash of '29 no longer were able to maintain careers in music. Of course, many black professional musicians had a difficult time as well following the crash. Not all early jazz musicians celebrated by jazz enthusiasts, however, were illiterate musicians. Bessie Smith, herself a successful vaudevillian singer, made several recordings coveted by jazz enthusiasts with the Jazz Hounds, a unit comprised of the best professional musicians in New York City including Coleman Hawkins. Pianist Lil Armstrong who performed with King Oliver, Freddie Keppard, and her husband Louis Armstrong on the most coveted hot jazz recordings was a graduate of Fisk University, while Keppard was performing in professional orchestras since the early 1900s. Certainly many of the New Orleans jazz musicians were not musically trained like their professional brethren in early society orchestras. But many of the black artists included as premier genuine jazz musicians were literate musicians and joined professional orchestras before or during the

Jazz Age. Louis Armstrong when playing on riverboats after leaving New Orleans learned to read music in order to perform in these more professional orchestras. And of course, Armstrong did not simply play on riverboats for the pleasure of free expression, but to earn a livelihood like all early jazz musicians whose skills were used as a means to earn a living. The idea of early jazz as non-commercial was a purely romanticized view. The pleasure of jam sessions also was not the exclusive reserve of uncultivated musicians freed from the burden of musical training. As we have seen, during the 1920s and 1930s jamming was part of black professional musicians' artistic lives as well.

The crucial point in terms of the new jazz art world was how the romantic narrative constructed the authenticity of jazz and how important this construct was to many jazz enthusiasts. This romantic narrative was not full of the same primitivism found in jazz discourse during the 1920s, but it did refract what jazz historian Ted Gioia (1988) calls the "Primitivist Myth" of jazz. This myth during the 1930s, as both Gioia and Gennari (1991) argue, was strongest among French language critics like Hughes Panassié and Robert Goffin – a strong association of authentic jazz as *primitive* culture and authentic jazz artists as *primitive* musicians. For American critics and enthusiasts, *primitive* was used only in reference to African music practices; the Primitivist Myth appeared more as antimodernist and a romanticizing of an urban black *folk* culture distinct from critics' and enthusiasts' own culture. The authenticity of genuine jazz, however, was still wrapped up in a view of a less *cultivated* Other – both in the romantic portrayal of jazz life and in the vernacular styles associated with genuine folk culture. Neil Leonard (1987) points to how jazz critics were rebelling against traditionalist tastes and values – similar to the rebellion of white hepcat musicians. "Genuine" jazz represented an authenticity lacking in the staid cultivation of traditionalist culture. A certain primitivism, therefore, remained behind the folk ideology of early jazz criticism in jazz's celebration as an uncultivated, vital, and free expression, and in the construction of who was an authentic black artist. As B. S. Rogers wrote in *Esquire* in 1939, "an appreciation of Mozart doesn't preclude an appreciation of jazz, intelligent people can and do enjoy it. They do it not in the spirit of slumming, but because no matter how cultivated you may be you are also capable of unsophisticated emotions – of raw tempers, simple melancholy, violent passion, and slapstick comedy, and even moments of vulgarity. And surely you are capable of being delighted and moved by fantastic musical colors and extremely complex yet basically savage rhythms, colors and rhythms which go far beyond the trickiest schemes of the most sophisticated of modern composers. If you aren't, you are too refined to live in this world." (*Esquire* 4-1939: 120)

Running parallel to the new jazz art world was a folk music movement that also constructed a romantic narrative of authentic folk culture. This folk movement intersected with the jazz art world since both had the majority of their influential critics and producers living in New York City. As historian Robert Cantwell (1996: 63) argues, the folk movement "arose from the interplay of the ethnomimetic culture of New York, through intellectuals, artists, and entrepreneurs, with the popular and provincial cultures that lay beyond it to the south and west." And the search for the folk roots of jazz resonated with the mission of the folk movement – "in this respect the contemplation of the black cultural Other both epitomized and essentialized the contemplation of 'the folk.'" (Cantwell 1996: 69) These two movements, of course, crossed paths as jazz enthusiasts wrote about and produced "folk" music. The intellectuals of the folk movement, however, rejected any urban-based jazz as authentic folk. As John and Alan Lomax wrote in *American Ballads and Folk Songs* in 1934, their "purpose was to find the Negro who had had the least contact with jazz, the radio, and with the white man." (Cantwell 1996: 69) Of course, jazz enthusiasts viewed the folk movement as somewhat corn-fed in its tastes. Charles Edward Smith in reviewing Alan Lomax's collection of folk songs for the Library of Congress felt that "there is a world of difference between the blues as collectors know them and the folk stuff as waxed for the archives... Most of us are sectarian. We think folk music went into a decline in the last century to make way for a few bright blasts on a golden horn." (*H.R.S. Rag* 1-1939: 11) In contrast to the folk movement, jazz enthusiasts combined a folk romanticism of both rural and urban life with a high art appreciation for jazz. For jazz enthusiasts, jazz became a *sophisticated* folk music as it developed from the field hollers and blues of rural blacks to the jazz of urban blacks in New Orleans, Chicago, and New York City.

The jazz art world also reflected the progressive politics of the New Deal Era and the American Left. At the center of this progressive agenda was the question of Jim Crow in America. Progressives and radicals also viewed jazz and blues as a genuine voice of the people uncontaminated by commercialism. For the American Left, folk music in general became an important part of their view of authentic working class life. The different worlds of jazz connoisseurship, jazz romanticism, and radical politics crisscrossed through jazz enthusiasts who had progressive to radical sympathies – those jazz critics whose mission included supporting the music of black artists and fighting against Jim Crow in America. John Hammond later expressed the progressive ideals that motivated his efforts as a jazz enthusiast. "My dissent from the social order started with my objection to the discrimination I saw everywhere around me. New York private schools might enroll one to two Jewish boys whose families were too prominent to ignore, not more... I did not revolt against the system. I simply refused to be part of it. The jazz I liked best was played by Negroes. My two best friends, Edgar Siskin and Artie Bernstein, were Jews ... the strongest motivation for my dissent was jazz. I heard no color line in the music... The fact that the best jazz players barely made a living, were barred from all well-paying jobs in radio and in most nightclubs, enraged me... To bring recognition to the Negro's supremacy in jazz was the most effective and constructive form of social protest I could think of." (Hammond 1977: 67–8) Viewing jazz as an urban folk music often intertwined an idyllic romanticism with an idealistic radical critique of American culture.

Unfortunately, the preference for "genuine" jazz led to conflicts between those who championed it and those who championed swing musicians. Professional musicians, who were unionized musicians and mostly members of either an oppressed race or class, unfortunately held a false consciousness of being sophisticated artists. Jazz traditionalists, as opposed to jazz modernists, viewed any movement away from genuine jazz as suspect, and jazz traditionalists dominated the early vanguard of jazz enthusiasts. Professional swing musicians performing in small swing ensembles were acceptable, since they did improvise, as long as they did not try to be too cultivated in their technique and improvisational melodies. Merrill M. Hammond in "Is Jazz Dying Off?" presented the common traditionalist view of a younger generation of professional musicians who were swept away by cultivated techniques. "At no time in the history of jazz music have there been so few men qualified to play in a forthright jazz manner as there are today... The result was that while technically he was inferior to the modern swing musician, artistically he was miles ahead of him... No one, except some whacky record collectors and self-styled critics of jazz, appreciates his talent." (*Jazz Information* 3-15-1940: 4) The *H.R.S. Rag* acknowledged that a "frequent complaint against the so-called 'jazz purist' is that he is interested only in illiterate raggedy musicians from various parts of the country as far from New York as possible." (*H.R.S. Rag* 1-1941: 18) Hughes Panassié in his second jazz book, *The Real Jazz*, explicitly revealed the traditionalist, anti-modern view of genuine jazz. "That is why musicians who are untrained in musical theory and who have no preconceived notions often express themselves with a naturalness which, granted an equal talent, makes them far more interesting than cultured musicians who are more or less consciously victims of theories of their age. In general, such independence is impossible except in a primitive music... As we have seen, jazz music has gotten further and further away from its original simple and pure form... It remains to be seen whether jazz will be strangled by that civilization, or whether it can adapt itself to new forms and can continue to live. But truth obliges me to point out that several signs seem to indicate that the vitality of jazz music has been profoundly affected... no great musicians arising in the younger generation. All of the greatest jazz musicians began playing before 1925 and 1926..." (Panassié 1942: 15, 232)

The traditionalists' rejection of any further cultivation of the jazz vernacular was even more explicit as they criticized any modern embellishment of jazz. This anti-modernism articulated a rather strange contradiction where jazz connoisseurs enjoyed genuine jazz as a "serious" aesthetic art form, but ridiculed professional musicians for any artistic pretensions. Jazz traditionalist William Russell argued that an "amateur is not to be regarded however with condescension. A perusal of the history of music and other arts shows that many important creative innovations have been due to the amateur. Usually in art a new style has its inceptions with the people, and not with cultured performers." (*H.R.S. Rag* 11-1940: 12) Hughes Panassié again expressed in *Real Jazz* the common anti-modernist critique of contemporary professional musicians. "The so-called 'artistic conscience' took hold of the jazz musicians, doing their art great harm... the Negro musician became increasingly aware of his own importance, or at least the importance of his music. That music which had been up to then an amusement took on the aspect of fine art. And the inevitable occurred. These musicians who had infallibly played in a perfect manner, and had never digressed for an instant from the pure tradition of their art as long as they blindly followed their instincts, now rejected their tradition and began to reason and to 'improve' their music... Another unfortunate error made by jazz musicians was to suppose that progress was necessary and that their art must be in continuous motion... 'It's not modern' was their disdainful cry when they listened to an old recording or to an excellent musician who had not modified his style for several years... We can see then why jazz, under the influence of these various factors, began after 1930 to lose all its purity and became injected with foreign elements which could only do great damage." (Panassié 1942: 53–7)

This anti-modernist position led jazz traditionalists to criticize the efforts of black professional swing musicians like Coleman Hawkins, Roy Eldridge, and Art Tatum who continued developing new techniques and harmonies in jazz performance. In the magazine *Jazz Hot*, Panassié criticized Eldridge for letting his "theories spoil his music. He seems to think that young players must inevitably forge ahead and improve on the old, and that's the rub. He has reached a point where his technique gets in his way instead of helping him." (*Jazz Hot* 2/3-1939: 9) In *Jazz Information* the comparison of boogie-woogie pianist Jimmy Yancey and swing pianist Art Tatum again revealed the anti-modernism of jazz traditionalists. "While Yancey, working with the simple elements of his folk music, creates a pure style of successful variations, Tatum – favorite son of many modern musicians – has developed the original jazz style of James P. Johnson, with its many European influences, to fantastic extremes. Tatum's superb technique and his extraordinary harmonic invention, win him the applause of jazz musicians who would call Yancey corny... the whole Tatum style seems to be directed toward an improvisation uncontrolled by conceptions of form; a kind of loose-minded, piano-tinkling that makes good listening for other pianists, or good background music at a sophisticated bar." (*Jazz Information* 7-26-1940:13) Coleman Hawkins also was criticized for his innovations in jazz following his return from Europe in 1939. Hawkins' recording "Body and Soul" in 1940 became the most influential modernist jazz recording of the period and eventually was elected to the National Academy of Recording Arts and Sciences Hall of Fame. In "Coleman Hawkins Is Declining" in *Music and Rhythm*, Duane Woodruff pointed to Hawkins' 1940 recording of "Body and Soul" as evidence of his decline as a jazz musician and his pretensions to being modern. "The greatest tenor saxophone virtuoso in all jazz is declining. His best days have passed. He attained his mature style about 1927... But since his return from Europe about a year ago, something has happened to his tone, his manner of phrasing... Another recently recorded Hawkins disk, *Body and Soul* (Bluebird 10523) in no way compares with his feeling, beautifully played chorus on the Fletcher Henderson version of *It's the Talk of the Town* (Columbia 28245)." (*Music and Rhythm* 12-1940:27) Bob White in noting that "the hot solo as a personal *creation* has gone steadily down hill" also noted that "Hawkins' great choruses on *Body and Soul* were the work of a marvelous instrumental virtuoso. But somewhere along – about the fifth or sixth bar they ceased to be hot solos." (*Down Beat* 11-1-1940: 6) As William Russell pointedly observed, it was "a generally accepted fact that refinement and elaboration in any art are accompanied by a corresponding decline in vital ruggedness, spirited abandon, and in genuineness and intensity in power of expression." (*H.R.S. Rag* 11-1940: 10) Hughes Panassié in *Real Jazz* summarized the jazz traditionalists' view of the modern innovations of swing musicians. "If you want to measure the melodic hiatus which separates the contemporary musicians from the men who play in the older style, you need only compare the recordings of *Body and Soul* and *Star Dust* recorded by Chu Berry and Roy Eldridge, with those made by Louis Armstrong. Armstrong's improvised melody line is clear, singing, and agreeable to hear, while Roy Eldridge and Chu develop over-elaborate and complicated phrases which are stripped of all significance." (Panassié 1942: 234)

Jazz traditionalists faced the contradictory position of claiming for themselves a connoisseurship of aesthetic appreciation and refinement – a natural predisposition of their class – while rejecting such cultivated connoisseurship among jazz musicians. For the sophisticated jazz connoisseur, the genuine jazz musician had to remain untainted by cultivated techniques or pretensions to transform an already ideal art form. Modernist professional musicians and modernist jazz critics, however, would challenge the romanticism and anti-modernism among early jazz connoisseurs. And ironically, the general appreciation of jazz as a serious art promoted by enthusiasts influenced the development of a modern jazz paradigm among professional musicians as they performed jazz as a serious art for appreciative listening audiences. And while jazz traditionalists held a romanticism that eventually pitted them against most professional musicians, they were instrumental in validating earlier vernacular jazz music and its artists. Jazz traditionalists in their own way challenged the cultural distinctions of status in America at the time. They were the first major writers and consumers to claim vernacular music as worthy of aesthetic appreciation equal to any other music including the European cultivated tradition. They presented some of the first social histories of popular music and popular musicians. They positioned African Americans as artists who created and performed the best homegrown music in America. And finally, their efforts assured that as the jazz narrative evolved in constructing a history of a great authentic American art form that the black jazz vernacular would be positioned as its first significant expression.

Modern swing: professional musicians and the modernist ethos

Situation Between the Critics and Musicians is Laughable

The dominating attitude has been that of the musician who questions the right of musical amateurs to pass judgement upon their efforts... The critics on the other hand, feel it is their duty to constantly 'expose' all musicians attempting to earn their living in any other manner than a strictly musical one... Give us critics who by *constructive criticism* will help to elevate former standards, whose sympathetic and encouraging advice will inspire the artist to strike out for higher levels, with the assurance that his efforts will not go unappreciated. (Duke Ellington, *Down Beat*, April 1939: 4)

Duke Ellington like many professional swing musicians was not particularly happy with the evangelical and pretentious ravings of jazz critics. Jazz critics' relentless attacks against the commercial capitulation of swing

musicians had taken their toll. Ellington in discussing the situation between critics and musicians also expressed the modernist ethos held by
most swing musicians. He dearly hoped for a constructive jazz criticism
to aid in the further development of jazz. The early romanticism of jazz
enthusiasts ran squarely against the modernist ethos of professional swing
musicians, not just against these musicians' unpardonable sin of serving
the commercial music market. This ideological conflict eventually crys-
tallized into a Jazz War between jazz traditionalists and jazz modernists.
As jazz enthusiast Bob Thiele later remembered, it was "a very strange era
in jazz where every musician and fan was vehemently loyal to his personal
preference ... everyone had their own inviolate, favorite category, musicians, and recording, and nothing else could co-exist with these personal
icons. It was like an endless brawl between fanatics." (Thiele 1995: 12)

From the beginning of the swing craze, jazz critics constantly combined
anti-commercialism with an anti-modernist ideology. This traditionalist
viewpoint peppered *Down Beat* magazine as well as the smaller special
publications for jazz enthusiasts. Critic George M. Avakian in 1939 expressed the common and combative viewpoint of traditionalist critics in
Down Beat. "Take most of the swing idols and chuck them down the drain
and maybe there'll be some hope for hot music! But the money's good
and so jazz will have to hit the skids. That's what will happen. Who are
the hot musicians today? Well, there's hardly a real one left, and all of
those have been going since the year one. The twenties were the golden
age of jazz, and it's the same crowd a decade later. The younger musicians don't play the same way. Which is a mistake, because you can't
improve on the old boys. Jazz is jazz; it can't be modernized or stream-
lined." (*Down Beat* 9-1939: 9) Swing bandleader and hepcat musician
Tommy Dorsey expressed the feelings of many professional musicians at
the time. "In the first place, during the last couple of years your writers seem chiefly interested in taking pot-shots at everybody. They don't
seem to offer constructive criticism but rather try to divide bands into two
groups – the one's they like and the one's they don't like. The latter, to use
one of their favorite words 'stink,' according to their views... *Down Beat*
should for the most part be current news, not opinions. Joe Public might
be interested in what your critics think but musicians as a whole form their
own opinions ... the ideas in most of your articles infer that anyone who
doesn't agree with your alleged critics is strictly an 'ickie'." (*Down Beat*
8-1938: 2) *Down Beat* editor Carl Cons was more adamant on this issue
in his editorial "What the Hell Good Is a Swing Music Critic." "There
are no intelligent critics! There are only press-agents for their own artistic prejudices. And finding an impartial and intelligent piece of criticism
is like finding a period in a haystack of adjectives... But our would-be

critics are so busy labeling everything either superbly magnificent or un-
believably sad, according to their personal taste, that they have no time
to examine their precious preachments or justify any of them with reason." (*Down Beat* 8-1938: 4) Critic Ted Locke responded to Cons with
the usual nonchalant attitude of early jazz critics. "We can only label the
finished product excellent, good, fair, poor, lousy, or stinking, as the case
may be." (*Down Beat* 12-1938: 6)

Duke Ellington, however, while not pleased with the state of relations
between professional musicians and critics did support the role of critics in jazz. It was "an established fact that any art worthy of the name
requires its own critics, whose responsibility it is to 'maintain and elevate standards,' the same principle applying to any respected profession."
Unfortunately, Ellington believed critics' "lack of impartiality" and "lack
of experience, youth or impulsiveness" rendered "their criticisms inef-
fectual." Critic John Hammond "identified himself so strongly in certain
directions that he no longer enjoys an impartial status which would entitle him to the role of critic," while critic Hugues Panassié preserved "a
closed mind on many musical subjects, judging all things according to
certain preconceived conceptions." (*Down Beat* 4-1939: 4 & 5-1939: 14)
While Ellington acknowledged the need for jazz critics, he conveniently
failed to name a single critic who was practicing this profession in an
appropriate manner. Needless to say Ellington and Tommy Dorsey were
not alone. Benny Goodman in *Colliers* in 1939 expressed his view of jazz
connoisseurs. "I'm ready to shoot when the ickies kick swing around
with professorial non-sense... Swing critics who would exterminate all
jitterbugs on sight remind me of art critics who would guillotine the ad-
dlepatters who draw mustaches on pretty girls in subway ads. All ickiness
is a form of sickiness. To me the swing icky is as dismal as the high-brow
music icky." (*Colliers* 2-25-1939: 60) Bandleader Gene Krupa argued
against critics' lament of the loss of artistry in swing bands, "there are no
Pulitzer Prizes in dance music!" And in a reference to the jazz art world,
he added, "I want capable musicians who can play the kind of music we
are paid to play. And that kind of music is listenable and danceable music.
The Bohemians in jazz can hide away in the confines of the swing clubs."
(*Down Beat* 2-1-40)

While swing musicians were critical of the harsh judgments of jazz critics and their continual belittling of these musicians' attempts to serve
the commercial market, swing musicians themselves were not necessarily pleased with certain aspects of the commercial music industry. The
anti-commercialism of most swing musicians, however, was focused on
the commercial market's undermining of jazz music within their modernist ethos. The commercial market undermined the development and

appreciation of modern swing. As Duke Ellington argued in 1939, the "most significant thing that can be said about swing music today is that it has become stagnant. Nothing of importance, nothing new, nothing either original or creative has occurred in the swing field during the last two years... What is important is the fact that Jazz has something to say. It speaks in many manners, taking always original and authentic form. Still in the throes of development and formation, it has fought its way upwards through the effortful struggles of sincere and irate musicians... It has striven in a world of other values, to get across its own message, and in so doing, is striving toward legitimate acceptance, in proportion to its own merits... Once again, it is proven that when the artistic point of view gains commercial standing, artistry itself bows out, leaving inspiration to die a slow death. (*Down Beat* 1-1939: 2, 17) Benny Goodman expressed similar feelings in his article "Is Swing Dead?" in 1941. "Swing, far from dead, has not yet been completely born. It is not yet halfway understood by the vast majority of its countrymen. If it were, there would be fewer tripe bands getting away with coast-to-coast murder – with pay. If it were, some of our finest artists like Benny Carter, Teddy Wilson and Art Tatum could make a million dollars. The only swing musicians worth their salt are the ones who aim over the heads of the layman and not at his midriff... Great swing music today rotates on the same axis as before the outside world discovered it. That axis is ideas – fresh, new and spontaneous composition set to steady rhythm." (*Music and Rhythm* 8-1941: 10)

While the anti-commercialism of critics certainly angered swing musicians, more important to the development of the jazz art world was the clear conflict over these musicians' modernist ethos. Since the jazz craze professional musicians prided themselves on cultivating the jazz vernacular. While swing music represented a further adoption of this vernacular professional musicians like Duke Ellington and Benny Goodman still retained the modernist ethos of artistic sophistication and innovation. In this sense, "modern" jazz existed since the Jazz Age only to be articulated in new ways through each generation of professional musician. Duke Ellington expressed the modernist ethos in *Metronome* as early as 1933. "I have always been a firm believer in musical experimentation. To stand still musically is equivalent to losing ground... My belief is that the new form will be 'sophisticated jazz' – a more subtle, a more clever, a more startling form than ever before." (*Metronome* 12-1933: 23) Teddy Wilson presented the modernist ethos of professional musicians in his prediction for the future of jazz in 1941. "Jazz will probably advance quite naturally, and it will take a long time to get anywhere near perfection. However, it is progressing all the time, and each man is adding his bit. Good hard study will speed up the process of advancement." (*Music and Rhythm* 4-1941: 37) Lionel Hampton certainly agreed with Ellington and Wilson on the constant improvements in jazz brought about by professional swing musicians. "What is happening to jazz music today is obvious and should have happened long ago. Jazz is becoming respectable and better and better musically all the time... But today jazzmen are becoming better musicians, trained in harmony and in the technique of their own instruments. And the music they play is becoming richer, and for my money, better." (*Music and Rhythm* 5-1941: 5) Coleman Hawkins presented the modernist perspective in terms of improvisation. "To really improvise a musician needs to know everything not only his instrument, but harmony, composition, theory, the whole works. You've got to know a whole lot more than just your instrument to jam." (*Music and Rhythm* 6-1941: 80) Swing musician Red Norvo was clear that "swing, to me, stands for something fresher and younger, something that represents progress... I certainly hope it isn't jazz we're playing, because jazz to me means something obnoxious, like that Dixieland school of thought ... the musicians that it stands for are corny by today's standards. You see, time has passed those people by, just as it's passed by the critics who still believe in that stuff and can't catch up with the newer ideas." (*Metronome* 4-1944: 23)

How to be a Jazz Critic

A formula of how to become a great critic might run something like this: spend four years at least in an exclusive eastern college. Become acquainted with Old Bix and Louis records and talk about these men in hushed whispers. Never listen to a record made after 1936 ... it just can't be good, it's too new. Get to know a few old musicians and give them publicity... Above all, remain completely ignorant of the technical aspects of music. Don't know anything about chords, about tone, or keys. That's all *commercial*. In short, become a romantic, a charlatan, a poseur, a pseudo-intellectual, an aesthetic snob, and you are well on the way to success. (Bob White, *Down Beat* August 1, 1940: 9)

Bob White as the newest member of the *Down Beat* staff, and fresh out of Dartmouth, immediately joined the heated debates about jazz. White presented an emerging modernist critique of jazz traditionalists as fanatics living in a romantic past uninformed by any real musical sensibility. White was not alone as some jazz critics began to fight back against the anti-modernist fanaticism of jazz traditionalists. Critic Paul Eduard Miller complained that the "esoteric hot jazz fan waxes so emotional over his beliefs that he has hardened them into an unshakable faith. This faith is imbedded in a deep, narrow groove, from which point he can see or hear nothing save *his* kind of jazz." (*Music and Rhythm* 2-1941: 70) Critic D. Leon Wolff in "Critics Are Sentimentalists With Faulty Emotional

Values" agreed with Miller. "Among the strange characteristics of this crew is a holier-than-thou hypocrisy. Their favorite trick is to 'puff' certain second-rate old-time musicians (most of whom are dead or out of tune, or both) so that when the average listener in all honesty is forced to subordinate them to their betters, he at once is supposed to commit musical suicide by classifying himself as one 'who has no understanding of the spirit and goals of true jazz' ... another characteristic of the lunatic fringe – their nostalgia for the early days of jazz, partly, but mostly their clannishness, their desire to seem elite, not to be included with the mass of jazz-lovers who refuse to idealize previous low standards. How these collectors hate to recognize the creative genius of Goodman, the colossal violence and technique of Eldridge ... the incomparable tone of Lawrence Brown, the beauty and assurance of Teddy Wilson! How it infuriates them to see young upstarts like these outclassing their gods by a mile in all the requisites, *including inner feeling*, that go to make great jazz musicians! But the more they're assailed by doubts, the more their icons are proved to be inferior to present-day jazzmen." (*Down Beat* 6-1-1941: 8) The modernist critic Leonard Feather remarked in 1944 that "there is absolutely no dividing line between swing and jazz... The devotees of the old time jazz, whose nostalgic yearnings for the idols of a generation ago involves an indiscriminate contempt for anything they class as modern swing, claim that the musicians of today pay too much attention to technique and too little to style; that the fundamental simplicity of jazz has been lost in the evolution of swing and the young stars of the swing era. This is an unrealistic argument." (*Metronome* 4-1944: 22)

These early stages of a jazz war highlighted a conflict between traditionalists championing the jazz vernacular of artists who mostly performed outside the world of professional music making and modernist professional swing musicians. As swing musicians performed in smaller jazz ensembles and jam sessions for the rising jazz art world they brought their modernist ethos to bear on improvisational performance to the displeasure and miscomprehension of many jazz traditionalists. But along the way, they attracted a new audience for modern swing and a new group of modernist critics who became spokespersons for professional musicians. As modernist critic and *Metronome* editor Barry Ulanov made clear. "Jazz is a great art because it accepts standards of musicianship, because it is progressive. We are not the lunatic fringe of jazz fandom and jazz critics who look merely for lameness, halting delivery and blind devotion to the jazz of thirty years ago in a jazzman. We are with and for the great jazzmen who look ahead, who play ahead, who are projecting their music and propelling this art to a brilliant future. We are not frightened because the men we like are famous, young, and healthy." (*Metronome* 2-1944: 8)

Groovin' high: bebop, hipsters, and the modernist revolt

Now that bebop has been absorbed into the mainstream of jazz, the major question that remains is how it will expand, escape its limitations and cliches, lead the way into something still richer in musical texture and finer in artistic concept. . . The story of bop, like that of swing before it, like the stories of jazz and ragtime before that, has been one of constant struggle against the restrictions imposed on all progressive thought in an art that has been commercialized to the point of prostitution; of struggle against reactionaries who resent anything new which they can neither understand nor perform themselves. (Leonard Feather, *Inside Bebop*, 1949: 45)

A new and more radical modernist ethos was adopted by a younger generation of professional musician in the 1940s. Led by young strident beboppers, "modern" jazz appeared as a radical transformation to even swing music. While Feather and other modernist critics supported older swing musicians like Art Tatum, Coleman Hawkins, and Roy Eldridge, they also championed a younger generation of "hipsters" who were refashioning their professional ethos into a modern jazz paradigm that became the foundation of the jazz renaissance of the 1950s and 1960s. Led by "hip" black beboppers like Dizzy Gillespie, both black and white young professional musicians adopted a high art ideology that incorporated elements of the jazz narrative of the swing era. Like previous white hepcat musicians, hipsters adopted a disdain for popular audiences, a contempt for commercial music, and a view of jazz as an unappreciated art. Hipsters' contempt for commercial music also articulated the anti-commercialism of jazz traditionalist critics. But like previous modern swing musicians, hipsters adopted innovation – new applications of technique, rhythm, and harmony – as their ethos. Needless to say, hipsters did not like old-style jazz. Hipsters also incorporated elements of swing populism, they claimed modern jazz as progressive, and for some, a radical rebellion against Jim Crow. And, unfortunately, like some swing musicians, some hipsters adopted a deviant life-style. Jazz traditionalists who battled modern swing music in the late 1930s into the early 1940s suddenly confronted an even more aggressive rejection of their romantic ideology – a new modernist ideology that co-opted traditionalists' elitist condemnation of commercial music and unappreciative fans. Dizzy Gillespie later remembered the hipster attitudes of boppers. That "beboppers expressed disdain for 'squares' is mostly true. . . A 'square' and a 'lame' were synonymous, and they accepted the complete life-style, including the music, dictated by the establishment. They rejected the concept of creative alternatives, and they were just the opposite of 'hip,' which meant 'in the know,' 'wise,' or one with 'knowledge' of life and how to live.

Musically, a square would chew cud. He'd spend his money at the Roseland Ballroom to hear a dance band playing standards, rather than extend his ear and spirit to take an odyssey in bebop at the Royal Roost. Oblivious to the changes which replaced old, outmoded expressions with newer, modern ones, squares said 'hep' rather than 'hip'." (Gillespie 1979: 296-7)

Ira Gitler's oral history of the transition to bebop, *Swing to Bop*, shows how bebop developed as a style and spread out among young professional swing musicians. (Gitler 1986) Young black professional musicians in New York City including Dizzy Gillespie, Charlie Parker, Thelonious Monk, Bud Powell, Milt Hinton, and Max Roach developed the modernist bebop style. These musicians congregated in Harlem at Minton's Playhouse and Monroe's Uptown House to jam and try out the ideas they were formulating. Other musicians came to Minton's and Monroe's to check out the new sounds including older swing musicians like Benny Goodman, Coleman Hawkins, Ben Webster, and Don Byas. Bebop spread as musicians moved from one big band to another and traveled around the country. Musicians Dexter Gordon, Wardel Gray, and Illinois Jacquet heard bebop while in New York City and on the road in big bands composed of bop musicians. By 1944, they were educating young jazz musicians in Los Angeles about bop in the jamming scene on Central Avenue. Small swing bands of older black musicians like Don Byas, Ben Webster, and Coleman Hawkins also used young boppers. The temporary hiring of black bebop musicians by a few white big bands in the early 1940s as well as the use of bop arrangements exposed bebop to white musicians. Big bands like Charlie Barnet's and Boyd Raeburn's placed young boppers in close contact with young white musicians. Charlie Barnet's big band, for example, had black boppers Howard McGhee, Trummy Young, and Oscar Pettiford, and a number of white musicians who became part of the first clique of white modern jazz musicians: Chubby Jackson, Buddy De Franco, Pete Condoli, Ralph Burns, and Neil Hefti. White musicians also constantly moved in and out of bands and traveled extensively. The white musicians in Barnet's band, for example, eventually performed in the first "modern" big bands of Woody Herman, Boyd Raeburn, and Stan Kenton. While the first bop ensemble did not perform commercially until late 1943, and the first bop recording did not occur until early 1945, bebop had already spread wide and far, capturing the imagination of a large number of young musicians. By the mid-1940s bebop had arrived on the jazz scene as a distinct new style and bebop bands were performing in a number of nightclubs and jazz concerts. In only a short period, a new national clique of modern jazz musicians emerged all initially influenced by bop.

The impact of bebop as a modernist revolt against jazz traditionalists was immediately evident as modernist critics adopted bebop as their
own. In May 1945, the New Jazz Foundation, founded by modernist critics Ulanov and Feather, had its first concert and featured boppers Dizzy
Gillespie and Charlie Parker. Feather set the tone for the modernist revolt four months later in "On Musical Fascism." "There are the extreme
right-wingers of jazz, the voice of reaction in music. Just as the fascists
tend to divide group against group and distinguish between Negroes,
Jews, Italians and 'real Americans,' so do the Moldy Figs try to catego-
rize New Orleans, Chicago, swing music and 'the real jazz.' Just as the
Gerald L. K. Smiths regard America as a private club to which refugees
and members of various races cannot be admitted, so does the right-wing
jazz group limit itself to a clique in which a nineteenth-century birth cer-
tificate from New Orleans is almost the only admission ticket, while all
young, aspiring musicians of today are barred and branded as 'riff musicians' or jump and jive men." (*Metronome* 9-1945: 16) As Gillespie's
publicist, Feather attacked traditionalists by co-opting the progressive
ideals held by early jazz critics and using these ideals against them. In an
early promotion for Gillespie in 1944, pianist Mary Lou Williams agreed
with the political positioning of bebop. "People who are progressive politically, should support progressive music and forget about all that old-time
Dixieland... And I believe every musician, no matter what or how he
plays, should always try to advance." Teddy Wilson stated that it was "a
funny thing, but that always has been a sore point with me too, how progressives support reactionary music. They want music to stand still, yet
they should know that one of the basic principles of Marx's philosophy is
that nothing stands still... jazz can't stay in that primitive groove, and political progressives ought to wake up and learn more about modern jazz."
(IJS File, Gillespie) A 1948 profile on bop in *The New Yorker* pointed
out that "beboppers occasionally describe themselves as progressives and
their opponents as reactionaries. They call themselves 'the left wing'
and their opponents 'the right wing.' Friends of the older music call the
beboppers 'dirty radicals' and 'wild-eyed revolutionaries'." (*New Yorker*
7-3-1948: 21) A column in the *Chicago Sun-Times* on Gillespie again referred to the modernists political attack against traditionalists. "Just in
case you came late, bop is the newest sensation in the music world. It
has split jazz music fans into more splinters than the Democratic party
had in the last elections. In fact, the musicians are even split along political lines. Those who favor the old Dixieland jazz, are considered right
wingers, or reactionaries, like the Dixiecrats. Those who go for bop are
left-of-center, or progressives, like the New Dealers." (*Chicago Sun-Times*
12-31-1948: 7)

Part of the progressive or radical politics of bop musicians was their race consciousness against Jim Crow America. As the *New Yorker* profile on bop pointed out, "Bebop, according to its pioneer practitioners, is a manifestation of revolt. Eight or ten years ago, many Negro jazz musicians, particularly the younger ones, who were sometimes graduates of music conservatories, began to feel, rightly or wrongly, that the white world wanted them to keep to the old-time jazz. They held the opinion that the old jazz, which they called 'Uncle Tom music,' was an art form of a meeker generation than theirs. They said it did not express the modern American Negro and they resented the apostrophes of critics who referred to them, with the most complimentary intent, as modern primitives playing an almost instinctive music. A lurid and rococo literature grew up around jazz, the work of writers who were delighted by the idea that this music began in New Orleans sporting houses, which was a notion that, whatever its merits, aroused no responsive spark in younger Negro musicians." (*New Yorker* 7-3-1948: 23) Arnold Shaw remembered the race consciousness of beboppers in the early 1940s. "And it was no secret that part of the adventure was to create something that 'Charley couldn't steal.' 'Charley' meant the white musicians who had reaped the rewards of black-oriented swing. 'Charley' meant the white musicians who still monopolized the top jobs in radio, in the recording field, in the Hollywood movie studios and in American symphony orchestras. . . Bop was not divisive but expressive of a divisiveness that still existed and had intensified." (Shaw 1971: 267) Mary Lou Williams later described the ambivalence of many boppers about co-optation and the success of bop moving "downtown" to white nightclubs. "And in no time, the commercial world from downtown was coming in on it, and they tried to learn it. I heard some of the guys speak about not wanting to play downtown or play in the open so everybody could take it from them. Because you know the black creators of the music have never gotten recognition for creating anything. . . I don't think anybody is looking for any big applause or anything about what they've created. But after a while, you get kinda really disgusted and dried out because everything you create is taken from you, and somebody else is given recognition for it." (Gillespie 1979: 149) White trumpeter Johnny Carisi later remembered the radical attitudes of black beboppers in Harlem. "I remember one time Joe Guy – we had a love-hate kind of thing – he grabbed me by the lapels. He said, 'You ofay cats come up and you steal all our shit.' It was like half mad, and at the same time it was like really a tribute. He was like saying, 'You're doing it'." (Gitler 1986: 85)

While modernists claimed a progressive cultural politics and rejected traditionalists as reactionary romantics, they also would refer to the upper-class origins of early jazz enthusiasts. The swing drummer Dave Tough slighted the class proclivities of early jazz enthusiasts as well as their "slumming" in Harlem during the Jazz Age. "Dixieland jazz was once revolutionary stuff. But now it's just straight Republican-Ticket kind of music. It's stuffy, musically limited and requested only by snobs who affect a 'pose'. . . Those Dixieland characters come here to live their youth over again. They like to think it's still prohibition and they're wild young cats up from Princeton for a hot time. All they need is a volume of F. Scott Fitzgerald sticking out of their pockets." (*Down Beat* 9-1946: 4) Since the Dixieland faction by the late 1940s was decidedly white, the racial divide also was hard to miss. Except for the old black jazz players from New Orleans and old Chicago boogie-woogie pianists, it was young hepcat white musicians who continued the Dixieland and Chicago styles and white jazz enthusiasts who were its critics and audience. Among small swing ensembles, it was Bob Crosby's Bobcats and Tommy Dorsey's Clambake Seven that continued the older jazz style while other swing ensembles adopted the modern swing ethos. White hepcat musicians like Eddie Condon, Lu Watters, Turk Murphy, Doc Evans, and Bob Wilber organized new Dixieland or Chicago style bands. Critic Amy Lee in 1949 pointed to the obvious irony of white proponents of the old black jazz vernacular while again pointing to early enthusiasts upper-class origins in places like upscale Westchester county. "In the midst of this heartening progress of the Negro musician from his 'natural' Dixieland to a more technically and intellectually advanced musical expression, is a quite less edifying example of reaction in the white camp. Even a devotee of Dixie and its Chicago and Condon derivatives, must look in dismay at the moldy fig jazz preoccupations of Bob Wilber and his Wildcats. . . When Bob and the boys, in their mid-teens were filling Westchester living rooms with earnest appropriations of Dodds, Bechet, Morton, and Armstrong, the effect was exciting. . . But as time goes by, and some of the new bop sounds become acceptably recognizable, there is something definitely disturbing in the Wildcat adherence to antique jazz." (*Down Beat* 5-6-1949: 2)

While bebop modernists attacked the politics of jazz traditionalists, the core of their aesthetic ideology was an avant-garde modernism. As the historian Scott DeVeaux (1997) argues, often the various associative meanings of rebellion in bop overshadow how this style was a logical extension of the modernist ethos of older swing musicians like Coleman Hawkins. While DeVeaux is absolutely correct in redirecting our attention to the modernist ethos of professional musicians, bebop still represented in its aesthetic ideology a more radical avant-garde orientation. *Down Beat* acclaimed the nation-wide modern revolution of bebop and its champion

Dizzy Gillespie in 1946. "The revolution caused by Dizzy's advanced conception was inevitable if Jazz were to keep progressing, for with the waxing of Hawk's *Body and Soul* and others in its class jazz reached a pinnacle of development. The human imagination has its limitations ... and Jazz had reached the point where musicians' imagination could no longer function effectively without the added stimulus of new horizons for exploration." (*Down Beat* 2-11-1946: 14) In 1947, *Down Beat* asked several boppers "What is Bebop?" Trumpeter Howard McGhee responded that "I just say be-bop is progressive music. It's the younger generation's idea of the right way to play." Trumpeter Tad Dameron believed that "Be-bop is music that's fresh and alive. It leads the way for new sounds in music." Charlie Parker claimed bebop was "advanced modern music." (*Down Beat* 9-10-1947: 6) Boppers like Parker also made reference to modernist and experimental classical composers as role models. (*Down Beat* 9-9-1949) The "somber, scholarly, twenty-one-year old" Thelonious Monk in *The New Yorker* pointed to these composers' influence. "We liked Ravel, Stravinsky, Debussy, Prokofieff, Schoenberg, and maybe we were a little influenced by them." (*New Yorker* 7-3-1948: 23) Ross Russell, owner of Dial Records one of the first labels to record bop, in the late 1940s explained to the mostly traditionalist readers of *The Record Changer* that bebop was both a true expression of jazz and a modernist revolution that rejected the dictates of the commercial market. "Bebop is music of revolt; revolt against big bands, arrangers, vertical harmonies, soggy rhythms, non-playing orchestra leaders, Tin Pan Alley – against commercialized music in general. It reasserts the individuality of the jazz musician as a creative artist, playing spontaneous and melodic music within the framework of jazz, but with new tools, sounds, and concepts." (Williams 1959: 202)

Modernist beboppers also adopted a hipster image along with hipster attitudes about the preponderance of squares and bad music. Dizzy Gillespie with his goatee, beret, zoot suit, and patois became the symbol of the new hipster. *Down Beat* in 1946 noted the widespread adoption of not only beboppers' music practices by "the vast majority of sidemen in the hipper bands around the country," but the hipster style as well. "Musicians wear goatee beards because Dizzy wears a goatee beard; musicians wear ridiculous little hats that have been seen around lately because Dizzy wears one; musicians have started to laugh in a loud, broken way because that's the way Dizzy laughs; musicians now stand with a figure 'S' posture, copying Dizzy who appears too apathetic to stand erect – and so down the list. . . It seems logical that Dizzy should epitomize the flauntingly unconventional, over-hip musicians, for his many mirror-imaging followers are just that." (*Down Beat* 2-11-1946: 14) Of course, as Gillespie (1986) later remarked, the hipster image was as much reality as stereotype when the popular media picked up the bebop phenomenon in the late 1940s. When bebop first hit the press it was as a deviant hipster cult as bop musicians Harry "Hipster" Gibson and "Slim" Gaillard popularized the new music with eccentric behavior and suggestive lyrics – and boosted their record sales and audiences in the process. *Newsweek* referred to bebop as "hot jazz overheated with overdone lyrics full of bawdiness, reference to narcotics, and double talk." The article was on the banning of bebop on radio station KMPC in Los Angeles as its program director claimed "Bebop ... tends to make degenerates out of our young listeners." (*Newsweek* 3-25-1946) The general press, to the dismay of jazz musicians and jazz critics, focused on the hipster cult, image and deviance, more than the music. "Its feverish practitioners like to wear berets, goatees and green-tinted horn-rimmed glasses, talk about their 'interesting sound'." (*Time* 5-17-1948: 74) "Bebop is a new school of discordant, offbeat jazz which has mushroomed into as big a music cult as swing. Its devotees ape the eccentric appearance of bebop's inventor, Gillespie: horn-rims, goatee and beret." (*Life* 10-11-1948: 139) Bop did receive a slightly more sympathetic airing in *Colliers*. "Bebop represents a revolt, not only from the monumental corn of big band arrangements but from the rigidity of tradition. Consequently, the boppers have cast aside many traditional jazz ideas and forms and introduced new effects... Instead the boppers strive for dissonance, or as many boppers put it, "new interesting sounds'... You have to be an extremely accomplished musician to attempt bop. It helps too if you happen to be more than slightly neurotic." (*Colliers* 3-20-1948: 16)

Unfortunately, the hipster life did include the use of narcotics. As Gillespie later pointed out, while the general press stereotyping of bop exaggerated the role of narcotics in jazz, it was a fact that the new hipster culture was a drug culture. "That beboppers used and abused drugs and alcohol was not completely a lie either... Now, certainly, we were not the only ones. Some of the older musicians had been smoking reefers... Jazz musicians, the old ones and the young ones, almost all of them I knew smoked pot, but I wouldn't call that drug abuse... Dope, heroin abuse, really got to be a major problem during the bebop era, especially in the late forties, and a lotta guys died from it." (Gillespie 1986: 283) The modernist pianist Lennie Tristano, a supporter of bebop, criticized the hipster culture of many boppers. "Jazz has not yet found acceptance with the American public; and bebop, an advanced and complex outgrowth of that jazz, exists precariously above the uncomprehending ears of the average person. But it is the musicians themselves, the vendors of jazz, who in many cases make their own lives difficult ... the supercilious attitude and lack of originality of the young hipsters constitute no less a menace to the existence of bebop. These young boppers spend most of their time acquiring pseudo-hip affectations instead of studying and analyzing modern jazz with the aim of contributing something original to it. . . They gaze indifferently at the uninitiate through dropping lids, muttering, 'It's cool, Daddy-o.' There is an unfortunate belief that to play like the great jazzmen, you must live like them. Close examination might reveal that the productivity of these creative minds has often been stagnated by self-destructive habits." (*Metronome* 6-1947: 16) Bob Livingston in a letter to *Metronome* pleaded for reform among hip modern jazz musicians. "For a long time now the public has scorned jazz, possibly because they have felt that the average jazz musician was a drug addict. Now is the time to wake them up to the truth about jazz musicians and now is the time to educate our future musicians and see to it that they do not make the mistakes that some of today's musicians have made. . . Use of narcotics by jazz musicians will only make the public scorn our music that much more." (*Metronome* 11-1947: 36)

While beboppers were the first to articulate a new modernist ideology, by the late 1940s the hipster or modernist ethos had spread widely among young professional musicians. "Beards" were everywhere: this was *Metronome's* label for the new "modern" jazz musician. The sociologist Howard Becker observed and interviewed white professional musicians in Chicago in the late 1940s. Like Carlo Lastrucci's earlier study, Becker found white professional musicians still retained the same attitudes of earlier white hepcat musicians. Except these musicians were hip not hep, and they viewed outsiders to the jazz fraternity as squares. " 'Squareness' is felt to penetrate every aspect of the square's behavior just as its opposite, 'hipness' is evident in everything the musician does. . . The musician thus sees himself as a creative artist who should be free from outside control, a person different from and better than those outsiders he calls squares who understand neither his music nor his way of life and yet because of whom he must perform in a manner contrary to his professional ideals." (Becker 1951: 139) A general modernist paradigm had infused a new generation of professional musician. Some white big bands would follow the example of Dizzy Gillespie's big band and do bop like the Woody Herman Orchestra. The modernist paradigm also was evident in white proponents of Progressive Jazz in the late 1940s. Pianist Lennie Tristano and bandleaders Boyd Raeburn, Claude Thornhill, Eliot Lawrence, and Stan Kenton led the progressive jazz movement in the late 1940s. The new progressive big bands incorporated new bebop innovations and the compositional experimentation of Duke Ellington, while pursuing a more symphonic jazz approach to big band composition and performance. They also were populated by hipster white musicians strongly influenced by beboppers and bebop music.

As progressive jazz pianist Lennie Tristano argued, "Bebop is a valiant attempt to raise jazz to a thoughtful level, and to replace emotion with meaning. It is successfully combating the putrefying effect of commercialism. It has been called mechanical, 'over-cerebrative,' sloppy, technical, and immoral. Beboppers have been accused of willfully promoting juvenile delinquency. All this prattle is due to a lack of understanding not only of the musicians who play bebop, but of the emotionally immature listeners... The development of jazz must be the concern of every musician who attempts to play it. Jazz is not a form of popular entertainment; it is art for its own sake." (*Metronome* 6-1947: 14, 31) Modernist critic Ulanov pointed out that the progressive Boyd Raeburn Orchestra was "by no means a dance organization. The music it plays is designed for listening: it's modern music, cast in new molds out of old classical forms and jazz rhythms and harmonies. It follows no conventions of beat or melody or harmonic organization... This is the way music will be played from now on by the really hip and talented and profound and musically healthy." (*Metronome* 30-1946: 18) Stan Kenton in the liner notes for his boxed set recording "A Presentation of Progressive Jazz" was clear about the future direction of jazz. "The reason we are seeking the concert field today, is because I believe jazz must grow beyond the rigid disciplining of dance music. For years jazz bands and orchestras presented their music for dancing or good listening – whichever the patron preferred. We believe that for jazz to progress – and it most certainly shall since it is now an established art form – it must move into the concert field... [J]azz is not just an emotional projection from an individual musician, not something always set to a definite beat, but instead a music of strong emotional impact even WITHOUT rhythm, or possibly in a five-four, seven-five, three-quarter, or even times rubato movement. This is one of many ways Progressive Jazz differs from jazz in its primitive forms." (Capitol H 172, 1948) Kenton suggested at the end of 1948 that it was time to establish exclusive halls for the performance of big band jazz concerts. "The Kenton plan, in brief, is the organization of a system of class spots where good jazz will be featured by top exponents in this brand of music for the exclusive enjoyment of persons interested in *listening* to jazz." (*Down Beat* 12-15-1948: 1)

In "Modernists Cop Top Poll Slots," *Metronome* celebrated its 1948 annual poll's demonstration that young "modern" jazz players like Charlie Parker, Buddy DeFranco, Charlie Ventura, Dizzy Gillespie, Bill Harris, and Nat Cole were garnering the top votes of its readers. "We've got a pretty good idea, just from looking at the following results, that jazz enthusiasts and participants are looking ahead, that they want their music modern and imaginative." (*Metronome* 1-1949: 24) Annual Polls in both *Metronome* and *Down Beat* by the last years of the 1940s definitely showed modern jazz musicians had become among the most popular professional musicians. Modernist musicians also were performing in jazz clubs and jazz concerts across the country, recording on independent jazz record labels, and even were marquee players in jazz festivals in Europe. Benny Goodman even announced forming a bebop ensemble in 1949. The modernist revolt, however, did not eliminate jazz traditionalists or the demand for genuine jazz. The Dixieland faction of the jazz art world remained active throughout the 1940s and as the fortunes of modern jazz and the jazz club scene hit hard times by the end of that decade a Dixieland Revival in the early 1950s boosted the hopes of jazz traditionalists. Caustic repartees also remained between the two factions leading into the 1950s as modernists were accused of various evils from the decline in the jazz market, to the continued deviant image of jazz, to the collapse of the popular big band market.

The modernist revolt in the 1940s combined various distinctions active during the Swing Era. It articulated the modernist ethos of swing musicians, the outsider ethos of hepcat musicians, the connoisseurship of jazz enthusiasts, as well as the politics of the American left. This new aesthetic ideology in general positioned "modern" jazz musicians as creative artists struggling outside the mainstream of American music and culture. Certainly not all musicians of the new generation of professional musicians adopted as a whole the paradigm first developed by beboppers, and certainly rebellion for black musicians was distinctly different than for white musicians. While the new hipster jazz musician as a rebel from convention – musical, social or political – became a common cultural construct among modern jazz musicians, not all modern jazz musicians incorporated the entire rebel ethos. This was particularly the case in terms of the deviant hipster life-style that continued to haunt jazz coverage in the popular press into the 1950s and 1960s. By the late 1940s, however, jazz in general had been re-conceptualized as a distinct music genre and music aesthetic from popular music. While earlier professional musicians struggled with the commercial market to mediate between the cultivated and the vernacular, the new generation of professional "jazz" musician rejected the role of mediator, moving jazz into a new trajectory as an American music.

The art historian Sidney Finklestein in *Jazz: A People's Music* published in 1949 pointed to modern jazz as "a bundle of contradictions... Bebop and modern jazz have by no means settled the problem of jazz. In fact, they raise the contradictions inherent in jazz from its beginnings, to their

highest level." (Finklestein 1949: 148–9) Like many of his contemporaries, Finklestein viewed the new modernist ethos of jazz musicians as
unquestionably a rebellion, but also recognized this rebellion as full of
contradictions. The modern jazz aesthetic reflected the socially heterogeneous world of jazz during the 1930s and 1940s as well as the different
meanings associated with this music. It articulated class, race, aesthetic,
and moral distinctions of the Swing Era in new and often contradictory
ways, particularly in relation to the original romantic view of jazz as folk
music adopted by both jazz enthusiasts and the Popular Front. As jazz
critic Leroi Jones (1963) later pointed out, beboppers as middle class
blacks suddenly rejected the conventional values coveted by their class
and reflected in their professional culture up to that time. These musicians re-articulated both their predecessors' agenda to create a legitimate
black art form, but adopted the hepcat ethos as a radical rejection of Jim
Crow and assimilation to mainstream American culture. Not all black
jazz musicians would adopt this radical position, but the bop rebellion
shifted the ideological center of these musicians' ethos to a more radical position while reorienting the original debates on race and culture
of both the Harlem Renaissance and the Popular Front. White modern
jazz musicians re-articulated the earlier hepcat rebellion but adopted the
modernism of both swing and bebop musicians. Inspired by beboppers,
a new generation of white professional musician, who were mostly working class, reoriented their professional ethos with a radical modernism
as a rebellion against conventional distinctions of status and legitimacy –
the white hipster representing the most radical position. In essence, the
socially heterogeneous world of modern jazz brought together a diverse
community of musicians who in some fashion, whether aesthetics, values, or behaviors, worked "against the grain" of American culture at
mid-century. And at the center of this general artistic rebellion was the
modern jazz paradigm – jazz as high art – in which these musicians and
future jazz musicians would articulate their own music making as well as
the meaning of jazz music.

Conclusion: things to come

Rebop, Bebop, and Bop

Today the *avant-garde* of jazz is still very much alive, even though it flourishes for a
time under the far from flattering name of Bop. This music is the sharply outlined
reflection of the musicians who play it and, especially, of the environment in which
it is played. Born in protest, both social and artistic, and cradled in contradiction,
Bop mirrors the pace, complexity, and confusion of the times – frequently with
too much accuracy for comfort. (Marshall Stearns, *Harper's*, April 1950: 96)

Marshall Stearns, one of the original founders of the Hot Clubs of America in 1935, reflected on the "brief but busy" history of jazz up to the modernist revolt of the late 1940s. As one of the early politically progressive jazz enthusiasts, Stearns expressed the new reconfiguration of swing populism and avant-garde modernism found in the new modern jazz paradigm. The different distinctions active during the swing era and leading to the modernist revolt demonstrate the complex articulation of race, class, aesthetics, and values in American music during the 1930s and 1940s. While swing was celebrated as a populist art, affluent white jazz enthusiasts were claiming a connoisseurship of high art appreciation for black vernacular jazz. White hepcat musicians who continued performing genuine jazz buttressed enthusiasts' preference for this black folk music. Meanwhile, black swing musicians, middle class within their own community but definitely second-class citizens outside of it, maintained a modernist ethos seeking a continuous cultivation of vernacular jazz as an art form. Many white swing musicians, some former hepcats and most working class, also adopted the general modern ethos of their profession. And from these early configurations of meaning and practice emerged a new radical modernist jazz movement that co-opted the various distinctions of the swing era into a new "outsider" modern jazz ethos that spread widely through a new generation of professional musician.

The struggle between jazz traditionalists and jazz modernists, of course, again put center stage the relationship between the vernacular and cultivated traditions in American music. Jazz traditionalists posed a unique challenge to the practice of professional musicians of cultivating the jazz vernacular. Yet this challenge was steeped in a romantic narrative of genuine jazz that while articulating the progressive ideals of the New Deal Era reproduced in some fashion the primitivist ideology that haunted the African American community as it struggled against racial stereotypes. Nor did this romantic defense of vernacular jazz mesh well with the ethos of professional popular musicians, an ethos reflecting their own struggles over status and legitimacy in American music. Unlike jazz enthusiasts whose status was predicated on an easily assumed connoisseurship of sophisticated art appreciation whether genuine jazz or impressionist art, professional musicians' status was predicated on their ethos and music making, given that their race, class or education precluded any presumption of legitimate status on their part. The conflict between traditionalists and modernists, therefore, reflected both the different social backgrounds between jazz enthusiasts and professional musicians and the distinct positions they occupied as consumers and producers of American music. The modernist revolt succeeded because it reflected the specific struggles of professional musicians, and therefore, spread quickly within this community.

Regardless of the conflict between jazz traditionalists and jazz modernists, early jazz enthusiasts did create the foundations of a jazz art world that made in many ways the modernist revolt possible. Ironically, the high art appreciation promoted by jazz enthusiasts for genuine jazz was easily co-opted by professional musicians as they occupied the emerging jazz art world. This art world of concerts, clubs, and record labels also formed the basis of the spread of the modern jazz paradigm among professional musicians as well as developing an audience for modern jazz. As a decentralized commercial market, the jazz art world provided an open system of production that allowed different genres of jazz to find a niche within this market. The victory of the modernist revolt reflected the preponderance of modernist jazz musicians as opposed to traditionalist jazz musicians. As we will see, however, the modernist victory did not mean that vernacular jazz ultimately fell from grace in the jazz art world and more importantly in jazz criticism. The modernist victory assured that the new jazz art world presented a progressive jazz tradition from folk art, to popular art, to modernist high art.

As a new jazz art world gradually expanded during the late 1940s and grappled with internecine struggles, changes of a larger scale were occurring in American music that would assure the transformation of jazz music into a distinct music tradition and market in the United States. By the late 1940s, the big band market was slowly collapsing as various factors undermined professional musicians' ability to maintain big bands as financially viable. And as the big band market declined, another gradual change was occurring where a new set of genres and musicians were to replace professional musicians in the commercial market of "popular" music. The professional culture of musicians that had dominated the popular commercial music market since the end of the nineteenth century suddenly witnessed its replacement by a new artistic culture of popular musician performing a distinctly different set of music practices. Ironically, the same factors that made this revolutionary change in the popular commercial market possible, the Rock 'n' Roll revolution, aided in the success of the jazz art world in the early 1950s that led to the modern jazz renaissance.

5 The New Jazz Age: the jazz art world and the modern jazz renaissance

It is true that no one human being can keep up with the Niagara of jazz recordings, concerts, and festivals, as well as radio, nightclub, and television appearances of jazz musicians... It wasn't always so. To the old-timer of the 20s, who remembers when a few grooves of a few 78-rpm recordings held all the recorded jazz extant, we are swinging through an era of plenty, a renaissance of jazz, which we will some day look back upon with wonder and envy. The sounds of jazz are hitting the public ear from all sides, and, although the conscientious critic necessarily finds that keeping up with it is difficult, in the midst of this great quantity of music, a new and qualitative change seems to be taking place.

Marshall Stearns, "What is Happening to Jazz,"
Down Beat Music 1961, 1961: 28

As a founding member of the United Hot Clubs of America in 1935, Marshall Stearns was selected by *Down Beat* in its annual review to reflect on the state of jazz during the 1950s. An avid follower of jazz since the late 1920s, Stearns pointed to a musical renaissance in jazz performance. He also noted the success of the jazz art world that sustained this renaissance in jazz music. In the 1950s, this art world began a period of rapid expansion in production, audiences, and stylistic innovation. It garnered national attention in print and broadcast media. Even the State Department gave an approving nod to jazz as it sent jazz musicians abroad as American cultural ambassadors. The long quest of Stearns and others to make jazz a recognized, legitimate, and financially viable art form seemed to have finally been achieved.

The rosy picture painted by Stearns of the state of jazz at the end of the 1950s stood in stark contrast to the state of jazz as well as professional musicians at the beginning of that decade. Leading into the 1950s professional musicians were confronting a major decline in the big band market and far fewer opportunities for employment. The jazz art world remained economically unstable as jazz musicians, jazz clubs, and jazz labels struggled to survive. While the big band business never recovered, the jazz art world by the mid-1950s suddenly experienced an economic boom in live and recorded jazz music. When only a few years earlier dirges on the state of jazz could be found in *Metronome* and *Down Beat*, suddenly jazz critics and even the general press were hailing a New Jazz Age.

The New Jazz Age witnessed a modern jazz renaissance in American music. The victory of jazz modernists over jazz traditionalists meant that the expansion of jazz as an art form during this period was driven by a modern jazz aesthetic. This aesthetic led to widespread experimentation among jazz musicians that resulted in the rapid development of a number of stylistic directions and musical innovations in jazz performance. The modernist direction also included a claim to high art status and led jazz performers to expand stylistically, mostly in the direction of a fine art aesthetic and to look for new locations conducive to fine art appreciation. The modern jazz renaissance also occurred during a period of tremendous political, social, and cultural upheaval. In the jazz art world, the tenor of the times would express itself among a more race conscious and radicalized community of black jazz artists. These artists would begin to challenge the directions of jazz, musically and ideologically. An important characteristic of the jazz art world, however, was its decentralized form of organization with a large number of independent artists, producers, and writers. This characteristic prevented any style – traditional, mainstream, modern, radical or pop – from dominating the art world. With no centers of authority, the jazz art world remained innovative and diverse throughout the renaissance.

While jazz music went in a variety of stylistic directions during the modern jazz renaissance, the jazz art world also underwent significant change. This art world in various ways moved away from its original home in the commercial world of jazz clubs and urban popular entertainment. Beginning in the 1950s, jazz music would move to concert halls, art museums, outdoor festivals, and even college campuses. The jazz art world continued its quest for legitimacy by moving to venues and finding audiences that imparted to jazz a greater status as a high art music. This art world also moved beyond the borders of the United States establishing an international circulation of jazz music and jazz musicians. As the economic boom led jazz music to new venues and new audiences, it also spurred a tremendous growth in jazz writing whether in jazz magazines, jazz books, jazz instructional material, and in non-jazz print media. Jazz in the written word and written note transformed the jazz art world into a far more "literate" world of jazz critics, jazz connoisseurs and jazz musicians.

By the early 1970s the musical renaissance and the economic boom of the New Jazz Age was at an end. No single reason stands out as to the cause of the end of the renaissance. The recession in the jazz market by the late 1960s and changes in the music industry's interest in jazz certainly played a role. It also can be argued that the rapid stylistic changes during the renaissance led jazz music through all its potential directions as an art form. A generational divide also separated the jazz musicians in the 1950s and 1960s from those that would follow. New generations of jazz musicians would take on a more craftsman like approach to jazz performance, falling into one of the already established streams of jazz performance and building on their predecessors' achievements. Young and old jazz musicians alike, however, would continue to perform a diverse range of styles for a jazz art world whose foundations were firmly established by the end of the New Jazz Age.

Hard times: American popular music and the jazz cult

A lot of reasons have been advanced as to why the dance band business slumped after the war and has never since regained a firm footing. Things like high prices, television, emphasis on vocalists, the lack of any new dance crazes, kids not dancing much anymore, etc. None of these faults could be laid at the feet of the leaders themselves. Things just happened and they suffered. (Editorial, *Down Beat*, January 11, 1952: 10)

In the late 1940s, the big band business confronted a steadily declining market punctuated by announcements of famous big bands disbanding. In *Down Beat* and *Metronome*, big band leaders announced the formation of small units to adjust to the dismal condition of the big band market, while other leaders announced yet another attempt at forming a viable big band. Professional musicians certainly were facing hard times. The collapse of professional big bands reflected broader changes in the popular music industry as it faced hard times as well. By the late 1940s, record sales were dropping and the former integrated music industry of recording, radio, film, and music publishing underwent a major transformation. By the late 1950s, American popular music entered a new period as a new artistic culture of musicians supplanted the old professional culture of popular musician. The rhythm 'n' blues, country, and rock 'n' roll revolutions brought vernacular music practices center stage once again in American popular music. And the long reign of professional musicians in popular music was decidedly over.

While changes occurring within the popular music industry affected the decline of the big band business during the 1940s, the first major blow as mentioned previously was the onset of World War II. Bandleaders and musicians enlisted to fight the war effort at the same time in which domestic resources were focused on supporting the war. The rationing of gasoline, material for tires, and the need for buses for the military effort made touring a daunting task. And except for major military embarkation points and bases, there were no large audiences for dance bands. (Simon 1950; Eberly 1982) Before the war, *Down Beat's* regular listing of big bands peaked at a high of over 800 bands in 1941 just before the United States entered the war. By 1943, the number of bands fell to around one quarter of the previous high and by 1945 *Down Beat* listed only ninety-two active bands. (*Down Beat* 1-15-45) While hopes were ignited with the end of the war and the possible recovery of the big band business, *Down Beat* and *Metronome* covered a post-war big band business "slump" that remained a permanent condition. The number of active big bands increased following the war, but by the early 1950s less than 100 big bands appeared in national listings outnumbered by the new formation of small combos. From 1947 into the early 1950s, the terrible state of the big band business became a regular issue in *Down Beat* and *Metronome* as dance band revivals were occasionally anticipated and debates ensued as to the reasons for the lack of large audiences for big band dance. Critic George Simon in 1950, after informing readers of the various ailments leading to the decline in big band dance, like fellow big band revivalists still remained hopeful. "From the sound of things, it appears as though the public may start to dance again... From all outward appearances it seems that the dance band has declined as far as it is going to, and that in 1950, with the help of the record companies, the disc jockeys, the promoters, and, perhaps the musicians themselves, the dance band will rise again!" (Simon 1950: 64)

The big band business, unfortunately, never recovered. A number of factors made its revival a lost cause. The first was the popular music industry deserting big bands as their major stars in the 1940s and moving to popular singers like Frank Sinatra, Perry Como, Dinah Shore, and Jo Stafford. As George Simon informed readers in the "Decline of the Big Band," "when the bands, those that were coming out of hibernation and those that were being reorganized by returning vets, started making platters they found themselves playing second fiddle, trumpet and sax to the new rage, the singers." (Simon 1950: 58) With singers as their primary artist, major record companies also consolidated production by using a small number of big bands or orchestras more directly tied to the record company. These bands could back up the entire company's roster of singers. More importantly, this allowed a further shift in artistic control to the major companies' small number of artist and repertoire person-nel who arranged the recordings and chose the songs to be recorded. (Denisoff 1986) Top record executives by the end of the 1940s were not impressed by the record sales of former "name" big bands. Walter Rivers of Capitol Records was not too optimistic in 1950 citing the poor sales of Woody Herman and Charlie Barnet. "But the big band jazz records are still a question mark... Woody couldn't make it with his last band and neither could Barnet and they both had wonderful bands, too." (Ulanov and Simon 1950: 78) The music industry's abandonment of big band artists severed the lifeline to securing large audiences through radio broadcasts and recorded sound for a lucrative national circuit of live performances. The economics of the big band market also worked against touring big bands. As Simon remembered, "slowly, but very surely, that delicate balance of supply and demand was shifting from great demand and little supply to little demand and great supply... gradually, as one promoter after another, all over the country, started taking a licking, they, the buyers, refused to pay high prices." (Simon 1950: 59)

The shift to the use of singers as the primary artist of the music industry was in part affected by the militancy of the American Federation of Musicians in the last years of the 1930s and through the 1940s. Led by the controversial figure James C. Petrillo, the AFM made several challenges to the popular music industry. In 1937 and 1939, the AFM threatened radio networks with strikes over pay scale and the use of recorded music. Broadcasting of recorded music was still not covered by royalty rights and was viewed as a threat to union musicians in radio who had not yet forgotten the effect of sound film for theater musicians in the late 1920s and early 1930s. The AFM reached agreement with the radio industry, but the strong-arm tactics of the union was not received well by the members of the National Association of Broadcasters. (Sanjek 1988) Then in August of 1942, the AFM initiated a successful 24-month strike against the recording industry. This strike forced recording companies to rely on singers, since they were not members of the AFM. Record companies relied on a cappella singing group such as Frank Sinatra with the Bobby Tucker Singers. Of course, Frank Sinatra, along with Perry Como, Dinah Shore, and Jo Stafford led the new wave of star singers following the strike. (Whitburn 1986) The militancy of the AFM and its president eventually led to congressional action against the union with Truman signing the Lea Act, or Anti-Petrillo Act, in March 1946. This act significantly undermined the power of the union in the radio and recording industry. (Leiter 1974) The militancy and anti-union legislation, however, did not alone cause the shift to singers as the primary artists in popular music in the 1940s, other factors were equally important. But over the course of the 1940s, the record industry moved further and further towards a closed in-house system of production that concentrated production around a small number of artists and producers. (Peterson 1990)

Cat's Creed – Do Yourself No Good

The original guy who didn't know to come in out of the rain must have been a jazz musician. No one quite touches the typical hip cat in his determination to do himself no good, outside of blowing a horn or beating a skin. Being a successful musician is at least as much a matter of business as it is of art. Yet it's the fashion for Joe Blow who can take a hot chorus to be above and beyond the common sense requirements of making a living. He laughs at appointments, scorns publicity and is in the dark as to what goes on outside his own narrow world... Jazzmen are extreme cultists... Devout adherence to the doctrine is mandatory for those who wish to join the circle of the hip. Except for overwhelming geniuses, it's also a one way ticket to insecurity. And it keeps the genius from the really big time, too. (Editorial, *Down Beat*, July 2, 1947: 8)

The decline of big bands and the generally poor prospects for employment for professional musicians were blamed by some on the generation gap between older musicians and young cult-like modernists. Louis Armstrong entered the fray in 1948 claiming that "young cats" wanted "to carve everyone else because they're full of malice, and all they want to do is show you up... So you get all them weird chords which don't mean nothing, and first people get curious about it just because its new, but soon they get tired of it because it's really no good and you got no melody to remember and no beat to dance to. So they're all poor again and nobody is working, and that's what that modern malice done for you." (*Down Beat* 4-7-1948: 2) Bandleaders like Louis Armstrong, Fletcher Henderson, and Tommy Dorsey also began attacking the bebop style as the main culprit. Henderson believed that of "all the cruelties in the world, be-bop is the most phenomenal... it isn't music to me." (*Down Beat* 9-8-1948: 1) Dorsey told newspaper columnist Earl Wilson that "be-bop stinks. It has set music back 20 years." (*Down Beat* 2-25-1949: 12) Drummer Buddy Rich announced giving up on employing hipsters in 1949 because of their cultist attitudes. "It's not that I dislike bop. I like it as well as any other musician, but there are lots of other things I want to play. These fellows want to play bop and nothing else. In fact, I doubt if they *can* play anything else. Let's make clear that I'm not going commercial, however. Everything that isn't bop isn't necessarily corny, despite what some of these guys would have you believe." (*Down Beat* 1-14-1949: 1) Critic George Simon also warned modernist musicians of the consequences of their condescending attitude towards danceable music. "The boppers and the other uncompromising progressives had succeeded in building a following. It wasn't a big one, but it was a following, a following that did not come to dance (horrors, nothing as commercial as that!), but one which came to listen. But how many places are there in the entire country where people who come just to listen? Experience has proved the answer to be very few, certainly not enough to take care of the supply of musical but undanceable bands. And these bands soon found themselves unable to work either in hotel rooms, dance halls, theaters, or the majority of clubs." (Simon 1950: 59–60)

The cult mentality of young modernists also was blamed for the vicissitudes of the new jazz market. In an editorial for *Down Beat*, a reader pointed out that business problems in the jazz club scene were not the fault of unappreciative audiences. Besides club owners who preferred peddling drinks rather than creating an atmosphere for listening to jazz, musicians had "a great deal of the public apathy to blame on themselves. They don't seem to realize or care that the audience is aware of the musical snobbishness and the patronizing attitudes so many of them harbor. Jazz musicians have the idea that if the public doesn't catch on it's just their tough luck... Steady followers are developed slowly and are the only ones who can keep the business on an even keel. The cultists and the faddists are not only undesirable, but actually dangerous to the business because of their instability and their inability to know when they are being misled... Musicians should develop the art of rubbing elbows with the public and develop a sympathetic attitude toward the uninitiated who may never have been exposed to jazz previously." (*Down Beat* 7-29-1949: 10) Even modernist musician Chubby Jackson lamented his peers' cultist behavior. "It's our fault. Because there has to be some other way of selling our product than by leaning against walls and staring into space like idiots... Jazz is being plagued by a cult of young, non-thinking musicians, imitative musicians who'd do themselves good by staying home and practicing than by creating bizarre nightclub spectacles that cause the fingers to point at the innocent, good-thinking musician... To get a majority of the people interested – not just the small handful of dyed-in-the-wool jazz fans – you have to get up there and do more than just play great... Right now we're like zombies walking in a stagnant fog trying to find a breath of fresh air." (*Down Beat* 10-20-1950: 19)

Metronome and *Down Beat* presented a kind of schizophrenic picture of the jazz scene. While some editors, writers, and musicians lambasted the attitudes of modernist musicians, these musicians received virtually all the accolades of critics who mostly supported the modern jazz aesthetic. Critic Michael Levin in responding to Tommy Dorsey's comments to the press on bop wondered when was "all this bopoloney going to stop? When are well-known band leaders going to stop making fools of themselves in the press... All this noise puts those who like good music in a very uncomfortable position... for all their frightful clinkering, technical exhibitions, and pure plain honking, the boppists come up with something valuable. The kids are puttering around with harmonic intervals, rhythmic variations, and counterpoint far more complex than anything TD's generation messed with." (*Down Beat* 2-25-1949: 12) Critic Barry Ulanov made clear that boppers and other modernists were bringing fresh ideas and a bright future to jazz. "When the draft moved remorselessly into band ranks, lifting whole bands with its unyielding administration of 'greetings', a kind of pall was removed from jazz with the musicians who were summoned for service. It's no reflection on them, not even the least of the men who joined the army, navy, and marine fighting and playing outfits, that the musicians left behind reorganized and reshaped the music left in their keeping. The change was inevitable. A boom period, with its fresh minted audiences, and the need for new groupings of men and notes to replace old musicians and satisfy the new listeners, brought a great gust of clean air into jazz." (Ulanov and Simon 1950: 54) By 1950, jazz musicians who garnered the most attention in *Down Beat* and *Metronome* were part of the modernist trend in piano, ensembles and big bands. Readers consistently supported these musicians in readers' polls and many sent letters supporting modern jazz. Dance band revivalists and other critics of modernists faced a new jazz art world and the transformation of *Down Beat* and *Metronome* into its main organs of communication.

The debate on the jazz cult was less about attitudes and behaviors that supposedly alienated a potentially large audience for jazz and more about jazz as entertainment. While not all modern jazz musicians ignored and disdained their audiences, they all approached jazz as a form of high art. Performing a serious art form like jazz entailed an equally serious approach in self-presentation. The general transformation in attitudes and behaviors among modern jazz musicians was a final break from a consideration of the values of entertainment and popularity. These musicians were no longer interested in performing for a popular market, but for a jazz market based on high art appreciation. How musicians interpreted high art performance and appreciation varied from cool hipsters like trumpeters Dizzy Gillespie and Shorty Rogers to articulate sophisticates like pianists John Lewis, Billy Taylor, and Dave Brubeck. All these musicians also shared the view that modern jazz was not yet fully appreciated, but how they approached this problem ranged from, cool disdain like trumpeter Miles Davis, to eloquent spokespersons like John Lewis and Billy Taylor. A young bassist Charlie Mingus in 1951 pointedly revealed the expectations of modern jazz musicians. "True jazz is an art, and as with all the arts, it is the individual's means of expressing his deepest and innermost feelings and emotions... It may take 500 years for the average American audience to advance sufficiently out of the mental turmoil and anxiety of the atomic age to be able to concentrate more on the art of music and to understand and appreciate a musician's individual interpretation... At that point in the growth of jazz, it will no longer be necessary for a musician to jump up and down on a drum or to dance on the bandstand to receive recognition of his talent." (*Down Beat* 6-1-1951: 7)

While the general high art orientation of modern jazz musicians certainly presented difficulties in reviving the big band market, other changes in the music industry were leading to a radical transformation in American popular music by the mid-1950s. (Peterson 1990, Ennis 1992) Changes in broadcasting and recording created the opportunity for country, rhythm 'n' blues, and rock 'n' roll artists to record with small independent record companies and gain access to the airwaves previously monopolized by Tin Pan Alley composers and professional musicians. Just as independent record production following World War I helped initiate the craze for vernacular jazz, independent radio programmers and record producers helped initiate a new craze for more vernacular-based genres. A new music culture, distinct from the music culture of professional musicians, captured the popular imagination and the popular market. A new community of musicians and singers used performance practices in a distinctly different way than the professional musicians who dominated the popular music market during its initial expansion from the turn of the century to the late 1940s and early 1950s. At the same time, however, riding the wave of independent production in the 1950s were independent jazz labels and jazz disk jockeys promoting jazz music as a distinct genre from popular music. Professional jazz musicians entered the jazz market wedded to a modern jazz aesthetic that rejected claims to the popular. Just as a new set of genres and community of artists invaded popular music, the jazz art world would enter a New Jazz Age buttressed by an economic boom in recorded and live jazz.

The new jazz age: growth and change in the jazz art world

The history of jazz in 1955 is most obviously chronicled in that year's mass recording and in the continuing trend towards stage performances, both in concert halls and in the open air. But both these phenomena were mainly symptoms of, though they had their part in, the growing public acceptance of jazz. That Dave Brubeck and jazz made ad copy, that unprecedented publicity was given to The Newport Jazz Festival, that newspapers carried front page articles on the importance of jazz, that major record labels became interested once again in jazz, that records sold in numbers never before believed possible, that radio and television sometimes followed the newspaper lead, that, finally, the State Department began to take some interest in jazz as a propaganda device, was certainly proof that jazz had come into a new era if not necessarily come of age. (*Metronome Jazz* 1956: 7)

The years 1954 and 1955 marked a watershed in the evolution of the jazz art world. This art world was gradually expanding in the early 1950s in terms of jazz records, jazz clubs, jazz concerts, and other activities, but by 1955 it was enjoying unprecedented success. *Time Magazine* in 1954 heralded the changing fortunes of the jazz art world with the boom in live and recorded jazz as the "New Jazz Age." (*Time* 11-8-1954) This art world flourished as never before as the modern jazz aesthetic and jazz performance in general entered a renaissance of creative exploration, a dynamic jazz market, and greater recognition as an American art form. It also actively and successfully moved jazz out of its former center in the urban nightlife of American cities and into special concert settings, festivals, conservatories, colleges, and high schools. The quest for jazz connoisseurs and a high art appreciation for jazz continued to guide the directions of the jazz art world. Commercial labels and clubs, however, remained the core of the art world supporting traditional, mainstream, and modern jazz as they prospered during the boom. By the end of the 1960s, the boom in the jazz market had subsided. Fortunately, the jazz art world had developed a base that insured its continued viability at the national and international level. The jazz art world by the end of the New Jazz Age, however, had changed significantly from its original foundations in the 1930s, 1940s, and 1950s.

On July 17, 1954, the East Coast resort of Newport welcomed its first jazz festival. The national media, including the *New York Times*, *Time*, *Newsweek*, *Esquire*, *Holiday*, *Our World*, and *Saturday Review* gave the two-day festival glowing reviews. Needless to say, the social significance of a jazz festival among the environs of America's elite was not lost on either the press or the jazz art world. "The fine art of American jazz, which rose from humble beginnings in the bordellos of New Orleans before the first World War, has now reached the fabled social lawns of the Casino at Newport, R.I. Last week came the end of a two-day Newport Jazz Festival, a smash sell out, which saw the Casino greensward jammed with thousands of enthusiasts – and social pedigree be damned." (*Newsweek* 8-2-1954: 70) *Down Beat* celebrated the festival, which showed that "Jazz Concerts Have Come of Age." "America's first major jazz festival – the largest held anywhere in the world so far – has opened a new era in jazz presentation . . . a town more recently identified with the mansions of the 400 and championship tennis tournaments, now has become a historic site in the brief but vigorous evolution of American jazz." (*Down Beat* 8-25-1954: 2) Following the success of the first Newport Jazz Festival, the national media suddenly rediscovered jazz. *Life Magazine* celebrated the "New Life for U.S. Jazz: Young Innovators Share Boom with Old Hands" in 1954. "To the delight of an enlarging audience dedicated to the loudest

of the lively arts, jazz is having the biggest time of its 60-odd-year life. . .
Now at its peak, jazz stands half in the great hot past and half in the
promising future of "cool" counterpoint and heady harmonics. Its fans
see and hear the ranking players at work in small clubs and big concerts.
But it is largely the records, selling at seven times the rate they were selling
five years ago, that have given jazz the widest audience in its lavish history."
(*Life* 1-17-1954: 42) Jazz critic Leonard Feather celebrated the new life
for jazz in "Jazz Achieves Social Prestige" in *Down Beat*. "Jazz today is
enjoying an era of prestige and acknowledgement as an aesthetic force
that might seem incredible to Bix Beiderbecke or any of the early stars
who did not live long enough to see their kind of music emerge from the
speakeasies and cheap dance halls. If Bix were alive today he would find
jazz referred to constantly in magazines, books, and newspapers of the
type that were not more than dimly aware of jazz in general, much less of
Bix in particular during his time . . . the end result is that the society crowd
and the newsprint crowd between them are offering jazz the greatest
degree of exposure and discussion it ever had enjoyed in this country."
(*Down Beat* 9-21-1955: 11)

The New Jazz Age certainly signaled the start of an economic boom
and new image for the jazz art world. Jazz critic Nat Hentoff in *Harper's*
noted the burgeoning audience for jazz. "In the past decade, however,
a startling change has taken place in the status of jazz – or, more accu-
rately, in the extent to which its existence is admitted. Stimulated by the
expansion of the LP record industry, the audience for jazz has notably
increased. Among the indexes have been expanding attendance at jazz
'festivals' and the traveling all-star troupes – 'packaged shows' is the blunt
trade term – and the growth of nightclubs specializing in jazz, though this
segment of the industry is incorrigibly erratic. A further indication has
been the unprecedented space that jazz now gets in the non-specialist
press." (*Harper's* 4-1958: 25) As jazz enthusiast and beat novelist John
Clellon Holmes wrote in *Esquire*, the "jazz audience today is a group so
enormous and so diverse that about the only thing they have in common
is their feeling for jazz. It is a poet in San Francisco, a farm hand in
Iowa, an ad man on Madison Avenue, a hipster in Detroit, and a student
in New Hampshire. . . Its presence is loudly attested to by the ringing
of cash registers in nightclubs, concert halls, record stores, and music
schools; by the membership rolls of jazz societies, fan organizations, and
the several burgeoning jazz-record clubs; by the subscription lists of the
half-dozen magazines entirely devoted to jazz, and the dozen others which
feature it regularly. Its purchasing power is as much evidenced by the
twelve record Encyclopedia of Jazz that was recently offered to supermar-
ket customers across the nation . . . as by Norman Granz's multi-million

dollar concert-and-record empire, built wholly out of the marketing of this kind of music." (*Esquire* 1-1959: 100)

A major part of the New Jazz Age was a significant change in general press coverage of the jazz art world. News coverage of this art world increased while jazz critics began writing for a larger number of magazines. Besides previous magazines such as *Harper's, New Republic, American Record Lover,* and *Esquire,* jazz critics wrote articles for such diverse magazines as *Saturday Review, Evergreen Review, Atlantic, New Yorker, Holiday, House and Garden, Parents Magazine, Reporter, High Fidelity* and new "gentlemen" magazines such as *Playboy, Cavalier,* and *Rogue.* Regular coverage of the jazz art world also appeared in magazines such as *Time, Newsweek, Life, Vogue, Senior Scholastic, Theater Arts, Christian Century,* and *Look.* Daily newspapers like the *New York Times, Boston Globe, San Francisco Chronicle,* and *Washington Post* had in-house jazz critics. Jazz critics, and other reviewers, also wrote a larger number of jazz record reviews in the general press and music magazines. Jazz critics like Leonard Feather and Ralph Gleason began writing regular syndicated music columns for the daily news press. By the late 1950s, the jazz art world had finally gained exposure in a large expanse of print media in the United States. The *Readers Guide to Periodical Literature* shows general press coverage of jazz in the late 1950s compared to the first half of the decade increased three-fold in the number of articles with twice the number of periodicals covering jazz. While coverage would decline slightly during the 1960s, it still remained significantly high. The tremendous increase in press coverage in the late 1950s and 1960s was indicative of the success of the jazz art world and also had an independent effect in exposing jazz to a far larger audience. The coverage of the jazz art world in the late fifties and into the sixties, therefore, brought new audiences to live and recorded jazz who might not otherwise have been exposed to the new art form.

The future of jazz is inspiring for many reasons. Somehow at the close of the Second World War jazz was able to break the shackles of popular music and strike out on its own... In America we now have Classical music, Popular music, and Jazz, three separate musical expressions. Many record labels have become established as specialists in Jazz and existed on the music alone. Today even the major record companies are showing excited concern for the music and are endeavoring to get a foothold on the jazz market. (Stan Kenton, *Metronome,* August 1954: 34)

The extensive coverage of jazz in the general press, starting in 1954, coincided with major record companies discovering the new jazz market. Faced with a major recession in sales since 1947, RCA-Victor, Columbia, Decca, and Capitol were searching for new markets and looking at successful independent labels for inspiration and talent. Jazz music, therefore, attracted the big four's attention. Majors signed a number of jazz musicians who had been recording for independent jazz labels. (*Metronome* 8-54; Priestly 1991) This new enthusiasm was in part made possible because of several jazz enthusiasts' entrance into the majors during the 1940s such as Dave Dexter (Capitol), George Avakian (Columbia), Milt Gabler (Decca), and Bob Thiele (Decca). George Avakian informed *Metronome* readers that jazz had finally made it into the big time. "Jazz at Columbia is finally stepping out of the secondary place it was forced into by the top-heavy demand for other kinds of repertoire by the final arbiter of every business concern. The Public. What's responsible for the change? Nothing but the Public again. People are buying more records than ever before in the history of the business. And the percentage of gain is largest in the jazz field. Thus jazz has achieved a position of real standing in the plans of every major record company." (*Metronome* 8-1954: 15) Avakian certainly was correct about the incredible boom in the jazz record market. By 1955, the number of jazz records produced were ten times the number produced in 1950. (*Metronome Jazz 1956*) Overall, the jazz market was bullish. John Hammond noted the "ever-widening market" and how major companies as well as the independents were "each vying with each other in signing new talent, and literally flooding dealers and jockeys with far more material than can be absorbed by even an avid public." (*Down Beat* 9-21-1955: 15)

The production of jazz by major record companies meant that the jazz art world finally had attained at least the acknowledged support of the music industry. This support was crucial in the initial years of the renaissance in spreading jazz to a larger national audience. This production by majors also generated new audiences and consumers for the jazz art world where most jazz was still produced. The jazz roster of the big four included jazz musicians performing traditional, mainstream, and modern jazz. The big four, however, continued to play mostly a reactive role in producing jazz. The majors did sign important figures in modern jazz, but only after they had proven themselves on independent jazz labels. Miles Davis, for example, signed with Columbia in 1956 and recorded a series of innovative works in modern jazz. For brief periods majors also signed important modernists like Gerry Mulligan, Art Blakey, Sonny Rollins, Stan Getz, Thelonious Monk, and Charles Mingus, although independent jazz labels produced most of these musicians' recordings. The exception to the role of the major record companies was ABC-Paramount, which started a recording division in 1960. Like Capitol when it began in 1942, the infant recording division of ABC-Paramount did not have the institutional inertia of the majors. In bringing in the modernist jazz musician Teo Marcero and the jazz enthusiast Bob Thiele to its Impulse jazz label, this company was to record many of the more prominent members of the jazz avant-garde.

The roster of jazz musicians for the majors, however, was incredibly small compared to the roster for independent jazz labels. These labels produced a far greater number of recordings and supported a far greater number of jazz musicians. John Hammond's fear in 1955 of what would happen to jazz if only the majors were involved in jazz production was predictive of the crucial role of independents during the renaissance. "It's a pretty frightening thought, since by far the largest amount of good jazz appears on such post-war labels as Atlantic, Bethlehem, Clef, EmArcy, Fantasy and Good Time Jazz, right down the alphabet... Without the competition of the independent specialists, it's doubtful whether we would get the tiniest fraction of the jazz available today." (*Down Beat* 9-21-1955: 15) In 1961–62, for example, *Down Beat* listed 188 jazz ensembles with 78 percent recording for one of 60 independent labels and the other 22 percent with one of the major record companies. (*Down Beat* 6-22-61, 6-21-62) The annual reviews published by *Down Beat* from 1956 to 1969 show that during the renaissance, independent production represented around three-quarters or more of recorded jazz issues. Labels such as World Pacific, Prestige, Blue Note, Candid, Verve, and Riverside that were strictly jazz labels did most jazz recording. Other labels producing mostly for the rhythm and blues market also recorded jazz musicians. Atlantic, the most successful rhythm and blues label of the period actually produced as many jazz recordings as the biggest independent specialty jazz labels. Independent labels were essential in supporting a renaissance in jazz music in the 1950s and 1960s. These labels not only recorded the major innovations in jazz music during the renaissance, but also supported a diverse range of jazz styles. Nesuhi Ertegun, part owner of Atlantic Records and a jazz enthusiast since the early 1930s, expressed the common commitment of independents to diversity and innovation in jazz. "Jazz has never moved in so many directions all at once as it is now. From basic blues to atonality, from rediscoveries of traditional roots... to experimentations so daring they might shock the most confirmed modernists... jazz has never before been so thoroughly adventurous... I can frankly think of nothing more fascinating than to be in the business of making jazz records... We are attempting to preserve on records as much as possible of all the forms of jazz that can be heard today, performed by musicians who are, in our opinion, of great significance." (*Down Beat* 5-16-1956: 13)

The broadcast media of radio and television also supported the boom in jazz. Radio played an important role in the 1950s and 1960s. In 1957,

Down Beat listed 120 jazz programs broadcasting in 34 states in the United States, and by 1959, 214 jazz programs were listed broadcasting in 41 states. (*Down Beat* 10-3-57: 68, 4-30-59: 44–5) Jazz programs could be found on public radio stations like KPFA-KPFB in Berkeley, California which had three jazz programs, *The Jazz Review*, *Jazz Archives* and *Modern Jazz*; or WBUR in Boston where Father Norman J. O'Connor, Catholic Chaplain at Boston College, presented *Jazz Anthology* and *Jazz Trends*. Commercial stations also carried jazz programs like KSAN in San Francisco with *Showcase for Jazz*. Jazz music continued as an important part of radio programming in the 1960s. In 1969, *Down Beat* listed 170 jazz programs broadcasting from 70 cities in 36 states. (*Down Beat* 5-1-69: 34) The newer broadcasting medium of television also helped expose jazz to local and national audiences. (Museum of Broadcasting 1985) CBS's *See It Now* in 1955 featured Louis Armstrong on tour in Europe. Edward R. Murrow informed viewers that "Louis Armstrong is the Prime Minister of the world of jazz," and "one of our most valuable items of export." *Camera One* a CBS Sunday-morning series on the arts featured the Gerry Mulligan Quartet in 1956. CBS broadcasted the *Sound of Jazz* in 1957 featuring Red Allen, Thelonious Monk, Billie Holiday, Lester Young, Roy Eldridge, Coleman Hawkins, Ben Webster, Gerry Mulligan, Jimmy Giuffre, and the Count Basie big band. Other network jazz programs in the 1950s included four *Timex All Star Jazz Shows*, *Swing into Spring*, *The Subject is Jazz*, and *The Sound of Miles Davis*. Local television stations also featured jazz programs. In the 1950s, local station WNTA in New York City featured *Art Ford's Jazz Party*, while WBGH in Boston featured a jazz program *Jazz TV* hosted by Father Norman J. O'Connor. Also during the 1950s, the jazz enthusiast Steve Allen would feature jazz musicians regularly on his *Tonight Show*. In the early 1960s, several jazz programs were independently produced including *Frankly Jazz* and *Jazz Scene U.S.A.* The series *Jazz Casual*, produced by jazz critic Ralph Gleason for KQED in San Francisco, featured the John Coltrane Quartet, Modern Jazz Quartet, Dave Brubeck, and Dizzy Gillespie.

Within the community of jazz musicians, most young players feel that jazz had become a music primarily to be listened to rather than a background for dancing or drinking, or both; and it is, therefore, "art music" in that sense. The facts of nightly jazz life, however, hardly indicate to them that an era of triumph, respectability, or artistic fulfillment had yet arrived. The jazz musician, to begin with, continues to work mostly in nightclubs. There are several players, young and older, who prefer the informality of the nightclub and see as its alternative only the cold, intimidating concert hall. But the majority of the younger musicians do not enjoy playing in nightclubs, and will welcome whatever feasible ways are eventually realized to liberate them from a setting in which the music may have been the main attraction for some, but not for all... the nightclub is hardly an optimum place for listening... Without attempting to equate or even compare the two kinds of music aesthetically, it is as disturbing and ultimately as frustrating for many jazzmen to sustain invention in the middle of infinitely varied degrees of inattention as it would be for a string quartet to play Mozart at Birdland. (Nat Hentoff (Hentoff and McCarthy 1961: 327–8))

The New Jazz Age also witnessed jazz performance moving significantly beyond its origins in popular urban nightclubs. This transformation in the location of jazz performance was a result of attempts to present jazz in settings considered more appropriate to a high art appreciation as well as a result of attempts to find new audiences for jazz. The urban nightclub scene came to be vilified by some in the jazz art world for its atmosphere of casual music appreciation as customers drank, conversed, and attended to other activities. Trumpeter Red Rodney voiced a not uncommon view among modern jazz musicians in 1950. "You know, I sure would like to see a lot more respectability attached to jazz and jazz musicians. And I'd also like to see artists like Dizzy, Charlie Parker, Lennie Tristano, and Miles Davis playing only in concert halls, where they'd get a chance to blow their greatest and not have to make any concessions." (*Down Beat* 6-2-1950: 3) As *Metronome* noted on the jazz club scene in 1954, "more and more complaints were registered about the difficulty of working and listening conditions." (*Metronome Jazz* 54: 10) Jazz musicians sought listening audiences and some like Charlie Mingus and Max Roach were well known for reproaching nightclub audiences for talking. As Mingus said, "nightclubs mostly don't make it. I prefer the colleges and the concert halls... Another thing about clubs is that the audiences don't come to listen." (*Metronome Music* 58: 84)

Jazz nightclubs, however, remained an important venue for jazz performance around the country during the boom in the late 1950s and early 1960s. While the jazz club business remained unstable with clubs constantly opening and closing, the national scene was large. In 1964, with ten years of relative prosperity in the fortunes of jazz over 250 jazz nightclubs could be found in fifteen major metropolises in the United States as listed in the "Where and When" club date listings in *Down Beat*. Besides New York City, Chicago, and Los Angeles, Detroit, San Francisco, St. Louis, Cleveland, and Philadelphia had a large number of clubs featuring jazz. By 1965, however, an economic downturn began to hit the jazz club scene. (*Variety* 2-12-64: 64, 1-27-65: 49, 4-28-65: 53, 12-17-69: 58; *Down Beat* 5-20-65: 10, 7-27-67: 13; *Billboard* 3-22-69: 36) By the 1970s, a far smaller number of jazz clubs existed serving a more specialized niche market.

Musicians and critics actively sought locations for jazz performance outside the club scene for reasons of status, aesthetics, and money. As critic Don Heckman pointed out, the "only logical conclusion that can be reached from this is that jazz had come to the point where it must leave the nightclubs... Jazz musicians no longer consider themselves entertainers whose main object is to make an audience happily tap swizzle sticks... the jazz rebels are going to find other means and other individuals with the sympathy, understanding, and connections to lead them into more acceptable areas of employment. The most obvious possibilities are the concert and recital halls. Others are college and high school programs, foundation grants, and the establishment of resident jazz groups at conservatories and universities." (*Down Beat Music* 1961: 50) In the 1950s, special jazz concerts and other performance settings with a similar type of appreciation became regular events and grew in importance to become major settings for jazz performance. Besides special jazz concerts, the other important new settings for jazz performance were jazz festivals and college campuses. All three settings presented jazz for listening audiences and emphasized a high art appreciation. The seriousness of these new settings, like earlier jazz concerts in the 1930s and 1940s, were underlined with the inclusion at times of hosts or panels providing commentary along with the music.

The November Revolution

EARLY in November of last year, several musicians met with the idea of organizing a cooperative jazz concert in hopes that they and jazz would both profit... It is up to the jazz musician, with the help of the loyal jazz fan, to do something for himself and his art. Granted that it is difficult for a musician, or even a group of musicians, to start a jazz club, there is nothing really difficult about running a series of cooperative concerts, where a loss can only be a minimum amount, with more than a probability of some eventual gain for the pocketbook and a large gain for the prestige and progress of jazz. (Jazz critic Bill Coss, *Metronome*, March 1954: 20)

While special jazz concerts continued to be produced by jazz entrepreneurs like Norman Granz – who in the late 1950s was grossing more than a million dollars annually – jazz societies, musician collectives, and other art organizations also organized special jazz concerts. The prototype of the jazz musician collective was the Jazz Composers Workshop formed in 1953 in New York City which presented concerts at Carnegie Recital Hall in 1954 and the Modern Museum of Art in 1955. The Jazz Messengers was a jazz unit originally organized as a collective by Art Blakey and Horace Silver in 1953. Besides musician collectives, jazz societies performed a similar function. The Modern Jazz Society in New York City, for example, supported the concerts of the Jazz Composers Workshop in 1955. In 1956, Eleise Sloan led the formation of Jazz Unlimited that claimed a membership of 425 by 1957. This society was involved in a Billy Holiday concert at Carnegie Hall as well as a jazz series at the Brooklyn Academy of Music. It organized its first concert in 1956 in Brooklyn's St. John Recreation Center with modernists Thelonious Monk, Gigi Gryce, Wilbur Ware, and Ron Jefferson. (*Down Beat* 3-6-1957: 24) In 1959, *Down Beat* presented a list of seventy-two jazz societies active in the United States and another fourteen in Canada. (*Down Beat* 5-28-59: 22, 24) By the 1960s, numerous collectives, societies, and arts organizations were producing jazz concerts throughout the country. Collectives formed in the 1960s included the Jazz Composers' Orchestra Association in 1966 as well as a number of "black art" collectives like the Association for the Advancement of Creative Musicians in Chicago in 1965. The most active scene of collectives and concert performances was the jazz "loft" movement in New York City in the 1960s where jazz performances occurred in coffeehouses, small theaters, art galleries, churches, bookstores, and other locations. (Litwieler 1984)

Another important performance setting during The New Jazz Age was the jazz festival. Like the special jazz concerts organized by producers, collectives, and jazz societies, the jazz festival represented a major shift in jazz performance from its origins in nightclubs to performance settings emphasizing the type of appreciation accorded high art performance. Following the Newport Jazz Festival's success a number of special and annual jazz festivals were organized in the United States and Canada. *Down Beat* noted the new popularity of big and small jazz festivals following Newport in "Jazz Festivals Dot U.S. Scene" in 1956. "In no summer in American music history have so many jazz festivals and appearances by jazz musicians at other festivals been scheduled." (*Down Beat* 7-11-1956: 8) An annual jazz festival was inaugurated on Randall's Island in New York City in 1956, while the Monterey Jazz Festival inaugurated in 1958 also became a major annual event for the jazz art world. In reporting on jazz festivals in 1959, *Down Beat* covered festivals in Newport, New York City, Monterey, French Lick, Great South Bay, New Orleans, Boston, Los Angeles, Detroit, Philadelphia, and Toronto. Jazz festivals in the United States would become an even more important venue in the 1970s. While the jazz festival was an important development in the transformation of jazz performance to a more high art appreciation, not all jazz critics and jazz musicians held festivals in high regard. A common complaint of festivals was the large roster of artists rushed through performances in what critic Nat Hentoff called an "assembly-line circus." (*Harper's* 4-1958: 28) In protest to working conditions at festivals, for

example, Charlie Mingus organized a "rump festival" to run simultaneously and alongside the Newport Festival in 1960. Critic and editor
Dan Morgenstern commented on the state of jazz festivals in 1961 in
Metronome with a mixed review, but pointed to the importance of festivals for the future of jazz. "A jazz festival should be a high point in the
activities of both musicians and listeners. A jazz festival, at its best, should
result in an affirmation of jazz as the greatest popular art of our time – the
music of America and of the world. . . In bits and pieces, jazz festivals have
been all these things. But they have also been three-ring circuses, crass
commercial supermarkets of jazz, cold and uninspired variety shows, and
unseemly mixtures of pretentiousness and sham . . . the rise of the jazz
festival is a logical and generic result of the possibilities long inherent in
jazz." (*Metronome* 7-1961: 8–9) Barry Kernfeld, however, in retrospect
describes the importance of the festival in the transformation of jazz performance. "Festivals were a late development in the history of jazz. They
form a landmark in the shifting of the balance between jazz as a social
event and jazz as a concert music. . . The emergence of successful, informal festivals, maintained year by year, marked more than any other
large-scale development a new attitude towards the music because at such
events audiences were able to devote their whole attention to listening to
performers on stage." (Kernfeld 1988: 361)

The Dave Brubeck Quartet released "Jazz at Oberlin" in 1953 on the
Fantasy label. The album liner notes made clear the significance of the
concert recorded at Oberlin, home of one of the oldest music conservatories in the country. "Through the years the Conservatory has considered it its duty to maintain a policy of adhering rather closely to the
mainstream of established classical literature in its instruction and its students' performances, never having seen fit to include jazz in its curriculum. Toward the beginning of 1953 the few jazz enthusiasts at Oberlin,
having grown extremely tired of the situation, decided to do something,
to present, at Oberlin, jazz on an organized concert level. . . In spite of
early doubt, apprehension, and lack of encouragement, the concert was
a huge success. . . Jazz had found itself firmly and comfortably at home
in surroundings, where, in the past, it had been met with only apathy
and misunderstanding." (Fantasy 3-11, 1953) Fantasy immediately followed this album with "Jazz at College of the Pacific." After signing with
Columbia Records in 1954, the Quartet's first album was "Jazz Goes to
College" a recording of concert performances at several Midwestern colleges. The Dave Brubeck Quartet came to personify a new legitimacy for
jazz music as the jazz art world successfully pursued the college market
as a new source of income and prestige. The most successful foray into
higher education was commercial jazz concerts, supported by booking

agencies as well as student organizations involved in performance events on campus. As critic Bill Coss commented, "all over this nation this year jazz has seemingly taken one giant step from club to campus... Dave Brubeck, for example, has become a college attraction, blazing a trail only seldom followed before, made much easier now because of his great popularity. If he deserves no other validity, he deserves sincere thanks for that ambassadorship. For, during the past year or two, other musicians have begun to make inroads on the college trade... Such an innovator as Teddy Charles, for example, has played the campuses and with good results. Now there's a rush on. *A Kenton Presents* package will soon be underway; the *Lighthouse All Stars*, led by Howard Rumsey, will head East via the campus route; New York's Monte Kay, booker Joe Glaser and many others are lining up college tours for their artists." (*Metronome* 12-1955: 20)

Music Educators Take a Long, Close Look at Jazz

IT WASN'T UNTIL the 50th annual meeting of the Music Educators National conference at St. Louis that jazz caught the serious attention of the music teachers of America. April 18, 1956, marked the first program in this long series of meetings of American educators that was devoted to a serious consideration of jazz as part of the study programs offered in music to the young people of America. (George Avakian, *Down Beat* 6-13-56: 14)

As the comments by George Avakian suggest, the jazz art world, besides enjoying a college market for jazz concerts, also was looking at other ways to enter the world of education. The publisher of *Down Beat* Charles Suber was a major advocate of jazz education. In 1963, he noted the positive changes during the 1950s in music education and jazz. "The 1950s marked the turning point in the attitudes of educators towards jazz. For the first time educators began speaking in large numbers, and without apology, of jazz as an art form and began implementing their talk with courses in jazz history, officially sanctioned stage bands, and lectures and seminars on jazz... Throughout the '50s, articles favoring jazz began to appear in magazines such as *Music Educators' Journal, Music Clubs*, and *Educational Music Magazine*." Suber noted that North Texas State University initiated a four-year degree in jazz in 1956 and that the Institute of International Education recommended in 1957 courses in jazz at conservatories and colleges of music. Of course, "the acceptance of jazz was not total, and even today it is evident that a majority of colleges and secondary-school systems look uneasily on the prospect of jazz in the curriculum." (*Down Beat* 9-26-1963: 18) But as George Wiskirchen, CSC noted "expansion is the keynote of jazz in education institutions. In recent years it has been expanding at a hare-like rate, and this proliferation has continued during the last year at an even more rapid pace. The increasing number of college stage bands offers a never-before-available advantage to the aspiring jazz musician. Well-run programs offer much experience to the young musician, and it is often remarked by professionals that they wish they had had the opportunities now available." (*Down Beat* 9-26-1963: 15)

As the jazz art world was making inroads into music education in the 1950s, it celebrated every victory for jazz in its recognition as a serious art. The most celebrated victory was the establishment of jazz in the venerated environs of Tanglewood in Western Massachusetts, an area famous for its summer offering of classical music. As early as 1951, a panel series on jazz with accompanying recitals was given "dedicated to the belief that jazz is a significant contribution to American culture." It "thrilled an audience of connoisseurs" at the Music Inn in Lenox. "Situated next door to Tanglewood, the summer home of the Boston Symphony, Music Inn attracted many classical music lovers, who became staunch jazz aficionados by the end of the week." (*Down Beat* 9-7-1951: 18) In 1957, the panel series was turned into a School of Jazz with jazz musician John Lewis as music director. *Down Beat* was impressed that in "all the classes and lectures and ensembles there was a soberness and dignity of demeanor that was encouraging." (*Down Beat* 10-3-1957: 23) Such dignity also was celebrated earlier when Brandeis University's Festival of the Creative Arts in 1952 initiated under the directorship of Leonard Bernstein an annual jazz symposium and concert. (*Down Beat* 7-30-1952: 5)

Besides special concerts and workshops, music conservatories for jazz were established in the 1950s including the Berklee School of Music in Boston, Westlake College of Modern Music in Los Angeles, and the Advanced School of Contemporary Music in Toronto. Other established conservatories also began offering jazz courses. The college band movement, however, was the most successful foray into music education during the 1950s. The first national college festival was held in 1956. The National Collegiate Jazz Contest was held with the "primary" purpose "to provide an opportunity for college jazz groups throughout the country to gain public recognition." (*Metronome* 11-1956: 10) In 1958, two annual college festivals were inaugurated, the Collegiate Jazz Festival at Notre Dame University and the Big 8 Jazz Festival at the University of Kansas. In 1960, the first annual Intercollegiate Jazz Festival was inaugurated at Villanova University. In 1964, both the Notre Dame and Villanova festivals even released albums. The growth of high school and college stage bands led to the establishment of the successful National Stage Band Camps in 1959.

Charles Suber reviewed the growth of jazz education in 1976. (Suber 1976) While starting on a dour note, he showed that jazz had definitely entered the academy and established permanent residence by the 1970s. In 1960, while 5,000 high schools had stage/jazz bands, only forty colleges had jazz courses and only half gave academic credits. By 1975, around 20,000 junior and senior high schools had stage/jazz bands and around 400 colleges were offering for credit at least one jazz performance group or jazz course. Postgraduate programs in jazz were offered at Indiana University, North Texas State University, Wesleyan University, Northern Colorado State University as well as at the Eastman School of Music and the New England Conservatory of Music. In 1969, there were 75 college jazz festivals and 170 secondary and elementary school jazz festivals. The presence of jazz education in American educational institutions had unquestionably established itself in the 1960s culminating with the formation of the National Association of Jazz Educators in 1968. The success of the jazz education movement was the result of a number of factors according to Charles Suber. Its initial growth occurred when musicians who served in the armed forces during World War II took advantage of the GI Bill after the war to finance a college music education degree. This influx of music educators who began as musicians performing the popular swing music of their youth and as musicians familiar with aspects of the jazz art world instigated the stage/jazz band phenomenon in secondary education in the 1950s and 1960s. In turn, their students entering colleges and universities would form the backbone of support for jazz on college campuses. The movement for jazz on college campuses occurred mostly outside the university music establishment, but in time had established a major presence of jazz on campuses in terms of jazz concerts, extra-curricula jazz programs for students, and eventually, jazz courses. Also, by 1970 many people who had become jazz fans as youths had risen to positions of authority in higher education and were important in lessening the impact of the resistance to jazz at colleges and universities. (Kernfeld 1988: 605)

The presence of jazz in educational institutions had two important consequences for the jazz art world. First, like the music appreciation movement for classical music, the jazz education movement created a new audience for jazz. This audience was far different in class background, race-ethnic background, and conventional sensibility than audiences in the urban jazz scene. In a sense, the new jazz aesthetic, just as in the case of live performance settings, had shifted jazz to new audiences. The second consequence was that the recruitment of jazz musicians by the middle 1960s relied heavily on the exposure of jazz performance to students in educational institutions. With the break between popular and jazz performance, it was essential that the jazz art world find another way in which to develop and recruit musicians. While it would remain an axiom of the jazz art world that jazz musicians had to eventually hone their skills among veteran musicians, the jazz art world would become dependent on the influx of young musicians with some form of conservatory or higher education.

Accompanying the various changes in the jazz art world in the United States, was a phenomenal growth in the international dimensions of this art world, particularly in Europe. While jazz was attracting jazz enthusiasts in Europe in the 1930s, the advent of World War II was to delay the international growth of a jazz art world. The war, however, did expose a larger number of Europeans to jazz through the Armed Services Radio broadcasting of swing music. Not surprisingly, after the war there was a rapid growth in interest in jazz. Although due to its isolation from changes in the United States, it was first limited to traditional jazz and swing. This interest, however, spurred a major increase in jazz books and periodicals published outside the United States. (Kernfeld 1988) By the late 1940s, American jazz musicians began performing in Europe more regularly as the new modern jazz aesthetic was attracting audiences outside the United States. Voice of America with Willis Conover did regular broadcasts of jazz following the war. By the sixties, an exodus of jazz musicians to Europe began and continued through the decade. This in part was a response to demand for jazz in Europe where the competition among jazz musicians was far less a problem than the United States, and in part a response to the downturn in the jazz club scene in the United States. For many musicians the type of audiences in Europe compared to the United States and the level of prestige they received as jazz musicians in Europe also influenced their choices. (*Down Beat* 7-2-64: 64) For modern avant-garde players, Europe also provided a greater appreciation for their art form than audiences back home and by the late 1960s many avant-garde musicians took residency in Europe. (Wilmer 1980) Besides print media and jazz clubs, in the late 1960s and early 1970s production of jazz outside the United States would make a significant leap in importance. The international jazz festival circuit quintupled by 1974 from its level of 1960. By the 1970s, jazz musicians could earn a livelihood simply touring the global festival circuit. (Kernfeld 1988) This same period saw the emergence of a number of important international jazz labels, many of which were independently recording both non-American and American jazz musicians. (Priestly 1991) By the 1970s, the jazz art world was an internationally based art world. The internationalization of this art world meant a further diversification and even more decentralization of producers. At the same time, this process also meant the generation of new audiences and new musicians not connected to the urban culture of jazz in the United States in the 1930s, 1940s, and 1950s.

With the boom in the jazz market beginning in the mid-1950s the jazz art world began a significant process of transformation. Having established a market for the new jazz aesthetic, musicians, critics, and others embarked on an agenda to expand this art world beyond its initial foundations in independent jazz labels and commercial jazz clubs. At the same time, the entrance of an international base of support for jazz music also effected changes within the jazz art world. Ultimately, the modernist agenda was driven by the desire to locate jazz in more "legitimate" cultural spaces and achieve the high art status and high art appreciation considered still unattainable within the urban jazz scene of nightclubs. It was also driven by the knowledge that linking jazz to a major cultural institution like education would provide for its future in terms of audiences and artists. These changes suggest that the jazz art world by the end of the New Jazz Age had more affluent and more educated audiences enjoying jazz than during the 1940s and 1950s. This art world began in the 1930s supported by affluent college-educated white enthusiasts, but then saw the "democratization" of jazz connoisseurship during and following the swing craze. Then the jazz art world once again returned gradually to a more select audience.

During the New Jazz Age, the jazz art world also developed into a decentralized art world with a large number of independent producers. This contrasts with the process of institutionalization of classical music and its claim to a high art status. The success of this establishment came about with the rise of a small number of urban elite supported symphony orchestras and opera companies, higher education music programs, and professional organizations. The system relied heavily on the patronage of urban elite and higher education institutions. This centralized organization and heavy reliance on elite patronage created a homogeneous and traditional classical fare that mostly marginalized modern and experimental classical music, which barely survived on the patronage of a small number of colleges and modern art organizations. (Davis 1981; Cameron 1996) In contrast to the classical establishment, the jazz art world's rapid growth relied on the decentralized organization of a large number of independent producers. No national, state, or metropolitan organizations or corporations had significant control over jazz production. The only nationally prominent forces in the jazz art world were *Down Beat* and *Metronome,* and while significant forces in the jazz art world, their policy during the period was less one of maintaining control over the jazz art world than in promoting its growth and diversification. The diverse number of jazz labels, producers of live jazz performance, jazz print media, and jazz disc jockeys during the renaissance engendered a period of major innovation and a significant diversification of styles in jazz performance.

By the end of the 1960s, however, the jazz record and club markets were shrinking and dirges on the state of jazz were once again common in the jazz print media. The coverage in the general press also fell, again reflecting changes in the art world itself and magnifying these changes even further. While major record companies continued to record mainstream and modern jazz, their jazz roster shrunk while their interest shifted to jazz incorporating popular styles of music like Jazz Fusion which incorporated jazz and rock practices. The only significant support majors provided for jazz at this time came from Warner Records since it purchased the independent Atlantic Records in 1967 which maintained an independent roster. In 1972, Atlantic represented 50 percent of majors' jazz recordings in the top rated new jazz albums in the *Down Beat* annual review. Besides Atlantic, majors only produced 12 percent of these 133 top albums. (*Down Beat Music '73*) The situation for jazz in the radio industry fared poorly too by the early 1970s. Like popular music disc jockeys, the more independent disc jockeys in jazz were slowly replaced by the power of program directors and the use of radio formats. In the early 1970s, jazz programming became dominated by soft jazz and fusion jazz formats as directors looked to attract the appropriate demographics and rating bases. (*Down Beat* 1-20-72: 29; *Billboard* 4-22-72: 16) The marketability of jazz by the media industry was understood either as music linked to popular musical styles such as funk or rock, or as music in the "soft" jazz category favored by many jazz radio program directors. Major record companies also relied more on reissues for tapping the market for other styles of jazz. While the fall in support of majors for jazz was a significant blow, the jazz art world had at least established a large base of independent record producers that maintained a jazz market, albeit a smaller one than during the boom.

The decline of the commercial market for jazz in clubs, records, and radio by the end of the 1960s, of course, made the shift in the jazz art world to concerts, festivals, and educational institutions even more significant. It would be these new forms of support that gave a lifeline to the jazz art world as its commercial market suffered from an irreversible depression. During the New Jazz Age it was the commercial market that first spurred the growth of the jazz art world. The New Jazz Age, however, witnessed the transformation of jazz performance from its original base in urban popular entertainment, the recording market, and radio to a base in special concerts, festivals, and education. By the 1970s, jazz musicians also would begin to receive grants from the National Endowment of the Arts. Jazz had become a specialized music genre dedicated to a niche audience both nationally and internationally. Thirty years after the initial efforts of professional musicians, jazz had achieved the original dream of becoming an American "classical" music replicating the art world of European cultivated music in high art aesthetics, production, education, and audiences.

The modern jazz renaissance: new directions in jazz music and the modern jazz musician

Progressive jazz is the jazz idiom which is currently being used as a medium of personal expression by jazzmen who wish to widen the scope of music they play. Like all the jazz styles which have preceded it, progressive jazz is dynamic, varied, flexible, experimental, and constantly changing when played by creative musicians who are cognizant of the jazz tradition. Since many of these musicians have studied the classics, their technical facility and knowledge has enabled them to utilize techniques and devices which were heretofore used only by the composers of classical music... progressive jazz is the latest development in jazz. It adds new techniques and devices to the mainstream of jazz, yet does not ignore the jazz tradition. (Billy Taylor, *Down Beat*, March 7, 1956: 11)

The economic boom in the jazz market combined with the diversity of the jazz art world brought about a renaissance in jazz performance during the New Jazz Age. The basic practice of the new jazz aesthetic shared by all artists during the renaissance was that jazz was an art form for listening audiences. Many jazz musicians continued to perform styles of jazz music that preceded the modernist revolt of the late 1940s. A larger number of jazz musicians, however, followed the modernist agenda first articulated by boppers and progressives like the pianist and jazz educator Billy Taylor. As the modernist agenda prevailed during the renaissance, jazz musicians experimented in different stylistic directions completing the basic repertoire of jazz strategies of this art world up to the present day. Also as Taylor suggests, the make-up of jazz musicians also gradually changed during the renaissance as more college-educated and middle-class musicians entered the jazz art world.

During the modern jazz renaissance, modernist jazz musicians approached innovation following two basic patterns. One strategy emulated in various ways elements of the classical music tradition, the second strategy innovated more directly from within the modern jazz idiom first articulated by bebop and cool musicians. These approaches were not always easily distinguishable. Many jazz musicians openly experimented with jazz, sometimes moving from one orientation to the other. These two basic strategies, however, were evident in the general artistic directions in modern jazz. While they remained the basic modernist approaches during the renaissance, a movement of Free Jazz emerged from these two approaches eventually becoming a third distinct approach called "The New Thing." All these approaches produced a new standard of musicianship and a new repertoire that finally severed jazz from popular performance.

The birth of the New Jazz Age occurred at a time when modern jazz musicians from the progressive-cool school were receiving the most attention in the jazz art world. In the early 1950s, bop had faded somewhat in importance and bop musicians were having a difficult time finding work. The cool school was also referred to as West Coast jazz since many of its musicians were located in Los Angeles or San Francisco. The cool style was mostly a reserved soft version of the swing ensemble with influences from bop and European classical harmony and timbre used by progressive big bands. Most of the major cool jazz musicians came from the ranks of the progressive big bands of Claude Thornhill, Stan Kenton, Boyd Raeburn, and Woody Herman. Almost all the cool musicians were white modernists, although Miles Davis, John Lewis, Charles Mingus, Mal Waldron, and several other black musicians worked in the cool genre. Examples of cool jazz include *The Birth of Cool* (Capitol), Gerry Mulligan's *Mulligan Quartet* (Fantasy) and *The Gerry Mulligan Quartet with Lee Konitz* (Pacific Jazz), Chet Baker's *The Chet Baker Quintet* (Pacific Jazz), Stan Getz' *Stan Getz* (Prestige), and Lennie Niehaus' *Lennie Niehaus Quintet* (Contemporary).

Like their progressive big band counterparts, cool jazz musicians began to use the European classical tradition more directly in small ensemble performance in the early 1950s. For many modern jazz musicians in the 1950s, jazz as high art signified a breaking down of barriers between these music traditions, and needless to say, utilizing classical idioms articulated the legitimacy of these musicians' efforts just as symphonic jazz did during the Jazz Age. The lineage of the progressive big band also continued into the 1950s with "jazz orchestras" led by leaders like Stan Kenton, Bill Russo, John Lewis, and Gunter Schuller performing jazz compositions similar in design and intent as compositions written for classical symphonies. Cool jazz and classical jazz modernists borrowed form and harmony from the breadth of the classical tradition, from the Baroque to Renaissance to Modern. This approach eventually was labeled as "Third Stream" jazz. The classical jazz modernists were a relatively small number of jazz musicians, yet their impact in the jazz art world in the 1950s was far greater than their numbers would suggest. The popularity of classical jazz modernists was due to jazz critics at the time strongly supporting classical jazz and giving major coverage to this approach in *Metronome* and *Down Beat*. Major record companies were attracted to this "legitimate" approach to jazz performance and a large number of jazz musicians signed by majors in the mid-1950s were classical jazz modernists and their cool jazz peers. The most successful modern jazz musician of the 1950s, the pianist Dave Brubeck, was a classical jazz modernist. Examples of classical jazz ensembles include Red Norvo's *Red Norvo Trio* (Savoy), Teddy Charles' and Shorty Rogers' *Collaboration West* (Prestige), Teddy Charles' *New Directions* (prestige), Jimmy Giuffre's *Tangents* (Capitol), Shorty Rogers' *Modern Sounds* (Capitol), The Modern Jazz Quartet's *Fontessa* (Atlantic), and Dave Brubeck's *Time Out* (Columbia). Examples of classical jazz orchestras include the *Modern Jazz Concert* (Columbia), Bill Russo's *Rebellion* (Roulette), Stan Kenton's *Kenton Era* (Capitol), *Jazz Abstractions* (Atlantic), and *Outstanding Jazz Compositions of the 20th Century* (Columbia).

In viewing the classical tradition as the path to advancing jazz as a fine art form, cool jazz and classical jazz musicians emphasized form and harmony from this tradition and consequently also this tradition's use of composition and arrangement. The result was the gradual reduction of jazz improvisation, ironically the very practice considered in jazz criticism as the defining practice of the jazz tradition. Instead, cool jazz and classical jazz music emphasized the use of written melody and arrangement. While a number of classical jazz modernists equated modern jazz with modern classical music, the use of modern approaches such as tonal rows, fixed scales, atonality, and free form were limited mostly to special jazz concerts and a few recordings. It was when classical jazz modernists focused on emulating pre-modern classical forms that they were most successful in the 1950s. The two most successful groups in the 1950s, The Dave Brubeck Quartet and The Modern Jazz Quartet, both focused on pre-modern forms.

By the early 1960s, the classical approach was fading in importance within the jazz art world just as a large number of mostly black musicians were advancing the second approach to innovation in jazz. To many musicians, the classical approach seemed contrived and far removed from the jazz tradition. The classical jazz approach also proved to have little impact on the development of the jazz tradition during the renaissance. In part, its failure was due to viewing the "advance" of jazz as more derivative than innovative. Classical jazz modernists relied on pre-existing forms, harmonies, and timbres in the classical tradition. With such a pre-given structure to performance, most classical jazz was a mimicry of the classical tradition. An important factor behind the cool jazz and classical jazz modernist approach in jazz performance was the appearance in the jazz art world of jazz musicians with formal music education from music conservatories or colleges. Having a conservatory or college background had a strong influence on adopting a classical jazz modernist orientation. In a sense, these musicians' musical training provided easily available forms and harmonies to use as sources of "innovation" in jazz. To a large extent the fading away of the classical jazz approach was inevitable as most jazz musicians still had no formal music education and were not familiar with classical forms, particularly black jazz musicians brought up with jazz, gospel, and rhythm and blues. Like their bop predecessors, black musicians in the mid-1950s continued to approach jazz innovation based on creative experimentation within the jazz idiom and other African American idioms. These musicians did not look directly towards European classical forms, harmonies, and timbres for their application of the modern jazz aesthetic as did cool jazz musicians and classical jazz musicians. They did use compositional tools and concepts from European music, as was the case in general in the development of African American music, but they applied them to given jazz forms and harmonies. If these musicians looked to other forms, harmonies, or timbres, they looked to African American folk and popular music as inspiration.

The jazz idiom approach of black jazz musicians led in two directions. The basic practice in both directions was to apply innovations, harmonies, forms, and timbres to improvisational jazz performance. One direction headed towards more complex composition. The other direction was towards less complex composition. Both directions contrasted with the classical jazz approach that led to greater use of composition with written parts and non-unison melodic lines. Instead, they continued to emphasize improvisation in jazz performance. The jazz idiom approach retained the previous use in bebop of one or two choruses of melody, usually unison melodic lines, and then extensive improvisation over the song form.

The direction towards more complexity began in the 1950s and continued into the 1960s. This direction was a logical extension of the development of harmonic ambiguity in bop's use of chord substitutions and chromatic progressions that created ambiguous voicing and a weakened sense of tonality. This lineage also was evident in the label Hard Bop given this new direction in jazz innovation in the late 1950s. More complex chord progressions than in bop were created by black musicians moving even further from the harmonic structure and tonal grounding of the blues and popular song forms that boppers first transformed. (Kernfeld 1988) Essentially, these musicians experimented with different voicing and chord progressions as structures on which to improvise. This was aided by the use of simple unison melodic lines over the complex chord progressions and focusing on the ingenuity of the single improviser to play over the song form. Examples of this approach to the jazz idiom include Clifford Brown's and Max Roach's *Clifford Brown/Max*

Roach Quintet (EmArcy), John Coltrane's *Giant Steps* and *Coltrane's Sound* (Atlantic), Thelonious Monk's *Monk's Music* (Riverside), Sonny Rollins' *Saxophone Colossus* (Prestige), and Miles Davis' *Miles Ahead* and *E.S.P.* (Columbia).

Black jazz musicians during the renaissance also followed a direction in developing less compositional complexity and therefore providing fewer demands on jazz improvisers to focus on rapid chord progressions. This occurred in three approaches that appeared by the end of the 1950s. In the first approach musicians went back to blues and gospel songs in jazz composition. Songs influenced by this approach were part of what was called Soul Jazz. The second approach was Modal Jazz that further reduced the role of chord progressions. Inspired by the theory of tonal organization of black composer George Russell, Modal Jazz based composition on chords chosen in accordance with specific scales (modes). Modal Jazz allowed improvisers to freely play on a scale with little concern to the underlying chords. The final approach was Free Jazz that led to the elimination of the role of chord progressions in jazz. The first works in free jazz were based around improvising on a simple melodic line with either alternating chords creating a drone over which to improvise or no consistent chordal pattern whatsoever. By the mid-1960s, most free jazz eliminated even a commitment to a melodic line and was based on complete spontaneous collective performance. Examples of Soul Jazz include Miles Davis' *Walkin'* (Prestige), Horace Silver's *The Jazz Messengers* (Blue Note), Art Blakey's *Moanin'* (Blue Note), Lee Morgan's *The Cooker* (Blue Note), and Cannonball Adderley's *Them Dirty Blues* (Riverside). Examples of Modal Jazz include Miles Davis' *Kind of Blue* (Columbia) and George Russell's *Ezz-Thetics* (Riverside), while Ornette Coleman's *The Shape of Things to Come* and *Free Jazz* (Atlantic), John Coltrane's and Archie Shepp's *New Thing at Newport* (Impulse), and John Coltrane's *Ascension* (Impulse) are examples of Free Jazz.

The incredible breadth of stylistic creativity of black jazz musicians was a result of the shared modernist aesthetic among these musicians and an art world that supported the development of jazz as a fine art form. Unlike its classical jazz counterpart, however, the jazz idiom approach developed a large repertoire of music that was musically distinct from both the classical and the popular. Given the new aesthetic, these musicians applied it conceptually to popular music idioms with which most were familiar – jazz, blues and other African American music idioms. The collective nature of the jazz idiom approach is evident in the fact that music education did not determine who became a major innovator or performer. Some major innovators had no formal education, while others did. Nor did formal education, or lack there of, determine which direction in the jazz idiom approach a jazz musician took. This collective heterogeneity allowed for the gradual development of jazz and the ability of non-formally trained musicians in the black jazz community to take on the gradual innovations applied to familiar forms and harmonies. Many musicians in fact participated in a number of the directions taken in the jazz idiom during the renaissance. The musical community of black jazz musicians only split with the rise of a black avant-garde in the mid-1960s that performed Free Jazz. Since young black avant-gardists performed free form jazz, many never were "schooled" in the previous forms and progressions of the jazz idiom. Avant-gardists, however, still used the basic scales and timbres of African American music idioms, and again formal education was not a determinant of who was an avant-garde performer.

By the early 1970s, the jazz idiom approach of black jazz musicians had run its course. Moving in the twin directions of complexity and simplicity in composition these musicians set the basic parameters of modern jazz performance. After fifteen years of experimentation, jazz musicians continued along these parameters. New generations of jazz musicians were given an established modern jazz tradition in which to pursue the new jazz aesthetic as an art form. The end of experimentation also was in part a result of a move back to popular music in the late 1960s. Having led jazz music in a direction away from popular performance, many jazz musicians now returned to the popular in a more direct manner applying jazz improvisation to the basic rhythms and forms of popular music.

During the renaissance jazz as a musical practice and as a community of musicians had become separate from popular music. Popular musicians, black and white, performed a different repertoire, used a different rhythmic foundation, and used a different instrumentation than jazz musicians. Only the distant relationship of the blues and gospel to popular music and jazz music provided common ground. Jazz musicians, however, did "return" to the popular and applied the jazz aesthetic to popular music. While Soul Jazz used the idioms of the blues and gospel, jazz musicians in this style still maintained the rhythmic drive, basic meter, and timbres of the jazz idiom. By the late 1960s and early 1970s, jazz musicians began to apply improvisational performance to separate popular idioms.

Jazz Fusion electrified jazz instrumentation and introduced the rock beat and the use of rock scales to improvisational jazz performance. Jazz Fusion was quite successful and established major careers for a number of jazz musicians. The Jazz Fusion route also was taken predominantly by white jazz musicians and white rock musicians, although a number of black jazz musicians were part of this new style in jazz performance. Not surprisingly, Miles Davis again was at the forefront of another stylistic direction in jazz. His *In a Silent Way* and *Bitches Brew* (Columbia) in 1969 were one of the first albums featuring Jazz Fusion. Other examples of Jazz Fusion include *Return to Forever* (ECM), Mahavishnu Orchestra's *Inner Mounting Flame* (Columbia), Jean Luc Ponty *On the Wings of Music* (Atlantic). Jazz Soul or Jazz Funk was the exclusive reserve of black musicians and took two forms: a jazz group using the beat and form of popular funk and soul music, or a single jazz instrumentalist performing over the basic background used for singers in black popular performance. Similar to its rock counterpart, Jazz Soul and Jazz Funk were quite successful and again established major careers for a number of black jazz musicians. Jazz Soul was a continuation of the Soul Jazz popular in the late 1950s, but incorporated more of the stylistic elements of contemporary black popular idioms. Examples of Jazz Soul and Jazz Funk include Freddie Hubbard's album *Red Clay* (CTI) and Grover Washington, Jr's album *Inner City Blues* (Kudu), Herbie Hancock's albums *Fat Albert Rotunda* (Atlantic) and *Headhunters* (Columbia), and Miles Davis' *On the Corner* (Columbia).

Jazz Fusion, Jazz Soul, and Jazz Funk were mostly produced by major record companies and non-jazz independent labels. These labels heavily promoted these styles because they were viewed as commercially marketable. Except for the jazz boom in the late 1950s and 1960s, jazz was never considered a major commercial market. It remained a specialized niche and by the 1970s commercial enterprises such as the majors emphasized "commercial" jazz versus the jazz produced and promoted by the jazz art world. In effect, the jazz market bifurcated into a specialized niche market and a commercial market for jazz.

Most of the younger players now approach jazz as a career with as much seriousness as apprentices in classical music. More are coming from middle- and upper-class homes. Jazz has always had some children of skilled workers, businessmen, and professionals, and the percentage rose during the 1920's as more Negro children of solid bourgeois families (Coleman Hawkins, Don Redman, Duke Ellington, Fletcher Henderson) began to find in jazz an expanding area for their ambitions. Particularly in the past decade, however, many white and Negro children, whose families have the resources to support schooling for more conventional careers, are choosing jazz as a life's work. The young jazzman today often does attend an established music school because of the increasingly demanding requirements of jazz; but once he is trained, he still must – as has been true throughout jazz history – find his own way. (Nat Hentoff, *The Jazz Life*, 1961: 44–5)

As jazz music went through important changes during the renaissance, the community of jazz musicians also underwent change. Critic Nat Hentoff pointed to the changes among jazz musicians already apparent by the New Jazz Age. Part observation and part wishful thinking, Hentoff was directing readers to the new legitimacy of jazz music and its consequences in terms of attracting musicians with backgrounds previously not associated with jazz music. The idea of jazz as a legitimate career equivalent to a career in classical music was rather a new concept. Hentoff was certainly correct that the community of jazz musicians by the 1950s was gradually changing in its social make-up. As we have seen, an important factor behind the classical jazz approach was the arrival of jazz musicians with formal music education from music conservatories or colleges. Leonard Feather published *The Encyclopedia of Jazz* in 1960 that included a biographical listing of the top jazz musicians. (Feather 1960) In this listing just over half of the top white modern jazz musicians in the 1950s reported some form of post-secondary education, while around a third of the top modern black jazz musicians reported some form of post-secondary education. This transformation was spurred by the growth in post-secondary education in the post-war period. It also was affected by the increased status of jazz by the 1950s, and of course, a lucrative jazz market. While the top of the field was attracting college educated and middle class musicians, however, the community of jazz musicians still remained socially heterogeneous. The sociologists Howard Becker (1951) and William Bruce Cameron (1954) found the jazz community to be basically working class without a college education. But Becker and Cameron were observing the average jazz musician of the period, not the top white and black musicians who were listed in Feather's 1960 book. The historian David Rosenthal (1982) also found that the average black instrumentalist during the 1950s was attracted to the Hard Bop jazz style. During the 1950s, jazz was still part of the general world of popular music making, performed in small venues across the country by musicians not necessarily enjoying the benefits of being the top jazz musicians performing and recording for the booming jazz market. And even the top jazz musicians during the renaissance were a diverse group of musicians in terms of race, class, and educational background. The modern jazz renaissance, therefore, was not the product of middle class and college educated jazz musicians alone. And as I have shown, the modernist ethos that directed this renaissance developed during the 1930s and 1940s. This vibrant period of musical exploration occurred when this community was still socially diverse by class, race, and education.

Edward Harvey (1967) and Charles Nanry (1972), however, show that by the 1960s the social make-up of jazz musicians was going through a final stage as the jazz art world was recruiting more middle class and college educated musicians with a craftsman's approach to jazz performance. The jazz education movement in the late 1950s also certainly helped in moving the recruitment of jazz musicians to colleges and conservatories. Just as the jazz art world was moving away from the world of popular urban entertainment, and new music practices and instrumentation were occupying the popular music market, the recruitment of jazz musicians no longer came from the large world of popular music making. The decline of the jazz market also left less inducement for choosing a career in jazz. Jazz by the end of the renaissance had become a specialized field of music making similar to the specialized field of classical music. The competencies and repertoire of jazz no longer could be acquired performing popular music. The recruitment of jazz musicians, therefore, depended on a much smaller population of individuals who consciously sought a jazz education. Even informal jam sessions by the early 1960s had become far less common. Leonard Feather noted in 1966 the changes occurring in the community of jazz musicians. As for the past musician, "in preparing for this type of life in music he had no place to turn for specialized instruction... Nevertheless, he found it relatively easy to drift into the profession because of the great number of orchestras, most of them from 12 to 17 men strong, on the local, regional, and national scenes. Compare those circumstances with today's. Jazz is taught not only at such a specialized school as Berklee and at several summer jazz clinics but also at more and more colleges. Dozens of nationally known jazz musicians double as teachers so that the youngster may take private lessons with one of his personal idols... College and school stage bands are in the middle of an era of rabbit-like proliferation ... the parent is furnished with ample evidence that the son will be embarking on a 'respectable' career." (*Down Beat* 6-2-1966: 13) The jazz art world now entertained a more academic leaning jazz musician – a specialist performing for a niche national and international jazz market.

Jazz music went through a renaissance as new styles of jazz music emerged under the modern jazz aesthetic even as older styles of jazz performance continued to attract audiences. By the early 1970s, a basic jazz music repertoire was established. This tradition ranged from the traditional to swing to modern to pop styles, all recognized by the jazz art world. The creation of this tradition since its beginnings was centered on the work of African American musicians and remained so during the renaissance. These musicians' commitment to the fundamentals of the jazz idiom during the renaissance let the new jazz aesthetic transform the jazz idiom into new modern directions that remained distinct from both the classical tradition and popular music. Following the New Jazz Age, however, new generations of more specialized and educated jazz musicians had a given tradition of performance supported through jazz education, literature, recordings, and live performance.

Freedom now suite: black music and the politics of modern jazz

Yes, I have changed, but only in terms of content. I will never again play anything that does not have social significance. It is my duty, the purpose of the artist is to mirror his times and its effects on his fellow man. We American jazz musicians of African descent have proved beyond all doubt that we're master musicians of our instruments. Now, what we have to do is employ our skill to tell the dramatic story of our people and what we've been through . . . sit-in demonstrations . . . courage of our young people . . . how can anyone consider my music independent of what I am . . . reflection of all I feel . . . no one can stand against change . . . praise for the color of my music, prejudice for the color of my skin. . . (Max Roach, *Down Beat*, 3-30-1961: 21)

Drummer Max Roach was expressing a new militancy among black professional jazz musicians beginning in the late 1950s. Having just recorded his album *Freedom Now Suite*, dedicated to the struggle against South African Apartheid and American Jim Crow, Roach as a mirror of his times was expressing the growing militancy in the black community in the United States as it struggled for its basic civil rights. This militancy would express itself in a Black Arts Movement in the 1960s in which New Black Music would play an important part. As before in the history of jazz, the significance and meaning of this music intersected with broader political and cultural currents of the time. While Free Jazz would elicit grumbling among critics in the jazz art world during the renaissance, occasionally faulted for the collapse of the market in the late 1960s, the most heated debate of the jazz art world was over black militancy and what some white jazz critics called Crow Jim. While Black Music proponents took a radical position on jazz and black music, the articulation of jazz as "black music" during the renaissance was not simply limited to radical Black Nationalism. Also certain aspects of the Black Music critique of the jazz art world reflected similar critiques by other musicians and critics about the exploitive conditions of the jazz club scene and the difficulties of finding venues for the "free" expression of jazz. And as we will see, aspects of the ideology of Black Music had roots in the community of African American artists since the turn of the century.

The success of the modern jazz aesthetic and the claim to high art status brought with it a resurgence of the Black Nationalist agenda among black professional musicians. It also appeared following the predominance in the jazz art world of cool jazz and white cool jazz musicians in the early and mid 1950s. The rise of black consciousness was at first an immediate response to jazz gaining respectability and legitimacy by moving away from African American idioms and towards the classical music idiom and posing mostly white jazz musicians as the major artists of this genre.

When the New Jazz Age first began the classical modernist jazz approach dominated discussions of the future and significance of jazz in both the jazz press and general press. This discussion included both white and black jazz musicians as this approach was held as the best direction for jazz. The focus of the modern jazz aesthetic on black idioms by black musicians was an attempt at reasserting jazz as a fundamental expression of African American culture and African American musicians. It also was an effort to regain a foothold in the booming jazz market of clubs, concerts, and recordings as well as gaining a larger audience among black consumers.

The first moves towards Black Music occurred with the Hard Bop and Soul Jazz of the late 1950s. The significance of the new style of Hard Bop was immediately recognized in *Down Beat*'s article on the new Hard Bop ensemble The Jazz Messengers in 1956 whose members were Art Blakey, Horace Silver, Donald Byrd, Hank Mobley, and Doug Watkins. "The Jazz Messengers are a blazing band of jazz evangelists who believe that jazzmen advance most surely when their roots in the jazz tradition are deepest." And Art Blakey and Horace Silver made clear what constituted this tradition. Blakey informed readers that the group's name was a reference to the power of preaching he experienced as a child and "the spirit of music is sometimes stronger than the spirit in a church meeting." Silver pointed to how "we can reach way back and get that old-time, gutbucket barroom feeling with just a taste of backbeat as in *Doodlin'* and *The Preacher*. And in one number, the medium tempo *Funky Blues* even includes some boogie-woogie." (*Down Beat* 2-22-1956: 10) Hard Boppers retained the modernist aesthetic but asserted a "jazz tradition" of black music as the backbone of their "funky" and "soul" jazz. In fact, the lack of funk and soul was now used against cool jazz and classical jazz proponents. Critic Nat Hentoff in 1957 asked black jazz musician John Lewis what he thought of recent criticisms that his group the Modern Jazz Quartet was not "funky" enough. (*Down Beat* 2-20-1957: 15) Critic Dan Morgenstern, however, on vibraphonist Milt Jackson of the MJQ noted that the "intangible 'soul,' which distinguish Jackson's playing, can be traced to the early and lasting influence of the church." (*Down Beat* 11-27-1958: 17) As critic John Tynan noted, by 1960 in "a somewhat belated back-to-the-earth movement, an increasing number of Negro jazzmen are talking, thinking, and playing 'soul' music. Indeed, the word *soul* itself has become synonymous with truth, honesty, and yes, even social justice among Negro musicians." And one could "use the word 'funk' or 'funky' and rightly consider oneself the hippest of the hip." (*Down Beat* 9-15-1960: 20, 11-24-1960: 18) While Soul Jazz proponents emphasized the black roots of jazz, even avant-garde black jazz musicians began emphasizing jazz as black music. Cecil Taylor while recognizing the contributions of such avant-garde white jazz artists like Lennie Tristano argued that "the greatness in jazz occurs because it includes all the mores and folkways of Negroes during the last 50 years. No, don't tell me that living in the same kind of environment is enough. *You* don't have the same kind of cultural difficulties I do... Jazz is a Negro feeling. It is African, but changed to a new environment. It begins in the Negro community... (*Down Beat* 10-26-1961: 20–1)

Of course, critic John Tynan also noticed that the "catchword 'soul,' currently is riding high with jazz record buyers if one is to judge from the advertisements placed by some record companies." (*Down Beat* 11-24-1960: 18) Or as Prestige Records celebrated, "Despite Opposition of Critics, Prestige Gave Birth to Soul Jazz." (*Down Beat* 1-5-1961) Soul Jazz was decidedly a market niche geared not only to the jazz market but also to black consumers. Soul Jazz was not only performed by modernist jazz musicians but by older black swing musicians like Gene Ammons and Eddie "Lockjaw" Davis and black singers like Etta Jones and Shirley Scott. And as David Rosenthal (1982) shows Hard Bop and Soul Jazz were popular in the black community and among black musicians. But in terms of the jazz art world, black trumpeter Nat Adderley was clear about the significance of Soul Jazz. "If the term soul music has a leaning toward meaning Negro music, then the term cool or west coast music had a leaning toward being white. And the whole thing behind this thing is that there were a whole lot of guys – a whole lot of good Negro musicians who weren't working very regularly when the vogue was the cool west coast sound, because everybody who was cool and west coast was white. So you get a thing 10 years later that is a big commercial gimmick, soul music, and everybody involved in it is colored... Now we got something to go; we got soul music. And finally, I've got a job. I can work in the clubs, and already, they're trying to kill it... This label – soul music. He feels it has a racial implication that can keep him working." (*Down Beat* 6-8-1961: 22) The reassertion of black idioms in jazz was therefore a combination of reactions to the directions of jazz at the beginning of the New Jazz Age in terms of music, musicians, and the art world. In 1953, a year before the boom, the covers of *Down Beat's* twenty-six issues did not feature a single black musician or group of black musicians and only three covers featured white and black musicians together. In 1961 more black musicians were featured on *Down Beat* covers than white musicians.

With the rise of Hard Bop and Soul Jazz tensions emerged in the art world over race and jazz, what critic Leonard Feather called the "racial undercurrent" in the jazz art world. (*Down Beat Music* 61: 44) What white critics called Crow Jim included the question of whether black musicians performed a different and better jazz and the accusation beginning in the late 1950s that some black jazz musicians would not perform with white jazz musicians. The accusation of Crow Jim was not new to the jazz art world. As early as 1938, critic Otis Ferguson accused jazz enthusiast John Hammond in his preference and promotion of black artists as starting "the Jim Crow car all over again, but in reverse." (*H.R.S. Rag* 9-1938: 6) The term Crow Jim also was used earlier in critiquing European critics and audiences preference for black jazz musicians. In 1949, critic Barry Ulanov noted the preference at European jazz festivals for black jazz musicians. "To Europeans and to some Americans jazz is a Negro product. It can't really be played by white men... No, Crow Jim is no more correct and no more appetizing than Jim Crow, and jazzmen, who have done much to break down the ugliness of the latter, will do well to have nothing to do with the narrowness of the former." (*Metronome* 5-1949: 42) *Down Beat* editors in 1951 castigated European Crow Jim as evidenced in the readers poll of the French jazz magazine *Le Jazz Hot* where black musicians won honors among the top five in each category except for five white artists none of whom placed higher than third. "Crow Jim is just as evil and just as misguided as Jim Crow." The editors also pointed to the prevalence of the romantic jazz narrative among Europeans that gave black artists unique natural gifts in jazz. "It is comparable with the chauvinistic, patronizing southern cracker attitude that the Negro is supposedly a separate and distinct brand of human being... has a 'natural sense of rhythm' and so forth..." (*Down Beat* 3-9-1951: 10)

In the late 1950s, black jazz musicians also were accused by white jazz critics of practicing Crow Jim in their attitudes about "soul" and in their preference for black musicians. Critic Nat Hentoff in "Race Prejudice in Jazz: It Works Both Ways" in *Harper's Magazine* in 1959 informed readers "that at the heart of jazz there are many Negro musicians who are not yet ready to extend full musical and social equality to whites... Jazz has come to mean for many Negro musicians, therefore, a secret society to which American whites have to pay heavily to be admitted... but the Negro musicians often add the connotation that 'soul' and 'funk' are exclusively Negro qualities." (*Harper's* 6-1959: 73, 75) Critic Gene Lees in 1960 argued that "today we are seeing the equally melancholy phenomenon of discrimination against white musicians... a good many serious-minded musicians, both Negro and white, are worried about what this attitude augurs for jazz... Evidently the view is that while Negro musicians lack none of the abilities of white musicians, white musicians lack some of the abilities of Negro musicians... The idea of a racial difference in music is irrational at the root. I'm getting tired of hearing certain Negro musicians, obviously paranoic, claim that white musicians have stolen from the Negro and given nothing." (*Down Beat* 10-13-1960: 53) Some white jazz critics, especially Nat Hentoff and Leonard Feather, did point to how the experience of Jim Crow created Crow Jim. Leonard Feather noted that in "analyzing these developments, we must bear in mind that this form of prejudice would never have existed without the primary cause, the genesis of the whole chain, Jim Crow itself. That the Negroes antiwhite attitudes are a direct product of his own racial suffering enables us to explain and understand antiwhitism without condoning or justifying it." (*Down Beat Music* 1961: 46)

The controversy over Crow Jim within the jazz art world eventually found itself in *Time Magazine* in 1962 as well as in other non-jazz publications including the gentlemen's porno magazine *Rogue* in "Crow Jim: No Gigs for Ofays." (*Rogue* 1-1964: 54) *Time* noted that "it is shared in some degree by many Negro jazz musicians, and its major cause is anti-Negro prejudice in a field that Negroes regard as their own. Its result is the regrettable kind of reverse segregation known as Crow Jim – a feeling that the white man had no civil rights when it comes to jazz... What embitters Negro musicians is that they share so little in the management of the music they created... Moreover, many Negro jazzmen honestly feel that white jazzmen cannot 'feel' the 'soul' music that the 'soul brothers' and 'soul sisters' are producing these days." (*Time* 10-19-62: 58) Meanwhile *Down Beat* dedicated a two part special report and panel discussion on "Racial Prejudice in Jazz," since the "growth of ill feeling – based on racial difference – between Negro and white jazzmen has become distasteful to most, alarming to some. A few self-proclaimed oracles have warned that ill feeling would lead to strict separateness and eventually kill jazz. But these are the few; the many recognize the situation as one that will be resolved with understanding on both sides." (*Down Beat* 3-15-1962: 20) This issue was followed-up the following year by another special report and panel discussion on the "Need for Racial Unity in Jazz" in April 1963.

While some black musicians acknowledged Crow Jim among their ranks, white jazz critics mostly pointed to the "problem" of Crow Jim. Racial tensions obviously were rising in the jazz art world, but the extent of Crow Jim was hard to measure given that jazz musicians in general performed mostly in segregated ensembles. John Lewis who rejected the confines of "soul" as defining modern jazz and claimed jazz as a color-blind art nonetheless led the all-black ensemble the Modern Jazz Quartet. On the other hand, Soul Jazz and Hard Bop groups like The Cannonball Adderley Quintet and the Oliver Nelson Sextet had white jazz musicians. But racial tensions were evident in the jazz art world. Horace Silver told *Time Magazine* that "whites started crying Crow Jim when the public got

hip that Negroes play the best jazz." White west coast jazz musician Cal
Tjader told *Time* that "I don't think I'd very much like to be a white boy
just starting out in New York City now," while white jazz pianist Paul
Winter agreed that "we're right in the middle of a Crow Jim period. Out
in Chicago they told us, 'Don't go to New York – you're ofay'." (*Time*
10-19-62: 60) Not surprisingly, New York City, the center of the East
Coast Hard Bop movement, was held suspect by some white musicians.
New York City also would be a major center in the rising Black Arts
Movement, a movement that was part of a growing Black Nationalism.
Needless to say, *Time* pointed to "the angry young men who are passion-
ately involved in the rise of Negro nationalism" as a major factor in Crow
Jim. (*Time* 10-19-1962: 59-60)

I address myself to bigots – those who are so inadvertently, those who are cold
and premeditated with it. I address myself to those "in" white hipsters who think
niggers never had it so good (Crow Jim) and that its time something was done
about restoring the traditional privileges that have always accrued to the whites
exclusively (Jim Crow). I address myself to sensitive chauvinists – the greater
part of the white intelligentsia – and the insensitive with whom the former had
this in common: the uneasy awareness that "Jass" is an ofay's word for a nigger's
music... Give me leave to state this unequivocal fact: jazz is the product of the
whites – the ofays – too often my enemy. It is the progeny of the blacks – my
kinsmen. By this I mean: you own the music, and we make it. (Archie Shepp,
Down Beat, December 16, 1965: 11)

Racial tensions would continue to rise in the jazz art world as more radical expressions of Black Nationalism appeared in the New Black Music
movement. Radical jazz musician Archie Shepp expressed the new move
in the New Black Music movement to reject "jazz" as an appropriate term
for an art form created by black artists. (McRae 1967) As Max Roach
remarked in 1972, "let us first eliminate the term, 'jazz.' It is not a term or
a name that we, as black musicians, ever gave to the art which we created.
It is a name which was given to the Afro-American's art form by white
America, with and which therefore inherits all the racist and purient attitudes which have been directed to all other aspects of the black experience
in this country." (Roach 1972: 3) As historian John D. Baskerville (1994)
argues, the New Black Music movement articulated the radical Black
Nationalism of the period. As part of the Black Arts Movement, New
Black Music proponents both condemned the capitalist and Jim Crow
exploitation and co-optation of the work of black artists and sought to
define and create a unique "black aesthetic." While following in the line
of the earlier Harlem Renaissance, this new resurgence in Black Art occurred at a time when many in the African American community had
become radicalized through the long insurgence for civil rights as well

as the growing militancy against the Vietnam War. This agenda among black musicians, therefore, often included more radical aesthetic and non-musical claims than previous periods. (Wilmer 1980) A major voice in the jazz art world of this new radical position appeared with the publication of the jazz journal *Jazz Today* (1965 to 1967) which featured radical critiques of this art world from the pens of Frank Kofsky and Leroi Jones, who later changed his name to Amari Baraka. The new black militancy was evident in Jones' book *Blues People* published in 1963. "The most expressive Negro music of any given period will be an exact reflection of what the Negro himself is. It will be a portrait of the Negro in America at that particular time." As for the new black aesthetic, Jones argued that "what these musicians have done, basically, is to restore to jazz its valid separation from, and anarchic disregard of, Western popular forms... The emotional significance of most Negro music has been its separation from the emotional and philosophical attitudes of classical music. In order for the jazz musician to utilize most expressively any formal classical techniques, it is certainly necessary that these techniques be subjected to the emotional and philosophical attitudes of Afro-American music – that these techniques be *used* not canonized." (Jones 1963: 137, 225, 230) Steve Young, Music-Art Coordinator of the Black Arts Repertory Theater/School in New York City, expressed this new radical ideology in the liner notes for a recording of a New Black Music concert benefiting this new art organization.

New Black Music

It is through the Black Man's Music that the record of his Spiritual strivings are recorded for, from the time he was first introduced into this country as a slave he was allowed little more Freedom than the freedom of his Music. Into his Music he poured all the energy that was elsewhere blocked... through which his Spirit could express itself. The creators of the New Music have reached deep into their psyches, deep into their cultural origins to find a language of sound that conveys this sense of the world as feeling, as knowledge found through the logic of emotions... Here then is the music of a new breed of musicians. We might call them "The Beautiful Warriors" or witch doctors and ju ju men... astroscientists, and magicians of the soul. (Impulse-90)

The New Black Music movement was an avant-garde movement based mostly on the Free Jazz innovations of the late 1950s and 1960s. (Litweiler 1984) This movement viewed black avant-garde musicians like Ornette Coleman, John Coltrane, Sun Ra, Archie Shepp, and Albert Ayler as major proponents of the New Black Music. However, it also saw its lineage reaching to the early beboppers and hard boppers. Journalist Valerie Wilmer in her book on the Black Music movement also points out this movement attempted to distance itself from the jazz art world by not only calling their music New Black Music but also by establishing independent production of live performance and recordings. (Wilmer 1980) In the 1960s independent black art collectives like the Association for the Advancement of Creative Musicians (AACM) in Chicago and the Black Artists Group (BAG) in St. Louis formed to promote independent performance. White Free Jazz avant-garde artists also were articulating radical critiques of the commercial world of music making and radical politics. The formation of the Jazz Composers Orchestra Association in 1965 sought to promote Free Jazz through independent performance, and the formation of the Free Jazz ensemble The Liberation Orchestra in the late 1960s expressed the radical politics of the time.

The New Black Music movement, however, was only the more radical avant-garde expression of the question of jazz as an African American art form during the modern jazz renaissance. The importance of music as an expression of the African American community, of course, preoccupied black professional musicians since the turn of the century such as James Weldon Johnson, William Marion Cook, and James P. Johnson. Duke Ellington continued this agenda in his advocacy of Negro Music and in his extended compositions – work he continued to pursue during the modern jazz renaissance. Even within a more classical influenced approach to jazz music black jazz musicians articulated a Black Nationalism. Oliver Nelson described the importance of his suite "Afro/American Sketches" in 1961. "I have at last realized the importance of my African and Negro heritage and through this enlightenment I was able to compose 40 minutes of original music which is a true extension of my musical soul. For this vision I am eternally grateful." (Prestige 1223) Since Hard Bop, black jazz musicians regularly made references to both African and African American culture and politics. As jazz attained greater legitimacy as a high art form and the modernist jazz aesthetic captured the imaginations of young professional black musicians, the agenda of creating a music expressive of African American culture was re-ignited among what W. E. B. Du Bois called the "talented tenth" of the black community.

The Black Nationalist agenda, however, sometimes worked against the idea of jazz as an ideal inter-racial democratic American music, what critic Nat Hentoff called the "inner-democracy" of the jazz community. (Hentoff 1961) Was jazz a great American art form or a great African-American art form, or both. Of course, white jazz critics from the beginning of the jazz art world pointed to black artists as the major creators and innovators in jazz. More radical black nationalists like Leroi Jones, however, rejected these critics defining an African American art form. "Most jazz critics were (and are) not only white middle-class Americans, but middle-brows as well. The irony here is that because the majority of jazz critics are white middle-brows, most jazz criticism tends to enforce white middle-brow standards of excellence as criteria for performance of a music that in its most profound manifestations is completely anti-thetical to such standards; in fact, quite often is in direct reaction against them." (*Down Beat* 8-15-1963: 16) Or as Max Roach stated in 1972, "But beyond recognizing the esthetics and the learning processes involved in black music, we must cleanse our minds of false categories which are not basic to us and divide us rather than unite us... In all respects, culturally, politically, socially, we must re-define ourselves and our lives, on our own terms." (Roach 1972: 6) Jazz musician Donald Byrd, Chairman of the Department of Jazz Studies at Howard University, argued that "in order to survive as a culture (and our music is only a small part of it) we must not only be aware of our cultural contribution, but we must go so far as to define it." (Byrd 1972: 31)

The countervailing directions of framing jazz music during the modern jazz renaissance again reflected broader cultural currents in American culture. Just as Jazz Studies was to emerge as an academic discipline, the discipline of Black Studies also emerged in the academy. These disciplines were not distinctly separate, but actually were intertwined in their mutual interest in an African American art form called jazz. But an agenda of defining Black Music by black artists and scholars was a new development. Black music historian Eileen Southern's *The Music of Black Americans* first published in 1971 became the first in the rising discipline of black music scholarship. "A history of the musical activities of black Americans in the United States is long overdue. The black musician has created an entirely new music – in a style peculiarly Afro-American – that today spreads its influence over the entire world." (Southern 1971: xv) Earlier works by Harlem Renaissance writers in the 1930s also attempted to develop a distinct scholarship in black music, but the initial efforts of Maude Cuney Hare (1936) and Alain Locke (1936) were not seriously pursued until the 1970s and the rise of Black Studies. (Ramsey 1995) An indication of the new direction of black music studies was the new academic journal *The Black Perspective in Music* that began publication in 1973, and the initiation in 1981 of *Black Music Research Journal*. Again, however, the intertwining of Jazz Studies and Black Music Studies is demonstrated in scholars publishing in journals and books in both disciplines.

The racial politics of the modern jazz renaissance reflected the radical politics of the time and the long-term agenda of Black Nationalism among black artists during the twentieth century. The initial efforts of James Weldon Johnson to uplift the race through literature, music, and other arts was joined during the modern jazz renaissance by black jazz musicians from John Lewis to Max Roach to Charlie Mingus to Oliver Nelson to Archie Shepp. Not all black jazz musicians who articulated black idioms in their jazz music held a clearly defined nationalist agenda, but as a collective community of artists, black jazz musicians expressed this agenda in various ways. As the black jazz vernacular moved through its various transformations and associated meanings, the racial framing of this music went in a number of directions. But a crucial direction in the evolution of jazz music was the quest for legitimacy of black professional musicians and their cultural expression of the African American community. In Duke Ellington's 1956 suite *A Drum is a Woman,* the muse Jass traveled from the African continent along the African Diaspora to inspire future generations of African slaves to create the most profound music. For Ellington, his roots and his mission as an African American artist remained clear. It was during the modern jazz renaissance that the various efforts of black professional musicians in the twentieth century to establish a unique high art expression of African American music came to its fullest realization.

The literation of jazz: jazz criticism, literature, and the jazz tradition

It has been the fortune of jazz to elude any and all attempts to tie it down, even to words. For better or for worse, in sickness and in health, the very name of this music has resisted any really satisfactory explanation. (Barry Ulanov, *Metronome,* October 1951: 16)

While critic Barry Ulanov admitted to the difficulties of defining and explaining jazz, The New Jazz Age saw the proliferation of writing attempting this very task. Ulanov himself published a comprehensive *History of Jazz* in 1952. Ulanov actually was pointing to the earlier problem of jazz traditionalists defining jazz against a modernist aesthetic of constant exploration in jazz music. The problem in jazz criticism for Ulanov was in defining the parameters of a music still in formation, that is, defining what constituted the "jazz tradition." Jazz criticism during the renaissance was decidedly modernist with most critics celebrating innovative and creative modern jazz musicians while predicting the future of jazz in print and special symposiums. Underlying the growth of jazz criticism, however, was the construction of a basic jazz history. By the end of the renaissance, jazz criticism outlined a basic evolution of jazz from folk music to popular music to a modernist high art music – a narrative history that essentially prevails in jazz writings up to the present. The elaboration of a jazz tradition, however, was only part of what I call the "literation" of jazz, the increasing importance of the written word and written note. This transformation in literacy also complemented the general evolution in the jazz art world towards a more select community of jazz artists and jazz connoisseurs.

The economic boom of The New Jazz Age had an important quantitative and qualitative effect on jazz print media. As we have seen, jazz critics reached a broader audience in the larger number of non-jazz print media that featured their writing from *The New Yorker* to *Playboy* to *High Fidelity*. A quantitative change also occurred in the greater number of jazz books published. Jazz periodicals, however, were not to show numerical growth until the early 1970s. (Kernfeld 1988) Jazz print media after 1954 also presented a number of qualitative changes. In general, these changes were the result of the spread and continued development of the modernist jazz aesthetic and a result of changes in the educational background of audiences and musicians connected to the jazz art world. The "literation" of jazz signaled the movement of jazz music from a more aural experience in terms of the apprenticeship of musicians or audiences listening to live and recorded music to a music where the written note and the written word became a major part of its art world and commercial market. Of course, the early efforts of connoisseurship in the 1930s and 1940s also were based on the literation of jazz for jazz connoisseurs. But this process of literation increased significantly with the coming of the New Jazz Age. It also was accompanied with an increase in the spoken word as serious jazz panels of critics and musicians were to become common in festivals, concerts, and special events, and jazz education entered colleges and conservatories.

The boom in jazz books presented a qualitative change as these new publications moved beyond the narrative social history and descriptive music criticism of earlier works. Many jazz books included historical, musicological, and sociological analysis, some of which were published by university presses. Works such as Barry Ulanov's *History of Jazz* (1952), Marshall Stearn's (1956) *The Story of Jazz*, Andre Hodier's (1956) *Jazz: Its Essence and Evolution*, Leroy Ostransky's (1960) *The Anatomy of Jazz*, and Hentoff and McCarthy's (1961) *Jazz* presented a new level of historical and musicological analysis in jazz literature. More general interest jazz books also were published, like Barry Ulanov's *A Handbook of Jazz* (1957), Leonard Feather's *Encyclopedia of Jazz* (1960), and Dave Dexter's *The Jazz Story* (1964). Nat Hentoff's (1961) *The Jazz Life*, Neil Leonard's (1962) *Jazz and the White Americans*, and Leroi Jones' (1963) *Blues People* were examples of the new sociological analysis in jazz writing. Jazz literature now posed jazz as not only the concern of the hot jazz enthusiast, but as an art form worthy of general intellectual interest. From 1955 to 1959, the number of jazz books published in the United States equaled the number of jazz books published from 1935 to 1954. By the early 1970s, the rate of publication of general and instructional jazz books was twice that of the first five years of the New Jazz Age. (Kernfeld 1988: 1335–46)

The major jazz magazines *Metronome* and *Down Beat* were to go through changes during the New Jazz Age as the modern jazz aesthetic and jazz art world gained in popularity. The most striking change was the transformation of *Down Beat* from a tabloid-like news format to a more professional presentation similar to *Metronome's*. The initial changes occurred in the early 1950s as jazz critics and instrumental jazz ensembles and soloists received a larger share of the regular coverage. In 1955, however, *Down Beat* changed from its large newspaper format, with news, reviews, commentary, photos, and advertisements scattered throughout the publication to a magazine format with just four separate sections. The first change was the disappearance of tabloid headlines and stories, swimsuit clad or seductively posed females, and comic photos. The previously large number of news items, often tabloid in nature, were condensed into a smaller news section absent of tabloid news. A features section became the major focus presenting longer articles on jazz musicians, styles and movements in jazz, other issues in the jazz art world, and popular music. The other two sections were music reviews and a section of regular columns.

Besides *Down Beat's* move away from its tabloid presentation, this magazine and *Metronome* would both move through similar changes in coverage and content as major organs of the jazz art world. By the early 1950s with the collapse of the big band business the emerging jazz art world had reached a point where jazz critics were no longer busy critiquing commercialism at every opportunity or elucidating the difference between jazz and popular music, but shifting to an exploration of the future of jazz as a recognized market and high art genre. Popular music and popular singers were still covered during the 1950s, but the distinction between jazz and popular music first set out by jazz critics in record reviews and columns in the 1940s was now part of all sections of these magazines. And by the end of the 1950s, coverage of popular music virtually disappeared with popular singers like Eddie Fisher, Patti Page, and Perry Como no longer gracing the covers of these magazines. Both *Metronome* and *Down Beat* had become "jazz magazines" geared to both musicians and connoisseurs.

Metronome and *Down Beat* played a crucial role in the renaissance with their promotion of a modernist agenda. While still supportive of traditional and mainstream jazz, these national organs of the jazz art world applied an open policy to the different directions of jazz performance, whether traditional, mainstream, or modern, at the same time in which the growth of jazz as an art form was a major preoccupation of both jazz critics and jazz musicians. In articles, columns, and special panels, critics and musicians discussed the state of jazz, new styles, jazz education, the importance of classical music in jazz innovations and growth, the ever-present danger of commercialism, and the struggle to find venues and support for jazz performance as a high art form. These magazines became intellectual forums for the promotion of the different ways that jazz performance both moved out of its original location in jazz clubs in urban entertainment districts and developed a more refined high art aesthetic.

The open policy of *Down Beat* and *Metronome*, however, never let the modernist agenda overwhelm their pages. As much as these journals were used as a forum for this agenda, they followed all the currents within the jazz art world. One way in which these journals allowed for this diversity was in giving a large number of jazz musicians a greater voice in their pages with extensive interviews, musicians' panels, and articles written by the musicians themselves. In a sense, these journals through musicians' voices allowed the jazz art world to speak for itself as musicians discussed their styles of performance, the state of jazz, and other topics. This open policy meant that these magazines played an important role in supporting the innovation and diversity that characterized the jazz art world during the renaissance.

With the closing of the *Record Changer* in 1956 and *Metronome* in 1961, *Down Beat* was to be the only jazz periodical to span the jazz art world from its initial beginnings through the renaissance and beyond. Other jazz journals, however, gradually appeared to take up the loss of the *Record Changer* and *Metronome*. In the 1950s and early 1960s, new jazz journals, like most of their predecessors, were short lived. *Metronome* attempted to publish another magazine completely dedicated to jazz, *Jazz Today*, but this magazine lasted for only thirteen monthly issues starting in October 1956. Critics Nat Hentoff and Martin Williams edited *The Jazz Review* in an effort to guide the jazz art world in the right direction but this publication only survived just over two years. And as we have seen, the more radical jazz journal *Jazz* survived only two and a half years. By the late 1960s, however, more and more jazz journals appeared and remained in publication. By the early 1970s, a definite growth in jazz periodicals was evident and continued on in the 1970s and 1980s. (Kernfeld 1988: 1346–9)

Included in the growth of jazz print media was a new market for instructional books in jazz performance and theory. By the 1960s, books on jazz theory, jazz improvisation, jazz composition, jazz transcriptions, and jazz exercises became an important part of jazz literature and jazz education. The jazz composer George Russell's *Lydian Concept of Tonal Organization* written in 1953 was an early theoretical work that had a major influence on jazz musicians. John Mehegan wrote a four volume series of books on jazz improvisation beginning in 1959 that were a template for later jazz instruction books. Jazz composer Bill Russo's *Composing for the Jazz Orchestra* was published in 1961, while Jerry Coker's *Improvising Jazz* was published in 1964. Up to the 1960s, jazz was music learned by example and experience, even for those with formal music education and the ability to read musical notation. This change in part was a reflection of the entrance into the jazz art world in the 1950s of a far greater number of musicians educated at college or conservatory level. It also was an outgrowth of the jazz education movement and the changes in the recruitment and education of jazz musicians in the 1960s.

Similar to the literation of the art world of European cultivated music, the literation of jazz constructed and legitimated a distinct music tradition called jazz for artists, audiences, and educators. This literation occurred not only in print, but in the various panels and lectures seriously discussing jazz at festivals, colleges, conservatories, art museums, and even on television programs. As Howard Becker (1984) argues, criticism is an essential part of legitimating a particular high art genre or high art practice as well as defining its parameters, what distinguishes a genre or practice from others. During the renaissance, jazz criticism in its various forms was constructing a jazz tradition from folk music, popular music, to modernist high art as well as defining a jazz connoisseurship. In the process, jazz criticism also was gradually moving into academia establishing the discipline of Jazz Studies.

Scott DeVeaux (1991) argues that the process of constructing a jazz tradition for the jazz art world entailed certain difficulties given the wide variety of musical directions taken by jazz musicians during the renaissance. This difficulty is evident in the way jazz critics who earlier promoted the classical jazz approach adjusted to Hard Bop, Soul Jazz, and Free Jazz. Free Jazz elicited a short but heated conflict in the jazz art world. Some critics referred to Free Jazz as "anti-jazz." But this conflict, like the conflict over bebop, subsided as a supposedly incomprehensible music became comprehensible to jazz critics, and also attracted audiences and record buyers. Jazz criticism, however, was able to incorporate the different directions in jazz music including Free Jazz within the general modernist paradigm of innovation and exploration. Jazz histories written following the renaissance like Frank Tirro's *Jazz: A History* (1977) and James Lincoln Collier's *The Making of Jazz* (1978) incorporated Free

Jazz as part of the jazz tradition and canonized John Coltrane as a jazz visionary. During the renaissance, the modernist aesthetic prevailed in the jazz art world. The greatest violation of the jazz tradition actually was not in avant-garde explorations whether those of the Jazz Composers Workshop and Jimmy Giuffre during the 1950s or those of John Coltrane in the 1960s, but in the "commercial" popular turn among jazz musicians.

The incorporation of the various styles of modern jazz into the jazz tradition also pointed to how critics were not alone in defining this tradition at the time. Jazz musicians in interviews, articles, and in their musical choices were defining this tradition as much as critics. While Krin Gabbard (1995) and Steven B. Elworth (1995) correctly highlight jazz critics' role in constructing the jazz tradition, they ignore how musicians during the modern period from Bebop to Free Jazz were actively defining this tradition too. Nor do they acknowledge how producers of recorded and live jazz were also constructing this tradition in the diverse directions of jazz. As Howard Becker (1984) argues, an art world is a collective endeavor in which critics are beholden to producers and artists, as much, if not more so, as producers and artists are beholden to critics, all of whom are beholden to their audience for support. DeVeaux (1991: 528) argues, however, that what constituted a jazz tradition always would remain open to challenges within the jazz art world – a struggle over the "*possession* of that history, and the legitimacy it confers." The New Black Music movement in the 1960s, of course, was one such challenge. This challenge in some ways was eventually incorporated into the jazz art world, although tensions still remained in the jazz art world over the place of the jazz avant-garde and jazz as black music in the construction of its tradition. As the renaissance came to an end, the jazz tradition was established ironically in both the basic stylistic approaches in jazz as well as the basic conflicts over the jazz tradition that would define this art world up to the present. And as was the case in its first thirty-five years, not only musicians, producers, and critics would shape these distinctions and conflicts, but also the commercial and institutional structures in which these individuals would produce jazz music and jazz criticism.

The literation of the jazz art world was part of the more general transformation in jazz performances, jazz musicians, and jazz audiences during The New Jazz Age and Modern Jazz Renaissance. It represented one part of the transformation in the jazz art world towards a connoisseurship of high art appreciation and high art education. The literation of jazz continued past the renaissance as the number of magazines and books continued to grow, even as the market for live and recorded jazz confronted a declining market. That jazz would eventually become such a literate world might seem ironic given the original view of jazz as the lowbrow art of illiterate folk musicians as well as the primacy given improvisation over the written score. At the same time, however, the literation of jazz combined with jazz education certainly fulfilled the dreams of professional musicians since the Jazz Age that jazz would become a legitimate American high art music worthy of the same criticism, history, and instruction as European cultivated music.

Conclusion: the end of the modern jazz renaissance

A different death assailed jazz during the 60's: economic strangulation... More and more, jazz was becoming an accepted art form; i.e. it was no longer the music of the day but rapidly moving toward the inevitable status of a cultural asset – something in need of artificial life supports. Such supports, without which classical music, contemporary painting, sculpture, poetry and dance, etc. could not have survived en masse in today's world, were not forthcoming for jazz. (Dan Morgenstern, "Farewell to the Sixties," *Down Beat Music '70*, 1970: 9)

Critic Dan Morgenstern was not alone in viewing the state of the jazz art world by the end of the 1960s as not particularly healthy. The vibrant commercial market that spurred on the New Jazz Age was faring poorly by the end of that decade, while many jazz musicians were leaving for Europe to earn a living performing jazz. Morgenstern also was not alone in seeing the future of jazz residing in the patronage of generous individuals and institutions. Many in the jazz art world preferred not to rely on an unpredictable, and for some corrupt, commercial market. While Morgenstern viewed "artificial life support" for jazz as not an immediate glowing prospect, the jazz art world had established a strong enough base of support to remain a viable art world.

By the end of the renaissance the jazz art world transformed itself significantly, building on the phenomenal success of jazz as a genre and market beginning in the 1950s. This art world over a period of twenty years moved jazz performance out of its origins in the urban jazz scene of clubs and dance halls into locations distinctly separate in terms of aesthetic appreciation and type of audiences. Individuals in the jazz art world also were aware of the crucial importance of independent production in the success of this art world. They actively sought to maintain established forms of production as well as find new forms. This need drove the jazz art world to look for alternatives to the commercial music industry such as musician collectives, arts organizations, annual festivals, a greater number of jazz concert productions, and institutions of secondary and higher education. In general, individuals in the jazz art world, after the boom in the jazz market, wanted to expand as much as possible the independent production of jazz. Whether at outdoor festivals, concert halls, college campuses, art museums, music conservatories, summer camps, cafés, or lofts, jazz performance was moving to new locations and new audiences. This trajectory of performance would continue past the renaissance, particularly in the increasing growth of jazz education and the discipline of Jazz Studies.

While the jazz art world moved towards non-commercial settings and support, the basic economics of the jazz art world during the renaissance was the commercial market. Besides jazz clubs and jazz concert tours, it was the commercial independent production of recorded jazz that would have the greatest long-term effect on the jazz tradition. Since the days of hot collectors in the 1930s, jazz records presented the most prominent documentation of this music tradition. Since improvisers for the most part defined this tradition, jazz performance dominated over jazz composition, and the jazz instrumentalist dominated over the jazz composer in the delineation of this tradition. Unlike the classical tradition that is written mostly as a history of composition, the jazz tradition is written and enjoyed mostly as a history of recorded performance, although social history was a concern among jazz writers since the beginning of the jazz art world. During the renaissance, independent record producers created a rich documentation of a period of incredible creativity in American music.

During the New Jazz Age jazz musicians established a modern jazz repertoire that firmly established jazz as a unique fine-art music. The modern jazz renaissance, however, was not without conflict. The question of the direction and meaning of jazz was significantly challenged by black jazz musicians with some critics lending support. As the New Jazz Age began, the direction of jazz performance was decidedly away from its base in the community of black professional musicians who had been its major innovators up through Bebop. Just as the swing craze allowed white professional musicians to over-run the market for big band jazz, the New Jazz Age was first dominated by mostly white cool musicians and discussions of the classical turn in jazz. Black jazz musicians responded by emphasizing bebop and other black music idioms in an effort to reclaim the jazz tradition as well as the jazz market. And as both black and white jazz musicians applied the modern jazz aesthetic, it was mostly the community of black musicians whose innovations established modern jazz as a genre distinct from the classical and the popular. Black musicians chose to apply the modern jazz aesthetic to the jazz idiom and creatively tied new compositional tools or concepts to the basic forms and harmonies in jazz. This general approach by black jazz musicians reestablished their central role as the innovators and performers of the jazz tradition.

During the New Jazz Age professional musicians also relinquished their role as mediators of American popular music. The shifting patterns of the vernacular and cultivated traditions in American music had changed by the late 1950s with more vernacular influenced popular genres supplanting the Tin Pan Alley song and professional bands that dominated the popular market beginning in the late nineteenth century. Jazz would emerge from this transformation as a distinct genre and tradition positioned against popular music and classical music. The modern jazz renaissance was the final culmination of professional musicians' cultivation of the black jazz vernacular since the first cultivated styles of the Jazz Age. The initial efforts of professional musicians during the Jazz Age to lay claim to a unique American high art music finally came to full fruition.

Conclusion

The jazz art world and American culture

> The highbrow's friend is the lowbrow. The highbrow enjoys and re-
> spects the lowbrow's art – jazz for instance – which he is likely to call a
> spontaneous expression of folk culture. The lowbrow is not interested,
> as the middlebrow is, in pre-empting any of the highbrow's function or
> in any way threatening to blur the lines between the serious and the
> frivolous... When, however, the lowbrow arts get mixed up with mid-
> dlebrow ideas of culture, then the highbrow turns away in disgust.
>
> Russell Lynes, "Highbrow, Lowbrow, Middlebrow," *Harper's*
> February 1949: 23,25

Harper's Magazine editor Russell Lynes in a somewhat tongue-in-cheek
essay on the workings of cultural distinction in America certainly painted
a less than flattering picture of the highbrow jazz enthusiasts who embraced "genuine" jazz in the 1930s and 1940s. As editor of *Harper's*, he
probably was aware of the conflict between traditionalists and modernists
in the early years of the jazz art world. His magazine in 1947 published
"The Jazz Cult" by jazz critic Ernest Borneman that addressed this very
conflict. Lynes, however, was addressing the whole notion of cultural
distinction and cultural legitimacy in America at mid-century. He suggested to his readers that America was divided into a world of highbrows,
middlebrows, and lowbrows, a world in which middlebrows reigned in
numbers and wealth while highbrows – few in number and declining in
cultural influence – reigned mostly in their own pretentious imaginations.

Historian Michael Kammen (1999) argues that Lynes was not alone
in seeing the decline of the highbrow at mid-century. Critics Dwight
Macdonald and Clement Greenberg, for instance, also wrote at the time
about the demise of the authority of highbrow culture. Unlike Lynes,
who rather enjoyed the less than bright future of highbrows, Macdonald
and Greenberg were more or less appalled by this unfortunate development. The fall of highbrow culture was part of what Kammen calls the
"democratization" of American culture – the "blurring" of the boundaries of high art and popular art that reigned during the first half of the
twentieth century. Kammen notes that the blurring of such boundaries of

269

cultural distinction was occurring before the 1950s in certain instances, but that a more rapid democratization of culture began during that decade. Not surprisingly, he points to Paul Whiteman's 1924 Aeolian Hall concert as an example of such crisscrossing of distinctions before mid-century. The success of the jazz art world with the New Jazz Age certainly was partly responsible in dissolving the distinctions that supported the previous claims of highbrow culture. Modern jazz as Lynes subtly suggested was a middlebrow art in the minds of most highbrows. And its ascendancy in the New Jazz Age certainly was an example of what Lynes, himself editor of a middlebrow magazine, referred to as the "jockeying for position in the new cultural class order." (*Harper's* 2-1949: 28) For Kammen, however, Lynes' analysis did not go far enough. Lynes' idea of a new cultural class order still retained the old idea of distinct cultural brows with distinct cultural tastes when in fact the democratization of American culture undermined those very categories. Jazz music, for example, was not simply moving up the hierarchy from low to high. Rather the jazz art world and jazz music threatened to dissolve the very boundaries of low, middle, and highbrow culture.

Kammen's argument about the democratization of American culture points to two basic changes in American culture beginning at mid-century. Kammen first points out that mass media products began incorporating elements of high culture, while reaching an increasingly diversified market demographic. He then points to changes in the content of high art and academic scholarship such as the Pop Art movement in the 1960s and the rise of social history and the study of popular culture in academia. Kammen's thesis echoes Paul DiMaggio's (1991) argument that a general democratization of American culture began at mid-century with the "rise of a more open market for cultural goods" that blurred the formerly more distinct boundaries between high art and popular art. Diana Crane (1992) also shows that there is a consensus among sociologists that this general blurring of distinct social boundaries of cultural taste in America was occurring in the last half of the twentieth century.

Beginning with the modern jazz renaissance, the jazz art world certainly bridged the former boundaries between high art and popular art. Jazz music and jazz musicians entered concert halls, conservatories, and colleges. The State Department in the 1950s sent jazz musicians on international tours including Benny Goodman, Louis Armstrong, and Dizzy Gillespie. By the 1970s, the discipline of Jazz Studies was established, accompanying such new disciplines as Black Studies, Women's Studies, and Ethnic Studies. Meanwhile jazz musicians were receiving grants from the National Endowment of the Arts and other prestigious arts organizations like the Guggenheim. The Smithsonian Institute initiated a jazz oral history project in 1972 with support from the NEA. And in 1987, the House of Representatives passed House Resolution 57 declaring jazz "a rare and valuable national American treasure." (Walser 1999: 333) At the same time, however, jazz music gradually left its popular base. It moved into a more specialized jazz art world based on a niche market and the support of patron and government-supported art organizations and educational institutions. A new generation of jazz musicians were more academically trained and inclined with little connection to the world of popular music making. As mass media culture continued to grow in prominence, jazz musicians made rare appearances usually through the Public Broadcasting System while recorded jazz became mostly the reserve of specialized independent jazz labels. What place had jazz come to occupy in American culture by mid-century? Given the democratization of American culture, how does the social history of jazz speak to this transformation in the boundaries of cultural distinction in America? What story does the jazz tradition still tell us about American culture and society?

Besides answering these questions about the impact of jazz music and the jazz art world on American culture, I also would like to address how the social history of jazz informs the sociology of culture. I would like to address the general question of interpretation and practice in the production and consumption of culture in relation to social institutions and social class. What does the story of jazz in the twentieth century tell us about how individuals come to interpret and transform cultural practices? What does this story say about how the social organization of culture shapes the interpretation and action of individuals and groups of individuals producing and consuming culture? Finally, what does the interplay of the various distinctions brought to bear on jazz music in the twentieth century tell us about cultural distinction and social class?

Jazz and American culture

While jazz music no longer occupies a major place in the world of popular music and popular audiences, it has continued to signify an alternative history of our culture and our society. The jazz tradition incorporates folk, popular, and modern jazz as both a music tradition and a social history of America. It has continued to challenge Americans on questions of cultural distinction, cultural legitimacy, and national identity even up to the present. As Lawrence Levine argues, jazz music urges us "to make that empathetic leap and allow ourselves to see jazz as an integral vibrant part of American culture throughout this century; to realize that before even the most prescient Europeans and long before any appreciable number of Americans thought of jazz as an indigenous American contribution to the culture of the world, jazz was precisely that. Jazz tells us much about what was original and dynamic in American culture even as it reveals to what extent our culture, or more correctly, our cultural attitudes had not yet weaned themselves from the old colonial patterns of the past. Jazz has much to tell us about our history and, indeed, much to tell us about ourselves if only we have the wisdom and the skill to listen to it and learn from it." (Levine 1989: 20)

While the modernist revolt led jazz down a high art path, the jazz tradition has continued in the written word, in recorded music, and in live performance to tell a broader story about American music in the twentieth century. Since the earliest jazz criticism, the jazz tradition has validated folk and popular music and its practitioners as worthy of aesthetic as well as social respect. The jazz tradition created the first extensive written and recorded history of popular culture as a legitimate and praiseworthy part of our American heritage. In its claims to the full rights of high art, this tradition also remained a challenge to the exclusive claims of European cultivated music and demanded a more democratic conception of music in America. In other words, the jazz tradition has reshaped in various ways our understanding of American culture. This is particularly clear in the way that this tradition has shaped our collective memory of black music and black artists in the twentieth century. From a contemporary perspective in which popular culture and black culture are now studied as serious academic subjects, it is difficult to appreciate how the jazz tradition created one of the first radical alternative histories of American culture. While this tradition has carried the contradictions of its history of cultural distinctions between high and low, legitimate and popular, cultivated and vernacular, black and white, conventional and hip, working class and middleclass, in its full telling it fundamentally transforms our collective memory of American music.

While the jazz tradition as a written, recorded, and performed history has reshaped our collective memory of American music, the social history of jazz is an equally revealing story about American culture and society. As Eric J. Hobsbawm (1989) argues, a full accounting of jazz must entail its unique and compelling social history. Jazz in the twentieth century engaged a widely diverse community of social actors as well as signifying an equally diverse set of meanings. As jazz music attracted various artists, producers, critics, and audiences it articulated a breadth of cultural distinctions that shaped the meaning and practice of jazz. The social history of jazz, therefore, brings to light some of the most fundamental conflicts in American culture during this century. This becomes most readily apparent when in tracing the evolution of the meanings and practices in jazz music one clear theme emerges. Jazz music was viewed by those who adopted it as their own as always confronting some form of subordination or expressing some form of rebellion against one or another cultural orthodoxy. The rise of the jazz art world was a self-perceived struggle against various forms of social, political, and cultural subordination. Jazz music seemed in various ways always to be on the "outside" of dominant notions of cultural and social legitimacy. While the trajectory of jazz was towards high art performance and high art appreciation, it encapsulated struggles and contradictions in American culture and society along the way. And of course, jazz as high art was itself a direct challenge to cultural orthodoxy. As a young Hobsbawm wrote in 1960, the "point is not that the jazz protests can be fitted into this or that pigeonhole of orthodox politics, though it often can – mostly a left-wing one – but that the music lends itself to any kind of protest and rebelliousness much better than most other forms of art." (Hobsbawm 1960: 262)

Of course, there was no greater source of struggle and contradiction in American culture and society than its racial divide. The subordination of the African American community permeated every aspect of American life during the twentieth century. This racial formation existed in segregated communities, workplaces and institutions of worship and education. It was policed through legislation, legal authority, violent riots, and lynchings. And it was expressed in the very formation of our national identity. The history of jazz is the history of black musicians and singers struggling to survive and surmount the racial barriers and racist distinctions that permeated American life. It was more specifically a matter of confronting and transforming these barriers and distinctions in the world of music making. So while rebellion was a consistent theme in the evolution of jazz music, so was its signifying *racial* struggle and rebellion whether by swing musicians, hepcats, swing populists, jazz enthusiasts, beboppers, cool hipsters, hard-boppers, soul brothers and sisters, or black avant-garde revolutionaries. The very subordination of the African American community that limited economic opportunities brought some of the best and brightest of that community to the profession of popular music making. And as organic intellectuals in the truest sense, black professional musicians since the beginning of the twentieth century carried the hopes of a Black Nationalist art that could transform the subordinate status of their community. The power of this agenda persists today. Jazz music remains among black jazz musicians and black audiences a creative art expressive of their heritage as African Americans.

As both an authentic *American* art and authentic *African American* art, the jazz tradition continues to challenge our conceptions of the nature of a democratic culture. It forces us to reflect on our own and others' predilections to divide culture through distinctions which place certain art, artists, and audiences and in turn certain social groups whether class, race, ethnic, religious, or gender as suspect, inferior, or even dangerous. It makes us confront the nature of legitimacy and status in American culture and of the distinctions invoked in their name. It also confronts us with a world of cultural meaning and practice fraught with contradictions in which cultural "politics" is not a pure art, but an art always in the making, a collective engagement always shifting and adjusting within the social, political, and cultural context of its time. Maybe jazz music and the jazz art world no longer speak loudly of protest against cultural orthodoxy. But at one time no other art form in America spoke in so many different voices against the privileged self-ordained upholders of American Culture, Values, and Identity whose conception of culture was one of exclusivity.

The sociology of culture

I have looked at the relationship between the social organization of music and the meanings and practices social actors brought to the production and consumption of music. I have explored what the cultural sociologist Robert Wuthnow (1987) calls the *institutional, subjective, structural* and *dramaturgic* elements in the working of cultural meaning and practice. The institutional element in the history of jazz was the social organization of music making both in the popular music industry and the art world of European cultivated music. The subjective element was the way individuals experienced and understood these institutions as well as the world of vernacular, popular, and cultivated music. The structural element emerged from the way the meanings and practices generated by individuals and institutions in American music set out numerous opposing cultural distinctions such as good music and vulgar music, high art and popular art, highbrow and lowbrow, sweet and swing, or straight and hip. And finally, the dramaturgic element was evident in the way such distinctions articulated social group dispositions and identities whether class, race, ethnic, or gender. I was interested in how the social organization of music gave shape to certain meanings and practices in music, and in turn, how social actors worked against this grain, against the institutional structures which imposed particular meanings and practices. In this sense, I was interested in what the cultural sociologist Pierre Bourdieu (1993, 1996) calls the *field of forces* in culture – a hierarchical structure of cultural distinctions – and how individuals actively engaged and transformed this field.

Richard A. Peterson (1997) argues that when we look at the meanings and practices of individuals engaged in producing and consuming culture we must look for the organizational arrangements in which they do it. This approach to understanding culture is commonly referred to in American cultural sociology as the production-of-culture perspective. The basic premise of this perspective is that the relationship between art, artists, and consumers is not a direct relationship, but a relationship mediated through the social organization of production, distribution, exhibition, and consumption of art forms. This relationship also is influenced by the activities of other important actors in art besides artists and consumers, whether producers, critics, or patrons of the arts. The social organization of cultural production determines whose conventions and assumptions have greater power in shaping culture in terms of genres, aesthetics, prominent artists, and selected audiences. As Richard A. Peterson (1994: 163) in his review of the production-of-culture perspective argues, the general conclusion that can be drawn from work using this perspective is that the social organization of cultural production affects "the nature and content of the elements of culture that are produced."

The history of jazz certainly shows the way organizational structures and conventions in music marginalized certain meanings and practices while promoting others. This is particularly true when the social organization of music was predominately a closed system of production and consumption. A closed system is characterized by a more centralized organization of production, which inhibits innovation and diversity. (Lopes 1992) This type of system moves towards standardized conventions and assumptions about art forms, artists, and audiences. The rise of the art world of European cultivated music as well as the emergence of an oligopolistic mass media industry in the 1930s demonstrated the effects of a closed system. American music under these systems of production and consumption was less a reflection of the whole community of American musicians and composers, or the tastes of American audiences, than the standardized conventions and assumptions of those who controlled the means of production, distribution, evaluation, and exhibition.

Ironically, while the history of the jazz art world is littered with complaints about the commercial market, it was when this commercial market expanded and moved into a more open system of production that new meanings and practices entered the national imagination. Whether the New Jazz Age or the Rock 'n' Roll Revolution, these national phenomena were spurred in part by a more open commercial system of music making and a transformation in the power of previously institutionalized conventions. The conventions of the old system were no longer maintained by structural arrangements in the field of commercial popular music and American music experienced a revolutionary change radically challenging the prevailing cultural hierarchy. As Richard A. Peterson (1990) suggests, there always are cultural innovations, and I would add alternative cultural practices, but the extent to which innovations or alternatives capture a large national audience depends on the social organization of cultural production and consumption. More importantly, they also often depend on the development of an independent organizational base of production and consumption. The New Jazz Age was only possible through the earlier efforts of building an independent jazz art world that then could take advantage of the opening of the social organization of the commercial music market.

It should be stressed, however, that organizational structures and conventions are historical products in large part built by social actors bringing their own meanings and practices to producing and consuming culture. When such structures and conventions attain an organizational and ideological cohesiveness as they did in the art world of the European cultivated music and in the commercial music industry, they become institutionalized in practice. The race segregation in the social organization of music making, for example, was not the passive result of market and organizational forces. It was an institutionalized practice that was the product of social actors actively engaging in producing and consuming music. Of course, economic, technological, regulatory, and legislative changes can have both intended and unintended consequences which transform the social organization of music as well as the constellation of music practices. But participants actively engage these changes in the social organization of music making. Individuals generate their own as well as collective understandings of the nature of these structures, conventions, institutions, and their transformations, as well as music making and music consumption.

But does the social organization of music alone explain why and how a cultural movement developed around jazz or the particular trajectory this movement and music would take? Professional popular musicians since the nineteenth century certainly confronted a social organization of music making that positioned them as less legitimate than their brethren performing for the art world of European cultivated music. And it is true that the professional ethos of these musicians and their quest for a greater status in the world of music making eventually transformed jazz music into a modernist high art. These musicians actively refashioned the meaning and practice of music making in part in response to their subjective experience of the social organization of music and its ruling institutional conventions. At the same time, however, the rise of a jazz art world involved non-musicians and musicians bringing other meanings and practices to jazz not directly concerned with the status of professional musicians. This cultural movement, therefore, was a much broader collective interaction of meanings and practices within a broader context of social and cultural distinctions.

Jazz as a collective and socially heterogeneous cultural movement leads to the question of whether this phenomenon can be attributed to the subjective dispositions, cultural distinctions, and expressive identities of a specific social group by class, race, or education. How do we come to understand the subjective, structural, and dramaturgical elements of this cultural movement? I have attempted to show how social actors of diverse social backgrounds and experiences brought their own meanings and practices to jazz. I believe the rise of a jazz art world involved a *collective* refashioning of the meanings and practices of jazz that incorporated a diverse set of dispositions, distinctions, and interests of an equally diverse set of social actors. Sometimes in conflict and sometimes in harmony, the members of this socially heterogeneous community actively transformed the meaning and practice of jazz as they collectively engaged in the production and consumption of this music.

I certainly have shown how social class did inform the subjective, structural, and dramaturgical expressions of particular groupings of individuals within this movement whether white hepcat musicians, black bebop musicians, or white affluent jazz enthusiasts. But the collective nature of this movement was not merely the existence of clearly distinct expressions of particular social class positions, but a larger interactive collective formation that rearticulated these expressive elements among diverse social actors. Hepcats, enthusiasts, populists, beboppers, hipsters, and others were in active dialog. This is not to suggest that the dynamics of this interactive collective formation eliminated the effects and conflicts of social class. But to emphasize how individuals can come to rearticulate subjective dispositions and cultural distinctions in their expressive social identities within a larger social context and within a collective interaction of meaning and practice. Like the musicologist Richard A. Middleton (1990: 16), I was interested in showing how cultural forms are "assemblages of elements from a variety of sources, each with a variety of histories and connotations, and these assemblages can in appropriate circumstances, be prised open and elements rearticulated in different contexts."

We must therefore understand Pierre Bourdieu's *field of forces* – the interplay of cultural distinctions and cultural status – as a dynamic, contradictory, and open process of cultural meaning and practice. The story of jazz certainly affirms his view of how countervailing forces of cultural distinction articulate the social class order. So while jazz as a cultural movement articulated a diverse set of cultural distinctions and social class dispositions, it also faced a clear line of forces defending a cultural orthodoxy affirming a particular social class status hierarchy. My work demonstrates, however, that American culture was an incredibly dynamic field of cultural distinctions constantly balanced one against another while also generating new constellations. Individuals also were at times quite aware of these opposing forces, while at other times less conscious of them. The social history of jazz is a fascinating story of constant re-interpretation against given distinctions and structures in the production and consumption of culture.

In this sense, I hope my book contributes to recent scholarship in cultural sociology and cultural studies that emphasizes what I call the *interpretive turn*. (Lopes 1999) The expressive social identities of individuals certainly occur within a set of social structures as well as a set of cultural meanings and practices. But individuals actively interpret their social world, and in turn, can collectively transform the meanings and practices that constitute culture. One of the most influential scholars in cultural studies Stuart Hall (1986) challenges us to understand how meaning and practice are open interpretations not determined in the final instance by an objective social structure, but the interplay between social structure and human interpretation. The cultural and social history of the rise of a jazz art world shows how individuals refashioned prevailing meanings and practices against cultural orthodoxy. They also engaged in this interpretive turn while within the broader social, political, and cultural currents of their time. This refashioning was complex and often contradictory as diverse social actors came to articulate the meaning and practice of jazz music.

Bibliography

Ammer, Christine. 1980. *Unsung: A History of Women in American Music.* Westport, CT: Greenwood Press.

Armstrong, Louis. 1936. *Swing that Music.* Reprint, New York: De Capo Press, 1993.

Badger, R. Reid. 1989. "James Reese Europe and the Prehistory of Jazz." *American Music* 7:48–67.

Baraka, Amiri [LeRoi Jones]. 1963. *Blues People.* New York: Morrow Quill.

Basie, Count, and Albert Murray. 1985. *Good Morning Blues: The Autobiography of Count Basie.* Reprint, New York: De Capo Press, 1995.

Baskerville, John D. 1994. "Free Jazz: A Reflection of Black Power Ideology." *Journal of Black Studies* 24/4:484–97.

Becker, Howard S. 1951. "The Professional Dance Musician and His Audience." *American Journal of Sociology* 57:136–44.

1982. *Art Worlds.* Berkeley: University of California Press.

Berger, Morroe. 1947. "Jazz: Resistance to the Diffusion of a Culture Pattern," *The Journal of Negro History* 32/4:461–94.

Berger, Morroe, Edward Berger, and James Patrick. 1982. *Benny Carter: A Life in American Music.* Metuchen, NJ: The Scarecrow Press & the Institute of Jazz Studies.

Bernhardt, Clyde E. B. 1986. *I Remember: Eighty Years of Black Entertainment, Big Bands, and the Blues.* Philadelphia: University of Pennsylvania Press.

Bierley, Paul E. 1973. *John Philip Sousa: American Phenomenon.* Englewood Cliffs, NJ: Prentice-Hall.

Blesh, Rudi. 1946. *Shining Trumpets: a History of Jazz.* New York: Alfred Knopf.

1971. *Combo USA: Eight Lives in Jazz.* Philadelphia: Chilton Books.

Bourdieu, Pierre. 1993. *The Field of Cultural Production: Essays on Art and Literature.* New York: Columbia University Press.

1996. *The Rules of Art: Genesis and Structure of the Literary Field.* Stanford University Press.

Brawley, Benjamin. 1937. *The Negro Genius: A New Appraisal of the Achievement of the American Negro in Literature and the Fine Arts.* Reprint, New York: Biblo and Tannen, 1972.

Bushell, Garvin, and Mark Tucker. 1990. *Jazz From the Beginning.* Ann Arbor, MI: University of Michigan Press.

Byrd, Donald. 1972. "The Meaning of Black Music." *The Black Scholar* 10: 28–31.

Cameron, Catherine M. 1996. *Dialectic in the Arts: The Rise of Experimentalism in American Music*. Westport, CT: Praeger Publishers.

Cameron, William Bruce. 1954. "Sociological Notes on the Jam Session," *Social Forces* 33:177–82.

Cantwell, Robert. 1996. *When We Were Good: The Folk Revival*. Cambridge, MA: Harvard University Press.

Charters, Samuel B. and Leonard Kunstadt. 1962. *Jazz: A History of the New York Scene*. Garden City, NY: Doubleday.

Chase, Gilbert. 1987. *America's Music: From the Pilgrims to the Present*. 3rd ed. Chicago: University of Illinois Press.

Christian, Charles M. 1999. *Black Saga: The African American Experience*. 2nd ed. Washington, DC: Civitas Counterpoint.

Clayton, Buck, and Nancy Miller Elliott. 1987. *Buck Clayton's Jazz World*. New York: Oxford University Press.

Crane, Diana. 1992. *The Production of Culture: Media and the Urban Arts*. Newbury Park, CA: Sage Publications.

Craven, Robert R, ed. 1986. *Symphony Orchestras of the United States: Selected Profiles*. New York: Greenwood Press.

Cuney-Hare, Maude. 1936. *Negro Musicians and their Music*. Reprint, New York: G. K. Hall & Company, 1996.

Davis, Ronald L. 1981. *A History of Music in American Life*. Volume III, Malabar, FL: Robert Krieger Publishing.

DeLong, Thomas A. 1983. *Pops: Paul Whiteman, King of Jazz*. Piscataway, NJ: New Century Publishers.

1996. *Radio Stars: An Illustrated Biographical Dictionary of 953 Performers, 1920 through 1960*. Jefferson, NC: McFarland & Company.

Denisoff, R. Serge. 1986. *Tarnished Gold: the Record Industry Revisited*. New Brunswick, NJ: Transaction Books.

DeVeaux, Scott. 1987. "Conversation with Howard McGhee: Jazz in the Forties." *The Black Perspective in Music* 15/1:65–78.

1989. "The Emergence of the Jazz Concert, 1935–1945." *American Music* 7: 6–29.

1991. "Constructing the Jazz Tradition: Jazz Historiography." *Black American Literature Forum* 25/3:525–60.

1997. *The Birth of Bebop: A Social and Musical History*. Berkeley: University of California Press.

Dexter, Dave. 1964. *The Jazz Story*. Englewood Cliffs, NJ: Prentice-Hall.

DiMaggio, Paul. 1982. "Cultural Entrepreneurship in Nineteenth-Century Boston," *Media, Culture and Society* 4(1 & 2): 33–50, 303–22.

1991. "Social Structure, Institutions, and Cultural Goods: The Case of the United States" in *Social Theory for a Changing Society*, eds. P. Bourdieu and J. S. Coleman. San Francisco: Westview Press.

1992. "Cultural Boundaries and Structural Change: The Extension of the High Culture Model to Theater, Opera, and the Dance, 1900–1940" in *Cultivating Differences: Symbolic Boundaries and the Making of Inequality*, eds. M. Lamont and M. Fournier. University of Chicago Press.

Dodge, Roger Pryor. 1995. *Hot Jazz and Jazz Dance*. New York: Oxford University Press.

Dugan, James, and John Hammond. 1974. "An Early Black Music Concert From Spirituals to Swing." *The Black Perspective in Music* 2/2:191–208.

Eberly, Philip K. 1982. *Music in the Air: America's Changing Tastes in Popular Music, 1920–1980.* New York: Hastings House Publishers.

Elworth, Steven B. 1995. "Jazz in Crisis, 1948–1958: Ideology and Representation" in *Jazz Among the Discourses*, ed. K. Gabbard. Durham, NC: Duke University Press.

Ennis, Philip H. 1992. *The Seventh Stream: The Emergence of Rocknroll in American Popular Music.* Hanover, NH: Wesleyan University Press.

Erenberg, Lewis A. 1981. *Steppin' Out: New York Nightlife and the Transformation of American Culture, 1890–1930.* University of Chicago Press.

1989. "Things to Come: Swing Bands, Bebop, and the Rise of a Post War Jazz Scene" in *Recasting America: Politics and Culture in the Age of the Cold War*, ed. L. May. University of Chicago Press.

1998. *Swingin' the Dream: Big Band Jazz and the Rebirth of American Culture.* University of Chicago Press.

Feather, Leonard. 1949. *Inside Bebop.* Reprint, *Inside Jazz*, New York: De Capo Press, 1977.

1960. *Encyclopedia of Jazz.* New York: Horizon Press.

Finkelstein, Sidney. 1948. *Jazz: A People's Music.* Reprint, New York: International Publishers, 1988.

Floyd, Samuel A. 1990. "Music in the Harlem Renaissance: An Overview" in *Black Music in the Harlem Renaissance*, ed. S. A. Floyd. New York: Greenwood Press.

1995. *The Power of Black Music: Interpreting Its History from Africa to the United States.* New York: Oxford University Press.

Fox, Ted. 1986. *In the Groove: The People Behind the Music.* New York: St. Martin's Press.

Franklin, John Hope, and Alfred A. Moss. 1994. *From Slavery to Freedom: A History of African Americans.* 7th ed. New York: McGraw Hill.

Gabbard, Krin. 1995. "Introduction: The Canon and Its Consequences" in *Jazz Among the Discourses*, ed. K. Gabbard. Durham, NC: Duke University Press.

Gans, Herbert J. 1975. *Popular Culture and High Culture: An Analysis and Evaluation of Taste.* New York: Basic Books.

Garofalo, Reebee. 1997. *Rockin' Out: Popular Music in the USA.* Boston: Allyn and Bacon.

Gennari, John. 1991. "Jazz Criticism: Its Development and Ideologies." *Black American Literature Forum* 25/3:449–523.

George, Nelson. 1988. *The Death of Rhythm & Blues.* New York: Pantheon Books.

Gillespie, John Birks, and Wilmont Alfred Fraser. 1979. *To Be or Not to Bop.* New York: De Capo Press.

Gioia, Ted. 1988. *The Imperfect Art: Reflections on Jazz and Modern Culture.* New York: Oxford University Press.

1992. *West Coast Jazz: Modern Jazz in California.* New York: Oxford University Press.

1997. *The History of Jazz.* New York: Oxford University Press.

Gitler, Ira. 1966. *Jazz Masters of the Forties.* New York: De Capo Press.

1986. *Swing to Bop: An Oral History of the Transition to Jazz in the 1940s.* New York: Oxford University Press.

Goffin, Robert. 1944. *Jazz, from the Congo to the Metropolitan.* Garden City, NJ: Doubleday, Doran & Company.

Goodman, Benny, and Irving Kolodin. 1939. *Kingdom of Swing.* Reprint, New York: Frederick Ungar Publishing, 1961.

Grey, Herman. 1988. *Producing Jazz: The Experience of an Independent Record Company.* Philadelphia: Temple University Press.

Hall, Stuart. 1986. "On Postmodernism and Articulation: An Interview with Stuart Hall." ed. L. Grossberg. *Journal of Communication Inquiry* 10/2: 45–60.

Hamm, Charles. 1979. *Yesterdays: Popular Song in America.* New York: Norton & Company.

1983. *Music in the New World.* New York: Norton & Company.

Hammond, John, and Irving Townsend. 1977. *John Hammond on Record.* New York: Ridge Press.

Hampton, Lionel, and James Haskins. 1989. *Hamp: An Autobiography of Lionel Hampton with James Haskins.* New York: Warner Books.

Hansen, Chadwick C. 1960. "Social Influences on Jazz Styles: Chicago, 1920–30." *American Quarterly* 12/4:493–97.

Harvey, Edward. 1967. "Social Change and the Jazz Musician." *Social Forces* 46:34–42.

Hennessey, Thomas J. 1994. *From Jazz to Swing: African American Jazz Musicians and Their Music, 1890–1935.* Detroit MI: Wayne University Press.

Hentoff, Nat. 1961. *The Jazz Life.* New York: Dial Press.

Hentoff, Nat, and Albert J. McCarthy, eds. 1961. *Jazz: New Perspectives on the History of Jazz.* New York: Holt, Rinehart and Winston.

Hitchcock, H. Wiley. 1988. *Music in the United States: A Historical Introduction.* 3rd ed. Englewood Cliffs, NJ: Prentice Hall.

Hobsbawm, Eric J. [Francis Newton]. 1960. *The Jazz Scene.* New York: Monthly Review Press.

1989. "Some Like It Hot." *The New York Review of Books* 13/April 13:32–4.

Hobson, Wilder. 1939. *American Jazz Music.* New York: W. W. Norton & Company.

Hodes, Art, and Chadwick Hansen. 1992. *Hot Man: The Life of Art Hodes.* Chicago: University of Illinois Press.

Hodier, Andre. 1956. *Jazz: Its Essence and Evolution.* New York: Grove Press.

Hsio, Wen Shih. 1959. "The Spread of Jazz and the Big Bands" in *Jazz: New Perspectives on the History of Jazz*, eds. N. Hentoff and A. J. McCarthy. New York: Holt, Rinehart and Winston.

Huggins, Nathan Irvin. 1971. *Harlem Renaissance.* New York: Oxford University Press.

Johnson, James Weldon. 1930. *Black Manhattan.* Reprint, New York: Arno Press, 1968.

1931. *The Book of American Negro Poetry.* 2nd ed. Reprint, New York: Harcourt, Brace & World, 1958.

1995. *The Selected Writings of James Weldon Johnson.* ed. S. K. Wilson. New York: Oxford University Press.

Jones, LeRoi. *See* Baraka, Amiri.

Kaminsky, Max, and V. E. Hughes. 1963. *Jazz Band: My Life in Jazz*. Reprint, New York: De Capo Press, 1981.

Kammen, Michael. 1999. *American Culture, American Tastes: Social Change and the 20th Century*. New York: A. A. Knopf.

Kenny, William Howland. 1993. *Chicago Jazz: A Cultural History, 1904–1930*. New York: Oxford University Press.

Kernfeld, Barry, ed. 1988. *The New Grove Dictionary of Jazz*. Reprint, New York: St. Martin's Press, 1994.

Kimball, Robert and William Bolcom. 1973. *Reminiscing with Sissle and Blake*. New York: Viking Press.

Lastrucci, Carlo L. 1941. "The Professional Dance Musician." *Journal of Musicology* 3(Winter):168–72.

Leiter, Robert D. 1974. *The Musicians and Petrillo*. New York: Octagon Books.

Leonard, Neil. 1962. *Jazz and the White Americans*. University of Chicago Press.

    1975. "Some Further Thoughts on Jazzmen as Romantic Outsiders." *Journal of Jazz Studies* 2(Summer):45–52.

    1987. *Jazz: Myth and Religion*. New York: Oxford University Press.

Levine, Lawrence. 1988. *Highbrow/Lowbrow: The Emergence of Cultural Hierarchy in America*. Cambridge, MA: Harvard University Press.

    1989. "Jazz and American Culture." *Journal of American Folklore* 102:6–22.

Lewis, David Levering. 1979. *When Harlem Was in Vogue*. New York: Oxford University Press.

Litweiler, John. 1984. *The Freedom Principle: Jazz after 1958*. New York: De Capo Press.

Locke, Alain, ed. 1925. *The New Negro: An Interpretation*. Reprint, New York: Arno Press, 1968.

    1936a. *The Negro and His Music*. Reprint, *The Negro and His Music & Negro Art: Past and Present*, New York: Arno Press, 1969.

    1936b. *Negro Art: Past and Present*. Reprint, *The Negro and His Music & Negro Art: Past and Present*, New York: Arno Press, 1969.

Lopes, Paul. 1999. "Diffusion and Syncretism: The Modern Jazz Tradition" in "The Social Diffusion of Ideas and Things," eds. P. Lopes and M. Durfee. *The Annals of the American Academy of Political and Social Science* 566:25–36.

Mason, Daniel Gregory. 1930. *Tune in America: A Study of Our Coming Musical Independence*. New York: A. A. Knopf.

McDonald, William F. 1969. *Federal Relief Administration and the Arts*. Ohio State University Press.

McRae, Barry. 1967. *The Jazz Cataclysm*. New York: A. S. Barnes and Company.

Middleton, Richard. 1990. *The Study of Popular Music*. Philadelphia: Open University Press.

Miller, Paul Eduard. 1939. *Down Beat's Yearbook of Swing*. Chicago: Down Beat Publications.

    1944. *Esquire's Jazz Book*. New York: J. J. Little and Ives.

    1945. *Esquire's Jazz Book 1945*. New York: J. J. Little and Ives.

    1946. *Esquire's Jazz Book 1946*. New York: J. J. Little and Ives.

Moore, MacDonald Smith. 1985. *Yankee Blues: Musical Culture and American Identity*. Bloomington, IN: Indiana University Press.

Mueller, John H. 1951. *The American Symphony: A Social History of Musical Taste.* Bloomington, IN: Indiana University Press.

Museum of Broadcasting. 1985. *Jazz on Television.* New York: Museum of Broadcasting.

Nanry, Charles. 1970. "The Occupational Subculture of the Jazz Musician: Myth and Reality." PhD dissertation, Rutgers University.

　1979. *The Jazz Text.* New York: Van Nostrand Reinhold Company.

Nasaw, David. 1993. *Going Out: The Rise and Fall of Public Amusements.* New York: Basic Books.

Neuls-Bates, Carol. 1986. "Women's Orchestras in the United States, 1925–45" in *Women Making Music: the Western Art Tradition, 1150–1950,* eds. J. Bowers and J. Tick. Chicago: University of Illinois Press.

Ogren, Kathy J. 1989. *The Jazz Revolution: Twenties America and the Meaning of Jazz.* New York: Oxford University Press.

Osofsky, Gilbert. 1965. "Symbols of the Jazz Age: The New Negro and Harlem Discovered." *American Quarterly* 17/2:229–38.

Ostransky, Leroy. 1960. *The Anatomy of Jazz.* Seattle: University of Washington Press.

Panassié, Hugues. 1936. *Hot Jazz: a Guide to Swing Music.* New York: M. Witmark & Sons.

　1942. *The Real Jazz.* New York: Smith & Durrell.

Peretti, Burton. 1992. *The Creation of Jazz: Music, Race, and Culture in Urban America.* Urbana: University of Illinois Press.

　1997. *Jazz in American Culture.* Chicago: Ivan R. Dee.

Peterson, Richard A. 1972. "A Process Model of the Folk, Pop and Fine Art Phases of Jazz" in *American Music: From Storyville to Woodstock,* ed. C. Nanry. New Brunswick, NJ: Transaction Books.

　1990. "Why 1955? Explaining the Advent of Rock Music." *Popular Music* 9/1:97–115.

　1997. *Creating Country Music: Fabricating Authenticity.* University of Chicago Press.

Piazza, Tom. 1996. *Setting the Tempo: Fifty Years of Great Jazz Liner Notes.* New York: Anchor Books.

Priestley, Brian. 1991. *Jazz on Record: a History.* New York: Billboard Books.

Ramsey, Frederick, and Charles Edward Smith, eds. 1939. *Jazzmen: the Story of Hot Jazz Told in the Lives of the Men Who Created It.* Reprint, New York: Limelight Editions, 1985.

Ramsey, Guthrie P. 1995. "Cosmopolitan or Provincial?: Ideology in Early Black Music Historiography, 1878–1940." *Black Music Research Journal* 15/2:91–123.

Reig, Teddy, and Edward Berger. 1990. *Reminiscing in Tempo: The Life and Times of a Jazz Hustler.* Metuchen, NJ: The Scarecrow Press & the Institute of Jazz Studies, Rutgers University.

Roach, Hildred. 1992. *Black American Music: Past and Present.* 2nd ed. Malabar, FL: Krieger Publishing.

Roach, Max. 1972. "What 'Jazz' Means to Me." *The Black Scholar* 10:2–6.

Rogers, J. A. 1925. "Jazz at Home" in *The New Negro: An Interpretation,* ed. Alain Locke. Reprint, New York: Arno Press, 1968.

Rosenthal, David. 1982. "Jazz in the Ghetto: 1950–1970." *Popular Music* 7:1: 51–6.

1992. *Hard Bop*. New York: Oxford University Press.

Ross, Andrew. 1986. *No Respect: Intellectuals and Popular Culture*. New York: Routledge.

Sablosky, Irving. 1969. *American Music*. University of Chicago Press.

Sanjek, Russell. 1988. *American Popular Music and Its Business, From 1900–1984*. v. III. New York: Oxford University Press.

Sargeant, Winthrop. 1938. *Jazz: Hot and Hybrid*. New York: Arrow Editions.

Seldes, Gilbert. 1957. *The Seven Lively Arts*. 2nd ed (1st ed, 1926). New York: A. S. Barnes & Company.

Seltzer, George. 1989. *Music Matters: The Performer and the American Federation of Musicians*. Metuchen, NJ: The Scarecrow Press.

Shapiro, Nat, and Nat Hentoff. 1955. *Hear Me Talkin' to Ya: The Story of Jazz As Told By the Men Who Made It*. Reprint, New York: Dover Publications, 1966.

Shaw, Arnold. 1971. *The Street That Never Slept*. Reprint, *52nd Street: The Street of Jazz*, New York: De Capo Press, 1977.

1986. *Black Popular Music in America: From the Spirituals, Minstrels, and Ragtime to Soul, Disco, and Hip-hop*. New York: Schirmer Books.

1987. *The Jazz Age: Popular Music in the 1920s*. New York: Oxford University Press.

Shaw, Artie. 1952. *The Trouble with Cinderella*. Reprint, New York: De Capo Press, 1979.

Simon, George. 1950. "The Decline of the Big Band." *Jazz 1950*, eds. B. Ulanov and G. Simon. New York: Metronome Corporation.

Simon, George. 1981. *The Big Bands*. 4th ed. New York: Schirmer Books.

Smith, Charles Edward, Frederic Ramsey, Charles Payne Rogers, and William Russell. 1942. *The Jazz Record Book*. New York: Smith and Durrell.

Sousa, John Philip. 1928. *Marching Along: Recollections of Men, Women and Music*. Reprint, Westerville, OH: Integrity Press, 1994.

Southern, Eileen. 1971. *The Music of Black Americans*. New York: Norton & Company.

1997. *The Music of Black Americans*. 3rd ed. New York: Norton & Company.

Spencer, Jon Michael. 1997. *The New Negroes and Their Music: The Success of the Harlem Renaissance*. Knoxville, TN: University of Tennessee Press.

Spivey, Donald. 1984. *Union and the Black Musician: The Narrative of William Everett Samuels and Chicago Local 208*. New York: University Press of America.

Stearns, Marshall W. 1956. *The Story of Jazz*. New York: Oxford University Press.

Stebbins, Robert A. 1966. "Class, Status, and Power among Jazz and Commercial Musicians." *The Sociological Quarterly* 7:197–213.

1968. "A Theory of the Jazz Community." Reprinted in *American Music: From Storyville to Woodstock*, ed. C. Nanry, New Brunswick, NJ: Transaction Books, 1972.

Stein, Charles W. 1984. *American Vaudeville as Seen by Its Contemporaries*. New York: A. A. Knopf.

Sterling, Christopher H., and John M. Kittross. 1978. *Stay Tuned: A Concise History of American Broadcasting*. Belmont, CA: Wadsworth Publishing.

Stewart, Rex W. 1972. *Jazz Masters of the Thirties*. New York: Macmillan.

Stowe, David W. 1994. *Swing Changes: Big-Band Jazz in New Deal America*. Cambridge, MA: Harvard University Press.

Suber, Charles. 1976. "Jazz Education" in *The Encyclopedia of Jazz in the Seventies*. eds. L. Feather and I. Gitler. New York: Horizon Press.

Tawa, Nicholas E. 2000. *High-Minded and Low-Down: Music in the Lives of Americans, 1800–1861*. Boston: Northeastern University Press.

Thiele, Bob, and Bob Golden. 1995. *What a Wonderful World: A Lifetime of Recordings*. New York: Oxford University Press.

Thomas, Lorenzo. 1995. " 'Classical Jazz' and the Black Arts Movement." *African American Review* 29/2:237–40.

Tick, Judith. 1986. "Passed Away Is the Piano Girl: Changes in American Musical Life, 1870–1900," In *Women Making Music: the Western Art Tradition, 1150–1950*, eds. J. Bowers and J. Tick. Chicago: University of Illinois Press.

Tischler, Barbara L. 1986. *American Music: The Search for an American Musical Identity*. New York: Oxford University Press.

Toledano, Ralph de, ed. 1947. *Frontiers of Jazz*. New York: O. Durrell.

Tucker, Mark, ed. 1993. *The Duke Ellington Reader*. New York: Oxford University Press.

Tucker, Sherrie. 2000. *Swing Shift: "All-Girl" Bands of the 1940s*. Durham, NC: Duke University Press.

Ulanov, Barry. 1952. *History of Jazz*. Reprint, New York: De Capo Press, 1972.

Ulanov, Barry, and George Simon, eds. 1950. *Jazz 1950*. New York: Metronome Corporation.

Walser, Robert, ed. 1999. *Keeping Time: Readings in Jazz*. New York: Oxford University Press.

Welburn, Ronald G. 1983. "American Jazz Criticism, 1914–1940." Dissertation, New York University.

 1987. "James Reese Europe and the Infancy of Jazz Criticism." *Black Music Research Journal* 7:35–44.

Wells, Dicky, and Stanley Dance. 1991. *The Night People: The Jazz Life of Dicky Wells*. Washington: Smithsonian Institution Press.

Wexler, Jerry, and David Ritz. 1993. *Rhythm and the Blues: A Life in American Music*. New York: A. A. Knopf.

Whitburn, Joel. 1986. *Pop Memories, 1890–1954: the History of American Music*. Menomonee Falls, WI: Record Research.

Whiteman, Paul, and Mary Margaret McBride. 1926. *Jazz*. Reprint, New York: Arno Press, 1974.

Williams, Martin. 1959. *The Art of Jazz*. New York: Oxford University Press. Reprint, New York: De Capo Press, 1979.

Wilmer, Valerie. 1980. *As Serious as Your Life: The Story of the New Jazz*. Rev. ed. Westport, CT: Lawrence Hill & Company.

Wuthnow, Robert. 1987. *Meaning and Moral Order: Explorations in Cultural Analysis*. Berkeley, CA: University of California Press.

Index